CONTENTS

PREFACE

We wish to thank the Victoria and Albert Museum, the Royal Irish Academy, and Lord Rothschild for their kind permission to print the transcripts of the Swift account books in their possession.

Over many years we have incurred obligations to a number of libraries, and it is a pleasure now to acknowledge them. Our greatest debt is to the Victoria and Albert Museum. Consulting the Forster Collection there for periods of several weeks at a time was an inconvenience to the staff, and we remember with gratitude approaching astonishment the patient courtesy shown by everyone with whom we had to deal. We are under almost equal obligation to the British Library and its efficient and tireless staff.

For aid generously given during less protracted visits we must thank the National Library of Ireland, Marsh's Library, Trinity College (Dublin) Library, Cambridge University Library, Trinity College (Cambridge) Library, The New York Public Library, and the Huntington Library.

Among individuals who have supplied us with information, both at their libraries and through correspondence, are Miss M. Mi Dhomhnallain, Librarian of the Royal Irish Academy; Mr. A. S. Bell and Miss E. D. Yeo, of the National Library of Scotland; Geraldine Willis, Librarian of the Representative Church Body Library, Dublin; Reginald T. Crampton, Secretary of St. Patrick's Hospital; M. P. Pollard of Trinity College (Dublin) Library; Francoise Gardey, Conservateur of the Bibliothèque Nationale; and Mr. Van Hasselt of the Foundation Custodia, Paris. We deeply appreciate the help they have given us. We also remember the kindness of Dean Armstrong, who gave us the opportunity, at a busy time for him--the semicentenary observances at Easter 1966--to consult the chapter minutes and cathedral records at St. Patrick's.

We are particularly grateful to the University of Colorado, whose librarians have been cheerfully diligent in procuring research materials for us and whose program of Faculty Fellowships brought relief from academic duties and responsibilities and enabled us to enjoy a year of uninterrupted work on Swift.

Every reader of this work will recognize its indebtedness to Swift scholars of the past, especially Elrington Ball and Sir Harold Williams for their indispensable editions of the Swift correspondence. Swift's letters frequently explicate and illuminate the account books, and vice versa; indeed, we have often found the temptation to quote from Swift irresistible: even his briefest comment lights up a page. Since our investigation was concentrated upon Swift's daily life, we depended heavily upon the two leading contemporary scholars of Swift's life and career in the church, Professor Irvin Ehrenpreis and Professor Louis A. Landa. We are profoundly in their debt.

It gives us extreme pleasure to acknowledge our special gratitude to one Swift scholar. David Woolley has given us not only unrivalled professional advice but constant encouragement. Many of our readings we owe to his own transcripts of the account books, which he generously left with us in Colorado in 1968. The friendship which began at that time has been a source of joy as well as advantage to us ever since. Except for the editors themselves, who are solely responsible for all errors, the book owes more to him than to anyone else.

Paul V. Thompson

Boulder, Colorado — Dorothy Jay Thompson

The Account Books
of
Jonathan Swift

INTRODUCTION

1. The Account Books

Every year of his adult life, except for the tragic period at the end, Swift kept a small notebook in which he entered his daily expenses. For this we have the authority of Dr. John Lyon (1708-1790), a minor canon of St. Patrick's Cathedral and court-appointed guardian of Swift in his final years, whose marginalia in Hawkesworth's Life of Swift, 1755, are among the most valuable and reliable pieces of information in our possession. Lyon refers to them as

> ye Accompt Books, wch Dr. Swift always made up yearly, & on each Page entered minutely all his Receipts & Expences in every Month, beginning his year from 1st: Nov^r, He observed ye same Method all his life time till his last Illness (Prelims, f. 16).

Though the books are mainly lists of household expenses, Swift also included other matter, notably income from his livings and his cathedral property, as well as debts owed to him, wins and losses at cards, lists of letters sent and received, various memoranda, and stray remarks and notations. If not necessarily secret, the notebooks were private: no other hand is to be found in the monthly lists of expenditures. They have long been recognized as of considerable biographical importance, recording as they do Swift's movements about London and Dublin and other parts of England and Ireland, often noting his meetings with friends and acquaintances, and providing information about his daily habits and concerns. The prices of household items are of interest to the student of economic and social history, and there is source material for the ecclesiologist. Yet, though the books have frequently been cited and excerpted in biographical studies of Swift, and certain passages, like the moving tribute to his mother, have been often reproduced, the books themselves have never before been published.

Swift prided himself on his systematic handling of financial records, and often urged a similar method upon his friends. On 15 June 1735 he advised Thomas Sheridan, whose casual way with money distressed him, "I say again keep very regular accounts in large books and a fair hand, not like me who to save paper confuse every thing." Stella was, in this as in other ways, Swift's most obedient pupil. After her death he wrote, "She kept an account of all the family-expences, from her arrival in Ireland to some months before her death"(PW, V, 232). Several pages of these family expenses, in the hand of Stella's companion, Rebecca Dingley, are extant and show an almost finicky precision in itemizing their small household purchases. Similarities in the method of keeping the accounts testify to Swift's instruction.

If Swift kept his accounts in separate books, one to a year, as Lyon says he did, and if he preserved them, he must at one time have had thirty or forty of them. At present only nine are known to be in existence. The nine which we have cover the years 1702-3, 1703-4, 1708-9, 1709-10, 1711-2, 1712-3, 1717-

8, 1732-3, and 1734-5. As Lyon remarks, Swift begins his fiscal year in November, so November and December of the preceding year are included in the book, and the entries normally stop on 31 October. Of the extant nine books, seven are in the Forster Collection at the Victoria and Albert Museum (Forster 48. D. 34/ 1-7, 505-511); the volume for 1703-4 is in the Rothschild Collection at Trinity College, Cambridge (Cat. No. 2258); and that for 1734-5 is in the Royal Irish Academy (Cat. No. 24. C. 31).

In the Forster Collection are two other notebooks, not properly account books. One is a record of collections and charitable disbursements at St. Patrick's (Forster 513). The other (Forster 512) is a composite of two completely unconnected parts: (1) a note of Dr. Lyon headed "The State of the Weekly Collections at St. Patrick's Church Rec^{d} by ye Dean from 1730 to April 1742," clearly relating to Forster 513, the cathedral record; (2) five pages in Swift's hand headed "Debts and mortgages due to me Munday Apr. 11, 1736." These two notebooks, covering the years 1730-1742 and 1738-1741, have also not been previously published and are included in the present edition.

2. History of the Books

The account books are not mentioned in the earliest record, made in October 1742, of Swift's manuscripts: "Mss: found in the Dean's Study," f. 14^{v} of "Catalogue of Books belonging to Dr Swift taken about Oct^{br} 1742 - & compared June 2^{d} 1744."[1] Most of the pages, according to Sir Harold Williams, are in Lyon's hand. Lyon may have included the books among the "odd imperfect Fragments not mentioned in the above Acc^{t}, or a few Pamphlets not entered in ye foregoing Catalogue; they are thought to be of no value, and are still in the Study" (Williams, p. 34). No manuscripts of any kind were listed three years later in _A Catalogue of Books, the Library of the late Rev. Dr. Swift, 1745_.[2]

After Swift's death his personal papers--letters, memoranda, records, notes--as well as several manuscripts of literary works, seem to have followed two main lines of descent: through his cousin, Mrs. Whiteway, and her children, and through Dr. Lyon and his heirs.

Martha Harrison Whiteway, the daughter of Adam Swift and the trusted companion of Swift's later years, came naturally into the possession of many of his books and manuscripts. When she moved to England in 1761 with her daughter Mary and her son-in-law, Deane Swift, the Swift books and manuscripts still in their keeping presumably went with them. At her death in 1768 Deane Swift inherited these books and papers (Deane Swift to John Nichols, 7 June 1778, _Illustrations_, V.383).

Deane Swift's use of Swift documents, both literary and personal, is well known. All that need be said here is that there is no suggestion in anything he wrote or printed that he knew of the existence of Swift's account books. Nor did his erratic son Theophilus, who had abundant Swift material, ever indi-

---

[1] This manuscript, in the Abbotsford Library, is described in Williams, pp. 9-14.

[2] Williams reprints the sale catalogue at the end of his book.

cate that he possessed or had heard of such a book; and the manuscripts of Theophilus's son, Edmund Lenthal Swifte, now in the Forster Collection, did not include any of the little books.[3] The extant account books, then, did not come through Deane Swift.

It is conceivable that Mrs. Whiteway, if she had any of the books, gave some of them to her son John, who remained in Ireland. In 1808 Edmond Malone wrote in the Lyon-Hawkesworth volume, "The Notes in this volume, I suspect, were written by Mr Whiteway, a Surgeon in Dublin. The son of Mrs. Whiteway, Swift's cousin german . . . he had access, after Swift's death, to his small pocket books and books of accounts." Malone of course is wrong is his conjecture about the writer of the notes, but this does not discredit his statement that John Whiteway had access to the account books. By calling them small, which Lyon nowhere does, Malone speaks as if he himself had seen them.

John Whiteway died in 1798. His son, George, is said to have owned some Swift material, though no specific item can be traced to him. When George died, in 1806, J. Cooper Walker, the Irish antiquary, wrote to the Rev. Edward Berwick, "I learn from the public prints that my old friend George Whiteway is no more. . . Geo. Whiteway was the last of the sons of John mentioned in Dean Swift's will. Several of the Dean's books devolved to him." "The Dean's books" suggests printed books that once belonged to the Dean, not manuscripts. But the Walker letter concludes several pages later with an arresting postscript: "You will take care of Swift's little Account Book, I am sure" (24 June 1806, CUL, Box III). There is nothing in the letter, either in the wording or the tone, to suggest that the account book has any connection with George Whiteway, but since we know that Walker owned an account book and also at one time Swift's copy of Paradise Lost, which had belonged to John Whiteway, it is not impossible that both came from the same source (Nichols, XIX, vi).

The other main line of succession was through Dr. Lyon. In later life a distinguished Irish ecclesiastical scholar, who held a series of prebends in St. Patrick's Cathedral, Lyon, as a young man, was an esteemed friend and assistant to Swift (Swift to Delany, 22 October 1736), who employed him as almoner of the cathedral charities and explorer of the antiquities there, and in 1740 appointed him a minor canon (Mason, pp. 407, 418; Lawler, p. 204). He "is a sort of Favorite of mine," Swift told Lady Orrery in 1739 (HL, August [?] 1739). In 1738 Lyon occasionally acted as Swift's amanuensis,[4] and it may have been about this time that he actually came to live at the deanery, according to a story told to Scott by Robert Dealtry, a fellow prebendary of Lyon's at St. Patrick's:

> Dr. Lyons, with whom I was acquainted, told me that at his first going to live with Swift, the Dean showed him to a gloomy bedchamber, from the window of which nothing was to be seen but the cemetary of the cathedral. Swift led Mr. Lyons to the window and said: "Now do not be complaining, man, of a confined view; for I have given you a Prospect beyond the grave" (NLS, MS 3885, f. 56, 8 March 1814).

---

[3]Theophilus Swift material at NLS, MSS 881, 882, 911. On this whole subject see Mayhew, pp. 3-25, and Woolley, pp. 194-5.

[4]A copy of "The Family of Swift" that came to Walter Scott in 1812 is inscribed "Memoirs of my grandfather, Thomas Swift, by Mr. Lyons, April 1738." (Scott, I, Appendix, viii.)

At the time of Swift's death, Lyon possessed considerable personal material of the Dean's. Important letters, which were a present to him from Swift, he released for publication in 1765; as executor of Mrs. Dingley's will and as her heir, he acquired not only some of her personal property but her papers, including a large part of the Journal to Stella; and also his were various memorabilia, such as Swift's prayerbook, Guiscard's knife, &c., which he bestowed on worthy acquaintances (Williams, p. 61; Forster, Life, p. 570). It is most likely that he owned the Swift account books. He is the first to mention them.

In 1765, at the same time as he was authorizing publication of Swift's letters, Lyon was also making his notes in Hawkesworth's Life of Swift. The notes were clearly intended to be used in a new life of Swift, perhaps to be written by himself: on the title page of Faulkner's "Further Account" he wrote, "Many Hints may be taken from thence for the new Life." Among these annotations he described, in the passage already cited, Swift's method of keeping his accounts, and he substantiated some of his marginalia by reference to the books themselves.

It can be proved that Lyon had in his hands several of the account books. In 1765 he used material from five of them: from 1699-1700 or 1700-1 he took the details of the value of Swift's livings; from 1700-1, 1701-2, and 1703-4 he selected facts about Swift's journeys between Ireland and England, as well as the cost of taking his doctor's degree; and from 1709-10 he copied out Swift's account of his mother's death. Lyon also had the 1712-3 book: it contains a note in his hand. He must have had still others. He says of Swift's charity, "His Bountys were daily entered in his Acc^t Books & were there distinguished on each page of his weekly Acc^ts Grand Dons - Petites Dons" (Lyon, p. 151). Swift's charities are indeed entered in extant account books, but they are never so titled, though they are sometimes disguised in the later books as Great G[if]ts and Sm[all] Ch[arities]. But Lyon is a careful transcriber, and where we can compare his transcriptions, as in the 1703-4 book, we find he has taken his notes precisely. Swift's use of French in the later account books is not unusual.

Similar notes about Swift's movements were added by Lyon, probably in 1738, to a copy of Swift's autobiographical fragment: again from 1701-2 and from three more account books, 1707-8, 1708-9, and 1713-4.[5] Those from 1701-2 also give the date Swift received his Doctor of Divinity degree; those from 1708-9 can be checked against the actual account book. Finally, Lyon's reference in "Of Dr Swift's Effects" to the valuation of certain tithes made by "ye Dean in his own Accompts" may suggest a 1741-2 book (Landa, "Deanery," p. 164).

What Lyon did with all these books we do not know. Some of them are heard of, in the early years of the nineteenth century, as being in various hands, all apparently in Ireland. If they had not been given to friends during Lyon's lifetime, they would have passed along with his other effects to his heir, Thomas Steele, of Cullane Castle, co Clare, who had married Lyon's

---

[5]Forster, Life, p. 16. The copy was one made in Swift's lifetime by Charles Cobbe, then Bishop of Kildare, later Archbishop of Dublin. It was lent to Forster by Archbishop Cobbe's descendant, Thomas Cobbe of Newbridge, Donabate, Malahide, co Dublin, in 1855, as described by Cobbe in a series of letters now in the Forster Collection. According to information courteously provided by Alexander Cobbe, a descendant of the Archbishop, the MS is no longer in existence.

niece. Through intermediaries Scott obtained from Steele some Lyon Mss for use in his Memoir of Swift.[6] A shipment was sent Scott, 16 July 1812, of a "Box containing a good many of the Writings of Swift, account Books, account of the receipts of his livings &c &c" (NLS, MS 3652, f. 155). Nothing more is specified about the "account Books"; they were almost certainly the cathedral records, which carry many notations in Lyon's hand and of which Scott made considerable use. The "account of the receipts of his livings &c &c" would be a genuine account book, presumably the 1701-2 book which Scott bracketed with that for 1700-1. Scott complained to Constable that the contents of the box "are not of great significance," but he conscientiously made use of many "Dr Lyons papers" in the course of his Memoir (Grierson, III, 161).[7]

Thomas Steele, Sr., died about 1819. His heir, Thomas Steele, Jr., died in 1848, his fortune, according to the DNB, dissipated. Four years later a contributor from Dublin signing himself "J. F. F." supplied Notes and Queries with two Lyon manuscripts which he had found among "letters and other MSS of Dr. John Lyon," which "by some chance or another recently got into the possession of a shopkeeper in this city, by whom they have been for the most part used as waste paper."[8] The two items, of minor interest, may well have come from one of the Steeles, but J. F. F. obviously had not discovered anything so important as an account book.

Some time between 1820 and 1856 the seven account books and the pages of cathedral records now in the Forster Collection came into the hands of William Monck Mason. Before his History of St. Patrick's appeared in 1820, he had communicated through a friend with the elder Steele and received permission to use the Lyon MSS (Forster 573, Steele to George Waller, 16 February 1818). But they did not reach Mason in time for him to use them in writing his history. He may have obtained them later from the younger Steele. J. F. F.'s statement in Notes and Queries that "Lyon MSS" were being used as waste paper in Dublin in 1852 certainly implies that the account books had been rescued before then, and it is definitely a possibility that, attempting to realize what he

---

[6] Thomas Steele senior himself never communicated directly with Scott. The intermediaries were his nephew, Thomas Steele junior, and Matthew Weld Hartstonge, who "explored Dr Lyon's Library in Peter Street," Dublin, and finally obtained the papers from the uncle. Their many letters to Scott are to be found at the NLS (MSS 881, 882, 3882-3886).

[7] Scott's description of the account books implies that he had seen more than just two. "The system by which he regulated his expence was so very rigid, that, from many of his journals still existing, it is clear he could have accounted for every penny of his expenditure, during any year of his life, from the time of his being at college, until the total decline of his faculties" (Scott, I, 19). But Scott used no other account books, and there is no support for his assertion that Swift began keeping his books as early as his college years. In fixing the terminal date, Scott may have had in mind the cathedral records, which run until 1742.

[8] Notes and Queries, First Series, V, 292, 27 March 1852. J. F. F. is probably James Frederic Ferguson (1807-1855), in charge of the Exchequer records in Dublin and a frequent contributor on Irish history to Notes and Queries.

could to pay his debts, the younger Steele sold his collection of Swiftiana to Mason. In any case, at the sale of Mason's library in 1856, Forster bought all but two of the surviving account books as well as the two books of records. At his death in 1876 they came to the Victoria and Albert Museum, where they have remained ever since.

The history of the two account books not in the Mason sale--1703-4 and 1734-5--is given in the analysis of the individual books.

3. Method of Keeping Accounts

With slight variations, Swift's method of keeping his accounts and preparing his notebook remained the same throughout his life. He divided his financial year into quarters: November to January, February to April, May to July, August to October. At the beginning of each quarter he wrote a heading identifying the quarter by number and by the months covered, as "1st. Quarter, November to January," and he then divided the page into a number of subheadings. These covered larger and less frequent expenses, such as those for clothing, lodging, servants, &c. The totals for each of these categories he then added and entered in a later page summarizing the entire quarter. The second page was headed "Expences" with the number of the month, as "November 1st Month." This was subdivided into four weeks with an item "Remainder" for the rest of the month. Under each week, after the appropriate date, the little daily expenses were listed and the total for the week summarized. At the bottom of the page the totals for the four weeks and the Remainder were separately entered and added. This completed the second page. The third and fourth pages were devoted to the other two months of the quarter, and the fifth page was a summary of the whole period, with the entries consisting of the larger expenses from page one plus the totals of the daily expenses of each of the three months. Thus each quarter covered five pages. For convenience we will call the first page of the quarter the Quarterly Categories and the fifth the Quarterly Summary.

The other three quarters of the year were treated in the same way. After the Quarterly Summary for the fourth quarter, an additional page, headed "Totals of a Year," gave the grand total of the four quarters.

Normally, after twenty-one pages were thus filled with the record of expenses, several blank pages remained. Sometimes Swift would use them for lists of letters sent and received. His records of wins and losses at cards, which are entered in most of the books, are always on a blank page at the beginning and never included with either expenditures or income; he must have considered them as entirely outside his regular financial concerns. On other pages changes in servants or lodgings are given, as well as addresses to be remembered, commissions to be executed, reminders to himself of entries to be made later, or even significant events in his life.

Many pages contain marginal notes and comments. Records of journeys and visits are often entered in open areas in the expenses section. These are sometimes merely a name, as "Laracor" or "Windsor," sometimes a precise statement with times of departure and arrival. Other memoranda, mostly about health, are frequently squeezed in at the top of the page.

Most of the expenses listed in the account books are ordinary daily ones, those which are not subsumed under the expenses itemized on the Quarterly Categories page. The usual entry, therefore, covers food and drink, coach and chair fares, postage, board wages, tips or small charities, and minor household charges, such as coals and candles. Unusual purchases are more likely to be entered under the quarterly rather than the monthly groupings, often as "Extraordinarys," though occasionally books and pictures will be considered as daily expenses.

The other major use Swift made of his notebook was to record the income from his parishes and deanery and the professional expenses in connection with them. For this purpose he turned the book over and began at the back, even providing a new title page. This ingenious practice accounts for the occasional empty pages in the middle of the books. Swift's methods of keeping his ecclesiastical records will be discussed later.

4. The Format of the Books

The nine extant books vary in the size and in the number of pages. This suggests that Swift assembled the books himself.

Of the surviving account books, though several have the same history, each differs somewhat from the others in content and arrangement, as the following analyses will show. The first three books and three of the later ones here discussed can no longer be traced, but they are included because references to them give us some idea of their contents.

1699-1700

The existence of a 1699-1700 account book has been postulated from Lyon's marginal entry in 1765:

> In his Acc^{t} Book he returns ye annual value of ye said union about £230: & within ye first Year from Mar. 1699 to 1. Nov. 1700 ye Expence of his Titles, Crown Rent Curate &c amounted to £117 (Lyon, f. 29).

By "Mar. 1699" Lyon means March 1699/1700, as is shown on the next page when he gives the date of Swift's institution to his livings as "22nd March 1699." Swift was instituted 22 March 1700. He would not have been entitled to receive tithes nor would he have been responsible for the costs of his livings before March of 1700.

Lyon indicates the costs Swift had to pay in 1700 at his first entering upon his livings. "Crown Rent, Curate &c" reappear in subsequent account books, but the item of "Titles" is unique and must represent the expenses of Swift's preferment to his livings in First Fruits, the dispensation to hold Rathbeggan, and other charges.

The 1699-1700 book, as noted above, has now disappeared.

1700-1

The 1700-1 account book, also no longer extant, was in the possession of Dr. Lyon in 1765 and of Dr. Tuke, also of Dublin, in 1811. Lyon extracted from it only two details relating to Swift's journeys in 1701: "In April Swift went to London; return^{d} to Irel^{d} Sep^{t} following" (Prelims, f. 36).

We do not know how the book passed from Lyon to Tuke. But Matthew Weld Hartstonge's letters of 1811 to the Ballantynes and to Scott carry specific references to Tuke's ownership of it:

> Dr Tuke of S^{t}. Stephen's green has in his possession a Diary of household expences in the hand writing of Dr Swift (NLS, MS 881, f. 114, 17 April 1811).
>
> I now enclose you a Diary in the handwriting of Dr Swift from the year 1700 to 1701. . . . It belongs to Dr Tuke of St. Stephen's Green. . . he gave me leave to transmit the original to you. . . . At the end of the Diary is given the incomes of the Parishes of Laracor, Dunlaven, Agher & Rathbeggan &c &c. . ... At your leisure you can return the Diary, for Dr Tuke (NLS, MS 881, f. 74, 3 June 1811).
>
> I found in the Diary of Dean Swift now in Mr Scott's possession, that the.Church of Laracore had undergone repairs in the year 1700. or 1701.--one of the items in his expenditure of accounts being for "repairing the Chancel" of the Church of Laracore (NLS, MS 882, f. 72, n.d.).

Hartstonge adds that Dr. Tuke will introduce him to his friend Thomas Steele "of the County of Clare, who is married to a Niece of Dr. Lyon's," and, as we have seen, it was through this contact that Hartstonge eventually obtained some "Lyon's MSS" for Scott. Thus the 1700-1 book may have passed from Thomas Steele to Tuke some time before 1811, or it may even have reached Tuke from Lyon himself before the latter's death in 1790.

Nothing is known of Dr. Tuke's account book after it was used by Scott. If it was returned to him, it may have been among his effects when they were sold in 1826. Two volumes of a sale catalogue, for 12 and 28 June 1826, are listed in Lugt's Répertoire des Catalogues de Ventes, but only the 12 June volume can be traced, and the single Swift item it carries is a marble bust.

Scott, who nowhere credits Dr. Tuke as the owner of the book, though he does mention him in connection with other Swift memorabilia, took from it information about the livings of Agher, Laracor, and Rathbeggan, which amount to

> about L. 230 yearly. The prebend of Dunlavin being added in the year 1700, raised Swift's income to betwixt L.350 and L.400. . . . These facts are ascertained from his account-books for the years 1701 and 1702 (Scott, I, 61).

Scott also printed a page from the book, the "Account of expences from Nov. 1, 1700 to Nov. 1, 1701" (Scott, I, 61, n2), the only record that remains of Swift's expenses for this year. It can be found on page 315 of the present volume. Although later account books carry such yearly totals, the sums are never rounded off as they are here. The categories are much like those in extant books, with the exception of the inexplicable "Accidents." "Play" may be assumed to be "Won" and "Lost" at cards, although Swift never elsewhere added those amounts into his annual totals. "Shoes and books" is doubtless Scott's misreading of "Shoes and boots." Some items--payments for letters and common charity, for instance--later tend to appear among the daily expenses. The amounts spent are also much the same, although, as could be expected, there is no heading of "MC," Swift's symbol for Esther Johnson and Mrs. Dingley: they did not come to Ireland until 1701; thereafter the item appears in all account books until Stella's death. Also, as nearly as the items can be compared with those in 1702-3 and 1703-4, one can see that in 1701, when Swift was living at Dublin Castle with the Berkeleys, he naturally spent nothing for lodgings and considerably less than he did later for a servant, but more for clothes and gratuities. We may thus assume that the figures Scott printed, though they come to the improbable total of £100 even, are approximately correct.

The only sources we have for Swift's income from livings and the charges on them for this year are Scott and Hartstonge. We can accept most of them, though Scott's figures for Dunlavin are clearly wrong: according to his later books, Swift never received more than £13 5s 3d from his prebend. An interesting fact, given by both Hartstonge and Scott, is that during the first year of Swift's vicarship, while still living at Dublin Castle, he set about repairing his church. Repairs were still being paid for as late as 1705.

1701-2

The 1701-2 account book, which has since disappeared, was used by Dr. Lyon in 1738 and 1765 and was apparently also in Scott's hands. From it Lyon gives us facts about Swift's doctor's degree and his journeys. After Swift returned to Ireland in September 1701 he

> took his Doctor's Degree on 16. Feb: after, wch cost him in Fees & Treat £44 and upward. In April 1702 [he went to England]. He went first to Leicester to see his Mother - in May to London - in July to Moorpark - and in Oct^{br} to Ireland (Prelims, f. 29; Forster, Life, p. 16).

The book presumably reached Scott with the Lyon MSS in the summer of 1812. The only use Scott made of it was to bracket it with the 1700-1 book, already received from Dr. Tuke, in providing the value of Swift's livings: "These facts are ascertained from his account-books for the years 1701 and 1702." We know therefore that the book contained the usual two sections: one on daily expenses and one on income from the livings.

1702-3

Forster 505. 48. D. 34/1

i. Account / From Nov^{br}. 1st. 1702 / to / Nov^{br}. 1st. 1703

ii. Account / Of my Livings / from / Nov^{br} 1st 1702 / to / Nov^{br} 1st 1703

1-16 leaves   11.4cm x 17.8cm

i.	1.	Title page
	1^{v}.	Law; Lost and Won; Memorandum
	2-4.	First quarter expenses and Summary
	4^{v}-6^{v}.	Second quarter expenses and Summary
	7-9.	Third quarter expenses and Summary
	9^{v}-11^{v}.	Fourth quarter expenses and Summary; Memorandum
	12.	Totals of a year
ii.	12^{v}.	Charges for Rathbeggan and Dunlavin
	13.	Received from Rathbeggan and Dunlavin
	13^{v}.	Charges for Laracor and Agher, brought over
	14.	Received from Laracor and Agher, brought over

14^v.	Charges for Laracor and Agher
15.	Received from Laracor and Agher
15^v.	Charges for Grenoge
16.	Received from Reads-town and Stokes town
16^v.	Title page (twice); 6 sums; 2 proverbs

The seven account books and the two other record books in the Forster Collection appeared as two blocks of items in the 1858 Monck Mason sale catalogue. The provenance here given will therefore serve for the other eight books.

> Catalogue of the Literary Collections . . . of William Monck Mason, Esq. . . . which will be sold by Auction, by Messrs. S. Leigh and John Wilkenson on Monday the 29 March 1858 and Two following Days. (British Library copy, priced and named, S. - C.S. 444 [3])
>
> #511 Dean Swift, Books of Accounts of Receipts and Expences for Seven years, between 1702 and 1733, inclusive, and statement of Debts and Mortgages due to him, 1736.
>
> #512 Dean Swift, in account with the Poor for the money received in the weekly collections, 1738-1740, and Note of Dr. Lyon relating to the same, 1742.

The note of Dr. Lyon, now bound with the "Debts and Mortgages due to me," is here properly included with the cathedral records of "Money payd out" and "Charity-Money Received," and the "Debts and Mortgages" is appropriately placed with accounts of Swift's private income.

Forster is listed in the British Library copy of the catalogue as the purchaser of the two items, paying £4 10s for #511 and 7s for #512. His attention had been drawn to these items two years earlier by Edward A. Bond of the British Museum Manuscripts Department as "unpublished Swift autograph papers at Sotheby's including MS Journals which have never been published" (Forster 571, Bond to Forster, 22 September 1856). Monck Mason had given up his collection for sale at least three years before his death.

As previously noted, Mason acquired the books between 1820 and 1856. If they all came to him as a block, it may be of some significance that at least four are known to have been at one time in the hands of Dr. Lyon. The possible connection between Mason and the family of Dr. Lyon's heir has already been suggested.

The 1702-3 account book is the earliest extant one. In it Swift kept his accounts, both expenses and income, more faithfully than he was often later to do. The categories of anticipated quarterly expenses all appear, and are similar to the ones Scott printed for 1700-1, except that "Lodging" and "MC" have been added, and "Accidents," "Play," and "Letters" have been omitted. All pages have been headed and filled in carefully; all months carry weekly entries and the totals are given; and all the pages have been totalled except that for the fourth quarter and, consequently, the "Totals of a Year." Swift may not have had time to complete these totals, as he left Ireland on 11 November, as noted in a memorandum on p. 2. This page also carries the customary double column of "Lost" and "Won" at cards as well as the special category of "Law," which does not reappear, at least under that heading. There is no list of letters sent and received.

The accounts of livings are also carefully kept. For the first time since receiving his livings Swift spends a full year in Ireland. Frequently in Laracor, he is establishing his system of management and accounting. Old charges going back to 1688 are paid; unwarranted charges for the rectory of Grenoge are cleared.

The 1702-3 book proves, even more clearly than later ones, that Swift kept his account books available after the year they cover had ended. He makes a note not only of his visit to England but of his return to Ireland in 1704. He uses the back cover (25) for additions and subtractions which, in four of the six cases, have to do with the next year's account. Even as late as 16 November 1709 he is entering income from Rathbeggan.

1703-4

Rothschild 2258

i. Account / Of Expences / From Nov^{br}. 1st. 1703 / to No / Nov^{br}. 1st. 1704

ii. Account of my / Livings for / 1703.

1-19 leaves 15.2cm x 9.8cm Disbound

i.	1.	Title page
	1^{v}.	Memoranda
	2-3.	First half year expenses
	3^{v}-5.	Third quarter expenses
	5^{v}.	blank
	6-7.	Expenses for August, September, October
	7^{v}.	blank
	8.	Totals of a year
	8^{v}.	blank
ii.	9-13.	blank
	13^{v}.	Arrears of Laracor and Agher
	14.	Due from Laracor, Rathbeggan, Dunlavin
	14^{v}.	Charges for Dunlavin and Laracor
	15.	Received from Dunlavin and Laracor
	15^{v}.	Charges for Rathbeggan
	16.	Received from Rathbeggan
	16^{v}-17.	blank
	17^{v}.	Charges for Laracor and Agher
	18.	Received from Laracor and Agher
	18^{v}-19.	blank
	19^{v}.	Title page

Of the Swift MSS in the Rothschild Collection (2251-2276), provenance is provided for all but seven of the twenty-six items; the 1703-4 account book is one of the seven. The Catalogue states in the introduction that the books and manuscripts of the collection were acquired from booksellers or at auction between 1935 and 1948 (I, xx). Booksellers' names are not given; particulars of auctions are.

The first reference to the 1703-4 account book was made by Dr. Lyon in 1765. From it he drew information about Swift's travels:

> The next year [1703] in Nov^{r}: he went to Leicester; from whence to London - and on 30 May 1704 he returned to Dublin, from whence he went directly to Laracor - This he calls in his Acc^{t} Book his 16th voyage (Prelims, f. 36).

In 1808 an account book, almost certainly that for 1703-4, was in the hands of John Kearney, Bishop of Ossory.

> The present Bp of Ossory late Provost of Trinity College Dublin, is in possession of an account book in Swift's writing of his expences for some years (NLS, MS 881, f. 51, Mercier, Dublin bookseller, to Constable, Scott's publisher, 27 August 1808).

When he heard this, Scott evidently asked Lydia White's help--she was related to the Bishop--in obtaining the book.

> The Bishop of Ossory is now here and desires me to inform you with his best compts that Swift's account book does not belong to him. Tho it was once in his possession he does not deem himself at Liberty to say whose it is. . . . as far as he can recollect, it was a mere account book containing trifling expences (NLS, MS 3878, f. 39, Lydia White to Scott, 5 March 1809).

The wandering account book seems to have been the one J. Cooper Walker mentioned to Berwick in 1806. Neither Walker nor Miss White assign a date to it. "I met Cooper Walker, who after all has the Diary you mentioned so long ago" (NLS, MS 3878, f. 39, Lydia White to Scott, 20 June 1809). Walker was in direct communication with Scott in the summer of 1809, sending him Swift materials, but among the items he sends he makes no reference to an account book. In 1810 Walker died, and no account book is listed in the catalogue of the sale of his library: _Bibliotheca St. Valeriensis: A Catalogue of Books . . . of the late Joseph Cooper Walker . . . sold at Auction by R. E. Mercier_ . . . 30 June 1817 (Dublin).

In any case, the 1703-4 book was in Bishop Kearney's library when he died in 1813, as appears from _The Third Part of a Catalogue of Books, Being the Library of Rt. Rev. John Kearney . . . Sold by Auction . . . 7 June, 1815 . . . by Thomas Jones_. Item 3623 is

> A Manuscript, being Dean Swift's Memorandum Book, containing an account of his expences from Nov. 1st, 1703, to Nov. 1st, 1704: also an account of his Livings, Laracor, &c. for 1703; all in his own handwriting.

(The use of the unusual term "Memorandum Book" in the catalogue description suggests that the inscription "Dean Swift's Memorandum Book" on the title page was made at this time.) A copy of the _Catalogue_ in the New York Public Library does not list the names of the buyers nor the prices paid. Nevertheless, there can be little question that the book was bought by John Brinkley, later Bishop of Cloyne, then Professor of Astronomy at Trinity College Dublin and Archdeacon of Clogher. In the November after the sale of Kearney's books, Hartstonge writes Scott in the course of urging him to consider a second edition of his _Swift_:

> Professor Brinkley is now, himself, copying out for you a bit of the expences &c of Dean Swift in 1704, which had been in the possession of the late Bishop of Ossory, from these it would appear that the Dean had been sixteen different times in England (NLS, MS 3886, f. 236^v, 21 November 1815).

Again Scott failed to obtain the book.

Brinkley may have been reluctant to let it out of his hands. He provided

Monck Mason, his nephew, with extracts only.

> I have been favoured by the Rev. Archdeacon Brinkley, who was himself sometime Vicar of Laracor, with some extracts from an account book of Swift's for the year 1703 (Mason, p. 241, k).

Bishop Brinkley died in 1835. If his library was sold, no copy of a catalogue has been traced. Monck Mason's reference in 1820 is the last mention of the 1703-4 account book until it appears in Lord Rothschild's collection.

As far as can be ascertained, the 1703-4 book is as it was when it left Swift's hands, although there are the remains of a stub between leaves 10 and 11, which are blanks. In its account of expenses it is the least complete of any of the extant books, but this was Swift's doing. The title of the first Quarterly Categories page has been altered to "First Half Year." Of the first half year the page for November, with entries for the first two weeks, appears, but the totals only for the remaining five months are given. The title for the third Quarterly Categories has been changed to include the fourth. The June through September pages carry daily entries only, not separated into weeks; the October page is the single one in the book in which the usual system is observed. Finaliy, there are no Won and Lost page, no list of letters, and no pages for Quarterly Summaries.

It seems clear that Swift left the book in Ireland in his hurry when he made his unexpected trip to England 11 November and filled it after his return 1 June 1704. The entries for November cease abruptly; other notes on that page were obviously made later, e. g., "p^{d} by Mrs Brent in my absence." At that time the first Quarterly Categories title was altered to "Half Year," apparently to cover the payment "in all" to MC for six rather than three months. The totals of expenditures in the five months in England must then have been entered from summaries kept on other papers. The third Quarterly Categories heading was subsequently expanded to include the fourth quarter.

The interest of the 1703-4 book lies more in the memoranda than in the sketchy record of daily expenses. Swift jots down changes in servants and lodgings and facts concerning the journey to England and back, with the gifts brought to Ireland.

Of even greater importance is the information given in the "Account of my Livings." This is the earliest account book to show how Swift managed his financial affairs when he was out of Ireland. As in other account books, the dates covered extend several years back and ahead: in this one arrears as far back as 1700 are listed, and settlements are made as late as April 1706. Only in this book is the "Account of Livings" considerably fuller than the "Account of Expences."

1707-8

The 1707-8 account book, no longer extant, was used by Lyon in 1738 in his notes to the Cobbe version of the Autobiographical Fragment to provide information about Swift's movements during the year.

1708-9

Forster 506. 48. D. 34/2

i. Account: / Of Expences / From Nov^{br}. 1. 1708 / to / Nov^{br}. 1. 1709.

ii. Account / Of my Livings / For the Year / 1708.

1-20 leaves 9.5cm x 15.6cm

i.	1.	Title page
	1^{v}.	Won and Lost
	2-4.	First quarter expenses and Summary
	4^{v}-6^{v}.	Second quarter expenses and Summary
	7-9.	Third quarter expenses and Summary
	9^{v}-11^{v}.	Fourth quarter expenses and Summary
	12.	Totals of a year
	12^{v}.	blank
	13-14.	List of letters
	14^{v}-15^{v}.	blank
ii.	16.	Arrears of Laracor
	16^{v}.	Charges for Rathbeggan and Dunlavin
	17.	Received from Rathbeggan and Dunlavin
	17^{v}.	Charges for Laracor and Agher
	18.	Received from Laracor and Agher
	18^{v}.	blank
	19.	Rathbeggan set
	19^{v}.	Laracor and Agher set
	20.	Bills
	20^{v}.	Title page

Provenance, cf. 1702-3. The first use of the 1708-9 account book was made by Lyon in 1738 in his notes to the Cobbe version of the Autobiographical Fragment. No evidence of its existence thereafter has been found until 1855.

This is one of the more complete account books. When it came into the Forster Collection, nothing was missing, but at some time not long before 1965 the title page, with the record of wins and losses at cards on the verso, disappeared. Fortunately, a photostatic copy had been made and is now part of the book. The copy reveals that the upper right corner had been torn away, the lost portion carrying with it a few letters from the "Won" column.

In addition to the complete list of expenses for each month, with quarterly totals and a page of totals for the year, Swift has included three pages of letters sent and received. The "Won" and "Lost" columns have not only been totalled, but, for the only time, the difference between them has been given: "Won this Year." This carefulness in record keeping is the more remarkable since the book, begun in England, was kept up during a period of suspense and illness in London, a month in Leicester, a return to Ireland in June, and five months spent in residence at Dublin and Laracor. The already full pages, moreover, are crowded with memoranda: addresses of tradespeople, a ridiculous "Hatter's Rule"--an Irish bull told to Swift--the dates of journeys, a note of a debt owing to him, lists of presents for his mother and MD, and the terrible record of illnesses suffered in London.

As in the 1703-4 book the "Account of my Livings" provides valuable evidence of how Swift handled his financial affairs during a long absence from Ireland. He includes rent rolls of tithepayers in Laracor, Agher, and Rathbeggan parishes for 1708 sent him in London, the only Laracor rent roll in any account book.

1709-10

Forster 507. 48. D. 34/3

i. Account / Of Expences / From Nov^{br}. 1. 1709 / to / Nov^{br}. 1. 1710

1-19 leaves   1-11^{v} 10.2cm x 15.6cm   12-19^{v} 10.2cm x 15.9cm

i. 1. Title page
1^{v}. Memoranda
2. Won and Lost
2^{v}. blank
3-5. First quarter expenses and Summary
5^{v}-7^{v}. Second quarter expenses and Summary
8-9. Expenses for June and July and Summary
9^{v}-11. Fourth quarter expenses
11^{v}. blank
12-19^{v}. MD's expenses, 1711-1713, in Mrs. Dingley's hand

Provenance, cf. 1702-3. The 1709-10 book was in the possession of Dr. Lyon in 1765: he copied from it Swift's memorial of his mother's death, which he says was written "at the foot of that Page which includes his Expences at Laracor in the Month of May 1710." The page, which has never been traced, had been removed before Forster acquired the book in 1858: the analysis made by Richard Sims reports "May wanting." Later biographers, using the Lyon transcript as given by Nichols, have reprinted the memorial, the most famous passage from the account books.

The book is flawed and incomplete. Swift's expenses are fully entered during the first half year, all pages added up and totalled, with the exception of the expenses on the second Quarterly Summary, which have been entered but not totalled. Because it is on the recto of the leaf with the May record, the third Quarterly Categories page is missing; it may not have been completed: none of the rest of the pages for the last half year have been, although entries are numerous. Swift left for England 31 August, and the book went with him, where presumably it remained till June 1713. The frequent entries continue in England, but there is no totalling at the end of the third or fourth quarter; in fact, the fourth Quarterly Summary page, which would have come on the verso of the page for October, is blank. There is no list of letters sent or received.

The book carries several memoranda of interest in addition to the account of the death of Mrs. Swift: two addresses, records of trips to Laracor and Clogher as well as the momentous one to England, and on the last day of the book, a recurrence of the giddy fits. In September and October, after Swift arrives in England, the account book entries can be filled out and occasionally explained by the first of the letters in the _Journal to Stella_.

The whole "Account of my Livings" has been removed, taking with it possibly a list of letters sent and received. There must once have been such a record. Swift spent much time in Laracor in 1709-10, and we know from the 1708-9 book that he settled his accounts with Parvisol on 16 November 1709, that he was at the Pace with him on 3 January 1710, dealing with the tithes of the previous year; and even the 1709-10 book lists under expenses for June an importand settlement date with the agent. Instead of the usual record, however, there are eight leaves in Mrs. Dingley's hand of household expenses between 1 November 1711 and 21 March 1713. These leaves, which are slightly larger and somewhat darker in color, must have been bound in with the book later, perhaps in place of the "Account of my Livings." (Not printed in this edition)

1711-2

Forster 508. 48. D. 34/4

i. Account / Of Expences / From Nov^{br}. 1711 / to / Nov^{br}. 1. 1712.

1-14 leaves 10.2cm x 16.4cm

i.	1.	Title page
	1^{v}.	Won and Lost
	2.	Memorandum: death of Ann Long
	2^{v}.	Memoranda
	3-5.	First quarter expenses and Summary
	5^{v}-7^{v}.	Second quarter expenses and Summary
	8-9^{v}.	Third quarter expenses
	10.	blank
	10^{v}-12.	Fourth quarter expenses
	12^{v}.	blank
	13-13^{v}.	List of letters
	14.	Memorandum
	14^{v}.	blank

Provenance, cf. 1702-3. No evidence can be found that the 1711-2 book belonged to Lyon.

The book is in good condition, presumably with no missing pages. The "Account of Expences" has been carefully kept for most of the year; April is sketchy "During Sickness," and August, "Sick with Giddyness much." No quarterly totals are given, nor is there an annual one, although pages have been reserved for them. There are a "Won" and "Lost" page and a list of letters sent and received.

1711-2 is the only extant account book kept during an entire year spent in England. As in 1709-10 and 1712-3, the record in 1711-2 illuminates that in the _Journal to Stella_. In addition to these helpful details, the pages contain the memorial on the death of Mrs. Long, changes of lodgings and servants, reminders of gifts and commissions, and jottings about the severe attack of shingles in April and other illnesses.

There is no section on "Account of my Livings." Probably Swift did not keep one: he did not return to Ireland until the next year, and his settling of his accounts for his livings customarily took place after his return, as in 1704 and 1709.

1712-3

Forster 509. 48. D. 34/5

i. Account / From Nov^{br}. 1. 1712 to Nov^{br}. 1. 1713.

ii. Income and Deanery Charges

1-19 leaves 10.2cm x 15.9cm

i.	1.	Title page and memorandum in Lyon's hand
	1^{v}.	blank

2.	Won and Lost
2^v.	blank
3.	Memorandum
3^v.	Odd expenses
4-6.	First quarter expenses and Summary
6^v-8.	Second quarter expenses
8^v.	blank
9-10^v.	Third quarter expenses
11.	blank
11^v-13.	Fourth quarter expenses
13^v.	blank
14.	List of letters
14^v.	blank
15.	Charges of the Deanery
15^v-16^v.	blank
17.	Received from Parvisol
17^v.	blank
18.	Charges on entering the Deanery
18^v.	Commissions for MD [not reversed]
19-19^v.	blank

Provenance, cf. 1702-3. Though Lyon made no use of the 1712-3 account book in 1765, we know that it was at one time in his hands: on the title page he started to write a memorandum: "Mr Ridge dyed 8th March 1709 of an Apoplexy. He left . . ."

Presumably we have the complete book in so far as Swift filled it in during this troubled year. Pages of "Won" and "Lost" and of letters sent and received are included, both divided into two sections with a line below which the entries refer to Ireland. But the expenses are not fully recorded: the pages of Quarterly Categories have been set up but some categories are left blank; three of the pages for the Quarterly Summaries are blank, and the other one contains only the category titles. There is no yearly total. Daily expenses are entered in all months, but June, the month of Swift's journey to Ireland, is understandably thin.

There is no section for "Accounts of my Livings"; possibly there was not time to enter one during Swift's brief Irish residence. He reversed the book to begin such an account, but entered nothing for parish tithes under "Received from Parvisol" and only two pages listing a few "Charges" in connection with the newly acquired deanery. Some accounting there must have been with Parvisol after an absence of three years. In the account of daily expenses is recorded the settlement of a house bill in midsummer.

The 1712-3 account book, with its many blank or incomplete pages, reflects the disarray of Swift's life during this year, when he was chiefly concerned about his preferment. The daily expenses continue to be fully entered and, until June, when the Journal ceases, are valuable as annotating Swift's reports to MD. The record of the journey to Ireland and back gives us some precise details and dates. But most interesting are the terse memoranda telling of the events in April and May leading to his presentation to St. Patrick's.

1713-4

The 1713-4 account book, which has now disappeared, was used by Lyon in

1738 to provide notes to the Cobbe Autobiographical Fragment about Swift's movements this year.

1717-8

Forster 510. 48. D. 34/6

i. Account / Of Expences from / Nov^{br}. 1st 1717 to Nov^{br}. 1st 1718

ii. Account / Of Receits from the Deanry &c. / For the Year 1717 / And for Rents for the Year 1718.

1-19 leaves 12.1cm x 19.1cm

i.	1.	Title page
	1^{v}.	Lost and Won
	2-4.	First quarter expenses and Summary
	4^{v}-5^{v}.	April expenses and second quarter Summary
	6-8.	Third quarter expenses and Summary
	8^{v}-10^{v}.	Fourth quarter expenses and Summary
	11.	Totals of a year
	11^{v}.	Charges brought over
	12.	MC, JB, Small Charities
	12^{v}.	Great Gifts
	13.	Wine, coals, candles, soap
	13^{v}.	Deanery charges and repairs
	14.	Taxes and cesses
	14^{v}.	Charges for Laracor
	15.	Jo's account
ii.	15^{v}.	A Rent roll
	16.	Received rents
	16^{v}.	Received for customs, duties, &c.
	17.	Received from Rathbeggan and Deanery
	17^{v}.	Received for Laracor and Deanery
	18.	Brought over
	18^{v}.	Memorandum; received from the Deanery
	19.	Received from the Deanery
	19^{v}.	Title page

Provenance, cf. 1702-3. If the 1717-8 account book belonged to Lyon, he made no reference to it in his notes.

The leaf for February-March is missing and was so when the book was acquired by Forster: the Sims analysis lists it as "wanting." The two months were originally completed and are represented in the totals of the second Quarterly Summary. The rest of the expenses are unusually complete, with all four quarters entered and added, and the yearly totals given. Swift has made some slight changes in his method of account keeping. The Quarterly Categories are reduced to four: Clothes, Servant's Clothes, Extraordinaries, and Horses. There is no longer, of course, a need for "Lodging." Separate pages are now given to yearly accounts for MC, JB, and charities; recurring household supplies; expenses in connection with the deanery; and taxes. These expenses, together with other larger ones, such as plate, his sister's allowance, and money reserved for use on recently acquired Neals Town lands, were apparently all added together to arrive at a grand total. The lower part of "Totalls of a Year" has been torn away and the leaf repaired. Only two letters or parts of letters were left from the original entry.

Swift kept a full account of receipts of tithes and duties from his deanery, but a page set up for a roll of deanery tithe and rent payers and a page set up for receipts of rents from deanery lands and houses have not been filled. Receipts from Rathbeggan, running as late as 2 November 1719, are sketchy and confused, and Laracor for 1717 (altered to 1718) is accounted for only by the receipt of a lump sum and two payments of crown rent and one quarter's salary to Warburton, Swift's curate. The general disorder of the accounts may be owing to the necessity of dealing with new and inexperienced agents.

In making the unusually detailed entries in the 1717-8 book, Swift has squeezed and cramped his handwriting so that, as in the two later books, many passages challenge the transcriber.

1732-3

Forster 511. 48. D. 34/7

i. Account / Of Expences from / Nov^{br}. 1st 1732 to Nov^{br}. 1st 1733.

ii. Account / Of Receits from the Deanry &c / for 1732 / And of Rents, dutyes &c for / 1733.

1-18 leaves 12.1cm x 18.7cm

i.	1.	Title page
	1^{v}.	blank
	2-4.	First quarter expenses and Summary
	4^{v}-6^{v}.	Second quarter expenses and Summary
	7-9.	Third quarter expenses and Summary
	9^{v}.	Fourth Quarterly Categories
	10.	blank
	10^{v}-16^{v}.	List of Deanery tithe-payers
	17.	blank
	17^{v}.	Memorandum
	18.	blank
	18^{v}.	Title page

Provenance, cf. 1702-3. There is no evidence of Lyon's ownership.

The book is not complete. The fourth quarter, except for the introductory page of Quarterly Categories, is lacking. As there is evidence to suggest that the rest of the fourth quarter once existed, the probability is that the two leaves on which the records were kept and which would have followed f. 9 were removed at some later date. Other leaves may also have been taken out. The separate pages of annual categories, such as MF, DD, charities, household supplies, deanery expenses, as in 1717-8 and 1734-5, are missing here, as well as the almost inevitable table of wins and losses at cards.

The daily entries in 1732-3 are less full than in earlier years, seldom amounting to two lines a week, and consisting largely of house bills and payments for coaches and chairs. There are few marginal comments: the one in March recording a giddy fit and the names of places near Dublin at which Swift visited are the only ones. But records are kept with fair regularity and the sums are usually totalled. The Quarterly Categories are also recorded, under the same four divisions used in 1717-8. "Extraordinarys," largely because of the money spent to feed the dogs, swells to eight lines in the fourth quarter.

The careful entries on this page add to the likelihood that the fourth quarter was originally complete.

Pages may therefore be presumed missing from the "Account of Receipts." An alphabetical roll of deanery tithe payers is provided and recipts are fully checked off, but no records are given of tithes of livings, although the mistaken entry of two Rathbeggan payers in the deanery roll indicates that Swift also had such an alphabetical roll for Rathbeggan. There is nothing on Laracor. Nor is there any record of deanery rents, duties, &c., for 1733, as promised on the title page. These omissions, in combination with the presumed omission of the final pages of the Expenses section, which they would overlap, suggest the loss of several leaves in the center of the book.

1734-5

Royal Irish Academy MS. 24. C. 31

i. Account of Expences from Nov^{r} / 1st 1734 to Novr 1st 1735

1-27 leaves 12.7cm x 19.1cm

i.	1.	Wins and losses with title affixed
	1^{v}-2^{v}.	Small gifts
	3-5.	First quarter expenses and Summary
	5^{v}-7^{v}	Second quarter expenses and Summary
	8-10.	Third quarter expenses and Summary
	10^{v}-12.	Fourth quarter expenses
	12^{v}-13.	blank
	13^{v}.	Various payments
	14.	Annuities and larger gifts
	14^{v}.	Wine, corks, Deanery charges, &c.
	15.	Defalcations
	15^{v}.	Physic, brewing, &c.
	16.	Taxes, soap, &c.
	16^{v}.	blank
	17-23^{v}.	Deanery tithe-payers
	24.	Names that gave no bonds
	24^{v}.	Rathbeggan tithe-payers
	25.	blank
	25^{v}.	Received from Mr. Grattan
	26.	Payments of arrears
	26^{v}.	blank
	27.	Deanery land and ground rents, &c.
	27^{v}.	blank

The 1734-5 account book is now part of a volume of Swift material in the Royal Irish Academy, Dublin. Bound in with it and with a number of transcripts of poems, some by Swift, is a letter from Swift to William Walker, which was presented to the Academy in 1852. As the account book was given to the Academy in 1853, the present volume must have been assembled after that date. The book has been disbound and the pages guarded.

The date of presentation, 13 June 1853, is the first record of the 1734-5 account book. Whether Dr. Lyon ever had it, we do not know. Scott, Mason, and, surprisingly, Forster apparently never heard of it.

It is not possible to trace the history of the book with any certainty. It was given to the Academy by George Clayton Cowell (1808-1859), of Prospect House, Milltown, who presented at the same time a second volume, the collection of transcripts of verses now bound in with the account book. In the Proceedings of the Royal Irish Academy, the acknowledgment speaks of the gifts as including "an account of his [Swift's] daily expenses from May to August, 1735, and a list of his tenants in the Deanery and at Rathbeggan, with the sums payable by them in the year 1734"(Dublin, 1853, V, 468). This material was in one volume. The strange description of the expenses as running from May to August 1735 suggests that the third Quarterly Categories page was possibly in the title page position. For this reason and others, the order of subsequent pages is suspect.

Cowell may have acquired the book from one of at least two sources. His second wife was the daughter of William Hodges, bookseller of Dublin. A more likely source is John Wisdom, vicar of Lusk, Cowell's great-grandfather. Wisdom's name is on a list sent by Hartstonge to Scott of persons "known to have in their possession Letters of Dean Swift" (NLS, MS 882, f. 70). He was a relation of the Dr. Tuke who has already been mentioned as the owner of the 1700-1 book and as the friend of Thomas Steele, Sr. Thus, by making a good many assumptions, it is possible to trace the 1734-5 book from Lyon to Cowell. How it became separated from the others is not clear, though it may be significant that the other volume associated with Tuke was also not in the group owned by Monck Mason.

When the 1734-5 book was disbound, the second part was reversed so that, contrary to Swift's practice, the entries can be read continuously without turning the book over and beginning at the back. It is by far the largest of the account books. One leaf known to be missing is the title page: the actual title, in Swift's hand, was cut from it and pasted on to the lower half of the page for wins and losses. The expenses section is complete except for the fourth Quarterly Summary and the totals of the year. The other three Quarterly Summaries have headings but lack any entries. In the 1734-5 book Swift uses the same four categories for his quarterly pages established in 1717-8: Clothes, Servant's Clothes, Extraordinaries, and Horses. The additional annual categories, entered separately, remain much the same as in the earlier book.

Although much of Swift's writing continues strong, there are clear signs of advancing age. No single category and no page have been added up, and blunders are more frequent than usual. Bitterness has increased: a customary charge, the salary to Lightburne, the schoolmaster of Trim, is now listed under "Defalcations"; law charges come under "La Chicane." His marginal comment on 25 November, perhaps in anticipation of his birthday on the 30th, is a Greek word which may be translated "Would I were dead." Other marginal comments bear out the account of his health which Swift wrote his friends during this year. His belief in the efficacy of riding for his health is confirmed by the notes he keeps of the days he rides and occasionally the distance ridden.

The book lacks a title page for the accounts of the deanery and livings. As in 1732-3 an alphabetical rent roll of deanery tithe payers has been provided, and this year one for Rathbeggan also appears. But, in contrast to 1732-3, the names are not here carefully checked off, none after March 1735, in fact, although some payment of arrears is noted. The failure to keep his records fully was probably caused by the fact that Swift was changing his agent and does not argue any incompetence in his own management.

1741-2

That so late an account book once existed is suggested by Lyon's estimate of deanery tithes in 1742 in "Of Dr Swift's Effects": "which ye Dean in his own Accompts rates at 420£ p An" (Landa, "Deanery," p. 164). Such an account book, especially one known to Lyon, would corroborate his claim that Swift "observed ye same Method all his life time till his last Illness."

1738-41 [1742]

Forster 513. 48. D. 34/9

i. Money payd out / of the weekly Collections / of the Cathedrall of / St Patrick's / From Febry. 11th to 18 / 1738-9

ii. Charity-Money / Received out of of / the Cathedrall of / St Patrick's / Beginning

1-14 leaves 8.9cm x 14.8cm

i. 1. Title page
1^{v}. Memorandum [Lyon's hand]
2-3^{v}. Money paid out of the collections
4-7^{v}. blank

ii. 8-8^{v}. Collections in my Cathedral, May [10], 1741 to April 18 [1742]
9. blank
9^{v}. Account of collections, January 11 to May [3], 1741
10. Money paid by the Dean [Lyon's hand]
10^{v}. Charity received
11. blank
11^{v}-13^{v}. Poor money, February 11, 1739 to January 18, 1741
14. blank
14^{v}. Title page

1730-42

Forster 512. 48. D. 34/8

i. The State of the Weekly Collections / of St Patrick's Church Rec^{d} by ye Dean / from 1730 to April 1742 [Note of Dr. Lyon]

ii. Debts and mortgages due to me / Munday Apr. 11, 1736

1-5 leaves (i) 14cm x 16.8cm (ii) 9.2cm x 14.3cm

i. 1. blank
1^{v}. Title page
2-2^{v}. Disbursements to the poor

ii. 3-5. Debts and mortgages
5^{v}. blank

As the different sizes show, these two records do not belong together. The Note of Dr. Lyon of October 1742 belongs with Forster 513 and will be so treated.

For the provenance of both books, cf. 1702-3.

Scott refers specifically to the cathedral accounts:

> To the last moment of capacity, he kept an accurate account of the revenues of the cathedral, and even of the sums collected and expended in charity, of which his accounts are now before the editor. One is dated so low as 1742 (Scott, I, 404).

He prints three extracts from them. He must have had the Note of Dr. Lyon too, since only there is the date 1742 actually written out. As he does not mention Swift's impressive list of mortgages owned by him in 1736, it is clear that at this time the two parts of Forster 512 were separate. They were separate when Forster bought them, for they occurred in different lots at the Mason sale, and they were still separate when Sims completed his analysis a year later.

That the Note of Dr. Lyon belongs logically with Forster 513 is shown by the fact that he has added up Swift's totals (513, f. 11^{v}) and transferred the result to the State of the Weekly Collections (512, f. 1^{v}). There it appears as the collections of St. Patrick's from February 1738 to April 1742. This figure is then added to another, representing the collections from 1730 to February 1738, the records for which we do not have, and from the total of the two the charities disbursed are subtracted (f. 2). The figure finally arrived at is the surplus Swift had contributed to the poor and is dated October 1742.

In the summer of 1742 Lyon was listing Swift's personal possessions and deanery holdings for the lunacy commission, and this record would seem to be one more in his tabulations of Swift's affairs.

"At the chapter meeting of 17 March 174$\frac{1}{2}$," says Louis Landa, "Swift did not preside; and the state of his health was such that he may well have been insensible to the date or the occasion--and if not insensible, quite indifferent" (Landa, p. 95). This may be true, but it is surprising how conscientiously and how neatly he kept his records until and even beyond this final meeting. The last disbursement in Swift's hand is dated 20 December 1741 (294); the last entry under "Collected in my Cathedral" is dated 18 April [1742] (305).

The list of "Debts and mortgages due to me Munday Apr. 11, 1736" concerns Swift's private financial accounts. Many of the details expand the list of mortgages entered in the 1734-5 book.

5. Use of Books by Biographers

The earliest biographers of Swift--Orrery, Delany, Deane Swift, Hawkesworth--make no mention of any account books. The only information similar to that found in the books concerns Swift's income when he first received the livings of Laracor and Rathbeggan. Orrery says, "The first of these rectories was worth about two hundred, and the latter about sixty pounds a year" (Orrery, p. 31); Delany says nothing; Deane Swift, perhaps relying on Orrery, gives the same figures (Deane Swift, p. 121); and Hawkesworth simply remarks, "which together did not amount to half the value of the Deanery" (Hawkesworth, p. 30). But Dr. Lyon and Walter Scott, who were both working from account books, give the actual value of the union as not £260 but £230.

<u>Nichols</u>. The account books were first used by Dr. Lyon about the year

1738 and again in 1765 in his notes to the Hawkesworth volume. In 1779, in his supplement to Hawkesworth's edition of Swift's Works, John Nichols printed all Lyon's notes as "Biographical Anecdotes," even though he did not know the author, whom he calls "a person well informed, and probably an intimate of the Dean's" (Nichols, Supplement, I, xvii).[9] Thomas Sheridan, when he came to write his Life of Swift in 1784, incorporated into it some of the "Biographical Anecdotes" from the Supplement. But he made no use of the specific details taken from the account books.

When Nichols published his own edition of Swift's Works in 1801, using Sheridan's Life as Volume I, the only account book material he took from the "Biographical Anecdotes" was Swift's report of his mother's death (Nichols, X, 104). In the introduction to this edition Nichols refers to his printing the "Anecdotes" in 1779 but adds, "These formed a valuable article at the time, but are now in a great measure superseded by Mr. Sheridan's life of the Dean" (Nichols, II, xxvi). But in his 1803 and 1808 editions of Swift's Works, Nichols added two further Lyon account book references as footnotes to Sheridan's Life: the record of the value of Swift's livings (Nichols, 1803, I, 110, 112), and the list of his voyages (Nichols, 1808, I, 53, 56). In the 1808 edition he described the author of the notes as a "well-informed person who seemed to have had access to several of Swift's papers" (Nichols, 1808, I, cxiv,n).

Thus Lyon's references to Swift's account books had been available to all students of Swift from 1778 and 1779 and easily accessible in the Nichols 1803 and 1808 editions. The use of this particular material by nineteenth century biographers, therefore, affords no proof that they ever consulted the books themselves.

Scott. In his edition of Swift's Works published 1808-1814, Walter Scott made use of two of the account books (1700-1 and 1701-2) as well as of the cathedral record books, all of which were actually before him. He was unaware of the use Lyon had made of the two account books. He had not seen the Lyon-Hawkesworth volume, as Monck Mason, who used it extensively, was at pains to point out (Mason, p. 302).[10] It is thus not surprising that Scott and Lyon took different selections from the same account books. Lyon gives Swift's records of his voyages in the books for 1700-1 and 1701-2; Scott does not mention the voyages, but does use the same two books for Swift's expenses and income from his livings (Scott, I, 61).

---

[9]Nichols had earlier printed some of Lyon's notes, including the account of Swift's mother's death, in the Gentleman's Magazine, 18 November 1778, where he calls Lyon a friend of Swift's. This is the first published reference to the account books.

[10]During the first years when Scott was known to be preparing his edition of Swift, the Lyon-Hawkesworth volume was in the possession of Edmond Malone. Malone may have felt disinclined to help Scott. When Scott asked the Edinburgh bibliographer Richard Heber, 5 April 1808, to present Malone with a set of his newly printed Works of Dryden, for which he had drawn heavily on Malone's edition of Dryden's Prose Works, 1800, Scott wrote, "I don't care to write to him as I think he always treated me rather drily" (Grierson, XII, 301).

Scott makes no further use of the 1701-2 volume except to print the table of annual expenditures for that year, thus holding the distinction of being the first to print an extensive extract from Swift's actual accounts. Since the book in question is now missing, the table provides a valuable record. He is also the first to refer to the cathedral record (Forster 513) and the note by Lyon (Forster 512) and to print excerpts from the former.

One account book reference reached Scott from Lyon, without his being aware of the origin: "Dr. Swift's Account of his Mother's Death, 1710" (Scott, XV, 321). A footnote explains the source: "Copied by Mr Nicol from Swift's yearly Memorandum Book for 1710." Scott had picked this up from Nichols's 1801 edition. Working at first only with this edition, he would not have encountered any other account book references. Lyon's remaining quotations from the account books, which Nichols had reprinted in 1808, Scott apparently did not find useful when he came to write his *Memoirs of Swift* in 1814.[11]

Mason. Though before his death in 1859 he was the owner of seven account books, there is no indication in Monck Mason's *History of St. Patrick's*, 1820, that he had any in his hands or even that he had ever seen one. In fact, all the evidence is to the contrary.

Mason's references to the account books, as he acknowledges, were taken directly from Lyon's notes in the Lyon-Hawkesworth volume. It had been lent to him by "the late Lord Sunderlin, brother to Mr. Malone" (Mason, p. 304,w). Mason was the first person to identify Lyon as the author of the marginalia. He wrote into the volume a note giving the identification and his reasons for making it. (*Prelims*, f. 3). In his *History* he adds, "I had made considerable use of this volume before I was informed, by Mr. Nichols, that he had published the greater part of it, in his supplemental volume to Swift's works, printed 1779."

Mason makes two references to the 1703-4 account book, but in neither case is the actual book before him. One gives the figures of Swift's income from his livings, which were furnished him by Archdeacon Brinkley; the other is the record of Swift's "10th" voyage, which he took from Lyon-Hawkesworth.

Oddly enough, Mason does not use Lyon's final marginal quotations from the account books--Swift's description of his charities as "Grand Dons" and "Petites Dons"--even though he was interested in defending Swift's reputation against accusations of avarice by critics like Orrery and Scott. He quotes Lyon on the subject, stressing his importance as a witness since "he acted for a long time as Swift's almoner, and particularly in a period of unexampled distress, during the severe winter of 1739-40" (Mason, p. 418,n).

Mason was granted permission by Thomas Steele, Sr., Lyon's nephew, to use the same Lyon MSS that Walter Scott had used, but there is no evidence that he received them in time for his *History*. The only Steele paper he mentions is Swift's "State of my affairs," 1718, which he got directly from Steele. Thus when Mason refers to any of Dr. Lyon's MSS not in the Lyon-Hawkesworth volume,

---

[11] Scott's dependence on Nichols's editions of 1801 and 1808 is treated fully by Mayhew, p. 16, and Lee Potter, "The Text of Scott's Edition of Swift," *Studies in Bibliography*, 1969, XXII, 240-55.

he is forced to rely on Scott.

There is ample negative evidence that Mason had no direct access to the account books. For example, on p. 252,c. he states that "it appears probable, from his correspondence, that he resided in England from Feb. 1707-8." Had he seen the 1708-9 book before 1820, he would have known that Swift "was all this year [1708] in England" (85).

Forster. John Forster, in the one volume of his Life of Swift completed and published in 1875, the year before his death, listed in his Preface the Swift materials he had been collecting for many years. Among them are "Swift's note-books and books of account," which he had purchased "at the dispersion of the library of Mr. Monck Mason of Dublin" (Forster, Life, vii). With the exception of the missing page containing the memorandum on the death of Mrs. Swift, none of the ones Forster owned had been used previously by any Swift biographer. Forster had also bought the Statement of Debts and Mortgages and the record of cathedral collections and disbursements, the latter of which had earlier been used by Scott and only by him.

Soon after Forster bought the account books and the other records, he turned them over for deciphering and analysis to Richard Sims, a specialist in autographs and manuscripts.[12] On 25 October 1859 "the diaries" were returned to Forster with the completed analysis, neatly dividing the hundreds of entries into seventy-four categories, ranging from the specific ("Milk and Eggs") to the general ("State of the Diaries").

Unfortunately, although Forster wrote his publisher, Murray, in 1856 that he would allow himself to think of no other literary work but the Swift until it was done (Woolley, p. 195), many years and many other professional responsibilities were to intervene before he settled down to the writing of the book. When he did come to work with the account book material, in the last year of his life and in failing health, he naturally depended heavily on the Sims analysis. Sometimes, indeed, he simply cut sections out of Sims's manuscript, no doubt to send to the printer, such as the value and charges of Swift's livings for 1702-3, the record of the journey to Ireland in 1709, the list of letters from June-October 1709, and portions of Swift's wins and losses at cards (Forster, Life, pp. 117, 262, 268, 269).[13] The inaccuracies in these excisions may be Sims's or the printer's, though the reversing of the "Won" and "Lost" columns in 1708-9 and 1709-10 is more likely to be Forster's mistake.

Forster was so dependent on Sims that he was occasionally misled by him. For instance, Swift's marginal references to giddy fits are used by Forster to show, as indeed they do, the "dark background of pain and fears thrusting itself upon Swift in the years between 1708 and 1710" (Forster, Life, p. 253). The running list of entries clearly comes from Sims's category of "Health,"

---

[12]According to his obituary notice in the Times, 29 November 1898, Sims had been "long associated with the Manuscripts Department of the British Museum." The Sims transcripts are 47. C. Box 5 of the Forster Collection.

[13]Forster used no other account books but his own. His references on pp. 124, 125, and 127 to material in earlier account books, no longer extant, all come, as he there states, from the Lyon-Hawkesworth volume, which he had bought in 1858.

even to the unaccountable misreading of "swoon" as "swimming in the head." The most surprising error by Forster is on p. 131:

> Swift's entry in his note-book of his English residence, which began in the winter of 1707-8 and extended to June 1709, will be found to have special significance. "In suspense I was all this year in England."

In spite of the distorted language, so uncharacteristic of Swift, Forster was not suspicious and in fact found the entry so striking that he referred to it twice again (Forster, _Life_, pp. 213, 252). Yet there is no such entry in the account book. The note "In suspense" is to be found at the top of Swift's first Quarterly Categories page (61), twenty pages away from the simple factual remark on the title page of his "Account of my Livings for the Year 1708": "I was all this year in England" (85). Forster had found the two marginalia side by side under "Travels" and evidently assumed that they formed one entry in Swift's account book for 1708-9.

Examples of such inaccuracy can be multiplied. Speaking of Swift's frequent enjoyable meetings with Addison in 1708-9, Forster refers to the account book, saying, "A batch of entries clustered on the same page are dry enough; but vividly behind them rise the _noctes coenaeque deorum_." The five entries he then cites of "Tav^{rn} Addison 2_s_. 6_d_.," &c. (p. 159), occur in the account book for 1708-9 certainly, but they run, one or two to a page, through November, December, and January. They do occur on a single page, however, in Sims, under "Taverns."

Forster is sometimes inaccurate even when Sims is perfectly clear. He states correctly that Swift's use of the term "MD" is to be found in the account books as early as 1702. But he extends his reference to include "the Ppts, MD's, and Pdfrs, which appear in Swift's note-books as early as 1702" (p. 200n). "Ppt does not appear until 1710, "Pdfr" never.

Again, Forster speaks of Swift's meetings with Addison, Congreve, Halifax, and Steele:

> Swift's note-book contains entries of dinners to or with them all, and of frequent coaches to the houses of Halifax in New Palace Yard or at Hampton Court. We trace them dining at the "George," with Addison for host, at the "Fountain" with Steele, and at the "St. James's" where Wortley Montagu entertains (p. 221).

Yet the account books show only one meeting with Halifax, one with Congreve, and one with Steele. These references never coincide with the frequent "Addison" entries, no taverns whatever are named, and Wortley Montagu does not appear. Similarly, Forster states that, in 1710, "Swift's note books also tell us that he and Addison had passed several summer days at the bishop's [Ashe's] houses in Clogher and Finglas; and that, both there and at Laracor, 'little MD' was with them" (p. 265). The July page in the 1709-10 account book carries five "Addison" entries, one dinner at Finglas, and four "MD's," but they are never together or even on the same date.

Forster's dates are unreliable, possibly because of haste. Swift's letter to Archdeacon Walls about punning with the Berkeleys, dated 22 January 1708-9, is brought together with the account book entry of "At Cranford from 22 to 27" in January 1709-10. The confusion is increased when Forster makes this stay at Cranford lead to the writing of the _Argument against Abolishing_

Christianity and the Project for the Advancement of Religion, both written in 1708 (p. 213).

After reprinting the sentences given by Scott and Mason from Swift's memorandum about his mother's death--"after a long sickness, being ill all winter, and lame, and extremely ill a month or six weeks before her death"--Forster goes on to say that the same account book (1709-10) "has an entry which shows that she had been able to write to her son during the month preceding her death" (p. 268). There are three notices of letters on the April page for 1710, none from Swift's mother, and there is no list of letters in that particular volume. Probably what actually happened is that Forster confused the years, as in the Cranford entry, for in the 1708-9 account book Swift recorded a letter received from his mother on 24 April 1709, exactly a year before her death.

It is regrettable that the first biographer to see these particular account books and to appreciate the vivid detail in them should in the end have been hurried, because of ill health and fatigue, into using that detail, more often than not, incorrectly. If he had turned to the account books when he first got them in 1858, he might have used the information in them to good effect, especially since he wanted his Life of Swift to be based on Swift's own testimony in letters and journals (Woolley, p. 198). He might have used the entries of wins and losses, meetings, and letters as they were later used by Ball, Williams, Landa, and Ehrenpreis. His accounts of Isaiah Parvisol, Jo Beaumont, Archdeacon Walls, and the Ashe brothers might have been fuller and more precise. Yet Forster remains the first biographer who saw the implications and importance of the account books and who preserved them.[14]

Craik. Henry Craik availed himself of the Forster Collection and glanced at the account books, though he made less use of them than Forster did. He does give Swift's income from the 1708-9 book and mentions casually a few examples of Swift's social life which Forster had not used. He may be taking the record of Swift's journey to Ireland in June from the 1712-3 book, but if so, he is copying one of the dates incorrectly: the account book gives the 10th as the date of the arrival in Holyhead, not the 8th (Craik, p. 264). He prints Swift's comments on the death of Ann Long, taking a few textual liberties (p. 227); and when referring to the memorandum on the death of Swift's mother, he makes the astonishing remark that the entire 1709-10 book, not just the page for May, is now lost (Craik, p. 192).

Thus, though Craik consulted the account books, he seems not to have studied them attentively. Forster, for all his haste, used the information in the books far more extensively.

It is a mystery, by the way, why Craik does not refer to the two account books--1717-8 and 1732-3--in the Forster Collection which Forster himself did not live to use. If he had been able to complete the Life, Forster would unquestionably have added information to give the kind of personal detail the books alone provide.

---

[14]He was also the first and, apparently, still the only student of Swift to publish a facsimile of part of an account book. On p. 254 Forster reproduces the page for December 1708. Cf. p. 63 below.

Twentieth century biographers and editors have, as might be expected, studied the account books more painstakingly and have used them effectively to fill in the gaps in Swift's biography. Some passages have been reprinted, not only the memoranda on the deaths of his mother and Ann Long, which have frequently found their way into the prose works, biographies, and editions of the correspondence, but the lists of letters sent and received in the years 1708-9 and 1711-3. The fullest and boldest use to be made of them as yet is by Irvin Ehrenpreis in Volume Two of His Swift, The Man, His Works, and The Age. It is to be expected that the final volume of this monumental work will, for the first time, examine in all their aspects and with Professor Ehrenpreis's usual thoroughness the three last account books, 1717-8, 1732-3, and 1734-5.[15]

6. Stella and Vanessa

Among the interesting biographical details to be found in the account books, we learn something about the friendships which meant so much to Swift and about his relationships with those ordinary people--minor clergymen, tradesmen, and servants--with whom he was necessarily in almost daily contact.

Of Swift's friends the closest, Esther Johnson, is never referred to in the account books as Stella, the name Swift used in literary works during the last ten years of her life. In the first of the notebooks, 1702-3, she is called Tetty (20), which may be the name by which she was known as a child, when Swift first met her; after that she appears under the ciphers Tpt or Ppt. The most common reference is MD, but this seems always to include Mrs. Dingley. Mrs. Dingley alone is DD. The ladies use MD of themselves, as we gather from Dingley's pages of expenses. All these symbols, so well known from the Journal to Stella, 1710-3, were being used, as the account books show, as early as 1703 or 1708.

The ladies were the nearest thing to a family Swift had. When he is in England, there are reminders to himself of commissions for them. The raillery in the Journal about Stella's addiction to cards is given justification by the

---

[15]An interesting example of a biographical problem arising from the account books is the "16th voyage" controversy. Swift wrote, in the 1703-4 book, "Left Neston, Tuesd. May. 30th. 1704. landed at Dublin, Thursday morn. Jun. 1. 1704. being my 16th Voyage" (41). The "16th" is very clear; no one who saw it could possibly misread it. But anyone who saw it only in Lyon's marginal note in Lyon-Hawkesworth could easily mistake it for "10th." The figure runs down into the trough of the volume, and a "6" is superimposed on a "0." Nichols read Lyon's entry correctly as "16" and so printed it in his Supplement of 1779 and in his editions of Swift's Works in 1803 and 1808. In 1815 Hartstonge learned from the account book itself that Swift "had been sixteen different times in England," not, of course, what Swift said. Monck Mason and Forster, both depending on Lyon-Hawkesworth, misread the figure in the trough as "10." Ball accurately read Lyon's marginal entry and corrected Forster's "10" to "16." Arthur Case, however, not having seen either Lyon-Hawkesworth or the account book, conjectured that Forster had been right ("Swift and Sir William Temple, MLN, LX, 259). Finally, Irvin Ehrenpreis turned directly to the book itself and set the matter straight ("Swift's Voyages, MLN, LXV, 256).

appearance of her name, when he is in Ireland, in the lists of wins and losses. When apart, they wrote regularly, and Swift recorded and numbered MD's letters, now lost, in his correspondence lists. The frequency of his visits to Stella and Mrs. Dingley is clearly reflected in those parts of his accounts which cover his residence in Ireland, especially in 1717-8, a year except for the account books somewhat barren of biographical information, when coach and chair trips to MD and dinner with MD are entered as often as two or three times a week. Indeed, the most common item in the book for 1717-8 is simply MD followed by a small sum of money; whatever it may indicate, whether a visit or a dinner, it is clearly a proof that they were together on that day. His dependence on them in illness is shown in the particularly moving entry in December 1708, when, after noting that he had been "Horrible sick" on the 5th, he is able on the 12th to record that he is "much better. thank G^{d} & MD's Pray^{rs}." Similarly, in October 1710 he writes, "31 a small giddy fitt & swoon MD G^{d} help me."

It is accepted as a fact by recent biographers, beginning with Ball (IV, 452), that at the time Swift urged Stella to move to Ireland, in the summer of 1701, he promised to give her an allowance of fifty pounds a year to supplement the small income she received from Lady Giffard, Sir William Temple's sister, and from the leasehold lands in co Wicklow left her by Temple himself. The evidence for the allowance is drawn from the account books, where the item MC appears as one of the regular quarterly expenses.

No suggestions have been advanced as to what the cipher stands for, and in fact Ball is the only commentator even to mention that it is MC, not MD. MC does indeed mean MD, and is used as MD is in the Journal to Stella to refer to both women, not just to Stella. Once it even occurs in the account books out of the context of the quarterly expenses: on 17 July 1704 there is the entry "G[ave] Coff[ee] MC," where one would normally find MD. It does not appear before the ladies come to Ireland, in 1701, according to the page of annual totals printed by Scott (315), nor after Stella's death, when the symbol DD replaces it.

MC was used far more commonly by Swift than has been realized. The symbol "Me" has been read throughout the Journal along with "MD" and "FW" at the ends of the letters. Williams (JS, p. lvi) restricts it to Mrs. Dingley, with a suggestion that it stands for "Madam Elderly," while Ehrenpreis offers the translation "remember me" (II, 653). It is to be read "MC."[16] Whatever it stands for--"my children"?--it is used in the letters as in the account books in connection with money paid the ladies. The following passages, which are ambiguous in the Journal, become understandable if we substitute "MC" for "Me." 17 June 1712: "Remembr to write a due time before Me money is wantd." 7 August: "I remember onely there was something in your Letter about Me's money, and that shall be taken care of on the other side." 15 September: "I have clearly forgot whethr I sent a Bill for Me in any of my last Letters; I think I did; pray let me know, & always give me timely Notice." 11 October: "How the duce come I to be so exact in Me Money; just 17s & 8d more than due. I believe you cheat me . . . . I have dated your Bill late, because it must not commence ung oomens till the 1st of November next. O fais I must be ise iss

[16]The facsimile of Letter I, printed in JS, I, 4, shows the MC clearly at the end.

fais must I, else Me will cheat pdfr." 27 February 1713: "This Lettr must go to morrow, because of sending Me a Bill."

These examples, all relating to the allowance, could doubtless have been multiplied, but Deane Swift, in printing Letters II-XL, must have omitted some of the "MC's" in the body of the letters as he did at the end.

In two of the books, 1702-3 and 1703-4, the MC item totals fifty pounds. In 1708-9 the total is forty-four pounds; in 1709-10 the entries are incomplete, but since eleven pounds is recorded for each of two quarters, this is doubtless another forty-four-pound year; in 1711-2 and 1712-3 MC is listed as one of the quarterly headings, but there are no entries and no money is recorded as having been paid out in those years; in 1717-8 there is only the yearly total, given under the heading "MC &c &c &c," which is not fifty but one hundred pounds, the increase reflecting Swift's improved income as Dean of St. Patrick's.

The explanation for the discrepancies in the yearly totals may be found in the Journal. On 20 October 1711 Swift writes:

> Is the eight pounds from Hawkshaw included in the thirty-nine pounds five shillings and two-pence? How do I know by this how my account stands? Can't you write five or six lines to cast it up? Mine is forty-four pounds per annum, and eight pounds from Hawkshaw makes fifty-two pounds. Pray set it right and let me know; you had best.

He takes up the subject again on 30 November:

> 7l. 17s. 8d. old blunderer, not 18sh. I have reckoned it 18 times. Hawkshaw's eight pounds is not reckoned; and if it be secure, it may lie where it is, unless they desire to pay it: so Parvisol may let it drop till further orders. . . . I mean that Hawkshaw's money goes for an addition to MD, you know; but be good houswives.

It thus appears that from 1708 or earlier to 1713 Swift was paying the ladies fifty-two pounds a year, forty-four of it from his own income and eight of it from the interest on a loan he had made to Dr. John Hawkshaw. Hawkshaw apparently would pay Parvisol, who would then convey the money to the ladies. It is interesting that the account book for 1734-5 shows the allowance given to Mrs. Dingley after Stella's death to be fifty-two pounds.[17]

On 23 April 1713, when he had just been appointed to the deanery, Swift wrote the ladies, "[whatever comes on it, Md's Allowance must be encreased.]" This is Forster's interpretation and, according to Williams, "probably cor-

---

[17]According to Deane Swift (p. 365) Mrs. Dingley believed the fifty-two pounds allowed her by Swift came from money she had in the Funds. Lyon produced a receipt for thirteen pounds, signed by Dingley, for one quarter in 1737 (Prelims, f. 34) and qualified Deane Swift's statement only by saying she really did have sixteen pounds a year in the Funds (Lyon, p. 57). The fiction (probably fully understood by Dingley) may have been a continuation of one she and Stella and Swift had observed while they were all together in Ireland. Surely the public knowledge that Swift was supporting Stella's household with an outright grant would have caused scandal in contemporary Dublin.

rect" (JS, II, 665, n34). Swift continues, "I shall not part with Laracor: that is all I have to live on; except the Deanry be worth more than 400ll a year; is it? if it be, the overplus shall be divided [. . . . . . besides te usuall. . . . . .]" The sections in brackets have been scratched out, probably by Swift: the method of deletion is the same as in the account books. The first bracketed section, if it has been correctly deciphered, proves the fact of an allowance, whatever the amount of it may have been.

The Journal to Stella is full of references to Swift's and Stella's financial transactions. Sometimes when he orders Parvisol to pay money to her, he may be referring not to the allowance but to a loan. For example, on 10 May 1711, when the ladies are planning a trip to Wexford, he says, "I write here to Parvisol to lend Stella twenty pound, and to take her note promissary to pay it in half a year, &c." Three months later, 23 August, he adds, "When you think proper, I will let Parvisol know you have paid that twenty pounds, or part of it," and in September he refers once more to the matter, "send me word how my accounts stand, that they may be adjusted by Nov. 1. Pray be very particular: but the twenty pounds I lend you is not to be included." Like similar loans and like the complicated real estate dealings between the two, noted by modern biographers, these were outside the scheme of the account books and must have been entered in Swift's other records.

In 1702-3 and at other times whenever Swift was in Ireland, the MC payments are not made in lump sums but in driblets, indicated by entries ranging from three shillings to five pounds, or paid "at Sev[ll] times." Nor are the payments, of whatever size, made with any regularity: some are two days apart and others separated by as much as forty days, and they may be recorded under every day of the week. This may be explained if we think of Swift as handing over small amounts to the ladies when he called upon them. In contrast, when he is in England, MC is paid in round sums by Parvisol on Swift's authorization; for example, in 1708-9 under MC is the notation "p[d] to May 1. by Accounts &c clearing from Eng[d]" (66, and cf 90).

Whatever Swift's method of payment, it seems clear from the account books that there was some regular allowance paid to the ladies and entered under MC.

Many references to the Vanhomrigh family are found in the account books, beginning with a loss at cards on 20 January 1709 and thereafter appearing frequently in the three volumes 1709-10, 1711-2, 1712-3. Hester Vanhomrigh herself, under a variety of pet names, is mentioned nine times, first on 1 July 1709 as the writer of a letter to Swift, who had just arrived in Ireland. Another of her letters, listed in his correspondence record, is forwarded later in the year to Clogher, where he spent the early part of December. All other references to Vanessa are in the 1711-12 volume: in February Swift enters payments of fourpence to her and a shilling to her maid; in June two coach trips, one to visit her and another for which he paid the fare; in September card games. There are instances in all four of the volumes when the entry is simply "Van," marking occasions when Swift doubtless saw Vanessa with her family. From the warmth of their later relationship, one would expect her name to appear more often than it does, and it is noteworthy that it is not found after October 1712.

As Professor Ehrenpreis has pointed out (II, 641), Swift did not feel it necessary to report to the ladies of St. Mary's all his visits to the Vanhomrighs, and when he speaks in the Journal of dining with an unnamed friend, that friend is often entered in the account book as "Van." He probably hesitated to let them know how many times he was there because they, who must have known the family, disapproved of them as people of "no consequence" (*JS*, p. 202). Whether his suppression of the name also indicates a growing involvement with the elder daughter is less clear.

In the course of his brilliant use of the account books on this matter (II, 642-647), Ehrenpreis has come to the conclusion that the two June 1712 coach items noted above, in conjunction with boat trips by Swift to and from John Barber's, are evidence of assignations there, for what purpose is not stated. Ehrenpreis speaks of "rasher intimacies," but he also says that "Judging from Swift's habits over many years, I believe he made no improper advances to Hessy." Indeed, even if the two did meet at Barber's, no sinister explanation is needed. The visit might well have been in connection with Vanessa's financial affairs, about which Swift was advising her from this period on until the end of her life, using Barber as a sort of banker.

It may be worth looking in some detail at the relevant account book entries for the spring and summer of 1712, contrasting them with similar entries in the four other account books of the years during which Swift knew Vanessa.

In April 1712 Swift was extremely ill with shingles: he tells the ladies that he rarely left his room, though he did manage to dine at a neighbor's, whom they would recognize as the Vanhomrighs. He improved somewhat during May, and the account book shows that he was able to make visits, three of them to Barber, who was then engaged in printing some pamphlets of Swift's, notably the *Proposal for Correcting . . . the English Tongue*. The only entry involving the Vanhomrighs is on the 9th: "Co^{ch} &c Vans. 3^{s}-6^{d}," a large sum. In June, the month in question, Swift left his lodgings near the Vanhomrighs and, on the 5th, moved to Kensington. On the 8th he jotted down in his account book that he was ill with colic. Sometime in the second week, between the 7th and the 13th, the item "Boat to & from B-- 1^{s}" and another "to Miss hess for Coach 2^{s}" were written down on the same line. It is the collocation of these two entries, almost certainly relating to the same day, that is the key point of Ehrenpreis's thesis. It is the "simplest interpretation," he says, to assume an assignation at Barber's. If this was a meeting for rash intimacies, one would expect it to be followed by others, and Ehrenpreis finds the evidence for others in the account books. But this evidence is extremely tenuous. Swift certainly visited Barber again that month. He makes an entry, "Boat Bar^{br} 1^{s}" on the 13th, and probably the "Boat. 6^{d}." on the 27th was to the same place. "Boat" alone occurs on the 20th and 30th, but it is not inevitable that these trips were to Barber's. Swift went by water to other places than his printer's: he speaks in the *Journal* of dining on the 14th with the Duchess of Ormond near Sheen "and thought to get a Boat back as usuall." The item on the 24th, "Co^{ch} Hessy 2^{s}," if we judge by Swift's usual practice, is likely to mean that he went to her. His normal method is to indicate by this order of words the person visited, as the next item, two days later, "Co^{ch} Ld Mans^{l}," illustrates.

Ehrenpreis adduces the boat trips on the 27th and the 30th as evidence of other assignations. On the 27th Swift not only spends sixpence on a boat but on the same day loses at hazard to "M---y," which Ehrenpreis reads as "Misshessy." But "M---y" is far more likely to stand for Mrs. Manley, Barber's mistress and Swift's most active assistant in Grub Street. He rarely disguises names in this way in the account books and never Vanessa's: whenever the entry is not "Van," which seems usually to indicate the whole family, her name appears without concealment as "Miss hess," "Hess," or some other variant. In fact, on the 24th Swift has taken the pains to go back and insert "Hessy" into the item. His care was rather to conceal the extent of his political involvement. Should the account book be lost, the danger to him and to his subordinates, if their names were to be found in it, might be considerable. His decision was evidently to omit their names entirely. We know that he supervised pamphlets written by others--he speaks of "my understrappers"--yet except for Mrs. Manley their names do not appear in either the account books or the Journal. In the account books, Mrs. Manley, if it is she, is mentioned only this once, when it could hardly be avoided in the list of wins and losses, yet Swift was frequently with her, giving hints, dictating to her, and directing her writing. In the Journal she figures twice under her own name, elsewhere as "the author of the Atalantis," a "woman," an "under-spur-leather," &c.

As to the meeting on 30 June, Swift does record on that day a two-shilling coach fare and a boat fare, but since the latter is only sixpence, I assume he himself went one way by boat and returned by coach. If the coach were for Vanessa, he would presumably have said so, as he did twice before on the same page. Ehrenpreis also instances on this day an eight-shilling dinner at Pontack's, which he considers suspiciously expensive. But Pontack's was expensive: the previous September, according to the Journal, Swift had spent seven shillings there on dinner just for himself (JS, p. 371).

During May and June, then, Swift was going constantly by water, presumably most of the time to Barber's. In the first three weeks of July there are three boat trips, also possibly to Barber's. Yet never again is Vanessa's name, which at this time Swift is making no effort to conceal, found on the same day as one of the boat trips.[18] The theory of assignations in June 1712, then, is not proved by the account book. The conjunction of the boat trip to Barber's on the same day as a coach for Vanessa is probably an unremarkable coincidence.

It is a greater probability that the relationship between the two became more intense a few months later. On the 19th of July Swift went to Windsor, where he remained, though not without brief visits back to London, till the end of September. On 15 August he refers in a letter to Vanessa to a projected visit of "3 or 4 days" from the entire Vanhomrigh family. The visit took place in September, and Swift records in the account book playing ombre with Erasmus Lewis and "Mishess" on the 11th, with "Van & Hess" on the 20th, and piquet with "Van," presumably Vanessa's brother, on the 24th. Swift later claimed that the composition of Cadenus and Vanessa took place at Windsor in the summer or autumn of 1712 (Corres., III,130). His dating of the poem can hardly be correct, and he may be blending his visit to Windsor in 1712 with the one in 1713, by which time he was dean and could properly have called himself Cadenus. Actually, the composition of the poem may have extended over both

---

[18]It may be thought an argument in favor of the assignation theory that Swift uses "B--." At most other times Barber's name is clearly given. But one other "B--" occurs, on 10 March of this year, when Swift wins three shillings at whisk "at B--s," when there is no question of an assignation, on a day that as he tells the ladies, "I dined with a friend in the City, about a little Business of printing." The friend is obviously Barber.

Windsor years, but it is interesting that 1712 was the crucial year remembered by Swift.

No reference to Vanessa occurs in the account books after the third week in October. Although in 1712-3 Swift's wins and losses record four or five games with the Vanhomrigh family, Vanessa's name is not given, nor is it among the lists of letters written and received, as it must have been if Swift had been keeping as careful a list as in previous years. (The list for 1712-3 amounts to little more than a record of his correspondence with MD.) It is especially significant that Vanessa is not mentioned in the 1717-8 volume. During this year she and her sister were living either at Celbridge, a few miles west of Dublin, or in town, not far from the deanery. It is impossible to believe Swift never saw Vanessa, yet there is no hint in the account book of a single visit. The book proves that, as we have said, he was seeing Stella and Mrs. Dingley regularly, and other entries show a busy social life, but the Vanhomrigh name is conspicuously absent. According to the 1717-8 volume, the sisters, though they were known to Ford, Provost Pratt, Archbishop King, and others of Swift's friends, were never at the deanery. Although unfortunately their letters from 1717-8 have not survived, in Vanessa's and Swift's correspondence from previous and succeeding years, references to meetings are common. The conclusion becomes inescapable that Swift is intentionally avoiding naming her.

In three later letters, when Swift recalls for Vanessa occasions which were full of emotional resonance for them both, he mentions nothing which can be interpreted to suggest a meeting at Barber's, but twice he alludes to an incident at Windsor. It is after Windsor in 1712 that the tone of their relationship changes, and her name disappears from the account book. It is likely that, whatever happened at Windsor, Vanessa's name was deliberately suppressed after that.

7. Friends and Relations

A book of accounts does not, as correspondence may do, offer full information about the compiler's friendships. The people we see most often are not necessarily those we choose to see but instead business associates, tradesmen, servants, and the like, and our dealings with them are most likely to find their way into our financial records. Even a correspondence is incomplete. In Swift's case, some friends, like Mr. and Mrs. Wesley, saved none of the letters which the account books tell us he wrote nor did he keep any of theirs; others, like Thomas Walls and John Worrall, saved his letters, but none of theirs to him remain. For those acquaintances with whom he had business dealings, such as Walls and Worrall, the account books usually contain valuable material on these dealings, supplementing what we know from letters. The books are, naturally, less helpful when money is not involved.

The loss of most of the books also deprives us, we can be reasonably sure, of many facts about close friends which would help fill in the picture given in letters. Because we lack the 1713-4, 1725-6, and 1726-7 account books, we find out almost nothing about Swift's relationship with Pope, mentioned but twice, and Arbuthnot, mentioned once in the extant books, nor with Gay, Lady Suffolk, and the second Earl of Oxford, who do not appear at all. Nor does Knightley Chetwode, whose friendship with Swift is so fully documented in the letters: the one account book in which he might be looked for, 1717-8, covers a period during which he was apparently out of Ireland. Even the close friend of Swift's final years, his first biographer, Lord Orrery, is not mentioned, though he was in Dublin for part of the time covered by the last two books.

The account books, on the other hand, sometimes give us glimpses of people whose company Swift enjoyed but who appear only infrequently in his correspondence. Possibly his closest friends at one time were the Ashe brothers, especially St. George Ashe, his tutor at Trinity and later Bishop of Clogher. No correspondence remains on either side, but the account books tell of visits to Clogher and evenings at cards, as well as listing letters sent and received. Few letters have survived from the group centered around Laracor and Trim, who must have known Swift in the years before he became dean better than anyone in England and most in Dublin did. There are no letters, as we mentioned, from the Wesleys; none from the Barrys, with whom at the end of 1709 he played at cards twelve evenings within a five-week period; and none from John Percival, a dinner guest and opponent at cards from the first extant account book till his death in 1718.

In discussing what can be learned of Swift's friendships from the account books, we can arbitrarily arrange them into four categories: clergymen, literary men, political associates, and a remaining group which fits into none of these but which includes such important figures as Charles Ford, Jo Beaumont, and Swift's relations. As it happens, the clergymen are all in Ireland, whereas the writers and politicians are English.

Like the Ashes, most of Swift's Irish friends were members of the clergy. His relationship with Anthony Raymond, rector of Trim, must have extended from 1705, when Raymond assumed the rectorship, till his death in 1726. The account books enforce the impression of close association which is given by the numerous references to Raymond in Swift's letters to Walls. Whenever Swift is in Ireland, from 1708 through 1718, the last account-book year before Raymond's death, he records social occasions with the rector: wine or frequently punch, meals at taverns, evenings at cards, and several dinners, including the final Raymond entry on 30 January 1718, when he was entertained with MD, Percival, and "Grattan" (probably Robert). Swift stayed with the doctor and his wife when his Laracor house was in ruins (1714-7), as MD did regularly, and the doctor was of considerable service in assisting with the tithes of Swift's Meath livings and in occasionally preaching for him. The dean, on the other hand, was instrumental in securing for Raymond the living of Moymet, near Trim, and this is probably one of the great obligations he acknowledges to Swift in his will (Corres., III, 465, n2). In spite of this acknowledgment and the gift of a mourning ring, he was marked down in Swift's evaluation of his friends which Dr. Lyon preserved as "ungrateful" (Corres., V, 270).

Thomas Walls, Archdeacon of Achonry, like Raymond a friend whom Swift finally marked "ungrateful," was the schoolmaster of St. Patrick's from 1698 till 1710, at which time he became incumbent of Castleknock. Thus they would have known each other from at least the time Swift entered the chapter, but Walls is not named in either the letters or the account books before 1708. By that time Swift was already using him as he would continue to do for the next twenty years, both before and after he became dean, as financial manager and as general supervisor of livings and deanery affairs during the absence of the dean, including taking Swift's turns in preaching at the cathedral. The account books show that in 1708-9, when Swift was in London, the money from his livings was transmitted to him through Walls. Swift thought well of him, relied upon him unhesitatingly, and made vigorous if unavailing efforts to secure his advancement. "Whenever you see me fail in any part relating to you," he wrote Walls, "I desire I may hear of it" (Corres., II, 169).

Walls strikes one as a solid but owlish, humorless figure. He evidently did not share Swift's amusement at puns, and Swift once impatiently characterized him to MD as "a reasoning coxcomb" (JS, p. 336). Archbishop King's description of him as a grave and good man (Corres., II, 224, n2) is not incompatible with his being dull. Like Dr Raymond he embarrassed Swift by coming to London, if only for a few days, during the Tory years, and the account of the visit in the Journal to Stella shows Swift's annoyance and exasperation. After his return to Dublin, he sent Swift a pompous "literary" essay on the visit, from which Swift quoted ridiculous passages--the only bits of Walls's letters which we have (JS, p. 369). But the ladies were close to the Archdeacon and his wife and even lived for some years with them at their house in Queen Street. There was a running joke that at one time Swift had been in love with Mrs. Walls, whom he actually found tiresome. The evidence of the Journal and the account books shows that she and perhaps less often the Archdeacon were staunch members of the card-playing club with Stella, the Stoytes, the Manleys, and Dean Stearne, and during the period 1709-13, whenever Swift was in Dublin, he recorded a number of games of ombre with them, even during the brief time between his installation as dean and his return to England in 1713.

Swift's general correspondence shows that the close relationship between him and Walls continued at least until Stella's death. Walls, along with Sheridan, Worrall, and Delany, kept Swift in England informed about Stella's condition during the summer of 1726, though Swift's last letter to him was written the previous year. Thus it may seem odd that Walls appears only twice in the 1717-8 account book. One explanation is the absence from that volume of the page of wins and losses, where in earlier ones the Wallses were often found. Also Swift's letters to Walls, all of which, as far as we know, the Archdeacon preserved, show that by 1717 Walls is relinquishing, apparently by his own desire, his part in Swift's financial concerns. In November 1717 a dinner with MD and perhaps other guests is recorded. His name last appears in the account books on 30 August 1718. Two disparaging references to him by Sheridan in 1736 suggest that after the death of Stella Swift no longer found Walls's companionship agreeable or necessary. It is hard to imagine the irrepressible Sheridan, by now Swift's closest friend, and the reliable but stodgy Walls having much in common.

The account books throw some light on two problems in the Swift-Sheridan relationship: the date of their first meeting and that of the near quarrel in the early days of their acquaintanceship. The first reference in the account books to Sheridan is to a dinner, probably at the deanery, on 17 or 18 May 1718. On 25 December 1734 Sheridan says that they have known each other "above sixteen years, and I believe a little more," which could place the date of their meeting in the spring of 1718, at about the time of the dinner. But the account book reference is not the earliest. If we accept Faulkner's dating, that is Swift's poem "Ad Amicum Eruditum Thomam Sheridan" of October 1717. Furthermore, two months later, on 11 December, Swift records a gift of five shillings made "at the Greek play" (190), and it has been suggested that the play was given by Sheridan's scholars.

Yet the fact that from November 1717 to May 1718 there is no mention of

Sheridan in the account book implies that during that time the relationship was not a close one. In August of 1718 Sheridan again dined at the deanery, in company with MD, and he appeared for the final time in the 1717-8 account book at the end of September, at a dinner with MD, "Grattans," and "Jacksons." This was probably the dinner to which Sheridan had been invited in a note dated 20 September appended to one of the poems the two were beginning to exchange: "pray come to Dinner with the Company you met here last" (Poems, p. 968). If the August dinner is the one referred to, the company must be only MD, not the Grattans and Jacksons, but of course Sheridan may have been entertained at the deanery more often than Swift's entries show.

It was probably during September 1718 that Swift and Sheridan began the exchange of doggerel which continued for many years. In one of these first poems, now lost, Sheridan offended Swift by overstepping the bounds of raillery: "he writ a long poem, describing [Swift's] muse to be dead, and making a funeral solemnity with asses, owls, &c. and gave the copy among all his acquaintance" (PW, V, 222). This incident Swift places within "three months time" from Sheridan's becoming familiar at the deanery. If we assume this period to coincide with Sheridan's first dinner there, the offense could well have been committed the following August or, more likely, September. One of Sheridan's poems to Swift, an answer to Swift's of 20 September, has a passage beginning "Oft have I been by poets told, / That, poor Jonathan, thou grows old," which proceeds to describe the decline of the dean's poetic powers. There are no asses or owls in it, and it is not a long poem, but the general tone of jocular abuse suggests that it belongs to the same period (Poems, p. 970). On 10 October Swift wrote a poem to Delany and sent it to him a month later with a short explanatory letter, both poem and letter recommending that he speak to Sheridan about the proper limits of raillery (Poems, 214; Corres., II, 301). It is interesting that, if we judge by Sheridan's appearance at the deanery in late September as well as by the continuing exchange of verses, no interruption occurred in the friendship. It is true that Sheridan is not named among the guests at Swift's dinners during the next month, but verses dated 23 October (Poems, p. 980), before Swift sent the letter to Delany, shows that his resentment was not long-lived.

Sheridan appears only twice in the 1732-3 book, both times at dinner, once in April and once in June. Yet Swift certainly and Sheridan presumably were both in Dublin for most of the year, and other evidence exists of their meeting. The entry of "dinner" is less common than in 1717-8; it is likely that during this year, before the advent of Mrs. Whiteway, Swift entertained little. Furthermore, the absence of the record of wins and losses for 1732-3 may give the impression that the two saw each other less than they actually did, for they evidently enjoyed an evening of cards, as the record for 1734-5 shows.

Except for a period in April, when Sheridan was on vacation, they met frequently during the spring of 1735. In January Sheridan came to dinner twice, the only guest. In February at least four meetings are indicated, three of them within one week: on the 20th they had dinner and played cards, no dinner is mentioned on the 22nd but Swift won a shilling from his friend at cards, and on the 27th there is a dinner but no cards. On all three of these occasions, one notices, Swift paid for Sheridan's chair to the deanery. Swift also put down a dinner in March and an evening of cards in May. Soon after, Sheridan retired to Cavan, where he spent most of the summer, returning to Dublin for a fortnight at the end of August. If his plan to leave Cavan on the

23rd was carried out, he must have gone directly to the deanery when he arrived in Dublin, for he played cards with Swift and "Harrison" the next night. The dean visited Sheridan at Cavan in November, but the visit is not, of course, covered by the present account book.

From their letters it seems clear that Swift and Sheridan had some financial dealings, but they are not recorded in the account books.

Swift's clerical acquaintances in Dublin would inevitably include the members of his chapter at St. Patrick's, some of whom were among his closest friends. Seventeen or eighteen are mentioned in the account books. The Grattans and the Jacksons, whom Delany praised as "genteel, agreeable, and well-bred men and women, such companions as no wise man ever wanted, or at least could want, if he could help it" (Delany, p. 94), are conspicuous in the 1717-8 book, usually as dinner guests at the deanery in company with Stella and Mrs. Dingley. They appear again in 1734-5 but less frequently, though we know from the letters that the friendships continued as long as Swift's mind remained clear. John and Robert Grattan, prebendaries and minor canons in the chapter, and their brother Charles earned the distinction of "grateful" in Swift's list, and John, Robert, and another brother, James, were remembered in his will, as was John Jackson, prebendary of Howth. Delany himself, chancellor of the cathedral and so close a friend that at one time he lived for six months in the deanery, is but once--in September of 1735--mentioned in the account books, which thus give no true picture of his intimacy with the dean. Delany's gratitude is acknowledged with reservations, but he received a silver medal at Swift's death.

Other members of the chapter with whom Swift was at various times on terms of friendship and who are to be found in the account books are John Stearne, Francis Wilson, and John Worrall. Stearne, the Dean of St. Patrick's and later Bishop of Dromore and of Clogher, is noted in the early books as a frequent opponent of Swift's at ombre, a member of the card-playing circle in Dublin to which Stella belonged. Though Swift describes him in the _Journal_ as a "good pleasant man" with "a very good face, and abundance of wit" (_JS_, p. 156), the relationship was an uneasy one, and certainly the impression is that Stella was a good deal fonder of him than Swift was. The extant account books record no meetings after Swift succeeded Stearne in the deanery, but Swift attended his installation as Bishop of Clogher in 1717 and visited him there in the summer of 1722, and a friendly invitation to dinner in 1724, which seems to have been made at the request of the ladies, shows that the ultimate estrangement had not yet taken place. In 1733 Swift, writing to Stearne, says that they have not met for some years, and no doubt, as with some of his other acquaintanceships, this one altered after Stella's death. Stearne, who was advanced to his bishopric to make way for Swift at St. Patrick's, was stigmatized with ingratitude in the latter's list. Swift never forgave him for depriving him of the right to make the presentation of St. Nicholas Without.

Dr. Francis Wilson, whose physical abuse of Swift in June of 1742, as reported by Deane Swift and Faulkner, makes such painful reading, entered the chapter in 1727 or 1728 and soon became of service to the dean. He must have been the "Dr. W--" noted in the 1732-3 book as receiving the payment of some of Swift's tithes; he is mentioned as performing that office in 1734-5. Thus Deane Swift is inaccurate when he implies that the two men were not well known to each other before 1739: "Ever since his Acquaintance with _the Dean_, he has used all the means in his power to subvert _Doctor Wynne_ in the office of Sub-

Dean" (Corres., V, 210), a position to which Wynne was appointed only in April of that year. Wilson was at times resident in the deanery during Swift's last years and continued to assist him in tithe collections. Deane Swift and Faulkner strongly question his honesty, and it is true that Swift never made him manager, as Walls and Worrall had been. A note in the Cathedral Collections under 3 May 1739 (291) seems to indicate Wilson's humanity in adding two more to the list of charitable objects: "increas^{d} to Mr Lyon by the pernicious vice and Advice Of my daily Spunge and Inmate [not ingrate, as Williams has it] Will's Son to 12 Scoundrels." Williams (Corres., V, 176, n 1) interprets the statement as proof that Swift was not blind to Wilson's failings, but the record of Cathedral Collections was not private, as the account books were, and it may be presumed that the note, so typical of Swift, was intended for Wilson's eyes. Nothing in any of the dean's letters suggests any disapproval of Wilson. Swift made him one of his executors and generously remembered him in his will, which was, of course, drafted before the attack.

Swift's early biographers differ in their opinions of the Rev. Mr. John Worrall and his wife, Orrery and Deane Swift attacking them, chiefly on the score of low birth, and Delany presenting a favorable picture. Orrery, without giving names, says, "It is certain, that from SWIFT'S settlement in Dublin as Dean of St. Patrick's, his choice of companions in general shewed him of a very depraved taste" (p. 68). Delany, assuming this to refer, among others, to Worrall, thus defends him:

> He was nearly of [Swift's] own standing in the college; a good walker, a man of sense, and a great deal of humour. He was married to a woman of great vivacity, good-nature, and generosity; remarkably cleanly, and elegant in her person, in her house, and at her table. Where she entertained her friends, with singular chearfulness, hospitality, and good humour (p. 91).

Delany goes on to say that the dean dined with the Worralls "as often as he pleased, at a certain rate," and invited friends "upon the same terms." This picture is confirmed by Swift himself in a letter to Ford of 9 October 1733:

> I let no Company see me except Mr Worrall and his wife, who is a chearfull woman with a clear voice, She sends me vittels and they both generally dine with me, and sit the evenings.

Though Swift knew Worrall from his first association with St. Patrick's, the acquaintance may have been slight until he became dean: there are no references to Worrall in the early account books. The receipt of a letter, probably from Worrall (the writer's name is not clearly written and may be incorrectly read) is noted on 8 May 1713, possibly a word of congratulation to the new dean. The first mention of Worrall in the correspondence is in December of the same year. From then on, as dean's vicar, Worrall would necessarily have had close contact with his superior.

In the 1717-8 book there are but three references to Worrall, though two of them suggest that he is occasionally paid in connection with deanery services (192, 203). By 1721 Swift was addressing Worrall, contrary to his usual practice, by his nickname. During the 20's, when we have no account books, many letters attest to the reliance Swift had come to place on his vicar, who managed his personal finances as well as those of the deanery in the absence of the dean. He was even trusted enough to be asked to supervise the printing of pamphlets, Intelligencer papers, &c. But the closeness of the two men is best proved by Swift's letter to Worrall from England in 1726, describing with unusual frankness the depth of his feelings for Stella, then ill and under Mrs. Worrall's care. The following year, when Swift was again in England, the Worralls, along with Mrs. Dingley, signed Sheridan's "Humble Petition to Stella," urging her to recover, which Sheridan then transmitted to the dean. (Corres., III, 221, n 6).

Thus it is obvious that in the 20's and early 30's the Worralls were extremely close to Swift, though as with Walls, whose function as business manager Worrall took over, it may well have been a kind of master-servant relationship. The evidence of the 1732-3 account book confirms Swift's and Delany's statements about the sharing of meals: there are many dinners throughout the year, and in some months Worrall's name appears at least once a week, possibly in connection with the payment Delany says Swift made for his food. From 1732 on the Worralls resided next door to the deanery, so that the arrangement became almost inevitable, and there is some evidence that the £5 rent on their house was forgiven as a compensation. Mrs. Worrall may have performed some of the offices which formerly fell on Mrs. Brent: regular payments to her, perhaps for marketing ("She sends me vittels"), are listed monthly for every week Swift was in Dublin, and she appears from another entry to have made his shirts. At this time he may have been temporarily without a housekeeper; none is mentioned in the account book, though passages in the letters imply that both Mrs. Brent and Mrs. Ridgeway were occasionally employed.

Judging by the 1734-5 account book and the correspondence, it appears that the relationship changed after 1733, and that Swift became less dependent on the Worralls. The account book has a few Worrall entries, two of them recording card games, but they occur in November 1734 (possibly Mrs. Worrall is referred to in December), none afterwards. There are no more letters to Worrall, though he is mentioned, with some contempt, by Sheridan, and he continued his duties at the cathedral. The suggestion that Swift lost interest in him after his wife's death (Deane Swift, p. 311) does not explain the omission of their names from the account book for 1734-5, during most if not all of which period Mrs. Worrall was still alive. It may be that, as he grew older, Swift took fewer walks and thus needed Worrall's companionship less. Or, more probably, the advent of Mrs. Ridgeway, whose name appears fifteen times in the book, and Mrs. Whiteway allowed him to change his habits so that he no longer had to rely on the services formerly provided by the Worralls. From the virulence of Deane Swift's animus against the Worralls, one may assume that Mrs. Whiteway did not encourage the friendship. Nevertheless, Swift apparently remained on good terms with his vicar and in 1740 bequeathed him his best beaver hat.

In the last two account books is to be found a puzzling item which sometimes looks like "Ma^{d}" but at other times like "Mav" or even "Ma^{r}." With some misgivings we suggest that it is an abbreviation of "Madam" and that it refers to Mrs. Worrall, who is once actually called "Madam Worrall"(218). The sums are usually small, a shilling or two, though on two occasions they are somewhat more, once nearly two pounds, an amount which could cover an exceptionally large market bill. Furthermore, the entries parallel to a considerable extent the Worrall ones: the final Worrall entry is in November 1734; the last Ma^{d} comes the following April.

Ma^{d} could possibly be maid. However, the word maid, which occurs with some frequency throughout the books, is normally written out. Or it might refer to Mrs. Whiteway, who is sometimes called Madam in the letters though not in the account books, but the name Whiteway once occurs in the same entry as Ma[d] (211), and the reference is undoubtedly to two persons.

Swift uses Madam Worrall on 10 August 1733 under the category of "Cloaths": "Linnen cheated by Madam Worrall for 7 Shirts." In December 1734 in the same category he enters "Making, mending & cheating," and it seems possible that this entry also refers to Mrs. Worrall.

* * * *

Swift's literary acquaintances are mentioned only in the four account books which belong to the period between 1708 and 1713. Most of this time he was in England, where his literary friends lived: his only contact in Ireland with a prominent writer occurred during Addison's visit there as secretary to the lord lieutenant. Of the four account books under consideration, one and part of two others are covered by the letters to Stella, which show that Swift met his friends and acquaintances far more often than the account books suggest. This is not surprising: if the occasion involved no expense, no entry was made.

A good example is the association with Addison, Swift's closest friend for the three years 1708-11. His name appears well over thirty times in the books, most often in 1708-9, where both in England and Ireland Swift records visits, dinners, evenings at taverns, &c., as often as three times a month, and the account books are our only source for most of this information. Yet, frequently as they seem to have met, we may assume that they saw each other even more often if we compare the entries for September and October of 1710 with the same months in the Journal. The account book merely notes a coach on 19 October and a dinner on the 28th. Yet the Journal reports six occasions in September and eleven in October, including the two on the 19th and 28th, when the two men were together. Even after political differences drove them apart, they sometimes met, and the Journal mentions five meetings between July 1712 and April 1713, none of which is recorded in the appropriate account book.

The Journal is also full of references to Prior, with whom Swift was many times in company, yet there is but one mention of him in the account books, on 26 November 1712, a day not covered by the Journal, when Swift and he had occasion to take a coach to Lord Treasurer Oxford's. Arbuthnot is found only in the list of wins and losses, playing ombre with Swift and the Duchess of Shrewsbury on 28 August 1712, also a day omitted from the Journal. And beyond buying his pamphlet The Importance of Dunkirk Consider'd, Swift makes no mention at all, in the three relevant account books, of Steele, though he does appear in an earlier one, in April of 1709, as a correspondent and as a tavern companion.

Pope, whom Swift in his will was to call his dearest friend, appears twice in the books, when he and Swift dine together on 20 and 27 October 1713, shortly before the 1712-3 volume closes. This must have been early in their acquaintanceship. The one reference to Pope in the Journal (9 March 1713) does not prove that the two men had met at that time, but since Pope says the following August that he has painted Swift's portrait three times (Pope, I, 187), they had obviously seen each other before Swift left for Ireland in May. However, their close association must date from the nine-month period when Swift was back in London from September 1713 to June 1714, at which time their friendship, which was to last to the end, was solidly established.

*   *   *   *

Swift's political acquaintances in the Tory years, like his literary ones, are fully described in the Journal and other letters, and many of them appear in the account books. It is probable that every time Swift visited the Earl of Oxford, he mentioned it to the ladies in his daily summary. But when he could not keep up these summaries, it was not his usual practice to review the omitted days, and hence some visits are not mentioned. Thus the account books are our only record for a few meetings: 2 July, 15 August (a game of hazard), 30 September, and 26 November 1712. In the rush to leave England after his appointment as dean, he took a chair to the Lord Treasurer's on 23 May 1713, and a week later recorded a tip to his porter. When he returned to England, he noted five meetings, on 10 September and 8, 12, 22, and 28 October. At this point the account book stops. For the next seven months they met often, but except for two occasions mentioned in letters to Walls and two referred to in Bishop Kennett's diary (Corres., I, 411; II, 9; V, 228), we have no record of the specific days.

The account books are surprisingly meagre in their references to Lord Bolingbroke, whom we know from the Journal that Swift saw almost constantly from the time he met him in November 1710 till the Journal ends in 1713; yet in the two account books in which his name is found, it appears only ten times. Most of the meetings there noted are described in the Journal; indeed, the one entry not found there, that of 18 February 1713, probably does not refer to a meeting: "wine Lord Bolingbroke Servants. 7^s 6^d." The sum seems large for a tip. But in the previous April Swift had received a gift from Bolingbroke, then St. John, of a chest of Florence and recorded a payment of 5s to "George," and the further expense of 2s 6d "For Lock &c to the Chest." It may be that the 1713 entry refers to another such gift, though one would expect a mention of it in the Journal. Perhaps it was an annual remembrance. In 1714, when Swift was at Letcombe, the Secretary sent him three dozen bottles of wine, and John Barber, who told him of it, remarked, "I am afraid it will cost you 5^s to George, my Lord's Butler" (Corres., II, 55). Finally, one would look for Bolingbroke's name in the account book for September and October of 1713, when Swift was back in London and Windsor with the court, but it is not there.

There is almost no duplication between the Journal and the account books in the case of Erasmus Lewis, whom Swift saw nearly once a week from their first meeting, in early October 1710, throughout his London residence, and with whom he remained in touch for the rest of his life. These meetings, though probably not all of them, are given in the Journal, but almost none of them appear in the account books, presumably because for some reason no expense was incurred. Where Lewis's name is to be found is in the list of wins and losses: sixteen out of the twenty-one appearances of the name are there. Swift did not as a general rule mention to the ladies his opponents at cards. Furthermore, since Lewis was a friend of the Vanhomrigh family, discretion may have prompted him to omit the name. Two entries couple Lewis with "Van" and one with "Mishess," all three referring to games played at Windsor. Since Vanessa was not at Windsor on the first two occasions and since in any case Swift would not refer to her as "Van," the other player must have been her brother. Finally, it was Lewis, as noted in both the Journal and the account book (143), who was the bearer of the order from Lord Dartmouth on 13 April 1713 (the account book mistakenly says the 12th) which caused Swift to force the administration's hand and thus led to his promotion.

All four members of the Masham group--Lady Masham, her husband, her sister, and her brother--are mentioned in the account books, and again we know that Swift saw them more often than on these occasions. He knew the husband and brother first; it was not until 17 August 1711 that he met Mrs. Masham (JS, p. 335). He seems to have spent a great deal more time with Lord Masham than with his wife: the entries naming her and her sister are largely among the wins and losses. When the Journal ceases to be a daily record, we must rely on the account books for the dates of their meetings, as on 12 and 14 May, 28 and 29 July, 22 August, and 10 and 23 September 1712. But it is clear from the Journal that this list is incomplete. On 17 June 1711 Swift writes, "The worst thing here is my Evenings at Ld Mashams, where Ld Treasr comes, and we sitt till after 12," yet there has been no account-book mention of the Mashams since 14 May, over a month before. Similarly, the next month, on 17 July, he says, "I play sometimes too, at Picket that is, Picquett I mean; but very seldom.--Out late, why 'tis onely at Ldy Mashams, and that's in our Town [Windsor]," but the last game of cards with Lady Masham--Lord Masham apparently did not play--was also on 14 May. After Swift returned to England in 1713, he surely saw the Mashams often, but the account book records no meeting, and the list of wins and losses in this volume has no entries for September and October.

The number of Swift's meetings with John Barber, the Tory printer, is not complete in either the account books or the Journal, though the account books record more of them. No doubt Swift hesitated in his letters even to MD to risk betraying his authorship of the pamphlets Barber was printing; furthermore, the ladies had not yet heard of Barber when Swift introduced his name. That was on 26 December 1710, and he added, "There is an intimacy between us, built upon reasons that you shall know when I see you." The reference is to the Examiner, which he had been writing for some weeks without as yet telling the ladies, though he gave a clear admission of his authorship a few days later. From then on Barber is occasionally mentioned, not usually by name but as a "friend" or "my printer," or a meeting will be indicated simply by "I dined in the City." The account books, where Swift gives either Barber's name or an abbreviation of it, usually make it certain who on these occasions is meant.

When the daily record in the Journal breaks down, the account books add the dates of other meetings, as, for instance, 10, 20, 24 May 1712; 7, 13, 27 June; 8 July; 22, 31 May 1713. But there must have been many more than these. The printing of the Examiner and other works would necessarily have thrown the men together, not to mention Swift's occasional supervision of Mrs. Manley's writing, and the appearance of both Barber and Mrs. Manley in the list of wins and losses indicates a friendship beyond the purely professional. Barber also had a good many financial dealings with Swift--and with Vanessa--though except for a bill Swift owed him for chocolate, which he paid before leaving for his installation, none of these is recorded in the account books.

Swift had known Benjamin Tooke, the printer and bookseller, at least as early as 1701, when he edited Temple's Miscellanea, Part III, which Tooke printed. From then on until Swift left for Ireland in 1714 the two men were apparently well acquainted, though there is no mention of Tooke before the 1708-9 account book. They must have met during the English period of the 1703-4 book, but there is no record of it in Swift's hasty summation of these months. When Swift began using Tooke, as he later used Barber, as a kind of banker, we do not know, but it was before the time of the Journal to Stella. The first reference to Tooke by Swift is on 14 January 1709, when the two have dinner together, followed by "tavern" notations in March and April. After Swift left London in May, they exchanged letters, now lost, which were duly recorded in the correspondence list. The omission of Tooke's name from September and October 1710 is strange, since the Journal indicates at least three meetings during these months; probably no money was spent. But the lack of any reference to Tooke in the 1711-2 volume, except for a memorandum to be transferred to the next one, is stranger still, as the Journal reports a number of meetings. Tooke is mentioned in 1712-3 but only in November and December: on 2 November Swift spent a shilling "at Tooks," and on 19 December he tells MD that he "dined with some othrs with honest Ben Took by invitation"; the list of wins and losses reveals that they played whisk afterwards. This is the last reference to Tooke in the account books, but, along with Barber, he continued to act as Swift's banker, presumably until his death in 1716. He was succeeded by his son, also Benjamin, but he and Swift appear to have had no direct dealings, and by the time Swift returned to England in 1726, the younger Tooke too was dead. It is pleasing to know that Swift found the elder Tooke "grateful" for the many and valuable services he had performed for him.

Among Swift's English friends whom he had known before the momentous years 1710-4 and whose interest for him was neither literary nor political were several ladies. One of these was Mrs. (Miss) Catherine Barton. It is not known when they met, though it seems possible that Stella and Mrs. Dingley knew her; at least they knew of her. During the years of the Journal Swift tells them, "I love her better than any body here, and see her seldomer" (JS, p. 229). Her politics seem to have been whiggish. Swift does not mention her in the Journal after November 1711, but it is unlikely that politics kept them apart. He saw her for the last time in 1727, on his final visit to England (Corres., III, 391). The first record of their acquaintanceship is in his accounts for December 1708, when he lost to her at ombre. Shortly after, he notes a "bad fitt" at her house, which necessitated his taking a chair home (63). On 4 April 1709, still in London, he lists a letter from "Mrs. B---n." The dropped letters may indicate a momentary spasm of discretion. Swift's occasional practice of dropping letters from a name in the account books seems a form of disguise, to conceal political involvement (xl) or acts of generosity, as to Mrs. D---s in 1703 (39, 47) and 1709 (190). His similar practice of entering an initial letter only, sometimes followed by a dash, for a name often entered in full elsewhere, may also be a disguise, but it seems more like a hasty abbreviation: V. for Vanhomrigh (142) or Mrs. W-- for Mrs. Wesley. In any case, when Swift's correspondence with Mrs. Barton continues, in June, July, and August, he uses her full name.

Politics did drive Swift and Lady Catherine Lucy apart. They may have met through the Berkeleys, to whom her husband was related. By 1708 Swift was a frequent visitor at her home: the account book notes seven visits between 30 December and 9 March of the next year. When he returned to London in 1710, he saw her at Hampstead in September and dined there a week later with her and her sister, Mrs. Armstrong. This is the last reference to either lady in the account books. As he told MD, he found them "plaguy Whigs" and Mrs. Armstrong "the most insupportable of all women" (JS, p. 179). He announced in November 1711 that "Lady Lucy and I are fallen out; she rails at me, and I have left visiting her" (JS, p. 404), and , despite her being a friend of the Vanhomrigh family, he never mentioned her again, and they may never have met.

Except for her appearance three times in November and December 1711 in Swift's list of letters--she had retired from London to escape creditors--and for the tribute at the time of her death, Ann Long is found only in the 1708-9 book: in mid-January 1709 Swift records taking a chair "from Longs" and a few days later a loss to her at ombre. Two months afterwards he writes to Robert Hunter that he and she have "fallen out" (*Corres*., I, 133), but the tone is not serious, and there are doubtless other reasons why her name does not appear again. He may have met her through the Vanhomrighs. The point of "The Decree for Concluding the Treaty between Dr. Swift and Mrs. Long" (*PW*, V, 197), which probably dates from December 1707 or the next month, depends on their being new acquaintance. She is mentioned earlier in an enigma from the *Muses Mercury* of May 1707 (*Poems*, p. 912), but the poem, even if it is by Swift, implies no acquaintanceship, any more than it does with Moll Kerr, whose name also appears. Miss Long's virtues and her remarkable beauty excited Swift's admiration, and his paragraph in the account book when she died (117) bears out his words to the ladies, "I never was more afflicted at any death" (*JS*, p. 445).

Swift's Whig friend, Anthony Henley, to whom he seems to have been introduced by Addison and Steele and who is mentioned a number of times in the *Journal* until his death in the summer of 1711, is not to be found in the 1709-10 book. A wealthy man, Henley was inconsiderate, Swift felt, in putting his less well-off friends, like himself and young William Harrison, to expense in dining and drinking, but the evidence of the *Journal* and the omission of Henley's name from the overlapping accounts prove that at this time he successfully avoided joining Henley at eatinghouses and taverns. In 1708-9, however, he twice enters a shilling's coach fare, probably to visit Henley, as well as noting an exchange of letters in his correspondence list. Incidentally, the existence of an unrecorded letter from Henley in July 1709, like one to Charles Ford the previous November, proves that there are omissions in Swift's lists of letters.

Swift would have met Sir Andrew Fountaine when the latter arrived in Dublin in the entourage of the Lord Lieutenant, the Earl of Pembroke, in the summer of 1707. If Fountaine is really the dedicatee of the *Tritical Essay upon the Faculties of the Mind*, as Ehrenpreis suggests (II, 191), the friendship obviously progressed rapidly, since the *Essay* is dated 6 August 1707. The *Dialogue in the Castilian Language* and the *Dying Speech of Tom Ashe*, in both of which Sir Andrew figures, also belong to the period of the Lord Lieutenant's residence in Dublin, i. e., from 24 June to 28 November, when the viceregal party left Ireland. Swift, who accompanied them, was by that time close enough to Fountaine to be asked to spend a few weeks at his house during the Christmas season.

Fountaine appears, as might be expected, in the 1708-9 account book, though chiefly as a correspondent after Swift returned to Ireland in May. Before then there are two references, one in November 1708, when the men had coffee, and another in February, when they played ombre. Back in London in 1710, Swift twice dines at a tavern with Fountaine, at unusual expense, for which he reproaches himself in the *Journal*. "Among three of us, we had sixteen shillings to pay," he says, "but if he ever catches me again, I'll spend as many pounds" (*JS*, p. 48). He entered his share, seven shillings, under "Extraordinaries" with the description "Tav^{rn}. Sr A. F. fool." Sir Andrew did catch him again, however, and five days later Swift enters another seven shillings: "Tav^{rn} & din^{r} Sr A. F. fool ag^{n}" (111).

He continued to report to the ladies of their frequent meetings, often dining at Fountaine's lodgings or, much more usual--at least sixteen times--at the Vanhomrighs, whose acquaintance with Fountaine must also have dated from Dublin days. It is odd that Fountaine does not appear at all in the 1711-2 book, since Swift tells MD of several occasions when they met. He is to be found, however, in 1712-3, seven times within the two months of February and March 1713 as a player at cards, all but the one on 7 March acknowledged in the Journal. After 26 March Fountaine's name disappears from the account books.

If one relied exclusively on the references to Charles Ford in the account books, one would hardly suspect that he has some claim to be considered Swift's closest male friend, a claim sustained by the Journal to Stella and the Correspondence. Since Ford resided mainly in England, he is not to be found at all in certain of the account books, such as 1732-3 and 1734-5: he did not return to Ireland after the spring of 1732. He is also absent from the 1717-8 book, though he was in Dublin from July to October 1718 and it is hardly conceivable that he and Swift did not meet. At any rate, Ford's name is found only in the four books covering the period from 1708 to 1713.

Swift knew the Ford family, it seems, as early as 1705. Charles first appears as the recipient of a letter from Swift dated 12 November 1708, somewhat formal in tone and implying no close acquaintanceship as yet. The correspondence record in the 1708-9 book indicates that letters were exchanged throughout the spring of 1709, though only one of those listed survives. In the summer of that year, Swift notes a tavern expense in July and a sixpenny tip "at Mr Fords" in August. The next book gives only a single reference, a tavern bill on 25 August 1710, even though both men had been in Ireland since the previous entry, a year before. Most surprising of all, however, is the absence of Ford's name from September and October of 1710, when they were in England and according to the Journal seeing each other or dining together at least every week. The explanation, doubtless, is that until December they lived next door to each other and that they usually ate at Ford's lodgings, without cost to Swift for transportation or food.

The Journal tells of a number of meetings and dinners, sometimes with Erasmus Lewis, the Vanhomrighs, and other friends but most often alone; we lack the 1710-1 account book for that period. We return to the accounts in 1712, but even in that year it is not till September that Ford is mentioned, when a game of piquet with Swift and Lewis is recorded on the 18th. All the remaining references, in fact, come from the pages of wins and losses, one in October 1712, one in March 1713, and three during the hectic days of May following, just before Swift left. Only the one in March is referred to in the Journal.

Arbuthnot speaks of Ford as "honest sensible firm friendly" (Corres., II, 143), and undoubtedly Swift found him so. If in the 30's Mrs. Pilkington thought him a tiresome eccentric, she had to admit that the dean seemed not to share her opinion (Pilkington, p. 56). Swift's only impatient reference to Ford in all their long association occurs in the Journal on 1 July 1712, after he had obtained the gazetteer's post for his friend: "The puppy does not seem satisfied." The irritation was temporary, the friendship continuing as before, and Ford eventually earned the accolade of "grateful" in Swift's list.

Two other nonclerical Irish friends of Swift's, Peter Ludlow and Richard

Helsham, figure in the account books. For Peter Ludlow the 1717-8 book provides a good example of biographical information not elsewhere available. From Swift's correspondence alone it would hardly be suspected that the two men were as close as they were. None of his letters to Ludlow exist, and the only one from Ludlow, a mysterious and rather silly note, signed "Sir Politick-Would-Be," scarcely bears out the testimony of Mrs. Delany, later echoed by her husband, that he was a man of "a vast deal of humour" (Mrs. Delany, II, 320; Delany, p. 96). The letter is attributed to Ludlow on the word of Deane Swift, but the authorship has not been questioned by later editors.

We do learn from the letters that Swift had spent a few days in January 1717 with Ludlow at his home at Ardsallagh, a short distance northeast of Trim; that MD and possibly Swift himself had spent Christmas of 1722 there; and that there he had met his enemy, Richard Bettesworth, in the early 30's, some two or three years before the account of the Bettesworth incident which Swift wrote to the Duke of Dorset in 1734. And we know from the poem by Sheridan to Swift and the Rochforts in 1721 that Ludlow was a member of the group of Swift's most intimate Irish friends (Poems, p. 1019). But only the 1717-8 book gives us any idea how frequently the two saw each other. In 1718 alone Swift made at least four visits to Ludlow. In January he was at Ardsallagh for six days; in April for at least five (February and March are missing, and it is quite possible that the April visit had begun the month before); in June he settled down for a visit of nearly a month; and in August he returned for another five days. He includes, under "Great Gifts," the amounts spent at Ardsallagh, mostly, one assumes, gratuities to servants, but some identified as Christmas gifts, though Swift had almost certainly not gone to Ludlow's till 3 January. The sums are all, incidentally, surprisingly large, which may suggest something about the style of living at Ardsallagh House.

Ludlow, who outlived Swift, does not appear in the 1732-3 or 1734-5 books, and though there may have been no quarrel, the two seem to have drifted apart, possibly, as Ball suggests, because of Swift's attacks on the Parliament, of which Ludlow was a member (Ball, V, 351, n 3). In a letter to Ford in 1736 Swift says, "The Ludlows have quite forsaken me" (Corres., IV, 505). It is the final reference to his old friend.

It is odd that Dr. Richard Helsham's name is not found more often in the account books. Swift's references to him in his letters and poems are uniformly friendly, and he names him in 1737 as one of his executors, an office Helsham, dying the next year, did not live to fulfill. He was a fat jovial man, a friend of most of Swift's other Irish friends, especially Sheridan and Delany, and could bear his part in the exchange of doggerel among Swift, Sheridan, and the Grattans. He was Swift's doctor as early as the autumn of 1718, when Swift wrote Arbuthnot for a second opinion on the treatment he was getting (Corres., II, 303), and in a poem to Sheridan in October, Swift even refers to him as "Dick" (Poems, p. 980), but his name does not appear in the 1717-8 book. Nor is it to be found in 1732-3, though Helsham had taken part in various poetic exchanges during the 20's and early 30's, and in October 1733 Swift tells Ford that Helsham "visits me constantly" (Corres., IV, 197). In the same letter he calls him the best of the Dublin doctors.

Helsham is mentioned often in the last of the account books. He seems either to have assisted Swift in the purchase of wine or perhaps to have lent him the money: in December 1734 Swift notes the payment to him of the considerable sum of £34 (266). Also at various times during the year notations of card games with both the doctor and his wife are made. Three times in these lists Helsham is styled "Arrogant." This must have been a private joke, possibly by contraries, since nothing we know of the "fat joker" suggests arrogance. The identification, however, is clear: in July of 1735, about the same time as Swift notes a loss at cards and a small gift to the doctor's servants, he writes to Orrery, "Dor Helsham is as arrogant as ever" (Corres., IV, 367).

Joseph Beaumont, linen draper and general dealer of Trim, for many years not only supplied Swift with household necessities but also became a close friend. It is thus inevitable that he should appear in all the account books compiled during his lifetime, even in Scott's 1700-1 list--in other words, all but the last two. When Swift was living in Laracor or Trim, he paid Jo for items of food, such as sugar, coffee, sage, cheese, and even occasionally meat. When in 1703 he is furnishing his house at Laracor, it is from Jo that he buys his sauce pan, coffee pots, plates, cups, and basin. Soap, candles, and powder too came from Jo, and there is evidence that Swift got his wine from the same source, even after he moved to the deanery. At times Jo seems to have shared with Parvisol the care of Swift's washing, and it was through Jo that Swift often rented horses for the ride back to Dublin. Indeed it is hard to think of anything Jo did not provide: in Swift's poem, "On the Little House by the Church Yard of Castleknock," it is suggested that even bricks could be had from him (Poems, p. 128). Swift obviously was fond of Jo, even when Jo pressed him to solicit the government in his behalf or, later, when his mind became unsettled and his conduct increasingly eccentric. At Trim or Laracor the two men were much together: Jo, Swift mentions, was with him at Laracor when the news came of his mother's death.

When Swift made up his book at the start of his year, he began the page of recurring expenses with the category "JB," almost certainly "Jo Beaumont." "JB" appears every quarter in the first six books; it is not used in 1717-8, where a separate page, crossed out when it was transferred to a new book, is devoted to "Jo's Account." Except in 1703-4, where the figure is given as £8 a year, the sums, often paid in small amounts, total £6 or close to it. These annual payments have nothing to do with the supplies Swift buys from Jo, and they are made whether Swift is in Ireland or England. What were they for? Nothing in the account books or the letters gives us a satisfying answer.

In the "State of my affairs, Sept^{ber} 8th 1718" Swift records a debt owing to him of £100 from John Beaumont (probably a mistake either of Thomas Steele's or Monck Mason's for Jo), for which he has a mortgage on Jo's house in Trim. This is an additional debt to the one of £60, also listed in the "State of my affairs," which Jo owes him.

In spite of Swift's strictures on his relations--and those on his sister are particularly severe--he was genuinely fond of a few of them and on comfortable terms with several others. He was not only a dutiful but a loving son. His affection for his mother, so deeply felt at her death, is proved by the 1708-9 account book, the only one in which she is mentioned, where the list of letters shows that they wrote each other once a month until the end of April, at which time he set out, bringing a gift of tea, to see her at Leicester on his way back to Ireland. He did not remain in Leicester the whole time, but he spent a month in the neighborhood (71).

Though she is not mentioned in it by name, the 1703-4 book shows that Swift did not go to or from London without visiting his mother. In November

1703 he records a stay at Leicester from the 13th to the 24th, and on the way back to Dublin the following May he stopped off for a week (38, 41).

By contrast his references to his sister, Mrs. Fenton, are usually impatient and in his old age show anger and contempt. Nevertheless, at least as early as 1717 he is providing her with an annuity of £15 (Corres., II, 270). This is the logical explanation of his statement to Gay in 1730: "I pay an Annuity of 15ll per Ann: in Surrey" (Corres., III, 380). (Mrs. Fenton lived at Farnham, in Surrey.)

There are but three references to Mrs. Fenton in the account books. The first, in June 1710, records Swift's payment of coach fare to visit her. She was at that time in Ireland, as she had been the month before, when she wrote Swift of their mother's death. The other two references concern money paid to her. Under the symbol "MF" Swift enters a payment to her in 1717-8 of £11 (188), probably a part of her annuity. In 1734-5, on a page headed "Articles of Annuities and other larger gifts" (265), the same initials are given at the top of the page, preceding those of Mrs. Dingley. The latter's annuity is given, but there is no entry under "MF." The reason may be that on 25 October 1735, before Swift cleared his accounts the next week, he wrote Motte that he had paid ten guineas "lately" to a representative of his sister's who had complained that her money was in arrears. This was apparently untrue, as Motte, through whom the matter was handled, had written Swift earlier in the month, "As to Mrs. Fenton's annuity, I have punctually paid it" (Corres., IV, 401).

In 1730 Swift said of his cousin, Patty Rolt, that she "hath been my favourite from her youth" (Corres., III, 420), and five years later he compared her to his sister, to Mrs. Fenton's disadvantage, as one who was "always kind and obliging to me" (Corres., IV, 411). She seems to have been unremittingly unfortunate, and we find Swift assisting her financially over a period of nearly thirty years. Ignoring the list of letters, she first appears in the account books in January 1709 as the recipient of 10s 9d. The next month, on a visit, Swift gives her 1s 6d. Leaving for Ireland in May, he buys a coffee roaster for her, which, if he is being rigidly precise about the date, he must have sent from Leicester. On his return to England in September 1710 he dines with her several times where she lodges, at the house of another of their cousins. Then she leaves London in order to live more cheaply in the country, and they exchange letters, none of which exist. By July 1711, however, she is back and on Swift's conscience: "If I were rich, I would ease her, which a little thing would do. Some months ago I sent her a guinea, and it patched up twenty circumstances" (JS, p. 308). He gives her another guinea, the accounts tell us, on 3 January 1713, and a few months later, before he departs in May, he again visits her, giving on one occasion 1s 6d and on another 3s. She does not reappear in the account books, but Swift's letters to Gay and Motte show that he remained concerned about her all his life. When he was ill in England on his last visit, in 1727, he even considered retiring from London with her, now remarried but evidently no better off, as his nurse.

Swift's real favorite among all his relations was undoubtedly his cousin, Martha Whiteway, the daughter of his uncle Adam. Five or six years after the death of Stella, some of the social duties which she had performed for him, such as presiding over his table, were taken over by Mrs. Whiteway. As he grew older, she assumed the supervision of his household and even handled some of his correspondence, including letters relating to his literary works. As late as 1741 she was making--incorrectly, as Swift pointed out--an entry in the cathedral accounts, though this office was not normally hers. She may well have been, as she claimed, the last person Swift knew (Corres., V, 207). As far as we can tell, their relations were always amicable--"one whom I should more value if she were not a Cousin," he described her in 1738, "and the onely one (except her Daughter) whom I can endure in my Sight" (Corres., V, 89)--and, other than Mrs. Dingley, she and her children are the first legatees to be mentioned in Swift's will, in which they are generously remembered.

Mrs. Whiteway was in no sense a domestic, as Mrs. Worrall had come close to being. Deane Swift, her son-in-law, repudiates with scorn (p. 369) Delany's statement (p. 130) that a friend of hers "sometimes marketed for him [Swift]," insisting that nobody except Mrs. Worrall or the dean's own servants performed this duty. The point is a trivial one, but nevertheless Delany may be right. Mrs. Whiteway's friend, Mrs. Sican, is mentioned in a letter of Swift's in 1739 as planning to buy the dinner (Corres., V, 171), and in an undated note he asks her to do some marketing for him before coming to dinner that evening. But there is no hint that Mrs. Whiteway's obligations were other than those of hostess in the deanery and companion to the dean.

Swift would have known her most of her life, first as one of his many cousins and then as the wife of a member of his chapter, Theophilus Harrison, but she does not enter his story until the end of 1730, when he writes her a note acknowledging the return of a book. The tone of the letter, though friendly, suggests no more than a formal acquaintanceship: "You live so far off, and I believe are so seldom at home, and I am so ill a visitor, that it is no wonder we meet so seldom" (Corres., III, 431). At this time she was forty years old, the mother of four young children, and married to her second husband, Edward Whiteway. In 1732 Whiteway died, and his widow's name begins to appear in the account books. At least twice in the 1732-3 book she is entertained at dinner; on the three or four other occasions when she is mentioned, it is not possible to know how the expense was incurred; on a visit to her or from her, Swift may have paid for the coach or chair.

By 1737, unless prevented by ill health or inclement weather, she was coming to the deanery from her home in Abbey Street, north of the river, on a regular basis, eating dinner and supper with Swift three days a week, usually Mondays, Thursdays, and Saturdays. It is likely that this arrangement had begun at least two years earlier, as the references to Mrs. Whiteway in the 1734-5 book are numerous. All through the year, several times a month, her name is to be found in connection with card games, dinners, and coaches and chairs, but most commonly as the recipient of the kind of generosity Swift listed under "Great and Small Gifts." Not all the dates are precise, but among the more than sixty occurrences of the name, most refer to her regular visiting days. She never left her own house to live at the deanery, though Swift urged her to at the time of her eldest son's death in 1736 (Corres., IV, 464). But even when he was no longer competent, she visited the deanery twice a week (Corres., V, 207).

Not only Mrs. Whiteway but her four children were exempted from the scorn Swift felt for his relations. He thought highly of Theophilus Harrison, the eldest son, and mourned his death in 1736: "I had set my heart very much upon that young man," he wrote the boy's mother (Corres., IV, 460), and he spoke to Sheridan on the occasion of his "infinite sorrow and disappointment" (Corres., IV, 466). Of Mary, or Molly, Harrison, the only daughter, he was also fond, bequeathing her some of his most treasured keepsakes. When he was away, both brother and sister would share with their mother the supervision of affairs at the deanery. How often they were there when Swift was in residence, it is not possible to say, since the letters are silent on the matter and the evidence of the account books is difficult to interpret.

In his letters Swift refers to the girl either as Miss Molly or Miss (after 1737 Mrs.) Harrison. On only three occasions in the account books, all in 1734-5, does she unmistakably appear, each time as the recipient of a gift. But there are eight references to "Harrison," seven of them in the list of wins and losses, the other under "Small Gifts." Since Swift usually records her mother as "Whiteway," it is certainly possible that by "Harrison" he means the daughter. But he may mean the son. There is no reference to Theophilus under his given name, which Swift seems never to have used, but the entry under "Small Gifts," "Whiteway & Son," probably refers to him rather than to his younger brothers. ("Mrs. Whiteway's boy," presumably, is a servant, like "MD's boy.") (265, 104)

It is worth notice that Mr. or Miss Harrison's name never appears in combination with "dinner," as their mother's so often does. They must surely have dined at the deanery. It is conceivable that the symbol which we have hesitantly interpreted as "Ma^{d}," i.e., "Madam," and have suggested may refer to Mrs. Worrall, is in reality "Ma^{r}," i.e., "Mary." But we have no evidence that Swift ever called her Mary. (The entry of "Box Mrs. May" [208] under 9 January 1733 could hardly refer to Miss Harrison. *May* might well be *Mary*, but the *Mrs*. is clear, and Swift would almost certainly never have used it of her this early.) Furthermore, the "Ma^{d}" corresponds roughly with the period covered by the Worralls, not by Mrs. Whiteway, who almost replaces them in the account books. Like her mother, Miss Harrison remained one of Swift's favorites for the rest of his life.

A dozen account book references to other relations are of some interest; they show visits made and financial assistance probably received and certainly given.

Swift had only two uncles living in Ireland after 1700: Uncle Adam (died 1704) and Uncle William (died 1706). The former, of Greencastle, co Down, was a solicitor and probably resided for the most part in Dublin (*Corres*., I, 26, n 2). A friend of the Warings, he had asked Swift "one day in private, as by direction," what his designs were in relation to Jane Waring (*Corres*., I, 35), an act hardly likely to endear him to Swift. Uncle William, on the other hand, also a solicitor, had been addressed by Swift, 29 November 1692, as "the best of my relations" when he thanked him for obtaining the Testimonium from the University of Dublin. A gift to "Bil. Sw^{ft}" in November 1702 (3) would have been to Uncle William's fifteen-year-old son, who had just entered the University. Swift twice refers in the *Journal to Stella* to the young man as "Billy" Swift (*JS*, pp. 325, 367).

Visits with his uncle and with his cousin Godwin are indicated by gratuities given maids and "God^{ws} man" in February 1703, "Un^{cls} 2 men" in March, and "uncles m^{d}" in September (8, 20). The most interesting mention of an uncle, surely Uncle William, is the entry in Parvisol's account in 1704: "p^{d} in absence to Uncle" (50) while Swift was in England, which indicates that Uncle William represented his nephew in financial affairs when he was out of Ireland.

Swift's frequent passages through Chester are recorded in the books, and twice entries refer to a Chester cousin. In 1703-4 a sum of 19s may have been "Left with Coz Swift at Chestr abt Engl acct" (38) either on Swift's arrival in England in November 1703 or upon his departure the following May. The next time he returned to Ireland, in June 1709, there is another entry, "G[ave] Coz^{ns} maid. 1^{s}" (73), indicating another visit. This cousin was either Isaac Swift, merchant of Chester, or his daughter Abigail, to whom Swift refers in the Journal (p. 4) and in a letter to Mrs. Vanhomrigh (Corres., I, 366). Indeed Swift seems to stop with these Chester Swifts whenever he passes through the city. He writes Abigail, then Mrs. Greenfield, 23 November 1726, having recently returned again to Ireland by way of Chester, sending her a picture and conveying through her his thanks to Mrs. Kenna, his Chester landlady.

Two other Swifts appear in the account books, the Deane Swifts, father and son, both in connection with money Swift lent them. The loan to the father is noted in 1708-9: "Memd. Coz Dean's Bond commences Febr. 22^{d}. 1706/7" (72). Son of Swift's Uncle Godwin, Deane Swift senior, to whom Swift had sent a letter in June 1694, had returned from Portugal to Ireland in 1705, married, and settled in the parish of Castle Rickard, near Clonard Bridge, co Meath, within six miles of Laracor (Corres., I, 14, n 2). Swift visited him there in January 1710 on his way from Laracor to Dublin: "G Coz deans man 5^{d}" (101). He received a letter from him in December 1711 in London (137), and had dinner with him soon after his return to Ireland (157) during his summer at Laracor. Deane Swift's will was proved a year later, 17 May 1714.

The financial assistance Swift extended to the father he continued, in even greater measure, to his son, who succeeded to his father's estate at Castle Rickard. Account book records show a loan of £2000 to the younger Deane, who already owed Swift "near" £1000 more (288, 310-313). This aid granted to his cousin Deane's son resembles that to his cousin Willoughby's daughter Hannah and to Hannah's husband, Stafford Lightburne, who became Swift's curate.

Terse as the account book entries are, they attest to the consideration which Swift bestowed on those members of his family to whom he felt some obligation: his Uncle William and his cousins Willoughby and Deane and their children.

8. Servants

We read in the Journal to Stella and in an occasional letter about Swift's relations with his servants, particularly the infuriating Patrick and the exemplary Saunders. The account books give us the names and sometimes the terms of service of these and several more. The servant who stayed longest in his employ was Mrs. Brent, his housekeeper. His references to her are uniformly affectionate: his special feeling for her can be seen in the conclusion of a letter to Worrall in 1729: "My most humble service to Mrs. Worrall, Mrs. Dingley, and love to Mrs. Brent" (Corres., III, 310). His regard was apparently not diminished by constant association: in 1731 he says they dine alone together five nights a week (Corres., III, 434). In Ball's opinion, she is the "Woman who does Business for me" who felt able to take the liberty of reporting to Swift the Dublin gossip about his visits to Vanessa (Corres., II, 149). Her belief, as reported by Lyon through her daughter (Prelims, f. 14^{v}), that Swift and Stella were never married is virtually conclusive.

The first mention anywhere of Mrs. Brent is in the 1702-3 account book, when in January 1703 Swift repays her for certain small purchases. It is likely that at this time she had only recently become his housekeeper. In 1728 he stated that she had been with him "above thirty years" (*Corres.*, III, 286), but probably his memory is at fault. We should not take too seriously the story told by Lyon of Swift's mother's passing her son off as her lover to Mrs. Brent "after his Settlement at *Laracor*" (1700), but it could not have occurred if the two had been acquainted (*Prelims*, f. 9^{v}).

Until a year or so before her death in 1735, Mrs. Brent managed Swift's household when he was in Dublin, and he depended on her for many services whether he was in Ireland or England. He entrusts her to pay his landladies, Mrs. Felter and Mrs. Curry, and he even uses her as his representative in making his allowance to the ladies. The term "Mrs. Brent's bill," which occurs two or three times, shows that like Jo Beaumont, Parvisol, and the personal servant, she would present a bill to Swift from time to time covering her expenditures. Among the items for which in 1703 he repays her is a shuttlecock, perhaps for Stella's use, as he twice in the *Journal* urges the use of it upon her as a healthful exercise.

Surprisingly, considering the recurring item for board wages for the footman and other servants, there is no record in the account books of any wages Mrs. Brent received. Yet when in England he sends her sums of money, once saying, "I believe I have not payed her this great while" (*JS*, 547, 594), and money is allowed her in Parvisol's account. Furthermore, Lyon, after mentioning the 4s a week allowed to the servants for their board wages, adds, "As to the house-keeper, she was much better paid, and generally dined and supped at his own table" (Lyon, p. 151). Her wages must then have been recorded elsewhere. There is also no record of wages for the cook or the housemaid at the deanery, servants who would come under the housekeeper's supervision and who were perhaps paid by her out of a fund not now traceable.

Whatever the arrangement with Mrs. Brent, it would have been continued with Mrs. Ridgeway, her daughter, who succeeded her. Mrs. Ridgeway's name appears only in the last, the 1734-5, account book, first under the date of November 1734, where Swift records a "Small Gift" to her. Lyon, calling her the housekeeper, speaks of her finding the poem "On His Own Deafness" in September 1734, so she apparently took over some time before her mother's death the next year (Lyon, p. 112).

It is probable that Mrs. Ridgeway was responsible for presenting Swift with the house bill which is given in the account book almost every week, though usually without her name. Twice we find her mentioned: "H bill Ridg^{w} 7^{s} 8^{d}½" (247) and "Ridg^{ws} bill. meat. 11^{s} 1^{d}" (251). As *meat* is often at this time a separate entry, this too may have been a part of Mrs. Ridgeway's bill. Swift often gives her 6d½, three times for "dinner" but more often for a present, and larger sums for special occasions, such as Christmas or "for a Play" (243). Twice she is mentioned in the cathedral accounts, both times as suggesting particular objects of charity.

Though, like her mother, she did not live at the deanery, Mrs. Ridgeway and Swift dined together--he says "constantly" (*Corres.*, V, 64)--in his chamber. She remained with him throughout the dark years, always, according to Deane Swift (*Corres.*, V, 210), going with him whenever he left the deanery. In his will she received £100, the rents on two of his houses, three gold rings, and all his small pieces of plate.

Swift's practice was to pay his personal servant, or footman, board wages, a fixed sum per week, and this he entered in his accounts. The actual amount was subject to certain variations. For example, when they were at Laracor or when the servant accompanied Swift on a visit and the host was at the charge of feeding them both, an appropriate portion was stopped out of the board wages. (Thus a study of the board wages in the account books sheds an occasional light on Swift's movements.) Also, when Swift employed a servant in London, the base pay was adjusted to the higher cost of living there. Finally, after he became dean and expanded his household, the figure was more than doubled to cover the wages of two or three servants. These considerations make it difficult to state positively how much the wages improved over the thirty-three years of the records, but the impression is that the increase was slight.

For a few months at the end of 1702 Swift seems to be paying 4s a week, but with the hiring of a new servant in February 1703 he reduces the pay to 3s 6d, or 6d a day, which may be considered the "normal" amount. Five years later, in 1708, the servant, Patrick, like his predecessors, receives 6d a day until in September he accompanies Swift to England, when his wages are advanced to 5s a week. Back in Ireland in the summer of 1709, Swift hires another servant at the usual Irish rate and at the beginning of February rehires Patrick at the customary 6d a day. In August they leave for England, where after a few weeks Patrick receives the usual London salary of 5s a week.

The account book for 1710-1 is missing, but the one for 1711-2 shows us that Patrick is still receiving the same 5s, which is also paid, apparently, to Will, who succeeds Patrick when the latter leaves in April 1712. In the last week of July, however, master and servant go to Windsor, where board must have been more expensive, for during the entire two-month residence there, Will receives an extra shilling a week. When they return to London, he is given 5s 6d, the first actual increase in a decade. Another increase is noted in London and Windsor in the autumn of 1713, when the servant, now Tom, is given 6s a week.

In the 1717-8 volume the item for board wages has reached 11s a week, too much for only one servant. Two years before, on 28 June 1715, when Swift, now in the deanery, was describing his household in a letter to Pope, he had said, "My family consists of a steward, a groom, a helper in the stables, a foot-man, and an old maid, who are all at board wages." The 11s would cover the wages for three of these. In the first quarterly statement Hugh and Saunders are named under "Servants," and Hugh, evidently the groom, also appears under the item "Horses" and seems to be receiving 3s 6d a week. A third man, Will, is indicated in the fourth quarterly statement under "Servants Cloaths." Up to September the figure stays at 11s, even when Swift is at Laracor, which is explained by the fact that his house there was not available during this period. With the reduction of the figure to 7s 6d during September, when he has returned to Dublin, it appears that the staff has lost one member. The payment is further lowered, to 3s, when Swift visits Peter Ludlow or the Rochforts. The account book ends in October, but before then the implication is clear that an increase has been necessary: for the last three weeks of October the entry is 11s 6d.

The last two account books mention only one manservant by name, Jo, but the item for board wages is regularly included. Except when there are visits, the payment is 12s. Since Lyon, probably referring to this period, reports that 4s was the sum allowed the servants (Lyon, p. 151), apparently the total amount covers three. The increase, then, is only 6d a week over the entire thirty-three years.

A frequent entry in the early account books is "Pat's bill" or "Will's bill," usually followed by an itemization, including throughout the various books food (bread, butter, coffee, tea, sugar, wine, cakes), household and stable necessities (coals, candles, paper, penknife, cord, nails, oil, lard, washballs, powder and shot, brush), personal requirements ([hair]powder, tobacco, razors), and services (coach, carriage).[19] As might be expected, the itemization becomes more perfunctory as the years pass, and even before 1713 it is common to find simply "Will's bill" without any indication of what it covered. Like Mrs. Brent, the servant would be reimbursed for the staples he had bought. In 1718 Swift made a change in his method of entering these expenses: he now set aside a separate page headed "Wine, Coals, Candles, Soap," and put the purchases of these items under the appropriate date with no mention of who bought them. We assume that after he moved into the deanery, he did not expect the footman to make these particular purchases. Only three times in the body of the book itself does the familiar form "Sander's Bill" appear, twice with no specific items added and once with "tobacco." Those purchases formerly made by the servant but not listed on the special page, such as oil or powder, are given under the usual daily entry.

As we learn from the letters and poems, Swift had other servants than those referred to in the account books. These records do, however, give us the names of several not mentioned elsewhere. Since they are almost always identified by the first name only, we sometimes cannot safely distinguish between two men: during 1702-3 Swift seems to have had two servants named John, and the 1703-4 volume mentions both a John Bunting and a John Campbell. A Hugh is referred to in 1703 and in 1717-8; it may be the same man. The Patrick of 1708-12 is probably not the servant of that name whom Swift employed for a time in 1703.

In November 1702 the position is occupied by John Kemp, who, since on 14 January 1703 he is paid £4 for what was owing to him on his year's wages, would seem in the previous November to have served Swift for at least ten months. In spite of this comparatively long service, he evidently did not give satisfaction, for he either left or was dismissed at the time he received these wages; in either case, he is characterized as "Rogue" in the account book, and we hear of him no more. After a few days Swift hired another servant, perhaps on a temporary basis. This one, also named John, was given his wages on 31 January for ten days and, apparently, dismissed. He is called "Jon" and described as "t'other Rogue." On 2 February a Patrick was hired; the date is assumed from the entry of half a year's wages paid on 2 August. His successor was Hugh.

The 1703-4 account book indicates that Hugh remained in service only until the journey to England, which began on 11 November 1703. After Swift's return, he tells us precisely that John Campbell came on 23 July 1704, but there

---

[19]"The Servants to . . . Have a Pocket-Book, keep all the Bills, date the Time and Place; and indorse the Numbers," The Duty of Servants at Inns, PW, XIII, 165.

may have been an earlier John employed for three weeks before Campbell. On 14 July an item of 3s 7d to "J^{n}," a common abbreviation for "John," looks like a payment of board wages, and on 21 July another for "Wages 7^{s}" may be board wages for two weeks. John Campbell continues, usually as "J^{n}" but once as "Camp^{ll}," till the close of the account book in November 1704. He may have stayed with Swift during most of the next year, for on the same page with the note of his arrival (36) is the statement "John Bunting came. De^{cbr}. 2^{d}. 1705." The fact of Swift's having made the notation in the volume of two years before under the reference to Campbell implies that John Bunting succeeded John Campbell. Of John Bunting we know nothing, since no account book survives to cover his service.

The next account book, that of 1708-9, opens in England. Several payments are made to Patrick--this must be the Patrick of the *Journal to Stella*--in November 1708 and two in December, but neither board wages nor any entries under "Servant" in the quarterly statements are given. After December no references to a possible manservant are made until Swift returns to Ireland, except for the interesting note "Allowd Patrick for Wages in absence" amounting to 13s and dated 11 February 1709 or soon thereafter. The implication, in spite of the omission of board wages, is that Patrick was with Swift in London through December, at which time he was sent home, very likely for misconduct, and his wages paid for the rest of the quarter. If this was the case, for the remainder of Swift's stay in England, he kept no servant.

In his summary for the third quarter, Swift recorded "Ned came Jul. 15th. 1709." He remained till February of 1710. Then, on the page for the second quarter of 1709-10, Swift jotted down the note "Patrick came to me the 2^{d} time, Febr. 9. 1709/10." This time he was with Swift for two years and two months.

The *Journal to Stella* gives us a vivid picture of Swift's most famous servant. In spite of the opprobrious terms given him--*extravagant whelp*, *puppy*, *dog*, *son of a b----*, *intolerable rascal*--it is obvious that he is a man of charm: the ladies in Ireland and Mrs. Vanhomrigh in England are sensible of it. Nevertheless, his conduct grows increasingly outrageous, and his drunkenness seems to have been the final straw. When Swift is coming down with the shingles in March 1712, he complains to MD that Patrick "is drunk every day & I design to turn him off soon as ever I get to Ireld" (*JS*, p. 527). But he (or possibly Patrick) did not wait. In his account book for 1711-2, on a page of notations about his residences and his Christmas gifts, Swift wrote "Apr. 8. 1712. Patrick left me." The following October Patrick appealed to be reinstated, but this time Swift was firm, and the intolerable rascal is heard of no more.

Three days after Patrick left, Swift made another note: "---11 William came." There are at least three Wills among Swift's servants: the successor to Patrick; the drunken groom of the letter of 27 December 1714; and Will Geddes, who, one gathers from the letters of December 1716, is more like a steward than a personal servant. (Williams, *JS*, p. 529, n 37, identifies Patrick's successor, probably incorrectly, with Will Geddes.) The first Will turned out to be more satisfactory if less colorful than Patrick. The last mention of him in the *Journal* occurs when Swift is outlining his plan to walk to Chester on his way to Ireland, an expedition on which Will was to join him. The account book, however, shows that the trip was not made on foot. The entries are not completely clear, but they suggest that Will went with Swift to Chester and on to Ireland. For example, a notation that Will was paid £5 is dated

15 June, when Swift had been in Ireland ten days; on 23 June Vanessa refers to Will as Swift's servant; and there is a payment on 25 June labelled "Will's gods [goods]" following an item of "Custom House." Whether Will came over or not, by 1 July Swift had a new servant.

This was Tom, who, the accounts tell us, returned with Swift to England and remained in his service through October 1713, at which time the book ends. This may be the same Tom, still employed over a year later, of whom Swift speaks in the letter of 27 December 1714 to Archdeacon Walls and who seems to have shared Patrick's fondness for the bottle:

> It was near 3 before I crosst the Ferry. There Tom and the Groom waited. . . I found Will was drunk: I rode on, and found Tom did not come up. . . he was drunk as a Dog, tottered on his Horse, could not keep the Way.

Swift asks Walls to visit the deanery to be sure that Tom does not come there to rob him; he wants "his great Coat, Boots & Whip taken from him; let him have a Crown in part of his Wages." He is to be immediately dismissed. After such behavior it seems impossible that Tom would ever be heard of again; nevertheless, Swift describes in a letter to Chetwode the following July how he pulled Tom's locks for holding a dinner plate under his armpit while waiting at table (Corres., II, 181)--a trick excoriated in Directions to Servants. But we may well be dealing here with two or even three Toms.

In letters to Walls in December 1716, Swift mentions Will Geddes (Corres., II, 231-3). Witness to the deed transferring Nealstown land from Percival to Swift, he is obviously a responsible character, not the drunken groom of two years before. He probably left before the account book of 1717-8 begins. There are two references to a Will in that book, one as receiving 5s 5d on 18 March, listed under "Great Gifts," and the other, possibly in October, recording a payment of 17s 9d for "Wills' frock then." The 5s 5d might be board wages, though why called a gift is not clear, but the use of frock in the latter entry suggests another groom named Will rather than the personal servant. In any event, the manservant in November 1717, when the book begins, is Hugh. References to him are few, but a notation under 19 November that clothes are being altered for him and shoes and stockings provided implies that he has only recently been hired. He does not last long, and in January we find a new name, Sanders or Saunders. This is Alexander McGee--"the best servant in the world" Swift described him to Chetwode (Corres., II, 422)--who is referred to in certain of the poems and who, when he died four years later, was memorialized by Swift in an epitaph. Mary the Cook-Maid, in her "Letter to Dr. Sheridan," repeats a conversation she had with her fellow servant, and he appears also in "From Dr. Swift to Dr. Sheridan" (Poems, pp. 986, 1013).

On 18 December 1734 the account book gives the record of a small gift to "Jo," and in July of the year following Sheridan transmits the greetings of his servant to "your Jo," who, Sheridan implies, is a specialist in Irish bulls. This is all we know of the man.

Various Roberts or Robins, Williams, and Archys appear in the letters and poems but not in the account books, and we know almost nothing of their terms of service or Swift's opinion of them, except for an Archy whom he refused to rehire in 1726 (Corres., III, 139). We do get a vivid picture of a week in the life of Wat, the servant who accompanied Swift back to Ireland in 1727 and whose "blunders would bear an history" (PW, V, 203). A few of them are set out in the pages of the Holyhead Journal, but the account book covering the period has not survived.

9. Travels

Much of our information about Swift's travels comes from the account books, even from some no longer in existence. Often he is precise: "Thursd. Nov^{br}. 11 1703 I went to sea, landed in Engld on Saterd. 13. 1703," he records in 1702-3, and then underneath adds the same formula for the homeward voyage: "Tuesd. May 29 1704 I went to sea, landed in Ireld. on Thurd. June. 1. 1704" (2). The same two journeys are entered in slightly fuller form in 1703-4, where they belong: "Put to sea. Thurs^{d}. No^{br}. 11. 1703. landed at Chestr. Sater^{d}. No^{br}. 13. 1703" (38); and "Left Leicest^{r}. Mon^{d}. May. 29. Left Neston. Tues^{d}. May. 30th. 1704. landed at Dublin, Thursday morn. Jun. 1. 1704. being my 16th Voyage" (41). In 1707-8, according to Lyon's notes on the "Cobbe" autobiography, Swift had used the same form to note his crossing to England on 28 November 1707, his landing at Darpool, and his riding "next day" to Parkgate (Forster, p. 17). In 1708-9, on the way home, he makes the usual memoranda of his journey from London to Leicester (71), all the various stages of which--St. Albans, Dunstable, Newport, Northampton, Harborough--are traceable through the amounts spent at each place (72). With all his determination to keep a complete record, Swift occasionally forgets where he was on a particular day: in May, at the top of the page, he has jotted down "Ubi. 8?" and in June "Ubi. 12?." a convincing proof that he did not always write down his expenses on the day they were incurred. From Leicester it is easy enough to follow him to Chester and on to Dublin. The trip to Chester is amply recorded: he had dinner and spent the night at Burton on the Hill and the next day proceeded on by Stone and Nantwich (73) to his destination, which he reached on the 15th. Nevertheless, it was to be a fortnight before he arrived in Dublin, as a fuller than usual comment tells us:

> Sett sail from Darpool for Ireland June. 29th, 1709 at 3 a clock in the Morning being Wednesday, lay that night in the bay of Dublin, and landed at Ringsend the next day at 7 in the morning, and went strait to Laracor without seing anybody and returnd to Dublin July 4, wch was Monday following (73).[20]

The beginning of the momentous visit to England the following August Swift described with even more than his customary detail, as if he foresaw the decisive importance it would have in his career. "Sett out for Engl^{d} Aug. 31st on Thursday, 10 at night: landed at Parkgate Friday 1. at noon. Sep^{tbr}. 1st. 1710. came to London. Thursday at noon. Sep^{br}. 7th. with Ld Mountjoy &c" (112). Again he enters in the book the stages to London--Chester, Whitchurch, Newport, Coventry, Towcester, and Dunstable--even though very little was spent along the way, as "Ld Mountjoy bore my Expences from Chest^{r} to London." The 1712-3 book notes with the same definiteness the journey back to Ireland, for the purpose of being installed as Dean of St. Patrick's (156), as well as the recall to England less than three months later (159), with the usual route to

---

[20]The "anybody" was MD, with whom he may have been provoked, as he apologizes three years later in the Journal: "I expect to see my Willows a Month after the Parlmt is up; but I will take Md in the way, and not go to Laracor like an unmannerly Spreenekick Ferrow" (JS, p. 535).

London indicated by the expenses along the way. Swift was to return to Ireland in 1714, and the account book for 1713-4, which Lyon saw, furnished the usual details: "He set out to Ireland from Letcomb in Berkshire August the 16th, 1714; landed in Dublin the 24th" (Forster, p. 17).

Sometimes Swift enters a place name, either at the top of the page or more usually beside the appropriate week, to record where he has been staying at that period. In the summer of 1712, as we read in the Journal to Stella, he spent much time with the Court at Windsor. The concise notation in July in the account book--"Windsor 26. a week"--would remind him that he had stayed there for a week beginning on the 26th. When he returned to England in the autumn of 1713, a period not covered by the Journal, the account book tells us precisely that he spent the fourth week of September at Windsor, staying till 5 October, and that he passed two days a week there on each of the last three weeks of October.

The same method is used to indicate places visited in Ireland. As would be expected, "Laracor" is most frequently found. In November 1709 each week has a location attached, the first three marked "Laracor," the fourth "Going to Clogh^{r}. 19." and the remainder of the month "Clogh^{r}." He marks the period 1-10 December "Clogher" and that from 24 December to the first of the new year "Laracor," and there are a few expenses in the middle of the month which enable us to follow him as he travels between the two towns. In February and March of 1710 he was at Laracor, as also in April, where the third and fourth weeks have the addition of "MD," though Stella and Mrs. Dingley would be staying at Trim rather than Laracor. We know from the account of his mother's death that he was at Laracor in May, and the headings in June make it clear that he stayed there till the 5th. He was back again for the third week in July, apparently his last visit before he left for England at the end of August.

After he returned to Ireland for his installation as dean on 13 June 1713, he left for Laracor on the 25th and made the "Laracor" notation after each of the four weeks in July and the first week in August. Then he had to return to Dublin to prepare for his sudden journey to England at the end of the month.

After he became dean, trips to Laracor became less frequent, though he continued to go there, if mainly as a stop on the way to other places. He was there on 27 December 1717 before going to Ludlow's. In April 1718, between visits to Ludlow at the beginning of the month and to Sir William Fownes at the end, he was at Laracor or Trim. In June he travelled back and forth between Laracor and Dublin before going to Ludlow's, and in August he returned to Trim before running up to Ludlow's again. He seems to have stayed in Dublin for the remaining two months of the account book.

Judging by the two account books from the 30's, Swift seems, understandably enough, to have travelled less than he had been accustomed to when younger. A stay at Castle Rickard, four miles from Trim, in April 1733 is mentioned; he was at Trim from 15 to 19 May for the Bishop of Meath's visitation, and at Belcamp, the home of the Grattans, four miles north of Dublin, for three days in July. The only place notations in the 1734-5 volume indicate that he was at Belcamp from 11 to 16 November and for a longer time, from 20 November to 4 December 1734, at the Grange, near Belcamp, and that he paid one of what must have been many visits to Howth Castle on 16 December. But these are all close to Dublin, and Swift's travelling days were nearly over. In May of 1735 he wrote to Pope, "I . . . dare not venture to be a days Journey from this Town, for fear of taking a fit of giddyness that sincks me for a month" (Corres., IV, 335). At the end of the year he was to pass a month or so with Sheridan at Quilca, but this seems to have been his last long expedition.

All these notes have been separately entered. Yet they are by no means the only clues in the account books to Swift's movements. The settlement of his tithe collections with his agent, either at Laracor or at the midway station of The Pace, took place in November, midwinter, and spring. Then the individual expenses sometimes betray his whereabouts. "Bill at Virginia," for example, "Candles at Trim," "Dunlary," "Leslip," "Coach MD at Donybrook," "Dinner & Coach Finglas. Mr Addison" are of great value in helping us to follow him. But also some idea of where he is can be gained, as we have said, from the item of board wages paid to his servant, who did not ordinarily receive them at Trim or Laracor. Using this method we find that, to take the 1702-3 book as an example, Swift and Pat spent Christmas at Trim, specifically from 19 December to 9 January. Board wages were also not paid at other times during the year--4 to 14 February, 20 March to 1 April, 17 April to 22 May, 24 July to 18 September, and during the week of 16-23 October--and it is probable that at these times Swift was staying in his parish. Some support is given to these dates and to similar periods in the other account books by the records of card games with opponents from Trim or Dublin or of his attendance at visitations and chapter meetings. His statement to Walls in 1708 that "2 Satyrdays in four I was at Laracor" (Corres., I, 108) would seem to be roughly accurate for the time he spent in Ireland before he became dean.

10. Health

In much the same way as he entered place names, Swift sometimes put down, usually at the top of the page, an abbreviated record of his health. It is not clear why he did this. The account books were not diaries, where such notations might be appropriate. In his constant and justifiable concern about his physical condition, he may have been making a rough study of his attacks of illness to compare the frequency and violence of them. This seems especially likely in the 1708-9 book, in which there are more memoranda about sickness than in the other books. Here it may be that, since he was in England at the time, he was using these entries as aide-mémoires when describing his health in letters, now lost, to the ladies; however, similar jottings, though not as numerous, occur in the Irish books and even in those compiled after Stella's death.

The giddiness or vertigo from which he suffered to the end of his life began while he was still a young man. "I have had my Giddiness 23 years by fits," he tells MD on 9 October 1712, which would place the onset of it as early as 1689, when he was twenty-two. The first mention of it in the account books occurs in 1708, when he is in his early forties. In November of that year he writes, "From 6 to 16 often giddy G^{d} help me so to 25th less," the form of which suggests an attempt to summarize the whole month. A notation for 16 November gives "Brandy for Giddiness"; we read in the Journal to Stella a year later that he is drinking a pint of it "at Mornings" (JS, p. 123). In December he is rather more detailed: "5 Horrible sick. 12 much better. Thank G^{d} & MD's Pray^{rs}. 16 bad fitt at Mrs Bartons," a severe enough attack, we learn from the day's records, to force him to the unusual expense of a chair and to the payment next day of the considerable sum of 7s 6d to Mrs. Barton's servants. It is this attack which he describes to Archbishop King in his letter of 6 January 1709:

> I should have acknowledged your Grace's letter, if I had not been ever since persecuted with a cruel Distemper, a Giddiness in my Head, that would not suffer me to write or think of any Thing; and of which I am now slowly recovering.

He refers to it again as late as 26 March, calling it a "cruel illness, that seized me at Fits." On 6 December he had attempted to cure himself by taking a vomit, a method he used with little success all his life; and it is likely that the two items of "broth" on 8 and 13 represent efforts, also made frequently in later years, to improve his condition through diet. "24 bettr, but dread a Fitt" is the next comment, but he was spared, and throughout December he is "better still to the End."

The improvement continues through the early part of January 1709, but for a period of about three weeks beginning on the 21st he experiences slight recurrences. "An ill fitt but not to excess" we read on that day, and a week later, on the 29th, after a visit to Cranford, he mentions that he is "out of order," and on the 31st, giving the monthly summary, he has to note "not well at times." On 7 February there is a "small fitt abroad," but after this the problem cleared, for he describes his condition in February, somewhat confusingly, as "Pretty well to th end, & bet^{r} still." In March and April there is no dizziness, but they bring other ailments. "Head ake frequent," he says in March; "toward th end Cough a week, but end in a cold," which lasts for the first week of the next month. "I am extremely afflicted with a Cold," he writes Archbishop King on 26 March, "and Cough attending it," and on 2 April he buys licorice and perhaps even consults a doctor, as on that day he pays a "Quack" 3s 6d. In June, the day before he leaves Leicester for Ireland, he pays 4s 5d to an apothecary, but we have no letters identifying the illness, nor are we told why he buys brandy in August or pills in September, though we may guess that they were to relieve giddiness.

In the next two account books the brief notices of ill health are expanded, often in some detail, in the _Journal to Stella_. Judging by the volume for 1709-10 and by the absence of complaints in his letters, Swift's condition seems to have been good during the winter and the first two thirds of the new year. There is a purchase of drugs in the first quarterly summary, and the rather large sum of 18s 6d is paid to an apothecary in February, but these are apparently all.

When the _Journal_ begins, in September 1710, we find proof of Swift's comparatively robust condition. "They tell me I am grown fatter," he says on the 9th, and a week later adds, "My health continues pretty well." However, on the last day of October he writes at the top of the page for that month, "a small giddy fitt & swoon MD G^{d} help me." On the same day he gives a full account of the attack to the ladies:

> Now I'll tell you what I would not in my last, that this morning, sitting in my bed, I had a fit of giddiness: the room turned round for about a minute, and then it went off, leaving me sickish, but not very: and so I past the day as I told you; but I would not end a letter with telling you this, because it might vex you: and I hope in God I shall have no more of it. I saw Dr. Cockburn to-day, and he promises to send me the pills that did me good last year, and

likewise has promised me an oil for my ear, that he has been making for that ailment for somebody else.

The account book for 1709-10 ends on this day, and the next one is missing, but the _Journal_ finishes the history. The next day he reports, "I had no giddiness to-day, but I drank brandy, and have bought a pint for two shillings," and on 2 November he gives another bulletin: "I took my four pills last night. . . . I have had no giddiness to-day." Finally, on the 3rd he merely mentions "no giddiness," and that is the last we hear of this particular seizure. They were to be more severe and to last longer as he grew older.

During the year covered by the account book of 1711-2, Swift suffered from his usual giddiness, as well as from a persistent cold and a most painful attack of shingles. He began the year (November 1711) with some alleviation of the vertigo. "My head has had no ill returns," he tells the Dublin ladies (_JS_, p. 409), but he was ill the next week and had got "a swinging cold" (_JS_, p. 411). "I am going on fairly in the common forms of a great cold," he tells them on the 16th; "I believe it will last me about ten days in all." It was to last all winter. His only remedy appears to have been licorice, which according to the account book he bought on 29 November and again on 11 February. It was, we can assume, inefficacious, as the cold, although better, is still with him on 21 March.

At this time a more serious illness struck him, so painful and incapacitating that he gave up his system of daily reports in his letters to the ladies and could not bring himself even to jot down regularly in his account book what few expenses there may have been. As an added burden it was while he was stricken that Patrick left. On the page for April of the account book, a page with only a handful of items, Swift has written "Shingles begun Mar. 27. Sick all this Month." The next day he informs the ladies, "I have a Pain these 2 days exactly upon the top of my left Shouldr, I fear it is something Rheumatick, it winches now and then." On the 29th it is still not serious enough to be mentioned to Archbishop King, though the ladies are told, "I am got into bed and have put some old Flannel for want of new to my Shouldr, and rubbed it with Hungary water." The next day he is in such distress that he can not go to church or court, though he does dine at Mrs. Vanhomrigh's, going the short distance in a chair, an expense duly recorded in the account book. During the entire month of April he is, as he reports to Dublin, in great discomfort. He is not absolutely confined to his room during this period, as he tells MD he is, since the account book gives the cost of chairs, doubtless to Mrs. Vanhomrigh's, on the 16th, 17th, and 18th. He is still uncomfortable on 10 May: "My Pain continues Still in my Shouldr and Collar I keep Flannel on it, and rub it with Brandy; and take a nasty dyet Drink." The nasty diet drink and other drugs cost him, we find by his accounts, as much as 17s, and the apothecary's bill came to a crushing £1 4s 6d. On 8 June, before he was finally rid of the shingles, another complication arose: "Colick sadly for a day."

In August Swift went to Windsor, but he was no better for the change of air, and the page that month is headed "Sick with Giddyness much." There are no further references in August, but on 3 September he tells Vanessa that he is "not very well in my Head," on the 15th and 18th he complains in the _Journal_ of giddiness, on the 23rd he tells Stella he is "vely kick," and on the 28th he pays 11s to the apothecary at Windsor.

Except for the usual winter cold, for the first part of the year 1712-3

Swift was in reasonable health, though not without some giddiness. In early November of 1712 he pays 2s 6d to Lord Orkney's man for "Spaw water," which he used to combat his giddiness. Since he tells the ladies the following March that "Ldy Orkney is my Physician" (JS, p. 645), it is probable that she had sent him the water. It was not helpful. An attack came in January. On the page for that month he writes "Giddy 26th," the only direct reference to his health in the whole 1712-3 book. On that day he describes the seizure to the ladies: "This morning I felt a little Touch of Giddyness, which has disorderd & weakend me with its ugly remains all this day, poo poo pdfr." Four days later he is still unwell: "I have drank Spaw Waters this 2 or 3 days; but they do not pass, and mak me very giddy: I an't well fais, I'll take them no more." On 5 February he reports that "I have left Spaw-water: it makes my leg swell," and on the 17th he notes an improvement: "I have given away all my Spaw water, and take some nasty steel drops, & may head has been bettr this week past." There is no reference in this or any other account book to steel drops; he may have got them from the apothecary along with other unspecified medicines.

Soon after Christmas he tells the ladies of a "great Cold," which lasts about a fortnight; but then a second one arrives, which is "almost off" in early February (JS, pp. 589, 616). No medication for these colds is indicated in the account book, and it is likely that he merely endured the discomfort. "Colds," he says; "why we have been all dying with Colds" (JS, p. 616).

On 23 May, as he is making plans to leave for Ireland, he complains to Archbishop King that he has been "out of Order for these ten Days past," and a week after that he remarks to Vanessa that he hopes the coming journey will restore his health. But at Chester on 6 June he tells her mother that there has been disappointingly little improvement. On that day he registers the sum of 16s 11d to the apothecary, which may have been paid, not in Chester, but as the final settling of the bill for his London medicine.

This was the prelude to a bad summer. During the rest of June and through half of July he suffered greatly from his old enemy, giddiness. The illness finally abated in early August, and by the time he returned to England at the end of the month and in September and October he seems to have been in good condition. The only medicine recorded in the account book during this period is "Milk wat^{r},"[21] for which he paid a shilling on 21 September, but we have no information from other sources about what he was suffering from.

According to Williams (Corres., II, 302, n 1), "During that year [1718] Swift appears to have suffered acutely from vertigo," and he cites for proof the entry in the account book for 3 May: "-terrible Fall G^{d} knows what may be th Event. bettr twards th End." This is, in fact, the only direct comment on his health to be found in the twelve months covered by the 1717-8 account book as well as in the few letters he wrote during the same period. There is a payment of "Physick 1^{s} 6^{d}" on 17 May, possibly connected with the dizziness that we may assume caused the fall two weeks before, and another for 7d on 25 August, made, if the date is reliable, during a visit to Peter Ludlow. Again, on

---

[21] Milk water, according to Hannah Glasse, The Art of Cookery, London, 1765, is made as follows: "Wormwood, carduus, rue, mint, balm, angelica. Put in a cold still and add 3 qts of milk. Quick fire then slacken. Draw off 2 qts."

9 May, a few days after the fall, he records "seeds [carraway?] & Brand. 1^s 8^d"; no doubt the brandy was his old remedy for giddiness. Also, his purchases of bitters for 1s 6d on 17 June and 17 July were certainly to cure some stomachic disorder. But that is the extent of the information we have about his state during this period: it seems to indicate a year comparatively free of illness.

We learn almost nothing about Swift's health from the 1732-3 volume. There are no expenses at all which can be definitely related to attempts to cure his twin evils. Yet we know from his correspondence that during much of the year he was not well, and that both in the spring and the autumn his giddiness was severe. The account book does give us the date when the spring attack began. "Giddy from 4th," he notes at the top of the page for March, and that same month he adds, "--14. very ill." He mentions this disorder in several letters to friends, the Duchess of Queensberry (23 March), Sheridan (27 March), Pope (30 March), Ford (5 April), Orrery (16 April), and Oxford (31 May). To Sheridan he says that he is taking "daily Drops and Bitters," and to Ford that he has put himself "into the hands of Deally and taking daily medicines." Yet nothing in the account book indicates the purchase of medicine or payments to doctors or apothecaries. He complains, also to Ford, that "I always totter in the dark, and have within this twelvemonth spent more money in chair-hire than in any ten years before." Since we have no account books during the previous ten years, we have no way of knowing whether this is an exaggeration; there are, indeed, expenses for a chair on an average of at least once a week during the year. In any case, the illness lasted far enough into the summer to make Swift give up his plans to visit England in August and spend the winter there.

It was well he did so. The autumn attack was a very severe one. It may be the explanation for the fact that, though we have the summary for the fourth quarter, August to November 1733, the three separate monthly entries themselves are lacking. We know of a few payments and transactions during this period from the quarterly summary, a memorandum at the back of the book, and a list of deanery expenses following that; but we have little knowledge of Swift's daily expenditures. On 12 December he tells Stannard that he has been confined three months by his deafness and giddiness, and nothing in the account book disproves this statement, though his remark to Ford on 20 November that he rides as far as Howth every fair day suggests that <u>confined</u> is not to be taken strictly.

For a small part of the period covered by the 1732-3 book, Swift had an additional problem, lameness, following a strain in the leg in February 1732, but it too is not hinted at in the book itself.

We know from the letters that during 1734 Swift was seldom out of pain, and indeed, as might be expected, his illnesses continued with increasing rigor to the end of his life. In November, when the 1734-5 book opens, he tells Pope that the deafness is "pretty well off" but that the giddiness makes him totter "towards Evenings" (<u>Corres</u>., IV, 262). In December he becomes really ill. On the 16th he twice notes "Deadly sick at Howth" (242, 247). We learn the details from a letter to Blachford written the next day:

> The Weather yesterday being very fine, I rode to Howth House, and as I was getting on horseback to return, I was seised with so cruel a fit of that giddyness which at times hath pursued me from my youth that I was forced to lie down on a bed in an empty house for two

> hours before I was in a condition to ride. However I got home safe, but am this morning very weak, as I always have been for many days after such fits. . . . I must fence by taking Vomits and other Medicines prescribed for me by some Physicians who happen to be my Friends.

The following day he makes a brief comment in French which we have been unable to decipher: it looks like "Enfin resblee pour le feu Vague," and we suggest somewhat hesitantly that it indicates a recovery. If so, it was a temporary one, for on the 20th he enters "2 giddy fits in 3 minutes Took a Vomit." That is all we hear of this December seizure, unless the frequent item of "chairs" means that he is unable to ride or walk as usual. It is not quite safe to assume this, however, since the entry may here refer, as it often does, to the chair Mrs. Whiteway took to the deanery and for which Swift paid.

On 7 February Swift writes to Humphrey French that he will be unable for reasons of health to attend the Blue-coat Board that evening, and the next day there is an entry in the account book, "Feb^{r}. 8. Surge^{n} 11^{s} 6^{d}." Later in February he tells Mrs. Pendarves that he has not had "one single hour of health" in three months (Corres., IV, 297). He continues riding for his health, and he begins in May to record in his book those days on which he rides. He tells his friends that he does not dare go farther than a dozen miles from home two or three times a week (Corres., IV, 378), and to Barber he admits in September that "I very seldom go to Church for fear of being seised with a Fit of Giddyness in the midst of the Service" (Corres., IV, 381). Nevertheless, after February the account book has few indications of malaise. There are purchases of brandy, licorice, carraway seeds, and milk water, all of which doubtless were used for medicinal purposes, but they are among the usual domestic pharmacopeia and prove very little about Swift's physical state. Finally, under the entry "Physick For my self and Servants" he has written "To Mr Staunt^{n} in all 13^{s} 6^{d}½." We do not know the occasion for this payment nor even the identity of Staunton; he cannot, one would think, be Swift's legal adviser, Thomas Staunton.

11. Wins and Losses

Swift was by no means an inveterate or heavy gambler. In October 1711 he thinks he has not played above four times during the year (JS, p. 375). Daily card-playing, a habit with such of his friends as Lady Betty Germain, Lady Acheson, and Stella herself, was, he thought, almost the only social activity open to ladies, and he regretted, in "The Hardship put upon Ladies," that they "should want the Privilege of Men" and "slave at Cards from Morn to Night" instead of reading and writing (Poems, p. 622). But he was an occasional player, and "The Journal of a Modern Lady" illustrates how well he knew not only the rules of quadrille but the common methods of cheating at it. He played on a small scale all his life. The account books quite disprove the younger Sheridan's statement (p. 487) that "he wholly left it off [playing for trifles] when he appeared in Ireland in the character of the Dean of St. Patrick's."

In all but two of the account books he set aside a page at the beginning to list his wins and losses at cards (basset, ombre, piquet, whist) or dice games (tables or backgammon, hazard), though the sums won or lost were not included in the monthly, quarterly, or yearly totals. The two account books without the lists are those for 1703-4 and 1732-3. If, in 1703-4, Swift originally kept a page of his wins and losses for the London period, he may have neglected to transfer it, and then, with no record in his book from November to June, saw no reason for keeping one for the remaining four months of his year. As to the 1732-3 book, it seems likely that the page has been removed, as have other pages. It is hardly conceivable that Swift played no games at all during the year. In 1729 he writes to Pope, in reference to the Worralls, "I give my vicar a supper, and his iwfe a shilling, to play with me an hour at backgammon once a fortnight" (Corres., III, 314). This fortnightly play must have continued for the next several years. In a letter full of Irishisms, Sheridan writes on 20 December 1733, two months after the conclusion of the 1732-3 account book, "I would go and play a game of back-gammon with Mr. Worral's tables, and be after winning some of Mrs. Worral's coin." And in the 1734-5 account book a win and loss in November to "Worrall" are duly entered. Hence, it seems certain that the play, at least the games with the Worralls, was carried on during 1732-3 and that the page recording Swift's success has been lost.

Another anomaly is in the 1717-8 volume, in which the page of wins and losses is empty except for the totals, placed in the lower right-hand corner, as if Swift intended to fill in later the individual entries. If he had done so, the page would probably have been a full one: the sum involved is fourteen pounds, a larger total than in any of the other extant Irish books, and one implying a good many evenings of gaming. He must have kept the itemization on a separate sheet but have found no opportunity of transferring it to the account book. This is unfortunate because 1717-8 falls in a period when we would like to know more about Swift's life.

It may be added that the 1734-5 volume differs from earlier ones in omitting the game played and giving only the opponent and the sum involved.

Since the pages of wins and losses tell whom Swift is seeing and where he is, they furnish some helpful pieces of biographical information. For instance, he plays with three major groups of friends, each of which is associated with a different place. In Dublin in the early years--that is, before 1714--there are the Stoytes, the Wallses (mainly Mrs. Walls), Dean Stearne, and the Bishop of Clogher; and in the 1730's the Helshams, Sheridan, Charles Grattan, and especially Mrs. Whiteway and her two older children. The lists give no evidence of games at Trim or Laracor after 1713--by 1735 Swift had virtually ceased to go there--but before that year the Barrys, the Wesleys, Percival, Raymond, Morgan, and Warburton were his principal opponents. In London he played with his friends about the court, such as Dr. Arbuthnot, Mrs. Masham and her sister, the Duke and Duchess of Shrewsbury, and the Lord Treasurer himself; with professional associates, like Tooke and Barber and Mrs. Manley; and most often with a group centering around the Vanhomrigh family, including Ann Long, Sir Andrew Fountaine, and Erasmus Lewis. He also gambled with Irish friends who were more or less permanently settled in London, like Charles Ford, or were visiting there, like Provost Pratt and the Ashe brothers.

These records, then, give us some idea of his acquaintance not only for the well-documented period covered by the Journal to Stella but for the years before and after, when our information is more scanty. Additional proof of the frequency with which he saw the Vanhomrighs, as we said earlier, is given by the list of wins and losses. With Stella and Mrs. Dingley, listed under the symbols "Tpt" and "Ppt," he played both in Dublin and Trim. In the Journal there are so many references, usually jocular, to the ladies'--or at least to Stella's--playing cards that one realizes it was their regular evening occupation. A vivid picture of the Dublin group is given under 27 June 1711. After describing an evening at the Vanhomrighs, Swift adds, "It put me in mind of the dean, and Stoyte, and Walls, and Stella at play, and Dingley and I looking on." He was frequently a watcher: his lists, of course, give no information as to how often he was present simply as an observer. In 1710, soon after he arrives in London, he tells the ladies,

> Today at last I dined with Lord Montrath, and carried lord Mountjoy and sir Andrew Fountain with me; and was looking over them at ombre till eleven this evening like a fool (JS, p. 51).

And in 1719 he writes Ford,

> I think as little of Publick Affairs as I can, because they concern me as one of the Multitude; and for the same Reason I dare not venture to play at threepeny Basset, because it is a Game where Conduct is of no use, and I dare not trust to Fortune as the younger Folks do, and therefore I divert my self with looking upon others at Play mea sine parte pericli (Corres., II, 312).

When he does play, the sums of money involved are usually trivial, seldom reaching to a pound, and Swift was correct in referring to himself in October 1711 as a small gamester (JS, p. 375). In London, naturally, the stakes were higher, and in 1712 the total amount of his gambling transactions there came to seventeen pounds, the largest total of which we have record. In the poem "To Charles Ford, Esq." we read

> So--let us now for Whisk prepare;
> Twelvepence a Corner, if you dare (Poems, p. 315).

and earlier he speaks of "playing at twelve-penny picquet" with Lewis (JS, p. 375). In Ireland a sixpence appears to have been the usual stake. In 1729 he writes Pope and Bolingbroke:

> If I play at piquet for six-pence with a man or woman two years younger than my self, I always lose; and there is a young girl of twenty who never fails of winning my money at Back-gammon, though she is a bungler, and the game be Ecclesiastic (Corres., III, 329).

In 1733, in the letter already cited, Sheridan implies that Swift played backgammon with the Worralls for an Irish sixpence. The sums grew even smaller: by the time of the 1734-5 book, he is playing with Mrs. Whiteway for as little as a penny, and the total for the year, during which he nevertheless played frequently, is the tiny sum of £1 6s 3d½.

The names of Swift's opponents include several which are indecipherable and others which, though readable, are not identifiable. The two most baffling cruxes occur on 27 and 30 March 1710, in Dublin, both in connection with losses to or perhaps by Tpt. They may in fact not be names at all but comments, since both entries begin, quite unusually, with "Lost for Tpt." Also in Dublin in 1710 is what appears to be "Mrs. Tigh," but it is not clearly enough written to allow a guess at identification. Nor is it known who "Lady Tint" at Trim is or, in 1709, "Lady Tant" at Epsom (Forster omits her from his transcription of the entry). The 1734-5 volume also presents two slight difficulties. If "Jax^{sn}" is the Rev. John Jackson, the letters "B. G." following it elude explanation. Likewise what appears to be "S. Grat" suggests one of the Grattans, but unless the initial should be read as "J," for either John or

James, or "C" for Charles, who is given as an opponent two or three months later, it is unclear which member of the family is meant.

12. Clothing

A regular entry in the quarterly list of expenses is clothes, which may include as well as articles of wear such accessories as handkerchiefs, wig boxes, bootirons, and once--perhaps in error--razors. Judging from the nine books only and taking into consideration the greater proportional cost before the days of machine tailoring, it does not appear that Swift spent a great deal on his clothes. The largest outlay is in 1708-9, when the yearly total is over twenty-eight pounds, and for six of the nine years it falls under fifteen pounds. Perhaps a more helpful figure would be the ratio of the cost of clothing to the total expense: this averages out in the extant books to somewhat over ten per cent, probably not a high proportion, even for a clergyman, in the eighteenth century.

Oddly, Swift's expenditures on clothing show no progressive increase over the thirty years. The amounts spent, as given in the nine books, are: £10 18s (1702-3), £21 10s (1703-4), £28 8s (1708-9), £11 7s (1709-10), £9 11s (1711-2), £17 7s (1712-3), £13 8s (1717-8 and 1732-3), and £9 15s (1734-5). The ratio to total expenses ranges from eighteen percent (1708-9) down to seven (1702-3).

However, we cannot rely entirely on the figures given in the books. Some expenditures mentioned in the Journal to Stella are not reported in the account books for the same period. For one example, on 31 January 1713 Swift mentions that he paid William Harrison "while he was with me 7 Guinneas, in part of a dozen of Shirts he bought me in Holland." This large sum is not found in the account book, though there is a note the previous September of 5s for shirts brought from Holland, possibly a payment for delivery.

Some of Swift's clothing was required by his calling. In the Project for the Advancement of Religion he regrets that "The Clergy are the only Set of Men among us, who constantly wear a distinct Habit from others" (PW, p. 54), and adds, "In my opinion it were infinitely better if all the Clergy (except the Bishops) were permitted to appear like other Men of the graver Sort, unless at those Seasons when they are doing the Business of their Function" (PW, p. 279). Some clergymen did occasionally dress like other men. Archdeacon Walls did not even bring a gown with him to London (JS, p. 318). But Swift apparently always appeared in clerical dress. No clothing inconsistent with a prelate's habit is listed in the books.

The gown and cassock are among the most common items under Clothes, sometimes as new garments but more often as articles requiring mending or other renovating. When new, the gown and cassock were expensive, coming to over six pounds for each of three purchases out of four recorded. We are told in unusual detail about one particular set of garments in 1708-9: "French. Gown & Cass. 4^{s}-6^{d} p^{r} y^{rd}; 24 y^{rds} 5^{ll}-8^{s}. mak. 18^{s}-0^{d}." for a total of £6 6s. At another time, by using a cheaper material, he is able to limit the cost to only five pounds. Obviously, so expensive a piece of clothing required considerable care in the maintenance: seven or eight times Swift pays to mend gowns and cassocks as well as to "swap old gown" or "alter camlet gown."

Among other articles of clerical wear Swift twice buys a girdle, three times a scarf, and twice bands. The "swelling scarf," as well as the "glossy gown" of a dean are contrasted in "The Parson's Case" with the pitiful clothing worn by a poor curate (Poems, p. 676). The scarf was not inexpensive: twice Swift pays over a pound for one, though he manages to get a crape one for fifteen shillings. As he reports in the Journal, he asks both Mrs. Vanhomrigh and Lady Abercorn to buy him a scarf--"mine is all in rags"--and a week later he is paying Mrs. Vanhomrigh for hers (JS, p. 118).

Most of Swift's clothing consists of the staples of ordinary wear--shoes, stockings, breeches, nightgowns, hats, caps, shirts, waistcoats, and periwigs. Among the two most common items are handkerchiefs and gloves. Though the quantity purchased is not always specified, we can with some accuracy estimate the number from the price. Since at various times Swift lists two handkerchiefs for 5s, four for 14s, and six for 16s 6d, we assume that he paid between 2s 6d and 3s 6d apiece. Thus he bought perhaps half a dozen handkerchiefs a year, hardly an excessive number in a snuff-taking age. A "gard," for 6s, placed directly after "handkerchiefs," is, one supposes, a device for preventing theft.

Gloves were cheap, and Swift bought them frequently. They seldom cost him more than 1s 6d a pair, so that when he records paying 3s or, in 1734-5, 5s 5d, he is undoubtedly buying more than one pair. They could be had even more cheaply: in 1702 Blundell (p. 42) paid 15s for a dozen pairs, and in 1712 Thomas Tyldesley (p. 58) was able to get a pair for 8d. In every year except 1732-3 Swift bought a pair, usually oftener than once and in some years almost every quarter.

Shoes also he bought often and paid little for them. In 1700-1 and presumably in earlier books, he used a separate quarterly entry for Shoes; during 1702-3 he began combining Shoes with Clothes and continued this practice from then on. He evidently bought shoes in quantity: in 1702-3 he pays for seven pairs at a price of less than 5s a pair. Later in the same year he buys one pair for 4s 6d and later still two pairs for 9s. Again, these low prices are to be expected: Tyldesley in 1712 pays 5s a pair (p. 38), and a year or two earlier the Archer accounts record 4s (Halliwell, p. 63). A second 9s purchase by Swift, if it represents two pairs, makes a total of eleven pairs of shoes in one year. Every year, except 1711-2, he buys shoes, though never again in the quantity needed in 1702-3. One can estimate, very roughly, that about seven pairs are indicated in 1703-4, four in 1708-9, three in 1712-3, five or six in 1717-8, only one in 1732-3, and four or five in 1734-5.

In addition to shoes, Swift occasionally buys slippers and galoshes. As these are never listed separately, we cannot tell what he paid for them, but Blundell's Diary suggests that slippers at any rate cost about as much as shoes, i. e., 4s (p. 8). There is no record of Swift's buying boots (except in the yearly summary for 1700-1), though three times he lists the few pence paid to have them mended. Two of the three times the expense is under Horses; they may have belonged to the groom. The gambadoes which Swift began to wear in 1732 are not mentioned in the account books.

We can often estimate what Swift paid for other articles of clothing, though it is not always possible to separate the cost of the material itself from the cost of having it made up. Stockings, usually thread, come to about 5s a pair. He sometimes bought several at a time, for we find him twice paying nearly £1 10s. Like his caps, they were mended by servants: in "The Cook-

Maid's Letter" Mary pictures herself mending her master's stocking (Poems, p. 986), and the manservant was probably expected at times to do so too.

Breeches run from 9s 6d to over 15s a pair, the difference possibly depending on the material: cloth ones seem to be cheaper than knit ones. At one point Swift pays £1 6s 4d for two pairs of cloth breeches, a figure which includes the cost of making them. Mending breeches, a frequent necessity, was apparently beyond the skill of the servant, for six times the payment of 6d or 1s is listed for this service. The 15s which once appears must have included more than just one mending.

Shirts, made up, may have come to about 10s, but there are too few entries to be certain. Swift pays £4 13s for six, and once he lists the "Cloth for 4 Shirts & Hol^{d} [Holland]" at £1 10s. The unrecorded seven guineas for part payment on a dozen shirts has already been noted. Late in his life he pays Mrs. Worrall 13s 2d½ for making seven shirts, but he omits the cost of the linen, which he thought too high, as he accuses her of cheating him on that score. Linen, which occurs twice, was probably used for shirts. One is a payment to Mrs. Manley; we know that Swift bought clothing through John Barber, with whom Mrs. Manley lived, as he tells Charles Ford in 1714 that he owes Barber for a hat and a nightgown. In his accounts he distinguishes between clerical bands, which he calls simply bands, and wristbands for shirts. These latter are small items: wristbands for two shirts come to 1s, and at other times he pays as little as 3d or even 1d½. Shirts, like breeches, were often mended; except for one charge of 8d, the cost was 1s.

Something like six nightgowns--the dressing gowns of today--are recorded in the nine books. The price for making them strikes us as pitifully small. Mrs. S., who seems to have done Swift's sewing in 1708-9, is paid 2s for making one, and others received 2s 6d and 3s 4d, this last for an India one, which may have been a more expensive article altogether, though the total cost is not given. One nightgown costs as little as 14s 9d, but a stuffed (quilted?) one comes to £1 13s; and for another, along with cap and slippers, Swift pays the great sum of £4 12s 6d. There are two small charges for cleaning and scouring a nightgown.

Swift seldom buys nightcaps: he often received them as gifts. In the Journal he refers to one made by Mrs. Dingley (p. 85) and another given him by Lord Herbert (p. 149). In 1728 he asks Worrall to give his wife "a thousand thanks from me for her kind present and workmanship of her fairest hands in making me two night caps" (Corres., III, 302). The complete absence of any mention of caps in the 1703-4, 1708-9, and 1709-10 books suggests that they were made for him by someone, Mrs. Dingley or Mrs. Brent or another, who was not being paid for them. In 1711, a year after he landed in England, he writes, "Patrick tells me my caps are wearing out; I know not how to get others. I want a necessary woman strangely; I am as helpless as an elephant" (JS, p. 407). The Mrs. S. of two years before is now apparently unavailable. Four months later, at the beginning of the new year, we find from the account book that he bought caps for 5s, and the next week he describes them to the ladies: "I have got four new caps, madam, very fine and convenient, with striped cambrick, instead of muslin; so Patrick need not mend them, but take the old ones" (JS, p. 458). When the servant did not mend the caps, perhaps the woman who made them did. The two times Swift pays for caps to be mended, he classifies the payment as "caps & mend," which suggests that he ordered new caps and brought old ones at the same time to be mended.

The waistcoat was expensive. The only one listed by itself in the account book comes to £1 10s, but another combined with breeches is £2 3s and still another along with "wristband," which in itself could not have been much, cost Swift the large sum of £4 12s 4d. A waistcoat "with 1^{s} 7^{d} to JB" may indicate either that Jo Beaumont provided the waistcoat or possibly mended an old one. A fustian waistcoat is once mended and at another time lined. A separate entry for fustian comes to only 1s 10d, probably too little for waistcoat material.

Only twice in the books does Swift mention the purchase of a riding coat, which must have been a more common and necessary garment than that would imply, and on only one of these occasions does he give the cost, £1 3s. This coat, even when worn by a clergyman, was not necessarily drab. He describes one he wore when riding with the maids of honor--of "light camblet, faced with red velvet, and silver buttons" (JS, p. 376). We lack the account book to give us the cost of this splendid garment.

Hats and wigs were important parts of Swift's wardrobe. He records buying a hat five times. One of them comes to only 9s. That is the least he pays, but hats could be had for less: in 1705 John Scott pays only 5s and in 1706 6s (Stevenson, pp. 349, 351). But clerical hats may have cost more. Once Swift pays £1, and three times he pays £1 13s. Since he describes one of these latter as a beaver, it is likely that the others were too. He died possessed of at least three beavers, which he willed to three friends, all clergymen. The care he took of his hats is indicated by the frequency with which he had them dressed. Four times the entry occurs, and the cost is usually 1s or under, though once it reaches 2s 6d.

One of the most expensive items was wigs. In the account book Swift mentions purchasing five, and the least he paid was £2 7s 6d, from which they ranged up to £3. He tells of paying even more than this in a passage from the Journal in January 1711, a date not covered by a surviving account book:

> It has cost me three guineas to-day for a periwig. I am undone! It was made by a Leicester lad, who married Mr. Worrall's daughter, where my mother lodged; so I thought it would be cheap, and especially since he lives in the city. Well, London lick-penny: I find it true (JS, p. 165).

Once he bought two at a time, paying £5 5s 6d for the pair. Wigs had to be kept in good repair, and several entries give the cost of mending them, sometimes as much as 3s. Keeping the wigs presentable from day to day would have been the servant's care: the item powder occurs constantly, usually in connection with coals and candles and other articles for which the servant presented a bill. In 1728, when Swift decided to extend his stay with the Achesons at Market-Hill, he had to ask Mrs. Brent to send him a periwig, but he was not pleased with it when it came:

> Your Periwig maker is a cursed Rogue, the Whig he gave you is an old one with a new Call, and so long that I cannot wear it, and the curles all fallen. I just tryed it on my head, but cannot wear it (Corres., III, 302).

Two accessories for wigs are itemized under Clothes. Three times Swift pays 1s or less for boxes, two of them specified as wig boxes, and the 1732-3 book records a wig block for 8d.

Smaller items include a collar, for 2d, and two large purchases of cravats, which he evidently bought in quantity: one payment of 10s covers four, we are told, and it is likely that the other, of 12s, includes at least as many and probably one more. Thomas Tyldesley gets his cravats for less--1s 4d (p. 126)--but Blundell in 1702 pays what Swift does (p. 42). Swift once pays 6d to have a cravat mended.

Bootirons, buttons, towels (he lists both making and mending them), and razors appear once or twice among the commoner articles. Several times Swift itemizes materials, to be made up into articles of wear, such as cambric, probably for handkerchiefs; flannel; linen; lutestring; muslin; serge; silk, twice specified as for his India nightgown; thread; velvet; worsted; and once simply cloth. Either a tailor or a necessary woman would do the sewing; there are payments to both. Except for one payment of 17s 6d, explained as an old debt to a "Rogue," and another of 14s, the outlay to the tailor seems too slight--1s 6d is the most--for work done, and may represent a gratuity to the man who brought the garments. Once the money is definitely said to be for the tailor's man, at another time for "man"; elsewhere the notation "small" is used, suggesting a service too trivial to be otherwise described. Other persons paid for sewing and thus listed under Clothes or Servant's Clothes are Mrs. Manley, Mrs. Parvisol, Mrs. Worrall, and a Mrs. Tool, possibly a connection of one of the deanery tenants whose tithes are given in the 1732-3 and 1734-5 books. That still others besides these did sewing and mending for Swift is evident from the Journal and other letters: in 1714, for instance, he speaks of a woman in Westminster Hall who made handkerchiefs for him when he was in London. (Corres., II, 72).

It was Swift's custom, when leaving London for Ireland, to buy an unusual amount of clothing, which he may have felt was of superior quality to any he could get in Dublin. In 1704, for instance, in addition to stockings for MD, he takes with him a periwig, a hat, two scarves, gloves, handkerchiefs, as well as muslin and camlet. In 1709 he lays out over thirteen pounds for clothing and accessories during the month before he departs. When he is planning to leave London in 1712, he tells the ladies:

> I have been packing up some Books in a great Box I have bought; & must by another for Cloaths & Luggage: This is a beginning towards a Removall. I have sent to Holld for a dozen Shirts, & design to buy another new Gown & hat, I'll come over like a Zinkerman, and lay out nothing in Cloaths in Ireld this good while (JS, p. 500).

And the day he leaves for Ireland in 1713, when he expects to return and hence buys few things to take with him, he does go to the unusual expense of paying ten shillings for a cap.

In the earlier account books, before he became dean, Swift sometimes uses the heading Servant in his quarterly summary to cover both the wages and the clothes the man required, though the wages normally are recorded every week. However, beginning with the 1717-8 volume or more likely in an earlier missing one, he changes his method slightly, restricting the heading to Servant's Clothes. By the arrangement with his servant, Swift was to provide the clothing or livery, a circumstance mentioned by Lyon as an example of his indulgence to his servants, since they were thus enabled to save something out of their wages (Lyon, p. 151). If we are to judge Swift's practice by Directions to Servants, the groom and the other liveried servants were to keep their clothes in good condition for a year. "If it [the master's riding coat] get more Hurt than yours, he can afford it better, for your Livery must always serve its Year's Apprenticeship" (PW, XIII, 49). The only reference to livery in the account books is to the payment for cloth used in making and trimming liveries and frocks, which probably--it is not completely clear--comes to £2 16s 2d. This seems small. In 1711, expressing to the ladies his annoyance with Patrick, Swift says, "I am making a livery for him will cost me four pounds; but I will order the taylor to-morrow to stop till further orders" (JS, p. 279). A month later, when threatening to dismiss him, he says,

> I have been ten times sending him over to you; yet now he has new cloaths, and a laced hat, which the hatter brought by his orders, and he offered to pay for the lace out of his wages (JS, p. 302).

In a third reference to the new livery, Swift gives the total cost as £5. We cannot always be certain what the figures include. Clothes for a new servant when Swift returned to England in the autumn of 1713 came to only £2 15s 6d; but other articles bought about the same time and probably not covered by that figure are breeches, boots, shoes, a hat, gloves, and stockings, which would bring the total to well over £4. At the same time Blundell spent about the same amount--£4 5s 8d--on his servant, but this may be merely a part of the expense, since he specifies only outside lining, two hats, silver lace, and blue livery stockings (p. 103). Swift's servant Saunders was apparently outfitted for £4 4s 8d, and this is "in all, hat, shoes, &c." In 1734-5 the large sum of £8 9s for "Clothes, &c." is given, but it is unlikely that this refers to clothing for only one servant.

The individual items for the servant, naturally, tend to be less expensive than Swift's. Shoes, cheap enough for the master, are even less for the servant: 4s 6d is the highest recorded price--except for 7s 6d, when the entry also includes stockings--and they are at one time as low as 2s 6d. Stockings vary from 10d to 3s 3d, in contrast to the 5s a pair Swift seems to have paid for his own. An entry of 6s and another of 7s must refer to more than one pair. It is difficult to tell much about the price of boots. In 1709-10 there is an entry of 2s 6d and in 1708-9 3s 2d, both of which seem impossibly low, not much above the cost of mending a pair. In 1712-3 Swift did pay 11s, but that also included shoes; 12s is the price by 1734-5, but whether that covers more than one pair we are not told. In 1732-3 occurs the unusual sum of £1 1s for boots, with the parenthetical addition "not allow^{d} but charg^{d} to them tho payd." The use of the word them certainly implies more than one pair.

As we gather from Patrick's willingness to pay for it himself, the lace on the hat was a mark of considerable distinction. According to Directions to Servants, "A Master ought always to love his Groom, to put him into a handsome Livery, and to allow him a Silver-laced Hat" (PW, XIII, 50). Hats, with or without lace, are a frequent item under Servants, but they do not seem to have cost Swift a great deal. The three hats for which he pays less than 3s each may not be new: the one bought of Ned is among these. An earlier hat of Patrick's than the laced one comes to 4s 6d. In 1712-3 Swift pays 9s 6d, and in 1717-8 13s, but the latter entry specifically says hats.

Other pieces of clothing and accessories for the servant are equally reasonably priced. Breeches, at the most expensive, are only 9s 4d, less than the cheapest of Swift's. Once they are as little as 4s, and twice they come to 7s. One of these is probably payment to Hugh for turning them over to Saunders; the other, some months later, is described as for "Saunders leather breeches." An Irish shilling is once paid for mending the servant's breeches. Only in the last two account books is there any mention of a greatcoat for a servant. In 1732-3 the cost is £2 8s 6d; since the item is clearly coats, it may refer only to the material itself. A similar expense, also for cloth for more than one coat, is £2 1s 1d in 1734-5. The single mention of a servant's shirt, "for Patt," at 2s 7d½, occurs in the first book. Six weeks earlier the same Patt had been given a waistcoat, along with breeches and hat, all for £1 2s, the hat alone being worth 6s. Like the shirt, this is the only time a servant's waistcoat appears in the account books. Among the larger purchases in the 1717-8 book, which reflects Swift's increased state as dean in its heavier expenses for servants, is a frock bought for Will, costing 17s 9d. Frocks appear again in 1732-3, when a sempstress is paid for making them. Finally, the entry Servants includes a few accessories. In 1703-4 1s 6d is paid for buttons. For gloves, which appear only once among the servant's wear, in 1712-3, when presumably Swift is outfitting a new man, he pays 1s. For 2s the same servant is also given a whip, an item often entered under Horses but only once under Servants. On the one occasion it is entered a stick cost 4d.

Swift does not put washing under Clothes but usually enters it separately in the monthly or quarterly expenses. Before he became dean, it is not entirely clear how the washing in Ireland was handled. In 1702-3 a payment is made to Mrs. Brent and a few times to Jo Beaumont, but customarily it is settled through Parvisol. Though Swift sometimes pays by the week, the bill is more often part of a larger sum covering five or six weeks. Naturally, the amount varies, but it averages out to about 1s 6d a week. Once he pays Parvisol £1 3s 6d to cover a number of items, including wash; yet at the bottom of the page he has added "JB more for wash ugly Slutt to Aug. 1" (16). At another time he pays Jo 13s for a quarter's washing. Thus he must have used both men for this purpose, whoever was more convenient. Except for the payment to Mrs. Brent in 1702-3 and another for three weeks in August 1713, washing in Dublin is not mentioned before 1732; it may have been written down in the housekeeper's book. Hence, it might be possible, as it is with board wages, to find out by studying the washing bills something concerning Swift's whereabouts.

During his six-month visit to England in 1703-4, he made no entry for wash in his highly condensed records; it was "Recknd with my Expences" (37), no doubt, along with his lodgings. In London in 1708-9 and from 1710-3, Swift records regular weekly payments, almost always made on a Saturday, the amounts varying slightly except during the three weeks in April 1712 when he was laid up with shingles and there is a consequent reduction in the bills. From 1709-10 on, the weekly payments are recorded on the pages of the quarterly summaries. Judging from the uniformity of the writing and from the color of the ink, as well as from Swift's error in once entering a whole quarter's washing bills on the wrong page, it is apparent that he transferred the entries at the end of the quarter from a separate record.

After he became dean, the item of washing is dropped from the quarterly summaries. It is undoubtedly being taken care of by the housekeeper. An entry in 1732-3 does read "For char[w] & wash" (214) and the payment of 11s 4d covers, at the usual rate of 8d a week, the seventeen-week period from the beginning of the book to the date of this entry. The same system is observed in 1734-5, at a somewhat higher rate, with either char or wash listed weekly. Swift evidently had to pay separately for such necessities as soap, starch, and blue. The large expense for one purchase of soap in 1734-5, £1 14s 2d, indicates a considerable quantity, and even a shilling's worth of starch would probably be at least three pounds.

Swift is careful to include his washing expenses when he is visiting, both in England and Ireland. In 1708-9 he makes payments at Thurmaston, Leicester, Chester, and perhaps at Stoughton Grange, where he is staying with Sir George Beaumont; and in 1713, returning to London, he pays for washing at Sir Gilbert Dolben's. Similarly in Ireland, in addition to Laracor, when he visits Clogher in 1709 and Gaulstown in 1718, he records his wash bills.

13. Food

Swift was not greatly concerned about food. We do not ordinarily find in his letters, to Stella and others, more than a passing reference to his eating, no loving enumeration of dishes nor any indication of fussiness concerning his diet. He was more interested in his dining companions; when St. John showed him the bill of fare as an inducement to dine with him, Swift said, "Shew me a bill of company, for I value not your dinner" (JS, p. 323), and was pleased enough with the riposte to repeat it to the ladies a few weeks later (JS, p. 350). It is unusual to hear him describe a haunch of venison as "mighty fat and good" (JS, p. 324); his ordinary comments on food and drink seldom range beyond the simplest terms of praise or disapprobation. In general, he seems to have been abstemious both in food and drink, and this in an indulgent age. In his last years, Lyon reports, "a couple of plain-dressed dishes of meat, generally roasted, with a plain bread-pudding, were his choice" (Lyon, p. 151), and Swift himself says in the Journal that, if he is not able to dine with friends, he often either sends to the alehouse for a slice of mutton and a pot of ale (JS, pp. 380, 403) or contents himself with a roll and butter (JS, p. 384). "You must know," he tells the ladies on 19 October 1711, "I hardly ever eat of above one thing, and that the plainest ordinary meat at table; I love it best, and believe it wholesomest."

Yet he had certain favorite foods. In spite of his belief that the giddiness from which he suffered had been caused by a surfeit of fruit in youth (Corres., III, 232), the letters and more particularly the account books show considerable fondness for fruit of various kinds. Orrery, asking for his receipt for preserving oranges, says, "Certainly the best Oranges . . . are the produce of your Table" (Corres., V, 157). Oranges he often bought, usually in small amounts, to judge by the sums paid, but in 1735 he must have been preserving them on an extensive scale, for he pays £1 8s 6d (250), enough one would think to buy several dozen. His famous receipt would have been used in the "Orangs preserv^d^" in the 1732-3 book (213). Apples appear only in the first of the account books; as they are said to be the offending fruit which caused the giddiness, the omission of them from the later books becomes understandable. Cider is mentioned only once, in 1703-4, though Swift does not avoid it completely, for in 1727 he blames it as well as champagne and fruit for bringing on a giddy attack (Corres., III, 221). Other fruits to be found in the books, though never in any great quantity, are cherries, olives, raisins (perhaps for puddings), and lemons.

Puddings, not only the plain bread ones mentioned by Lyon, were another favorite: Swift boasted that he was "not onely the best, but the sole perfect maker of them in this Kingdom" (Corres., IV, 556), and Lord Castle-Durrow, perhaps exaggerating, said that he had been acquainted with Swift's puddings since

1697 (Corres., V, 1). In 1734-5 among the "Deanry Charges" is listed fivepence for a pudding bag.

Coffee occurs with great frequency in the earlier books, along with three references to coffeepots and two to coffee roasters. No entry for coffee occurs after 1718: Swift had by then either given it up or was taking it at home. As early as 1712 he tells the ladies that he never dares to drink coffee or tea after dinner, as they keep him awake (JS, p. 581). In 1734, describing his "sickly man's" breakfast to Miss Hoadly, he says, "I am wholly a stranger to tea and coffee, the companion of bread and butter" (Corres., IV, 235). Yet Lyon declares, speaking of coffee, that

> He thought it good for raising the spirits; and valued himself much upon the making of it, for he never suffered it to be made in his own house out of his presence (Lyon, p. 151).

In his earlier years Swift puts down only the small amounts he pays for coffee at the coffeehouse; after he became dean, he seldom visited coffeehouses. Only twice in the 1717-8 book, both times in September, do we find what seem to be payments at coffeehouses. The other coffee entries, too large for this purpose, must indicate buying in quantity: on 22 October he buys seven pounds for £1 2s.

Only two entries in all the books might be called single servings of tea. The first, on 7 June 1710, is described as "Tea Mr Addis^{n}" for ninepence. In the second, in December 1712, a tenpenny charge is listed as part of "Will's bill." All other references are clearly to tea bought in bulk, usually in the execution of a commission. Leaving England in 1704, he takes with him, almost certainly for Stella and Mrs. Dingley, a pound of bohea (at sixteen shillings, though this seems an impossibly expensive price), a pound of green, and half a pound of imperial. On 27 April 1709, likewise before returning to Ireland, he again carries with him a pound of bohea and what must be at least two pounds of green (it comes to £1 5s as against 10s for bohea). In addition to these gifts, he brings five shillings' worth, perhaps half a pound, to his mother. Finally, on 9 June 1735 Swift makes the confusing entry of "China" or "China tea" three times in the same day, all of them for 10s.

Swift connected tea, as he did coffee, with his giddiness. He had presumably given it up before the 1734 letter to Miss Hoadly. As early as 1711 he repeats to MD Sir George Beaumont's opinion:

> I was telling him of my head; he said he had been ill of the same disorder, and by all means forbid me bohea tea; which he said always gave it him; and that Dr. Radcliffe said it was very bad. Now I have observed the same thing, and have left it off this month, having found myself ill after it several times (JS, p. 263).

Nor was Swift a heavy chocolate drinker. Among the few entries in the account books, two are such large payments made before returning to Ireland that they unquestionably cover the fulfillment of commissions for the ladies: twenty-three pounds in May 1704 (41) and £16 worth in June 1713 (154).

Swift seems to have eaten all kinds of flesh, fish, and fowl. Fish, without further identification, is mentioned only twice, both times in 1709, and one of those is listed as "Ale & G. fish," implying a treat. Oysters appear twice in the 1702-3 book (11, 21), and in 1717-8 form part of the menu at a deanery dinner given to MD, among others (172). With a shilling paid for a lobster in 1712-3 (159), the few references to seafood in the nine books are complete. The term meat in the books generally means food as distinct from wine. It appears once in each of the 1703-4, 1708-9, and 1717-8 books, but it is only in 1734-5 that it becomes a regular item in the lists of daily expenses, occurring in every month but June.

The butcher's meats most often mentioned are mutton and beef. We have seen that Swift sends out for a bit of mutton, and he mentions eating it at a chophouse (JS, p. 46). Lamb appears directly as a food only once in the account books: on 8 April 1718 he pays elevenpence for "Lamb, Bred. &c." Beef he ate less often than mutton: he tells the ladies after an attack of giddiness that he finds it, as well as some other foods, too strong (JS, p. 248). But it is listed seven or eight times in the 1717-8 book, always in connection with a deanery dinner and all but once in company with ale, and it occurs once in 1734-5. Pork is mentioned rarely, so rarely that one assumes it was not a staple food. There are only three references in the books, all in 1734-5 and all under "Small Gifts." One, given simply as "Pig," comes to a mere 6d½; it may not even be meat but one of Swift's impatient pejoratives describing the object of a small beneficence--most of the rest of the entries in this category are charities. About two weeks later he notes a shilling for "Hog's cheeks," which, as a gift, is not necessarily a part of his diet. The third reference is to bacon, listed the next month. Veal is never entered. Venison appears a number of times, always as a gift either to him or from him.

The most common fowl, then as now, was chicken, and Swift often dined on it. It was cheap: he promises Gay that he can get one for sevenpence in Dublin (Corres., III, 251), but his accounts suggest that he himself sometimes got it for less. Fowl appears only once, in 1734-5, and in spite of the larger price of 1s 3d is no doubt a chicken.

Swift had a fondness for gingerbread, to judge by the frequency with which he bought it. In Laracor Jo Beaumont supplied him: it is a part of JB's bill in 1702-3 (11) and of JB's "old sham debt" in 1717-8 (185). Several times it appears in connection with a dinner at the deanery. It is found frequently in the last three books, in 1717-8 as a part of the daily expenses, in 1732-3 and 1734-5 as an extraordinary. For the usual quantity of gingerbread, whatever it may have been, Swift pays 2s 2d.

Swift was at no time in his life, by the standards of his day, a heavy drinker of wine. There are few references, either by himself or by others, to his having had too much to drink--"I dined with Mr. Prior to-day at his house . . . and came home pretty late, and I think I'm in a fuzz, and don't know what I say" (JS, p. 271) is the nearest he comes to it--and if he was not as abstemious as Pope, he was apparently equally far from sharing in the common vice of the age. He strongly objected to the deep drinking at Oxford's or Bolingbroke's dinners. In his later years he often speaks of how much he drinks a day, but though this is probably less than he drank during the busy years in London, it may be a fair picture of his habits throughout his life in Ireland. The account books provide a little information about his drinking habits; there is nothing in them to suggest excess.

Many separate entries of wine are found throughout the early books. These are generally small, a shilling or so, and refer to drinks, probably with companions, in public places. But even added to the item of tavern, they do not occur often enough to suggest immoderation. During the years in London, he learns to avoid taverns, and in 1712 boasts to the ladies that he never goes to a coffeehouse or a tavern (JS, p. 580), and this, allowing for some exaggeration, is borne out by the accounts. After he begins to live in the deanery, he serves his own wine, bought by the hogshead and then fined and bottled on the premises. In the 1717-8 book he has made a separate page for "Wine," &c., on which he lists corks, bottles, porters, fining white wine, even eggs for wine. This separate page has evidently been removed along with others from the 1732-3 book; it appears again in 1734-5, where there are two sections on wine and one on brewing, including the purchases of hops, yeast, and malt.

Swift says to Gay that he loves ale better than wine (Corres., III, 446), and to Pope "I love Mault liquor," adding that he "dare not touch a drop" (Corres., IV, 135). The accounts support his claim. Whereas in his earlier years a pot of ale accompanied his dinners, the word almost disappears from the last two books, and the brewing carried on in the deanery must have been largely for the members of the household and for guests.

One item, which appears in the Extraordinaries for each quarter of 1732-3, is usquebaugh, for which Swift seems to have developed a taste. It is listed nine times and each time but one costs 5s; the exception is explained as "country usquebaugh," and the price is 6s. Possibly his interest in it grew from his desire to encourage Irish manufactures, since he often sends it to England as a gift.

Swift's first wine merchant was Jo Beaumont. After Jo's death he employed a Mr. Hall, to whom he pays £10 (266)--"an honest Catholic merchant here, who deals in Spanish wine" (Corres., IV, 469)--and John Shiell, often mentioned in both the account books and the letters.

14. Horses

Considering Swift's constant complaints about horses and his ill luck in riding them, his favorable presentation of the Houyhmhmns is surprising. The trouble horses were to him is vividly described in the Holyhead Journal (PW, V, 202), and throughout his letters he laments that he cannot get a satisfactory mount, he bewails the cost of hay and oats, and he dwells angrily upon the perfidies of grooms and stable boys. His problems were the harder to bear because, as we have seen, he had a strong faith--and his doctors agreed with him--in the therapeutic value of riding.

The account books record payments for a number of horses. The first book carefully lists the purchase of a bay nag for £4 5s on 30 January 1703 and of a chestnut horse for £3 15s 8d a few weeks later (10). For the journeys to Laracor, on which his servant accompanied him, two horses were required. Before the bay nag was bought we find the entry "2 Horses hird frō Trim" (6) for 7s, and on two other occasions previous to his buying the chestnut he records payments for horse hire (9, 33). For some years he seems to have had no more than two horses: thirty years later he dwells often in letters upon the necessity of his having three now that he is old.

In England he does not keep a horse, hiring them for the trips to and from Holyhead or Parkgate or for shorter visits near London. In 1709, in Ireland, at the end of October, he lays out £6 5s for a horse, possibly the "great ugly Horse" referred to in the *Journal* three years later (*JS*, P. 560). Back in England, he frets about the expense of keeping his horses at Laracor: Parvisol "keeps me at Charges for Horses that I can never ride" (*JS*, p. 560), he complains, and the following month he continues, "I am very much discontented with Parvisol, about neglecting to sell my horses, &c" (*JS*, p. 567).

In September 1710, arriving in England, he hires horses at Parkgate for £2 18s for himself and Patrick to make the journey to London, during which, he tells the ladies, he fell from his horse but sustained no injury (*JS*, p. 2). In June 1713, on the return to Ireland, he rides his own horse from London to Chester and hires another, for £1 4s, for his servant. Swift's mount is Bolingbroke, probably given to him by the secretary: the account book records no payment for a horse and the £4 3s 6d for "A saddle &c." (154), paid just before Swift left London, indicates that the horse had been presented for the trip. Esther Vanhomrigh asks how he performs (*Corres.*, I, 364). Unfortunately, he performed badly. "I mett no Adventures in all my Travells," he writes to Esther's mother, "onely my Horse once fell under me"--no wonder that he dreams at Holyhead some years later of getting twenty falls from his horse (*PW*, V, 203)--"for which Reason I will not ride him to Holyhead, I can assure him that" (*Corres.*, I, 366). The horse, however, was carried over to Ireland --Swift paid 15s for his passage (154)--and he remained in Swift's possession for at least three years, though Swift himself avoided riding him. On the return trip to England in September Swift hires horses at Chester, paying £2 10s.

The letters after 1714 tell of Swift's discouraging search for a horse. He bought one in 1717-8 for £10 10s, possibly from George Rochfort, as there is the notation on 27 May "to G. Rochforts Man with th Horse 9^{s} 2^{d}½" (190). This is not the same one complained of in a letter to Robert Cope two years later, a horse that Swift has been training for the past eighteen months; that one cost £26 (*Corres.*, II, 348).

There are no recorded purchases of horses in the last two account books, possibly because Swift may at last have found a satisfactory one. In 1730 Christopher Cusack

> let me have a little mare, which I have rode ever since. I often desired him to let me know the value he put on her. He answered, it was a present to him, and should be so to me; I protested I would suffer no such thing; he likewise sent me another young mare, which he was breeding up for me (*Corres.*, III, 433).

We no longer hear any complaints in the letters, and in 1736 Swift refers almost with affection to "my bay mare" (*Corres.*, IV, 455).

The expense of keeping horses was considerable. In 1702-3, probably a typical early year in Swift's Irish residence, he totalled £13 10s 6d½, exclusive of the payment for the horses themselves. Of this over £6 went for hay, not including hay received in tithes drawn, oats, straw, and grass. Incidental expenses were for mending saddles and bridles, shoeing, gelding, and grazing at Laracor, the latter also in part tithes drawn in kind. Page, either a stableman or a smith, presented a bill twice during the year, amounting to £1 4s 8d. These expenses would have been handled through Parvisol (45, 54). In 1703-4 the total was even more, despite Swift's being out of Ireland much of the time. When in 1717-8 he is keeping his horses in Dublin at the deanery, his expenses are higher than they have ever been or will be, more than any year of which we have record--£31. Among the items which made up the sum were hay (£18), oats (£2), bran, straw, grazing, stabling, saddler (£4), smiths, and various medicines.

The Horses accounts in 1732-3 and 1734-5 are somewhat thin and not always easy to interpret. It seems improbable that for 1732-3 Swift spent only slightly over £12 on his horses. Of even this small sum, thirty loads of hay account for two thirds. There are a few more entries in 1734-5, but Swift's casualness is shown by his neglecting to add up the totals and by the illegibility of his hand. Again, it is not likely that the care of his horses cost him only £10 10s for the full year. The largest part of the sum is, as always, for hay: Swift paid £4 16s 1d for twenty loads, including bringing it in.

By the time he made his will, Swift owned more than the three horses he mentions as his requirement. He says, "I bequeath all my Horses and Mares to the Reverend Mr. John Jackson, Vicar of Santry, together with all my Horse Furniture" (PW, XIII, 155). We do not know whether Jackson did, in fact, receive the horses after Swift's death. Lyon tells us that after his mind deteriorated, "it was neither safe or prudent to take him out & then his Coach & Horses were sold by the Committee" (Lyon, p. 123).

15. Lodgings

Swift lived with the Earl of Berkeley and his family from August 1699 until April 1701 at Dublin Castle and at the Lodge in Chapelizod, "obliged to a constant attendance," he wrote King, then Bishop of Derry, in July 1700. Understandably the earliest known account book carried, according to Scott, no expense category for "Lodging," as do all extant account books dated between 1702 and 1713. During the summer of 1701 he was in England, crossing with Berkeley in April and returning with the new Lord Lieutenant, Rochester, in September. In Dublin during the autumn and winter of 1701-2 he presumably was put to the expense of lodgings, but Scott does not record the categories of expenses for that year. In the summer of 1702 he was again in England, returning to Ireland in October, just before the 1702-3 account book begins. That year was Swift's first spent entirely in Ireland since receiving his livings, and the account book gives evidence that he was establishing his way of life there.

He took a lodging on 24 October 1702, as is shown by his paying £3 15s rent for a quarter "end Jan^{ry}. 24. 1702/3" (3). He stayed in lodgings for two more weeks at 6s a week and for another week at 5s 1d (8); during the unpaid week in February he may have stayed in Dublin with his relations, for he gave gratuities to maids and, at the month's end, tipped his cousin Godwin's man and his uncle's two men. Around 20 February he moved into new lodgings, paying a higher rent than before: £5 on 22 May for "a q^{rts} Lodging then expired" (13), and in August for a quarter ending on the 22nd (18). Mrs. Felter was his landlady, Mrs. Brent his housekeeper. In February, when he moved in, Mrs. Brent was paid for purchases of household equipment, dishes, plates, and glass; and he provided himself with coffee and a roaster, his basic requirements for a home. He continued a little while at Mrs. Felter's--£1 0s 6d is paid her by Mrs. Brent after he went to England 11 November (36)--but a great deal of his time was spent at Laracor, with a few days at Finglas (4s for lodgings). In Dublin he gave his uncle's maid a gratuity in September, paid 14s for three weeks of lodging in October and 16s more as he left Ireland (18, 16), a total this fourth quarter of £2 14s 6d.

Every account book of the years before 1714 shows that when in Ireland Swift regularly maintained Dublin lodgings, as was customary for an Irish cleric of his time and status, but also that he lived a great deal of the time in the Trim-Laracor area. In the first part of 1702-3 he even paid for second lodgings, these in the Trim-Laracor region with a Mrs. Andrew Malaly (28, 29). But after he equipped his own residence at Laracor with household goods, he required no more Trim lodgings. When he was in the area on concerns of his parish, he reports himself as "at Laracor." The costs of housekeeping there were taken care of by Parvisol and were settled with him under the Accounts of Livings. In 1704 and 1713 he spent almost the entire summer at Laracor and engaged no Dublin lodgings.

In England it was usually necessary to engage a "dear [expensive] scurvy London Lodging" (Corres., IV, 378), such as are recorded in four account book years. In the condensed record of 1703-4 the cost of Swift's London lodgings is entered only as "Recknd with my Expences" (37). On his return to Ireland 1 June 1704 he paid 2s 8d½ for four days in Dublin lodgings (40), and then left for a summer at Laracor and Cavan. He certainly returned to Dublin from time to time, but he did not bother to take Dublin lodgings until September. When briefly in Dublin, he may again have stayed with relatives: he gave Uncle's maids a considerable tip, 8s 1d½, just as he moved into lodgings in September (45). When he "came to Mrs Bradly Sep^t^. 19. 1704" (36), it cost him only £10 per annum. Mrs. Bradley's rent had to be paid in advance, however, even though Swift did not pay it until 28 October: "a Qua^r^ befor hand, to end de^cbr^. 19" (40). He left Mrs. Bradley's and came to a Mr. Close's 1 May 1705" (36).

When the 1708-9 book begins, Swift had been almost a year in London. For a time he lived with Sir Andrew Fountaine in Leicester Fields. "The Decree for Concluding the Treaty between Dr Swift and Mrs Long," written about this time, refers to him as "Dr Swift of Leicester Fields" (PW, V, 197). No other addresses are mentioned in any of the many letters exchanged the next year until 9 November 1708, when he tells King to send future letters to St. James Coffeehouse. For a time Swift may also have lived at Lord Pembroke's: some time before October 1708 he received a letter addressed to him "at Lord Pembroke's in Leicester Fields" (Prelims., p. 37. Swift's list of "Subjects for a Volume" was drafted on the back of it). Pembroke was married 21 September, and Swift wrote King 9 November that he had been in Kent "during my Lord Pembroke's absence with his new lady," and had returned to town for a few days, gone to Epsom, and "yesterday" had returned to London.

"From Nov^br^. 8^d^" lodging is paid at the rate of 5s 6d a week until Swift leaves London 25 April 1709 (61, 66). His lodgings were in the Haymarket (Corres., I, 139), and his landlady's name was Mrs. "Sa^ll^," if we may conclude as much from Swift's paying her for receiving a letter to him (63), a service performed by other landladies like Mrs. Curry of Dublin. He made "Mrs. S." gifts in January and April; at the end of April he paid her for making him a nightgown (66); and, as he left London on 3 May, he made her a final gift of 5s, reimbursed her for a gift or a purchase for MD, and paid an unusually large amount for lodging, £1 7s 6d, which he entered under "Extraordinaries" (71). After he returned to Ireland he remembered 5s which he had paid for "lodging in London a week" (75), which he had forgotten to enter and which would be the real rent. The large extra amounts paid Mrs. S. may represent services rendered him in his many illnesses while at her lodgings when he had no servant.

When Swift returned to Ireland 30 June 1709, he went straight to Laracor, staying there four days before coming to Dublin 4 July; he paid 5s 8 July for a week's lodging and "Then came to Mrs Curry" (71). Her rate was £5 for a half year. Mr. and Mrs. Curry's house was "over agst the Ram in Capell-Street" (Corres., I, 165). When he was in England, the ladies took over his lodgings, but Swift remained responsible for the rent: "If Mrs Curry makes any difficulty about the Lodgings; I will quitt them" (JS, p. 4). Stella and Mrs. Dingley stayed there only five months, until February 1711, four weeks beyond Swift's half-year term, and then moved back to Mrs. De Caudres in St. Mary's Street, where they had formerly lodged. Possibly they were more comfortable there; their lodgings cost almost twice what Swift's had, if he is accurate when he says they would have saved themselves £8 by staying at Mrs. Curry's five months. Furthermore, their removing causes problems: Swift fears that a box just sent them in February to Mrs. Curry's will now go astray, and when the times comes, in April, for Mrs. Brent to pack up his books and papers, he wonders what should be done with his bookshelves. All problems were settled, including rent, by the ladies and Mrs. Brent, but the Currys were "exacting people about those four weeks" (JS, p. 275).

Swift's payments for his own lodgings in London are precisely entered in the account books; other details are furnished in the Journal. The day he arrived in London, 7 September 1710, he took lodgings "in Pall-mall," where he stayed for two weeks at 5s a week (111) before removing to Bury-street (JS, p. 24). Here he paid 8s a week--"plaguy deep," but he had "the first floor, a dining-room and bedchamber" (JS, p. 34). Evidently the ladies commented on the high rent, for he answered them, "Impudence, if you vex me, I'll give ten shillings a week for my lodging" (JS, p. 87), but when he next moved at the end of December to new lodgings in St. Alban's Street, he paid the same rent for "an apartment two pair of stairs; but I have the use of the parlour to receive persons of quality" (JS, p. 143). It was "but five doors off" from the Vanhomrighs (JS, p. 216).

The Journal continues to recount Swift's subsequent removals through the months for which we lack an account book: from St. Alban's Street on 25 April 1711 to Chelsea, "six shillings a week for one silly room with confounded coarse sheets" but "just over-against Dr. Atterbury's House"; back to town on 5 July and "got into Suffolk-street," again near the Vanhomrighs, although Swift does not now say so. During the late summer--"the town is dull, wet and empty"--he spends much of his time at Windsor, where he lies in "one of the prebendary's houses. . . . Here am I all alone in the prebendary's house, which Mr. secretary has taken" (JS, pp. 251, 308, 321, 322, 327).

When the account book record picks up, Swift notes that he came to St. Martin's, Leicester Fields, 11 October 1711, at 10s per week (118)--"that won't hold out long, faith" (JS, p. 380). But he remained there eight weeks, and when he removed to Little Panton Street 29 November--"another lodging hard by, in Leicester-Fields"--it was at the same rate, and he continued there, with a Mrs. Crane, through his long bout of shingles, until 5 June 1712; on leaving he tipped her maids (118, 124, 129, 131). He was at Kensington, "Partly to be near the Court, where dinners are to be found" (JS, 538), from 5 June to 19 July, still at 10s a week (118, 129). He went to Windsor 19 July and remained all through the following weeks until 29 September (118, 129, 132-5). "My

Lodgings there look upon Eaton and the Thames, I wish I were Owner of them, they belong to a Prebend" (JS, p. 553). No charges needed to be entered under "Lodging" during this time (129) except 5s for a week back in London "in a hedge Lodging"; on leaving he paid "Woman at Wi^dr" 10s under "Lodging" (129) and paid "at Wind^sr to old woman" a gratuity of another 10s (133).

Thereafter, when Swift returned to London lodgings, he came to Mrs. Hubbots in Rider Street (118), where he paid only 6s a week (133): "an ordinary room two pair of Stairs," which was "over against the House in little Rider street where Dd lodged" (JS, 565, 581).

"Take no Lodging for me," Swift warns the ladies twice before he returns to Dublin for his installation. "What at your old Tricks again? I can ly somewhere after I land, & I care not where nor how," and again "the poor Dean can't afford it" (JS, pp. 669, 671). In Ireland he paid for only a fortnight in Dublin, 11 to 25 June, at 6s a week, and then escaped to Laracor and his "field-bed and an Earthen floor" (Corres., I, 373). He stayed all summer; all his letters are dated from Trim, Laracor, or The Country, and although there were obviously trips into Dublin, there is no more lodging paid until he returns to London in September. Stearne, the newly created Bishop of Dromore, stayed on in the deanery house for many more months. Swift addresses a letter to him "at his House in St Kevin's Street" in December 1713 from London (Corres., I, 419).

Back in London again Swift paid 6s a week for lodgings from 9 September 1713 to 1 November; there are trips to Windsor, the first for ten days, but thereafter for only two days each week (158, 160-1). With no more letters to MD, we know nothing of the location or character of these lodgings. The rate of payment is that of little Rider Street.

On Swift's return from England he instituted repairs and improvements at the deanery house in the fall of 1714 and is himself in residence there in December 1714.

16. Dogs

One reason for placing the short list from the Huntington MS (318) in the 30's is the item of 6d for "Dogs." There are no references to dogs in the account books before the 1732-3 volume, but in that one and the next "Dogs" appears regularly as an "Extraordinary." Each quarterly summary has at least seven of these entries over the three-month period, and they sometimes rise to as many as twice that. The amounts in 1732-3 are generally 7d, occasionally 6d or 6d½; once it is 1s and once 1s 2d, suggesting double payments; in 1734-5 the expense is almost invariably 6d. Often two or three of these items are listed under the same day. Since it is unlikely that, if they were all paid at once, Swift would not have combined them, we may assume that he makes the entry when he remembers it without regard to the exact date.

Only twice does the wording vary from "Dog" or "Dogs." Under a date between 27 June and 24 July 1735 Swift has written "Dog. Doc^tr 6^d½" and "Dog sick 8^d" (255). The explanation of this expense is given in a letter of 17 July 1735 to Orrery:

> My favorite Dog, your Acquaintance is in the same condition [with many pains in his bones] by his own fault, by pursuing one of his fellow servants round the Vineyard field, who yerked him a kick in the back, which forced him to keep his bed for some days, but is now better. His Physician is a Cobler of ninety two, who is likewise a Dog-Doctor.

It is possible that these were not the only times that Swift took a dog to the aged veterinarian. Some time between 1 and 20 May there is a scarcely legible record of a 6d payment, entered between two "Dogs" items. The word looks most like "Cob^{lr}."

Swift may not have been able to keep dogs before he had a Dublin house of his own, but the complete omission of them from the 1717-8 book implies that at that time he had none. Three years later he writes to Pope that the works he is now writing "contain nothing of present times or persons, upon which I shall never lose a thought while there is a Cat or a Spaniel in the house" (Corres., II, 367), but the reference need not be to particular animals. He soon provided himself with at least two dogs: in "Lady Acheson Weary of the Dean," which Williams places in the autumn of 1728 or 1729 and which was printed in 1730, we are told that he had taken a pair of dogs with him on his visit to Market Hill:

> His Brace of Puppies how they stuff,
> And they must have three Meals a Day,
> Yet never think they get enough. (Poems, p. 861)

In December 1735 Mrs. Whiteway, reporting on the state of things at the deanery while Swift is away on a visit, writes that she found the dogs "in high spirits" (Corres., IV, 444).

17. Marginalia

Most of the marginal jottings and comments which are found throughout the existing books have already been touched upon. The most common are the names of places where Swift is visiting or residing. Memoranda concerning his health are frequent, especially in the 1708-9 volume. There are also notes of the arrival and departure of servants; several addresses; records of the dates of voyages to and from England; and a few financial memory aids. Several commissions are given in the English volumes, purchases to be taken home as gifts to the ladies. Under marginalia we may likewise include the accounts of the deaths of his mother (319) and of Ann Long (117); two proverbs (25); an absurd Hatter's Rule (61); and a few items of considerable biographical interest. In some of these latter the writing is scarcely legible and consequently the interpretation is hazardous.

Of the addresses in the books, most refer to lodgings occupied by Swift during his English years. Some, like Mrs. Massy's or Mrs. Price's (61), may be lodgings recommended but not used. One of the two on p. 96, "Vandrheyden & Drummod Amsterdam Donvill," seems likely to be the address of Swift's correspondent and dining companion, Sir William Domville, who is said the next year to have "come home from his travels" (JS, p. 421). "Drummod" is probably John Drummond, one of Harley's agents in Holland.

We have already mentioned the tea and chocolate Swift sends back to Dublin. Another commission is "A large Bible for ppt" (139). There is no date, but a passage in the Journal under 17 July 1712 explains:

> Ppt shall have a great Bible. I have put it down in my memlandums, just now. and Dd shall be repaid her tother Book; but patience, all in good time; you are so hasty a dog would &c.

They needed patience: Stella had to wait a year for her Bible, which is mentioned again in the next volume along with half a dozen blue and white coffee cups with handles (164). These too are referred to in the Journal:

> I will buy your Eggs & Bacon, yr whadeecallit, your Cups & Bible, and pray think immediatly, & give me some Commissions, & I will perform them as fas as a poopdfr can (JS, p. 669).

Among the marginalia with biographical implications is the "In suspense" of the 1708-9 book (61), a condition Swift later described as "the worst circumstance of human nature"(PW, V, 205). It occurs at the top of the page for the first quarterly summaries, but there is now no way of knowing whether it is intended to refer to the whole year, the whole quarter, or merely the moment at which he wrote it. It probably is in reference to his professional prospects, his hopes of advancement under the Whigs.

A few times, as we have mentioned, Swift writes "Ubi?" at the top of the page. In 1708-9 this clearly indicates an attempt at a later time to remember where he was. The same query reappears in the 1712-3 book for April, May, and June. In this case the interrogatives were almost certainly written before, probably in March, as is shown by not only the form of the question for May and June--"ubi nunc?"--but also the similarity of the handwriting, the color of the ink, and the fact that Swift was in London for all of April and May and half of June. He is well aware that his future is being decided at this time. "Talk not to me of Deanry's I know less of that than ever by much," he writes on 1 March. The situation grows more tense in the next month, and on 13 April he tells the ladies, "oo may see me in Dublin before April ends." Quite probably, in this uncertainty, he wrote the three headings.

Three pages contain items referring to Swift's promotion to St. Patrick's. On the page following the wins and losses it a single memorandum, written up at the top of an otherwise blank page: Me^{md}-- / Mund. Ap^{r}. 12. 1713 at 10 in the morning. M^{r} L[ewis] came to me & showed me / the Order from L^{d} D-- [Dartmouth] for a Warrant for the 3 Deanryes" (143). The date is a mistake for the 13th, since under that day he wrote to the ladies of the end of his hopes for an English deanery. The three vacant ones were Wells, Ely, and Lichfield.

> This Morning My Friend Mr Lewis came to me, and shewed me an Order for a Warrant for the 3 vacant Deanryes, but none of them to me; this was what I always foresaw., and receive the notice of it better I believe than he expected. I bid Mr Lewis tell Ld Tr that I took nothing ill of him, but his not giving me timely notice, as he promised to do, if he found the Qu would do nothing for me. at Noon Ld Tr hearing, I was in Mr Lewis's Office, came to me, & sd many things too long to repeat. I told him I had nothing to do but go to Ireld immediatly, for I could not with any Reputation stay longer here, unless I had somethink honorabl immediatly given to me; we dined togethr at D. Ormds, he there told me, he had stopt the Warrants for the Deans, that what was done for me, might be at the same time, &

> he hoped to compass it to night; but I believe him not. I told the D. Ormd my Intentions; He is content Stearn should be a Bp, & I have St Patricks; but I believe nothing will come of it; for stay I will not.

The fact that Swift made so precise a record in his account book indicates the depth of his disappointment and hurt. The warrants were not signed by the Queen until the 23rd, in a group which included one making Dean Stearne Bishop of Dromore and thus releasing St. Patrick's for Swift. The history of the process is given in the briefest possible form on the April page, at the top following the "ubi nunc?," to which, incidentally, it bears no relation: "--23^{d}. / Warrant sign^{d}, sent / 25th." These dates agree with those in the Journal. On the 23rd he writes there, "This Night the Qu--- has signed all the Warrants," and on the 25th, "the Clerk at Mr Lewis's message sent the Warrants for Stearn & me."

On the page for May occur two notations, in addition to the "ubi nunc?" The first, dated 6, is difficult to read. It may consist of six words, or it may be two items of three each. The first three, which are on one line, follow the "ubi nunc?" and seem to refer to it: "ibid sed dubius." On the next line, below the 6, are three words, not one of which is safely decipherable. Professor Ehrenpreis ingeniously reads the six words as "ibid sed dubi ne. ob Red Sing" (II, 632). It may be said that in the last three words the letters o, R, d, i, n, and g are fairly clear. Ehrenpreis explains the note in this way: "I conjecture that the red-headed Duchess of Somerset was the red thing, and that Swift suddenly heard of some new move she had made to block his promotion, a move which was of course ineffectual." This reading lies open to several objections. What does the ibid refer to? It appears to be a clear answer to the "ubi nunc?" If the three questions were written at the same time, in March, it would be natural on 6 May to put a reply to the query. As to the identification of Red Sing with the Duchess of Somerset, it is unprecedented for Swift to use the little language, if that is what it is, in his account books, i. e., to himself. He certainly disliked the Duchess and doubtless attributed the loss of English preferment in part to her influence, but he never refers to her in the Journal as Red Sing, and the epithet is uncharacteristic. But perhaps most troubling is the assumption that Swift had heard of some "new move she had made to block his promotion." We do not have a letter to the ladies for 6 May, but there is no hint of any such move in the letter written ten days later. Furthermore, Swift's warrant was ready, as we know, on 25 April, and it is hard to imagine any move the Duchess could make after that date.

The first three words then may mean "In the same place, but I am doubtful [how long I will be here?]. This, by the way, justifies the stop after dubius. The three words on the line below resist satisfactory explanation. Whether they refer to the Duchess or perhaps to the struggle with Stearne over the Dublin livings (R^{cd} L^{ing}?) or other matters relating to the new appointment is still unsettled.

Following this notation is another, dated 16 May. Ehrenpreis reads this as "heard Patent past" (II, 632, n 2). But Swift had written three weeks before to Dr. Coghill to have the patent passed (JS, p. 666), and he must have been assured of it in the letters from Stearne or Coghill which he received on 8 May (162). The note may instead be read as "heard / I dont prst," the last word being an abbreviation of present. The remark would refer to the news he had received the day before in a letter from Stella that the new Bishop Stearne and the chapter of St. Patrick's had already presented the two livings of St. Luke's and St. Nicholas Without, which Swift had hoped to do himself. His anger is shown in his reply to Stella:

> Your new Bp acts very ungratefully, I cannot say so bad of it as he deservd. I beggd at the same Post his warrant and mine went over, that he would leave those Livings to my disposal (JS, p. 668).

For the benefit of the reader who may wish to examine these notations himself, the page for May has been here reproduced in facsimile.

Some of the side comments in the final book are also problematical. The Greek word on p. 246 and the French phrase on p. 247 have been already referred to. In addition, there is on p. 244 on the third of the pages assigned to "Small Gifts" what appears to be "Octr. 11: den: otè." Since this page lists the small gifts for October, it may belong there, though its position, some distance from the other entries, suggests no connection. There are no clues elsewhere in the account book nor in the letters of the time, and the entry remains unintelligible. Another marginal item is at the top right of the page for January: "--20. Lett^{r} from / Sh-- about Bs / knife." "Bs" is not certain; the rest is legible. "Sh--" may be Sheridan, though no letter from Sheridan to Swift written between 25 December and 25 February is extant. Furthermore, Swift records dining with Sheridan on 17 and 27 January, so that Sheridan was in Dublin during the period of the letter. Swift pays 6d for a letter on the 17th or 18th, the only such payment made in the last half of the month. This may not mean that he received no letters, of course: he was probably not scrupulous in entering all small payments, or the Sh-- letter may not have come through the post but have been handed in at the deanery.

ACCOUNTS OF LIVINGS AND DEANERY

Swift's income from livings and deanery is recorded in six of the nine extant account books. Three of them--1702-3, 1703-4, 1708-9--carry parish and prebendal returns. Three others--1709-10, 1711-2, 1712-3--contain little or no information about ecclesiastical income, though the first of them must surely at one time have had the usual record, and on two pages in the last deanery accounts have been started. The remaining three books--1717-8, 1732-3, 1734-5 --cover years when Swift was established as dean; in these we naturally find chiefly deanery income, although some parish returns, especially from Rathbeggan, are given.

In reading these books one is often reminded that the information in them does not provide a complete view of Swift's financial affairs. They are not even official records of ecclesiastical income, such as his agents and receivers were expected to keep. Swift refers to his tithing agent's "Great Account" (28), just as, in writing to Archdeacon Walls 13 December 1716, he refers to the agent's "Parchment bound folio of Accounts" and the "great Book" then in Walls's own possession. He also mentions other records of his own: "Refer what follows to my Table book" (90); and "All which I have entred in my severall Books as received" (284).

As for Swift's larger business dealings, his private loans and mortgages, the account books carry very little. Some hints appear over the years: "Left with Coz Swift at Chestr abt Engl acct" in 1704 (38); "Coz Dean's Bond commences" in 1707 (72). And on the last page of the last book appears a record of "Interest" paid Swift by four private borrowers. "It grows obvious," as Ehrenpreis remarks, "that he had resources, business dealings, and responsibilities which are not comprehended in the statements of the little notebooks" (II, 98).

Nevertheless, the account book financial records are significant for the light they shed on Swift's management of his ecclesiastical income. Although sometimes cryptic and often incomplete, most of the entries are comprehensible, once his systems of management and bookkeeping are accepted. If his financial situation is fully understood, one concludes that too much has been said of his penuriousness, preoccupation with money, and grasping after preferment; one is impressed instead with his competence, equanimity, and generosity.

18. Tithes

> The Farmers, spightfully combin'd,
> Force him to take his Tythes in kind.

The account books reflect the disturbed state of tithing in Ireland in the early eighteenth century. By Swift's time there had been many lay impropriations, the tithes of one parish had been assigned to another, and some tithes were in dispute, those of Rathbeggan, for instance. Swift wrote Chetwode, 27 September 1714, that

> Jourdain [Vicar of Dunshaughlin Parish, adjoining Rathbeggan Parish] has been often telling my agent of some idle pretence he has to a bit of one of my parishes worth usually about five pounds per annum, and now the Queen is dead perhaps he may talk warmer of it. But we in possession always answer in those cases, that we must not injure our successors. Those idle claims are usual in Ireland, where there has been so much confusion in parishes, but they never come to anything.

And certain deanery tithes were in dispute as late as 1735 (283).

Two categories of tithes are clearly specified in the account books: tithes paid in money and tithes drawn (i.e., tithes paid in kind). The latter might be received by Swift for his own use (hay and oats for his horse); otherwise his agent had to convert them into cash at local markets. This was a nuisance to the receiver, and required special knowledge and special honesty on the part of the agent who drew and marketed the tithes. Not surprisingly, account book records of "Tyths Drawn" are often confused: at one time a "Qu" is entered after "honey" (54); at another Swift writes "Mr Parvis^l^ alledges the Tyths drawn for part to be allowd. Some time when settl^d^. thy are 17^ll^" (30). Between 1702-4 and 1708 the percentage of parish tithes received in kind was reduced markedly, from about £36 to £3 10s. Inconvenient as tithes drawn in kind were, they were less troublesome if they were drawn from lands close to Laracor glebe, as the account books show they were: Readstown and Stokestown, Laracor, or Nealstown. No tithes were drawn from the more distant parish of Rathbeggan. In correspondence with Walls Swift observes that it would be convenient to rent a farm near his deanery lands "to dray my Tythes to on Occasion" (<u>Corres</u>., II, 243).

The chief source of Swift's tithes, on parish and deanery lands, was grain: winter corn, seeded the preceding November and grown during winter and spring, and spring corn, seeded in the spring and grown during spring and summer. The crops had their tithes set on them by Swift's agent in the early summer. On 28 June 1725 Swift writes to Sheridan, "It is one good Circumstance that you got such a living in a convenient Time, and just when Tythes are fit to be Let." Tithe payments on grain began to come in in November, after the corn had been housed, although arrears might be collected two or even three years later. In 1733 winter corn was worth 5s an acre, spring corn 3s.

What tithes of wool and lamb Swift received would be due in June, as he points out in letters to Walls about reckoning sheep and lambs on deanery land (15 June 1715) and to Sheridan (28 June 1725). Once in the account books "Tyth of Wool & Lamb" is specified (87).

A more important source of tithes came from summer pasture and from hay harvested in the summer months. Many of these tithes are recorded as drawn in kind. Hay from deanery lands, mentioned in the correspondence, may appear once in an account book, that of 1717-8 (200); meadow land was valued in 1733 at 2s 6d an acre (239).

Of the other tithes Swift mentions in the account books, "thatching" recurs regularly and seems clearly to be straw for the roof of his Laracor building; stone, wall, wood, and turf may also have been used for improvements to buildings and grounds--most came from tithes drawn. Even tithes of personal labor may have been received: "cleaning sallyes," "all for thrash," "work done." Other tithes are less easily explained, such as the quarts of honey and the barrels of beer from tithes drawn accounts in 1704; the former may have been of use in the stables; the latter may have been produced from grain and barley (and even hops, "that useful Plant") grown on Laracor tithelands.

Because grain and pasture tithes and glebeland rent were paid on crops grown the previous summer, Swift's accounts of tithes, whether from livings or deanery, always bear a date a year earlier than the November-to-November year in which they were collected; collections of the tithes and of glebe rent ran concurrently with the expenses listed in the front parts of the books. In all his bookkeeping Swift notes this carefully: 1703-4: "Accounts of My Livings for 1703."

Discouraging as was Swift's experience with his ecclesiastical income, he knew that the tithes of his livings in counties Meath and Dublin were in better shape than those of livings in other parts of Ireland. As Archbishop King pointed out when appealing for the remission of the first fruits and twentieth parts, a lamentable state of things existed outside the diocese of Dublin "save in the six counties of the north, where a more equitable tithing table had been established" (Corres., I, 60, n 2).

19. Temporalities

Louis Landa has described Swift's livings in co Meath most succinctly in his *Swift and the Church of Ireland*. Of help in understanding account book entries--indeed a necessity in deciphering certain of them--is some consultation with the records and maps used by Landa.[22] Since Down Survey maps of the mid-seventeenth century show parish and townland divisions, and since the purpose of the Civil Survey terriers was to describe the type and quality of the various lands for requisition and distribution among Commonwealth soldiers, these sources are peculiarly useful in reading Swift's Accounts of Livings.

Laracor, Swift's chief parish, provided his largest income. The Civil Survey reported the parish as about 66% arable land, 25% pasture, the rest meadow with some wood and very little bog; it is all classified as "profitable." In its townlands are two mills and two stone quarries, and in Laracor itself a stone bridge over the river Effernock. The tithes in 1654 were valued at £210 (Civil Survey, V, 173-6; 384).

The account books show that this valuable land returned tithes from a variety of crops: from the arable land chiefly corn and oats; from the meadows and pastures hay and grazing, wool and lambs; from the stone quarries "stone drawn" for "Wall" and "building."

Laracor townlands are mentioned first in 1702-3 when Readstown and Stokestown are entered apart from the rest of Laracor parish under a separate account, "Tyths Drawn" (26). In 1708-9, in a list which Parvisol must have provided Swift, thirteen Laracor townlands are named with the tithepayers and the amounts for which their 1708 tithes had been set: Somerstown (twice), the Glebe, Little Freffans, Umberstown, Dangan, Great Freffans, Collierstown, Clondogan, Summerhill, Knockbeg, Laracor, Stokestown, and Readstown, plus Brownstown "not returned," Nealstown, and Steacum "Tyths drawn" (87). It is such a roll as Swift requested from Walls in December 1716 of deanery tithepayers listed "both as to their names and habitations" (Corres., II, 233). Swift names the locations somewhat differently in letters to Walls of 13 and 27 December 1716, and the variants used by him and his agents make it impossible to assign and compare precise land valuations over the years.

With two exceptions, all the Laracor townlands mentioned in the account books and in Swift's letters to Walls may be found, in a variety of spellings, in the Civil Survey and on the Down Survey Barony and Parish Maps. The exceptions were important parts of Swift's parish: Dangan, residence of Garrett Wesley, and Summerhill, residence of Sir Arthur Langford. These two, being Commonwealth territory in 1654, would not have been included for forfeiture. Steacum has not been located.

Two townlands included in the account book list--Brownstown and Nealstown --show, in different ways, the confused state of clerical tithes in Ireland during Swift's life. Brownstown is listed in the Civil Survey as belonging to Laracor, lying just north of Collierstown and west of Effernock, but it does not appear on the Down Survey map of the parish, and the fact that the account book list shows it in 1708-9 as "not returned" indicates that its status was still uncertain. The inclusion of Nealstown in the 1708-9 list of Laracor tithepayers illustrates how the tithes of one parish might be assigned to another. Nealstown was in Trim parish, and in 1717 Swift secured some of it for

---

[22] Pp. 25-44. Landa draws his facts chiefly from documents in Marsh's Library and in the Representative Church Body, Dublin, Library; from the Civil Survey, A. D. 1654-1656; and from the seventeenth century Down Survey Maps.

Laracor glebeland. The 1654 Civil Survey shows that Nealstown had long paid tithes to Laracor parish: the "viccaridge of the sayd Parish beinge Endowed with the greate Tythes of Collierstown Nealstown and Tolloghcopp." Collierstown and Nealstown adjoined Laracor itself.

A year after acquiring Nealstown land, Swift purchased for Laracor on 14 June 1718 "the impropriate tyths of the parish and rectory of Effernock" in the parish of Trim (SPH documents, Reference Numbers 1F, 3F). Like Nealstown and Brownstown, Effernock lay just north of Laracor parish.

The parish of Agher returns are always reported in the account books with those of Laracor. The only time Swift distinguishes Agher lands occurs in the 1708-9 list of tithepayers, headed "Laracor & Agher Sett": Agher (two parts) and Ballintogher. In the 13 December 1716 letter to Walls, Swift lists "Both Guennets." The Civil Survey and the Down Survey map of Deece barony show four townlands in Agherpallis parish: Agherpallis, Ballitogher, Little Genedstowne, and Great Genedstowne (now Ginnets). All were contiguous to Laracor parish. The lands are about 63% arable and 18% pasture, but with a good deal of bog (14%), little meadow, very little wood. The townland of Agherpallis had five acres of glebeland, Ballintogher a mill. The Civil Survey lists the value of Agher parish in 1654 as £10 (Civil Survey, V, 156-7; 401). By the time Swift writes Walls in 1716, listing both Ginnets, the other Agher townlands (Agher itself and Ballintogher) had probably been absorbed into neighboring Laracor townlands.

Rathbeggan is always reported separately from Laracor/Agher in the account books. In the 1708-9 book ten townlands are named in the list of Rathbeggan tithepayers: Rathbeggan (three holdings); Parsonstown ("part"); Rainstown; Mill land; Pouderlagh (two); "Small Tyth. of Impropriation"; Glebe Rent (88). The Civil Survey and the Down Survey maps of Rathbeggan parish show ten townlands, including Pouderlagh, Rathbeggan, and five acres of glebe. The land is described as almost 75% arable, with an additional 25% of meadow and pasture, very little wood and less bog. There is no mention of a mill. The impropriated tithes and the vicarial tithes of Rathbeggan are each described as consisting of a moiety of both great and small tithes.

In the account books, the tithes of Rathbeggan exhibit the same confusions as those of Laracor. Swift in 1708 received a "small" part (£2 15s) of tithes which supposedly had all been impropriated to Lord Drogheda (Landa, p. 43). He also received tithes from some lands which lay outside Rathbeggan parish: the Civil Survey assigned to Rathbeggan the small tithes of "Rahinstown & pts of Parsonstowne" in Rathregan parish and located "a Mill" there. It is not surprising that his right to a "bit of one of my parishes" was pressed by Jourdain, the vicar of Dunshaughlin parish which neighbored both Rathregan and Rathbeggan. Because of these confusions it is hard to say exactly how the tithes of Rathbeggan were valued in 1654, possibly at £10 (Civil Survey, V, 83-5; 380; 386).

Rathbeggan had one drawback: only there was Swift responsible for paying the setting fee to the agent (Corres., II, 48). But he had none of the nuisance of tithes drawn, which would have been a special inconvenience at that distance from Laracor.

Although Swift's predecessor at Laracor, Dr. John Bolton, had held all three parishes, Swift found it necessary to petition the Primate for a dispensation to hold Rathbeggan together with Laracor and Agher. The petition was granted 9 March 1700 "for a composition of £20" (Craik, p. 78, n, from a MS in the Records at Armagh).

* * * *

In 1702-3 Swift names one other benefice: the rectory of Grenoge. The last page of the book lists ecclesiastical charges for it: Crown rent, fees to the receiver, and proxies, £6 2s 4d. This was not a benefice to which Swift was entitled. It belonged to Ratoath parish and would have been retained by Bolton when he kept Ratoath parish after his elevation to the deanery of Derry. Healy notes that in 1682 five parishes were joined to Ratoath, among them Grenock, and he shows John Bolton to have been the incumbent of them all from 1693 to 1720 (pp. 302-4). It is confusing to find these charges included three years after Swift had received his livings.

* * * *

Although, as Landa points out, the prebend of Dunlavin was of importance to Swift in introducing him to the chapter life of St. Patrick's Cathedral, he does not seem to have given it much consideration. On his preferment to the deanery, he wrote Archbishop King asking that Thomas Parnell "may have my small Prebend" (Corres., I, 344). This seems to be the only reference to Dunlavin in his extant correspondence. But the account books show that he did discharge his prebendal obligations to Dunlavin: in both 1702-3 and 1708-9 he records a payment of £1 to a vicar at Dunlavin. Lying on a main road south from Dublin in co Wicklow, Dunlavin may well have been visited by Swift, although he seems never to have determined just how much income it should bring him.

* * * *

The temporalities of the Deanery of St. Patrick's consisted of tithes, rents (land rents and house rents), and fees for services performed by the dean. The history of the deanery of St. Patrick's tithes and rents as given by Mason runs from the time of the establishment of the deanery in 1219 through the inquisition of Henry VIII, 1547, and on through 1660. The Down Survey maps describe the lands and show their boundaries in the mid-seventeenth century. But the most helpful document in connection with Swift's accounts of deanery income is the manuscript "Of Dr Swift's Effects," which "sets forth item by item the sources--rents, tithes, and fees--from which Swift's annual deanery income was derived, with the amount each returned" (Landa, "Deanery," p. 160). Landa believes that the document was compiled by Lyon in 1742.

Deanery tithelands lay in the southern part of co Dublin. The original lands annexed to the Deanery of St. Patrick's centered around the church of Tavelach or Taulagh, the church of Clondalkin, and the chapels of Rathcool and Esker (Mason, p. 26). Lyon in 1742 listed the "Rectorial Tythes of Tallaght, Esker, Clondolkan, Tassagard & Rathcool" (Landa, "Deanery," p. 164). Deanery land crops mentioned in the account books are corn, both winter and spring, and hay, never, according to Swift's letters, in sufficient supply.

When first appointed dean, Swift requested Archbishop King (in vain) to dispose of the livings of Saggart and Rathcoole to Thomas Warburton that he might have "a Vicar in one of my Rectories, and upon my Deanery, in whom I can confide"; and he suggests that a representative of his meet with his former agent Gillespy "at Tallow" to discuss rental of farmland nearby (Corres., I, 377; II, 240). At "Tallow-Hill" Swift, Orrery, and Sheridan measured stream flow in May 1733, according to Faulkner's Dublin Journal (15-19 May 1733, 798). In the 1717-8 account book Swift identifies two tithepayers as "of Tallow" and "of Job's Town" (a part of Tallaght) (199). He obviously knew the area well, and he discharged his obligations there: Tallow is mentioned both in 1734-5 and in 1735-6 in connection with the repair of the chancel (267, 317).

Swift received two-thirds of all the tithes of Saggart, the great tithes only of Rathcoole and Tallaght (Landa, "Deanery," p. 165). Lands in Tallaght parish and in parts of the parishes of Saggart and Rathcoole had been assigned to the estate of the Archbishops of Dublin since the thirteenth century, just as long as other tithelands had been assigned to the Dean of St. Patrick's (Ball, History, III, 2-47, 112). It was probably inevitable that some disagreement should arise over tithe allocations between the dean and the archbishop. In 1732-3 Swift lists "Ld A. B. Dubl." among three tenants who had not paid their tithes (239) and in 1734-5 "Arch Bishops Tyths" were placed among those "Disputed" (283). Yet Swift remained on reasonably friendly terms with Archbishop Hoadly (Corres., IV, 234).

Deanery Rents are on the title pages of the 1717-8 and 1732-3 account books, and in 1717-8 a page has been set aside for them, but 1734-5 is the only year when they actually appear: a payment of a year's rent by Mr. Stopford and a payment by Alderman Pearson of a half year's rent (288).

The land leased to Stopford was at Kilberry and Cloney near Athy in co Kildare. He was still leasing it in 1742 (Landa, "Deanery," p. 163). The lands and churches of Clonwanwyr (Cloney) and Kilberry had been the first endowments of the Deanery of St. Patrick's (Mason, p. 26). Swift visited his Kildare lands in November 1714, soon after returning to Ireland, examined the leases at St. Patrick's Cathedral, and then wrote to Chetwode, listing all the "manors, lordships and townships" and all the lands involved and estimating the worth of the "1700 and odd acres" and "all those hard names" as at least £475, "And it pays me only £120 . . . There was a great deal of young wood which has been horribly abused" (Corres., II, 155).

The lands leased to Alderman Pearson in 1734 were still leased to him in 1742: "Lands of Dean Rath, Priest Town, Ballibane & Angerstown containing 357 Acres near Clondalkan" in co Dublin (Landa, "Deanery," p. 164). Lands near "the grange of the Dean's-rath" had been part of the original endowment of the Deanery, and King Henry's Inquisition of 1547 listed the four lands of Deanrath, Ballybane, Angerstown, and Preiston (Mason, pp. 26, 28). Dean Stearne had re-leased the holdings to Benson, Archdeacon of Kildare, in 1709, an action Swift denounced by writing on the back of the lease, now among Cathedral records, "By Dean Lindsay (now Lord Primate) for 54l. per annum, never raised since! shamefull! it is worth at least on a full rent 250l. per annum (Mason, p. 26, n d)

When Swift became dean, the rent was therefore of necessity £54, and his dealings seem to have been with Benson's widow, the "importunate woman" of the letter to Chetwode, 3 December 1714; his renewal of the lease in 1720 was to Alice Benson, widow of the archdeacon. Our concern here is not so much with the historical background of Swift's deanery land leases, but with the improvements in them which he was able to effect during his deanship.

Deanery Groundrents, like land rents, are reported only in the 1734-5 account book (288); rents are paid by three lessees of deanery houses: Morgan, £5 for two years; Goodman, £5 for a half year; and Connly, £9 for a year. The houses stood on the Dean's Ground to the east and west of the Deanery House, in St. Kevin's Street or Mitre Alley. There is a plan of the deanery grounds in Mason, p. 11.

The two more important holdings leased to Goodman and Connly are specified in Swift's will: "Goodman's Holding" of "two Houses, or more lately built" and "two Houses let to John Cownly" (PW, XIII, 153-4). The rents are the same as in 1734, £10 and £9 respectively. The rents are still the same in "Of Dr Swift's Effects" of 1742: from "Mr J^n^ Connly for his Holding East of ye Deanry" and "Mr Goodman for his Holding West of ye Deanry" (Landa, "Deanery, p. 165).

The more modest holding of Morgan can be identified only as one of "certain Houses in St. Kevin's-street" named in Swift's will (PW, XIII, 153), or the "small Tenement somewhat ruinous now in Deanery Lane or Mitre Ally worth £3 p[er] Ann." listed in 1742 (Landa, "Deanery, p. 166).

Duties or income realized from services performed by the dean in his ecclesiastical role, such as funerals and the granting of leases and licenses, appear in separate account book listings: "Customs, Dutyes &c for the Deanry" in 1717-8 (203); "Perquisits" in 1734-5 (288). One other duty received as dean is indicated by the memorandum of 17 June 1735: "Rx from Mr R. Grattan as Proctor 23^ll^" (286). The explanation of this receipt of £2 on a £23 transaction is in the statement from "Of Dr Swift's Effects": "ye Proctor . . . also pays ye Dean's Duties reserved in all chapter Leases worth £10 p[er] Ann" (Landa, "Deanery," p. 166). The "Perquisits" in 1734-5 are very incomplete: only two fees (for leases) are entered and added. The customary fee for a lease both years was 11s 8d or 5s 10d for half a fee. The 1 October entry, "A Vicar 10^s^-10^d^" could be a fee received from a vicar for a license; the entry a day later of "Vicars fee 10^s^-10" as a Great Gift (265) suggests that Swift shared the fee, as in 1718: "For a Licence (half given Wa^ls^) (203).

In a letter to Walls Swift estimated that "duties" will be worth "eight pounds or something under"(Corres., I, 392). In 1717-8 they added up to £23 8s 9d; in 1734-5 (very incomplete) to 17s 6d; in 1742 they were valued at £10 (Landa, "Deanery," p. 166).

20. Bookkeeping

And Parvisol discounts Arrears
With Bills for Taxes and Repairs

Swift's private records of his ecclesiastical income, Accounts of Livings and later Accounts of Deanery Receipts, include some unitemized lump sums, many "&c's," and several untotalled columns of figures. Nevertheless, his system of bookkeeping presents an interesting body of information in a comprehensible and consistent form.

When investigating this system, it should be remembered that Swift kept at hand a complete file of all his account books. This is shown by late entries in all the extant Accounts of Livings. He meticulously entered receipts of arrears in the account book for the year in which they were due, not in that of the year when they were finally received. Some are entered two or three years later than the terminal date covered by the book, one--that for 17 November 1709 in the 1702-3 book--as much as six years. Examples of referrals to earlier books are "old account of Tyths drawn 1702" in 1703-4 (53) and "vide old book [i.e., 1716-7]" in 1717-8 (201). A referral forward is "transfer^{d} to new Book [i.e., 1718-9]. Aug. 5th. 1719. JS." in 1717-8 (195).

Once Swift retrieved an old account book and did various calculations on the back of it. The titlepage of the Accounts of Livings section in 1702-3 (25) carries sums in his hand of figures arrived at when he was preparing that page of his 1703-4 book which gives the arrears due from Laracor, Rathbeggan, and Dunlavin for the years 1700-3. The three sums in the lower left of the titlepage determine arrears of Laracor for 1703 and of Rathbeggan for 1703 and 1701. The results are all entered on page 56. When thus occupied, Swift must have had before him the earlier account books for 1700-1, 1701-2, and 1702-3. Incidentally, this tends to weaken Mayhew's argument that the presence of two proverbs on the 1702-3 titlepage proves that Swift was jotting down overheard clichés in his pocketbook as early as 1703 (Mayhew, "Two Entries," p. 49).

The Accounts of Livings titlepages in 1702-3, 1703-4, and 1708-9 are followed by double-page spreads, with "Re^{cd}" and "p^{d}" pages facing each other. There are separate spreads for Laracor and Agher, Rathbeggan and Dunlavin; and in the first two books a separate account for "Tyths drawn." The most extensive of the four accounts is Laracor/Agher:[23] in 1702-3 its receipts and disbursements have to be brought over to a second two-page spread (28-9; 30-1). Rathbeggan and Dunlavin accounts, however, require only a half-page double-spread each (32-3). "Tyths drawn" takes only one page in 1702-3 (26) and the beginnings of a two-page spread in 1703-4 (54-5). In 1708-9 there is only a subheading (87).

The "Re^{cd}" entries, under each of the four accounts, are of two kinds: receipts in money or goods, and allowances of receipts collected and already expended by the agent on Swift's behalf. These allowances, covering, as we have said, many sorts of payments made by the agent out of tithe collections, were acknowledged by Swift when the two settled their accounts. They are often, though not always, doubly entered, appearing a second time on the opposite page under "p^{d}." Since the "p^{d}" column is never completed nor entirely totalled, no attempt to balance "Re^{cd}" and "p^{d}" is made. A different wording in the "p^{d}" column is sometimes useful in explaining an entry listed under "Re^{cd}."

The fact that four separate accounts are kept by Swift (and therefore by his agent) does not mean that each account is strictly self-contained. Laracor/Agher routinely carries ecclesiastical charges for all three parishes. The Rathbeggan account, which never carries major charges, is pleasantly uncluttered, carrying after 1702-3 only cash receipts. "Tyths drawn" in 1702-3 and 1703-4 is, in contrast, a study in disorder. This account required much adjustment between Swift and his agent over which tithes had been received and

---

[23]The fact that the heading (29) "For Charges belonging to Laracor & Agher" originally read "to my Livings &c" shows that Swift was in the process of setting up this system of bookkeeping.

marketed by the agent and which used by Swift. Naturally, perhaps, it became a sort of dumping ground for other vexatious financial details, such as Rathbeggan setting fees, which are deducted over a six-year period (1702-1709) from arrears of tithes drawn in 1702-3 and 1703-4.

As for the Dunlavin account, Swift seems never to have quite organized it. In 1702-3 the amount set is not known, nor is the total collected--"Qu? what remains this year" (32). A year later what remains has still not been discovered and entered. Certain charges peculiar to the prebend, such as travelling expenses and payment to the vicar, are deducted. The "Tax for the Church" in 1703-4 is not an ecclesiastical charge; it is Swift's sarcastic comment on the amount still in arrears, as may be seen by comparing the figures on the opposite page.

Though the costs of improvements to the house and grounds at Laracor are regularly charged to the Laracor/Agher accounts, housekeeping bills and expenses for horses may be deducted from any one of the four, depending apparently upon which account Swift happens to be settling with his agent at the time. Including them in the Accounts of Livings is perfectly reasonable since they are incurred while Swift is staying in his parish discharging parish duties. Also, some pasturage and hay for his horses is a tithe drawn in kind. Obviously, it must have been a convenience for him to reckon the costs of his domestic arrangements at Laracor with a business agent who lived in the vicinity and allowed his bills to accumulate over several months. The fact that housekeeping and horse bills appear added <u>into</u> the expenditures in the Account of Expenses as well as deducted <u>from</u> the Accounts of Livings needs to be kept in mind when balancing Swift's income against his expenditures for any one year. This curious sort of dual entering may be found in every account book carrying an Account of Livings section. The clearest example is "Horses sent 6^{s}, Tongues 5^{s}, mend saddles 3^{s}-9^{d} Houskeeping 10^{s}-$8^{d}\frac{1}{2}$ For the use of his Horse 0 - 7 - 0" 1 September 1704 (45), which is reproduced almost word for word on page 54.

As soon as the deanery years begin, a different system of record keeping appears. In the summer of 1713 Swift drew up a page headed "Charges on entring the Dean^{ry}" and then began another page, "Charges of the Dean^{ry}." The latter page appears, as ecclesiastical payments always do from now on, not among accounts of receipts but among accounts of expenses--i.e., right side up. Thus deanery expenses appear among the costs of household supplies and repairs to the deanery. In 1717-8, for example, we find a page of "Taxes and Cesses" and one of "Dean^{ry} Charges and Repairs," among which the salaries Swift paid his agents may be found. In 1734-5 the charges are scattered: a category of "Taxes and Cesses" comes just before "Soap and Candles," repairs to the chancel of Tallow church under "Defalcations from Deanery," and the visitation dinner under "Houshold goods."

Records of the receipt of deanery tithes and rents appear, at least as headings, in all three of the later account books. Swift would enter a rent roll, provided by his agent, of all his tithepayers and the amounts for which their tithes were set. In the year 1717-8, when he was acting as his own financial manager, he optimistically headed two pages "A Rent Roll for the Year 1717 for Tythes, and the Year 1718 for Lands &c," faced by "Received Rents of Lands and Houses for 1718." His new agents that year evidently failed to furnish the rolls, and the pages remain blank. Lacking such lists to work from, Swift enters his tithepayers chronologically as they pay him. The deanery record spreads over four pages, crowding into the pages originally headed "Receiv^{d} For Laracor" and "Receiv^{d} From Rathbeggan."

But the last two account books carry neat alphabetical rent rolls, although neither gives the total amount set. Names are checked off on certain specifically recorded settlement dates. There is very little confusion. At the end of the earlier roll three names have to be added "Out of the Alphabet" as well as six names under "Tyths drawn without notice" (tithes to be paid in kind, with no bonds taken). In the later book three names appear under "Disputed," and twenty in a list of "Names that gave no Bonds."

Records of livings are scanted in the account books of deanery years. Gone, naturally, is any mention of Dunlavin. Especially thin are the records of Laracor. Pages have been headed for receipts from livings in 1713 and from Laracor in 1718, but no entries appear on the earlier page and only a lump sum on the later, and there are no balancing pages, as formerly, of "P^{d}." Instead, as in the deanery records, "Proxyes & other Charges for Laracor" are in the Accounts of Expenses section; the large sum "Layd out at Neals Town" is on a page of general expenses for the year; agents' salaries, presumably for livings as well as deanery, are under deanery charges. One assumes that the usual parish charges were taken care of as before, at settlement times with the agent, as the words "Account^{d} for wth Mr Bourne" in 1718 imply (201).

Rathbeggan accounts are fuller and in the form taken by deanery reports. In 1718 Rathbeggan tithepayers are listed, like the deanery ones, chronologically by date of payment, and the record is, unsurprisingly, as confused as that of the deanery. In 1732-3 and 1734-5 lists of Rathbeggan tithepayers, along with those of the deanery, were provided. None appears in 1732-3, but Swift probably had a list since twice Rathbeggan names have been alphabetically entered by mistake among deanery tithepayers (228, 233). In 1734-5, together with deanery collections, Rathbeggan money is turned in on 7 February 1735--all "enterd in my severall Books as received"--a tithepayer's name is checked off the list 14 March 1735, and names "that gave no Bonds" are added.

* * * *

On specific dates recorded in the books Swift cleared accounts with his agent, allowing dispersals the latter had made out of tithe collections. These are called settlement dates. Settlements took place wherever the agent brought his "Great Account"; at Trim or Laracor for Laracor/Agher accounts; at Rathbeggan or the Pace, midway between Rathbeggan and Dublin, for Rathbeggan accounts; in Dublin always for Dunlavin and, later, deanery accounts. They never occur when Swift is out of Ireland, and are usually not arranged until some time after his return.

It is well to remember, in using account book dates to prove Swift's whereabouts, that on settlement days he was definitely present at the time and place indicated--sometimes he even affixed his initials. He was probably present whenever and wherever cash is recorded as received: "in Dublin," "at Laracor," &c. He was probably not present when actual payments were made, such as to his curate, for work on his grounds, &c. These payments were made by his agent, a great many of them, indeed, during Swift's absences in England.

In 1702-3, when the account book opens, Swift has just returned to Ireland. During his absence Parvisol has paid his curate, Smith, two installments of back salary. But although Swift receives some money from Parvisol in

Dublin in early December, he does not go to Trim until the end of the month, and the first settlement date with Parvisol is not until 7/8 January 1703. Parvisol is allowed the amount of salary payments to Smith. Six more settlement dates follow. On all of them housekeeping and horse bills are settled along with ecclesiastical charges, land improvements, and agent's fees.

Swift leaves Ireland 11 November 1703 and returns 30 May 1704, but there is no major settlement until 1 September. On that day Laracor/Agher, Rathbeggan, and Dunlavin accounts are all cleared for "what was p[d] in absence, to Uncle, M[rs] B[rt], Crown rent, curate. ½ yr. Proxyes, &c," as well as for a house bill and the summer's costs of improvements to house and grounds (50). At the end of September another house bill is paid, but the next main settlement waits until 7 November. At that time Rathbeggan and Laracor/Agher year-end balances are figured out and arrears entered.

In 1709 Swift returns to Ireland on 30 June, but not until 12 October is there a settlement when all dispersals made "in absence" are allowed: ecclesiastical charges; bills to MD, Mrs. Brent, and Walls; horse costs and "a House bill to Sept. 27th" (90). A later entry, 16 November 1709, records the payment of costs of grounds and house improvements "from Dec[br]. 13 1707," the larger part of a house bill, and a past installment of the curate's salary. The 16 November date was an especially important one, as arrears due since 1703 were also being settled.(26). Later entries in the 1708-9 book show that settlement of Rathbeggan arrears occurred 3 January 1710 "At the Pace . . . wth Parvis[l]" (93); the last recorded Laracor arrears on 20 March 1710 (94). The 1709-10 book carries no Accounts of Livings, but the Account of Expenses indicates the identical settlement dates: 16 November 1709, 3 January, and 20 March 1710 (99, 101, 105).

The most important settlement dates came to be mid-November and early spring. Also common are late December for Laracor and January for Rathbeggan, but mid-November and March/April dates appear in all extant account books, except 1711-2, from 1705 through 1735. These times came to be identified with Laracor even when Swift was far away: "I'm weary of courts, and want my journies to Laracor" 15 November 1711; "I wish I were just now in my Garden at Laracor" 21 March 1712 (JS, pp. 413, 520).

During his Irish summer of 1713, between stays in England, Swift settled Laracor expenses 8 August, "House Bill at Laracor," his last settlement date with Parvisol on record. In 1717-8 there is an important settlement date, 19 November 1718, when his agent accounted to him for collections from the deanery, Laracor, and Rathbeggan. Earlier stops at the Pace in December and March in the same account book indicate other settlement dates for Rathbeggan tithes (169, 174).

Seven settlement dates appear in 1732-3: 3 May, 9 November, and 20 December 1733; arrears came in on 9 February and 19 May 1734 and on 14 March and 28 June 1735.

In 1734-5 collections of tithes from the deanery and Rathbeggan were turned in 7 February 1735, smaller sums on 24/5 February and 14 March. Thereafter no more names are checked off the rent roll, but payments of arrears are noted on a separate page on 1 May, 17 June, and 19 December 1735. The linked reporting of these two accounts suggests that one agent was responsible for both.

21. Ecclesiastical Charges

"Fifty [pounds] must go in a Curate and Visitation Charges and Poxes, Proxies I mean."

Swift's ecclesiastical charges find a place in almost every account book, including one no longer extant. From the 1699-1700 book Lyon extracted the information that "within ye first year from Mar. 1699 [1700] to 1. Nov. 1700 ye Expense of his Titles, Crown Rent, Curate &c amounted to £117" (Lyon, p. 29). Routine charges on livings, as recorded in the three earliest surviving account books, come to between £50 and £60: crown rent is always £15 3s 4d a year, the curate's salary £30 or £40 annually, twentieth parts about 14s, hearth tax 8s, and the frequent purchase of proxies £2 7s 9d. When Swift sent Sheridan his estimate of charges Sheridan would have to pay on his new living in co Cork, twentieth parts no longer had to be paid (thanks to Swift); possibly the living of Rincorran did not require the payment of crown rent (Corres., III, 66).

Few charges against livings are found in the three later account books, and routine charges against the deanery were comparatively slight. No crown rent was involved nor salaries to curates, and taxes amounted to only a pound or two. Initial costs were, of course, heavier. So were variable costs: Swift was expected to pay for entertainment at his chapter visitations, and his position as a dignitary of the church involved purchasing licenses for absence when he left Ireland.

Initial charges occurred, of course, only in 1700 and 1713. The £117 in 1700 must have included installation charges as well as the £20 composition Swift had to pay 9 March 1700 in order to hold Rathbeggan. Such initial costs were unavoidable upon advancements in one's profession. Two years later according to the 1701-2 account book, when Swift took his doctor's degree, it cost him "in Fees & Treat £44 and upwards" (Lyon, p. 36). At the time of his installation as dean, the patent was the most important expense, just under £20, but there were incidental charges--"Quire, Drums, Sexton &c" and treating the chapter; the total came to just over £29 (165). No account book records exist to show when Stearne was paid the £600 owed him on his leaving the deanery, about which Swift expressed his concern to Stella, 23 April 1713, and to Walls (11 June 1714), but Lyon noted in 1742 that it had been paid (Landa, "Deanery," p. 167).

As to First Fruits on his livings, we do not know what part of the £117 went for them in 1700, but in 1697, according to John Stearne's revision of the (1693) State of the Diocese of Meath, they came to £8 6s 6d (ML, MS Z. 3. 1. 4. [5]). There is no record of deanery First Fruits in the 1712-3 account book. Swift told Stella, in the 23 April letter, that they would amount to £150; they have still not been taken care of a year later when he writes Walls that he will be glad to begin paying them (Corres., II, 9).

Crown rent for Laracor parish was said by Stearne in 1697 to be £20, but as Landa points out, the account books show that £15 3s 4d was actually paid (Landa, p. 36). It was due at Michaelmas and Easter, but payments were sometimes delayed for a year or more. The 1702-3 book carries no crown rent payment on Laracor, but there is a baffling "Crownrent for the Year 1688, due by Dean Bolton" of £7 11s 8d (30) and an annual crown rent for the Rectory of Grenoge of £5 8s (27). The record of crown rent paid on a benefice to which Swift was not entitled is troublesome, especially three years after he had entered upon his livings. There would not have been "Fees to the Receiver" unless the payment had actually been made. Crown rent due in 1702-3 was evidently paid the following year: the 1703-4 account book includes among its payments "a Year Crownrent" of £15 3s 4d (i.e., to Easter 1703 and to Michaelmas 1703) and "½ y^{r} Arrear" of £7 11s 8d (i.e., to Michaelmas 1702); and after Swift's return to Ireland there is the payment of "½ years Crownrent due at Ester 1704" (50, 51).

Crown rent payments are spelled out clearly in 1708-9: "Crown r^{t} to Mich^{lmas}" and "Crownrent due Easter 1709," each £7 11s 8d (91). The same charge is last recorded for the livings in 1717-8, on 7 March and at Michaelmas 1718 (194); those due on the livings thereafter must have been allowed on the unrecorded settlement dates.

Swift's crown rents did not weigh as heavily on him as they did on the incumbents of other Irish parishes, where they sometimes consisted of "the third Part of the reall Value of the Living; and often, a full half" (_Corres._, I, 182). But every payment must have been galling, since he believed that, without the untimely interference of the Irish bishops in 1710, he could have gained remission of them as well as of the twentieth parts.

Twentieth parts, Swift wrote in 1710, "are twelvepence in the Pound yearly out of all Eclesiasticall Benefices, as they were valued at the Reformation . . . of much Trouble and Vexation to the Clergy" (_Corres._, I, 182). He told King that his personal interest in them was "about ten shillings a-year" (_Corres._, I, 184). Actually, they were slightly more: 14s 3d in May 1703 (29) and 14s 9d½ in June 1709 (90). They are not given in 1703-4; they would have been included in the sum allowed "for what was p^{d} in absence" (50).

Salary to a curate began as early as 1700, when Swift first assumed responsibility for his cure of souls at Laracor. Lyon records it among Swift's charges for 1699-1700. Bolton had not engaged a curate at Laracor in 1697, according to that year's diocese report, but himself provided "one duty performed there every Sunday." He did provide a curate, William Major, for Agher. During the period covered by the first two account books, the curate is a Mr. Smith. The records show that he received a salary, first of £40, later of £30, annually; both salaries fall within the customary range of salaries paid curates at that time in England and Ireland. In 1702-3 it is not easy to determine this salary because Smith is never paid by the quarter or half year. Swift writes "the remaind^{r} of a Quart^{r}" (£9 5s 2d), "in part for a Quart^{r}" (£8), and to clear "in full" (£14 5s). Yet since these sums total £31 10s 2d and cover a specified period of something over three quarters (12 April to 2 February 1703), the obvious assumption is that Smith was receiving £40 a year. This assumption is borne out by the 1703-4 book. Here Smith is paid £10 for "a 4^{r} end. Aug. 7. 1704"; the £10 is a part of £30 for "3 q^{rts}" (i.e., from 7 November 1703) (50, 51). For the final quarter, from August to November, Smith is paid, instead of £10, only £7 10s; no explanation for the reduction appears.

There is no indication of a salary to Smith for the three quarters between 2 February and 7 November 1703. Could Swift have been serving his cure himself from February until he left for England 11 November? He was at Laracor a great deal of that time.

Whatever the exact details about Smith's salary may be, it is clear that

Warburton was paid £30 in 1708. In the 1708-9 book the quarterly salary is twice stated as £7 10s. But the third quarter is different: "A Qua End. Aug. 19" is entered as "half cleard, & 10s more allowd . . . 6 - 15 - 0." This suggests an increase, possibly occasioned by Warburton's receiving priest's orders in September 1709 (Records of the Diocese of Meath in RCBL). He remained Swift's curate until January 1717, but we learn no more about his salary.

In 1717-8 £20 is recorded as paid to Mr. Warren "to Mar. 25th 1718." The time covered is not indicated, but it is likely to have been for a half year, i.e., from 25 September 1717. On 1 May 1717 Swift, looking for a replacement for Warburton, had written King asking that Warren, "Landlord of Galtrim," who had a living "in Clogher Diocese," might exchange it for the less valuable one of Galtrim and Kilmore, on the borders of Laracor parish. On 24 June Bishop Evans reported to Archbishop Wake that Dr. Swift "would put upon me a curate to be licensed who has a great living in the diocese of Clogher, which I have absolutely refused to do," citing moral and political objections to Swift's candidate (Ball, III, 37, n 4). Though Williams says that "Warren does not appear to have received either Galtrim or Kilmore" (Corres., II, 266, n 4), the account book entry is clear that he did act as Swift's curate for a time, in spite of Evans' refusal to provide him with a license.

No salary to a Laracor curate is recorded in 1732-3 or 1734-5, but the 1733 Visitation of the Diocese of Meath (RCBL) says that "Stafford Lightburn Curate of Laracor" received an annual salary of £40. The Visitation report also states that Swift's curate resided "in Trim within a mile" of the Laracor church, not in the "neat cabin" (Swift's own residence) "situated near the Church." The 1734-5 book credits Lightburne with receiving the 10s 2d which Swift paid his curate as schoolmaster of Trim. The same annual sum is also entered for the schoolmaster in 1702-3 and 1708-9. The position would seem to have been a perquisite of the curate: Swift reports to Vanessa in 1713 that "Mr. Warburton has a thin school" (Corres., I, 374).

An entry in the 1734-5 book mentions, for the only time in any account book, a curate for Rathbeggan: a salary of £8 is paid "Mr Jourdan for May 1. 1734." The 1733 Visitation report states, without giving the salary, that the parish of Rathbeggan was "served by Mr Jordon Vicar of Dunshaughlin." The two curacies are referred to in Evans' letter to Wake, noted above, in which, mentioning that "Dr. Swift has two rectories here, without dispensation," he speaks of "one of his curates."

The account books show a small charge paid to a vicar, regularly placed against the Dunlavin account. Since vicars choral enjoyed comfortable salaries from the cathedral, the small amounts entered in the account books may represent payments for sermons delivered in his place on the days when it was Swift's turn to preach. In 1702-3 two sermons are actually specified in the Dunlavin account; in this instance the money was paid to the Laracor curate, Smith, who may have travelled down and delivered them in person. Another entry this year lists the inconsiderable sum of £1 "to My Vicar for a Year." Though no charges are given in 1703-4 under the Dunlavin account, a block sum allowed there during Swift's absence may have included another such small payment to the vicar. In 1708-9 the Dunlavin account records £1 "P^d to my Vicar in Dublin for 2 Years. for him & late M^r $Buck^n$ to lady day. 1709." "M^r $Buck^n$" is Simon Buckton, vicar of the traditionally combined prebends of Maynooth and Dunlavin from 1696 to 1707. He was succeeded by George Rogers, who would have become "my Vicar in Dublin."

Visitation charges and proxies were always anathema to Swift. As incumbent of Laracor, Agher, and Rathbeggan, he was expected to be present at Trim for the annual visitation of the Bishop of Meath in the late spring and the triennial visitation of the Archbishop of Armagh in the summer. Since he was reluctant to attend any visitation but his own, the cost of proxies was a frequent expense. When in the Accounts of Livings a proxy is noted, we may conclude that he was absent from a visitation; when there is no such item, he may be presumed to have attended.

Proxies for the diocesan visitation are recorded as paid in the three early account books, always in May or June and always under the Laracor account; twice the exact sum is given, £2 7s 9d, with an additional fee to the bishop's clerk or apparitor. In the earliest book, though presumably not present, Swift paid a visitation charge: 10s 9d for "Two Dinners" (29). Proxies and a fee to the Bishop's Receiver are also entered in 1702-3 for the Rectory of Grenoge for a visitation which he could not have been expected to attend (27). Of particular interest is the situation in June 1718, when no proxy is purchased, although Swift has headed a page "Proxyes & other Charges for Laracor, 1718," a proof that he intended to absent himself as usual (194). Other entries show that he was "at Trim &c" on 5 and 6 June, that he then went to Dublin, but that on 9 June he returned to Laracor and remained there. The eventful visitation of Bishop Evans took place in the second week of June. The account book entries, taken together, suggest that Swift changed his mind at the last minute and appeared before the bishop for the express purpose of defending the clergymen whom Evans had censured. The latter complained to Archbishop Wake, 20 June, about "the insolent rudeness of Dr. Swift att my Visitation last week where he had never appear'd before" (Landa, p. 183). By the last part of his remark Evans may have meant only that the dean had avoided his particular visitations, but the account books give some evidence that Swift had never attended any since entering upon his livings. The following year Evans refused to accept his proxy, as we learn from Swift's letter to the bishop of 22 May 1719, reminding him that "I promised last year never to appear again at your visitations." After Evans' death in 1724, Swift's record of attendance at episcopal visitations improved. His courteous behavior to Bishop Downes in 1724 was acknowledged (Corres., III, 13, n 1), and in 1733, when Bishop Ellis was his diocesan, Swift notes at Trim in May: "15 to 19 Visitation."

The purchase of at least one proxy for the Archbishop of Armagh's triennial visitation must have formed part of Swift's ecclesiastical charges in 1700, the first year he held his livings; he excused himself to King, then Bishop of Derry and acting for the Archbishop, for his absence (Corres., I, 36). Thereafter he was more faithful. In the triennial years of 1703, 1709, and 1718, he was, according to the account books, at Laracor for all or part of August, when the visitations took place, and there is no record of proxy purchases. The 1717-8 book notes his return to Trim on 19 August, and the next day he writes Ford, "I am here upon a Clergy business called a Trienniall Visitation, which begins to morrow."

While a prebendary, Swift's record of attendance at chapter visitations by the Dean of St. Patrick's was better than at diocesan visitations in Meath. The dean's visitations were held in early January. During Swift's thirteen years as a prebendary he was present at five visitations (1701, 1702, 1703, 1705, 1707). On 7 January 1706 and 9 January 1710, when the chapter minutes show him absent, he was presumably in Dublin; but on the six other occasions (1704, 1708, 1709, 1711, 1712, 1713) he was in London on church business.

After he himself became dean, he anticipated his first visitation, January 1715, with unaccustomed eagerness. "My visitation is to be this day sennight . . . I design great things . . . and I believe my Chapter will join with me. I hear they think me a smart Dean, and that I am for doing good" (*Corres*., II, 154). He may have been basing his optimism, which seems excessive in view of his difficulties with his vicars choral and the political opposition in the chapter, on the healthy condition of the cathedral funds, for which he was responsible and which for the first time showed a redundancy of money in the proctor's hands (Mason, p. 296). The only references in the account books to his own visitations are to charges the dean was expected to incur. In 1718 he escaped with a modest outlay: "Jan^{r}. 13. Visitation dinner. in all . . . 1^{ll} 16^{s} 7^{d} Ale 2^{s} 2^{d}" (192). In 1735, however, the dinner on 13 January cost him £7 0s 8d (266). Swift always valued highly the power of the dean to visit his chapter, a power which he rates first among the dean's "great prerogatives" : "He visits the chapter as ordinary, and the Archbishop [of Dublin] only visits by the dean" (*Corres*., II, 198).

Swift did not, in consequence, feel himself bound to provide a proxy when absent from the Archbishop's visitations to St. Patrick's. These were held in April or May. During his thirteen years as prebendary of Dunlavin, he attended chapter meetings in these months only three or four times; he was in England during eight of the visitations. He notes his return to Dublin from Laracor in April 1703, to be present at the visitation on the 15th. Proxies for these ceremonies in 1704 and 1709 may be included along with those for diocesan visitations, but it is more likely that Swift ignored them. In April 1710, the one time he was in Ireland but planning to be absent from the visitation, upon Dean Stearne's urging him to send a proxy, his reply from Laracor sounds much as if he had never applied for one before: he has had to look in a "Book of Presedents" in order to draft "the Jargon annexed" (*Corres*., I, 162). When out of Ireland, prebendary Swift was excused for nonattendance if, as Archbishop King wrote in 1711, he was "on the public business of the Church" (*Corres*., I, 225). After Swift became dean, when in Dublin, he was present at most if not all of the Archbishop's visitations. When absent, he resolutely refused to furnish a proxy. At King's request for one in 1727, Swift wrote him from England, "I take my Chapter to be my proxy, if I want any: It is only through them that you visit me, and my sub-dean is to answer for me" (*Corres*., III, 210). Consequently, there is no mention in the account books of a proxy for these visitations. In 1739 and 1740 the cathedral records show that the Archbishop's visitations took place on 2 and 14 May. On these occasions the collections rose to well over a pound instead of the usual ten shillings or under (296, 298).

Taxes were slight. A small hearth tax was levied, possibly twice a year, on Swift's glebehouse: 4s is twice recorded in Laracor accounts: "Hearth money p^{d} May. 28" and "Smoak money due Jan^{r}. 1708/9" (29, 91); in the latter year a balancing entry reads "Oct. 12 Allowd . . . Hearth money &c" (90). So small an amount may well have been included under "&c's" allowed elsewhere. Deanery taxes and cesses amounted to £2 9s 9d in 1718 (193); to something over a pound in 1735 (269).

A *license for absence* from Ireland is often mentioned by Swift in his letters after he is advanced to the higher ranks of the clergy, usually when he is asking someone to renew it for him. The cost of his first license, recorded in the 1712-3 account book, was £5 19s 1d, paid on 15 September 1713 after Swift had returned to England (163). Swift wrote Walls the next month with some satisfaction, "I hoped, and was told, my license would be under six pounds though all was paid; and I heard, if Lord Chancellor had taken his fees, it would have been eight pounds" (Corres., I, 390). Six months later, on 11 February 1714, he wrote to Joshua Dawson, permanent secretary, "I must desire the Favor of You, to renew My Letters of Absence for half a year longer, and I will order My Agent Mr Parvisol to attend you with the Charges of it."

22. Costs of Maintenance of Church Property

Three years before Swift received his livings, the State of the Diocese of Meath reported that, while the churches of Agher and Rathbeggan had been in ruins "since 1641," Laracor had had "ye body of ye church repayrd in 1694" by the incumbent, John Bolton. The account books show that, from his very first year as vicar, Swift went forward with the work of restoration; Hartstonge directed Scott's attention to an entry in the 1700-1 book: an expenditure for "'repairing the Chancel' of the Church at Laracore" (NLS, MS 882, f. 72). Additional work on the chancel--or perhaps simply the clearing of the original expense--is recorded in the 1703-4 book: "Novb^{r} 6. 1705 Allowd to Mr Wesly for the Chancell, the 2^{d} Pay^{mt} of 10^{ll} . . . 5 - 0 - 0" (50). Although no later account book itemizes any of the improvements, Swift continued to keep his church in excellent condition. The 1733 Visitation report states it to be "a handsome well built church in very decent repair the Church & Chancel ceiled & flagged & furnished with all conveniences except a Surplice & carpet." At this time the church at Rathbeggan remained "ruinous."

The previous incumbent, Bolton, did not live at Laracor but at Ratoath, "within 8 miles," according to Stearne's 1697 report, which mentions no residence in the vicinity of the church. Earlier surveys (Civil Survey, 1654, and Barony of Meath maps) listed only "some thatch houses" and "cabbins." As Swift, writing from Dublin on 4 May 1700, told Jane Waring, "The place of residence for that [living] they have given me is within a mile of a town called Trim, twenty miles from hence; and there is no other way but to hire a house at Trim, or build one on the spot: the first is hardly to be done, and the other I am too poor to perform at present."

As a single man Swift continued to reside with the Berkeleys in Dublin and travel back and forth between Ireland and England; and when he came to the Trim/Laracor area in the account book year 1702-3, he hired not a house but lodgings at Trim. On 5 April 1703 he paid "for all acc^{ts}" one Andrew Malaly (29), whose wife, he tells Stella on 17 August 1711, "was once my landlady in Trim." At the same time he had been preparing a house of his own, not at Trim but at Laracor. Lacking funds to "build one on the spot," he evidently adapted to his use one of the thatch houses or "cabbins" located near his church. In March 1703 he equipped it with housekeeping necessities--sauce pan, coffee pots, plates, basket, cups--all bought from Jo Beaumont in Trim.[24]

The simplicity of the dwelling is evident from letters as well as from

---

[24]The previous month Mrs. Brent had bought dishes and plates and a roaster for him in Dublin, but no similar list of purchases can be found in the account books until furnishings for the deanery are recorded.

the account books: Swift refers to its "field-bed and an Earthen floor" and mud walls and straw-thatched roof in terms that also convey his deep regard for the house as a place of refuge and retirement (Corres., I, 373; II, 130). The straw roof needed frequent attention: thatching is paid for in the spring of 1704, the autumn of 1705, and in 1709. Swift paid a hearth tax, so we know there was a fireplace. The "cabin," to use Swift's description, was solely for his own use; the curate lived in the house provided for the parish residence, half way between the church and Trim.

After the spring of 1703 Swift records his presence in the Laracor/Trim area as "at Laracor." In December 1702 he still takes "Coach Trim" and locates himself "At Trim." But in August 1703 the entries "at Laracor" begin. In that month he receives money "at Laracor"; he is "At Laracor" in June 1704 on his return from England and is paid his money there in October; he goes "strait to Laracor" on his return to Ireland 30 June 1709. In 1710, though he writes down "Oats at Trim," "Treat Trim Peopl.," "MD being at Trim," he himself is at Laracor; and it is "in my chamber at Laracor"--his glebehouse, according to Lyon--that he records in May 1710 the receipt of the letter containing the news of his mother's death (319).

Simple as the dwelling was, it must have had a stable close by. In 1704 there is a considerable expense amounting to over £14 for building as well as repair: "for barn, stable," entered elsewhere as "Build" (54, 51).

In 1702-3 many expenditures were laid out for work on grounds and gardens: "Work done in the Garden . . . making Trenches & walks, and planting Sallyes"; "making the westside Ditch, & other work, sallys, &c."; "Cleaning Sallyes 3 times & drawing Stone" (29). Swift had arranged for his plantings to continue even during his absence in England: "Allowd for . . . Sallyes . . . to May 31, 1704"; "Allod setting Sallyes in Island, weeding setting Fruit trees &c from Febr. 19. 1704. to Oc^{tr}. 30. 1705" (54).[25] When he is again abroad, he pays for "Work done in th Garden from Dec^{br}. 13 1707 to Sep^{t}. 1. 1709" (91). When he was at Laracor for eight weeks in the spring of 1710, he must have occupied himself as he describes to Stella nearly a year later: "I should be plaguy busy at Laracor if I were there now, cutting down willows, planting others, scouring my canal, and every kind of thing," and Stella would "ride by and see Presto in his morning-gown in the garden" (JS, p. 197).

The house and grounds were kept in good condition during Swift's 1710-3 absence in England, but apparently they were allowed to deteriorate greatly the following year. On 14 September 1714 he lamented to Bolingbroke that his "country seat" had "gone to ruin." This was not exaggeration. His letters show that for the next three years, when he preached at the church or had business in the area, he stayed with Raymond at Trim and walked to Laracor.

A large part of that business was the revitalization of Laracor. During

---

[25]The "Island" was leased from Percival for 2s a year. Shortly after Percival's death, it reverted to his son, whom Swift angrily charged with having "cutt down more Plantations of Willows and Abeilles than would purchase a dozen such Islands" (Corres., III, 365). The fruit trees, as we learn from frequent references in the Journal, were apple and cherry (JS, pp. 175, 220, 472, 525, 555).

the summer of 1716 Swift negotiated with John Percival and with the Board of the First Fruits Fund to acquire for Laracor some of the land Percival owned at Nealstown. The Board in July paid fees for examining Percival's title and conveying the Nealstown tithes; then on 18 December £200 was authorized for the purchase (Synge, pp. 49, 51).[26] Swift wrote Archbishop King, 22 December 1716, about the £200 of First Fruits money, outlining a complicated plan whereby he would lease an additional twenty acres, "lay out the s[d] 200[ll] in Building," pay Percival a fine of £55 immediately ("out of my own Pocket") and £14 per annum thereafter "for ever." He purchased the land from Percival early in 1717, but the plans for building and for acquiring additional land never materialized; the 1733 Visitation report lists only the good garden and neat cabin at Laracor, worth £60, on the "original Glebe belonging to the Parish containing an acre."

Possibly the death of Percival in 1718 may have forced a change in plan. In his "State of my affairs, Sept[ber] 8th 1718" (316), Swift was still planning that the £200 "be layd out for building at Neilstown," but by November Percival was dead (Corres., II, 302). There is no mention of "building" with the £100 which the 1717-8 account book records as actually "Layd out at Neals Town" (188); since no house was ever built on the new land, the money may have gone to complete the land purchase. The £100 seems too great a sum to have been laid out merely on land improvements, although Swift wrote King 2 March 1717 in the first glow of ownership, "I shall make so many Plantations and Hedges, that the land will let for double the Value." The £18 for a discounted bill dated 8 May 1719 for Nealstown (195) may have been for land improvements or for a final settlement with the Percival estate.

Disappointment in his plans for Nealstown may have led Swift to his purchase of the tithes of Effernock the following year from Raymond.

In the spring of 1717, even before he had abandoned his plan to build a house on Nealstown land, Swift decided to refurbish his old quarters. By May he is grumbling that "There has not been one thing done to my Rooms at Laracor since I went" (Corres., II, 269). Few details are discoverable about what things were eventually done, but the 1717-8 account book notes that he stayed at Laracor in December 1717 and in February, April, June, July, and August 1718. Indeed, in April and July he entertained there at dinner, the only recorded occasion of this kind of hospitality at Laracor. Letters during the early 1720's show that he invited visitors there, and he even considered the house commodious enough to be offered in 1724 to Bishop Downes, whose own residence was under construction. On this occasion Sheridan ridiculed Swift's furnishings in "A True and Faithful Inventory," but even "A batter'd, shatter'd Ash Bedstead" is an improvement over a field-cot (Poems, p. 1044).

The Visitation report indicates that the house and grounds at Laracor were still in excellent condition in 1733, and Swift probably stayed there when he attended Bishop Ellis's visitation at Trim 15 to 19 May. But with increasing age Swift would visit Laracor less often, and by 1742 the then Bishop

---

[26]A document signed by Percival and Swift, dated 13 June 1716, obviously prepared for the Board's use, shows the twenty acres of Nealstown "being the part purchased by the Rev[d] Dean of St Patricks from John Percival Esq[r] for the use of the Church" (CUL, Williams Collection, Box iii).

of Meath, Price, complained of "the ruinous Condition" of the glebe-house at Laracor (BL, Add. MSS. 38671, f. 18r). But the land Swift left his successor was of greater extent and in better condition than when he had received it.

The Deanery House in Dublin, "the great House there, which they say is mine" (Corres., I, 373), had been built by Stearne between 1707 and 1711 at a cost of £900. Swift was to repay Stearne £600, leaving his successor responsible to his estate for £300. Stearne continued to reside at the deanery until shortly before Swift returned to Ireland permanently in 1714. When he left, Swift did buy some of his household furnishings, despite his earlier determination not to: "I shall buy Bp Stearns Hair as soon as his Houshold goods" (JS, p. 669). In March 1714 he is willing to take whatever his women friends recommend. On his return to Dublin, he began making imrpovements in the deanery, chiefly a new chimneypiece and a room shelved for a library. When not able to supervise the work himself, he depended for information from Walls:

> Why the whole room painted? is it not enough to have onely the new Panels & Edges of the Shelves painted; Do what you will, but pray let it be done before I come, that the Smell may go off. Is the Chimney-piece up, or onely finished at the Man's House (Corres., II, 145)?

Lyon in 1742 says that the chapter paid Swift £20 a year "by way of Repairs, because he laid out above £200 in improving ye Deanry-House" (Landa, "Deanery," p. 167). This sum of £200 must have accumulated over the years, and the chapter's £20 reimbursement never appears in the account books. But £20 a year would be a fair figure. In the 1717-8 account book, deanery repairs, separated out from other deanery charges, add up to about £25, of which over £10 is for painting rails and mending leads. In 1734-5 the total is over £14, consisting chiefly of £8 for painting, but also including repairs to windows, chimneys, and locks.

As for the deanery gardens, about £10 was spent for maintenance in 1717-8, under £3 in 1734-5. There is no reference in the 1717-8 book to the transfer of chapter land, 14 May 1718, which resulted later in the creation of Naboth's Vineyard. The development of the grounds and wall is frequently mentioned in the letters of the 1720's, and the spot is described at length in "Of Dr Swift's Effects" (Landa, "Deanery," p. 168). In 1734-5 a number of entries under "Garden & Vineyard," such as "ground near Vineyard wall" (268), must refer to the area, and a tax of 5d for "Naboth" is entered under January 1735 (269).

Swift strongly supported maintaining the building and antiquities of St. Patrick's, but the cost would have been no part of his personal expenses.

His personal responsibility for repair of the church at Tallaght was urged upon him by King, 19 December 1723: "You are Rector there and the repair of the chancel is incumbent upon you, but inasmuch as it was not ruined in your time, you ought not to be charged with it, but it ought not to lie in the rubbish, and I find the fifteen pounds you promised will finish the repair of it." The fact that Swift records 10s annually, in 1735 and 1736, for the Tallow chancel indicates that he accepted responsibility. Thus both the earliest known and the latest extant account books carry records of Swift's personal concern for the maintenance of church buildings entrusted to him.

23. System of Management

The account books, read in conjunction with his letters, illustrate Swift's management of his ecclesiastical income. He always employed a land agent (manager, land steward, proctor), experienced in judging crop values and in setting and collecting the various kinds of tithes. Sometimes an assistant would help with collections.

When away from Dublin for any length of time, Swift empowered a receiver or financial manager, a sort of surrogate of himself, to accept collections from his agents and to keep records. Occasionally he enlisted the help of clerical friends in tithe management, valuations, and collections.

The duties of land agent, receiver, assistant, and friendly clerical advisers tended to blur and overlap. Any one might be requested during Swift's absences to obtain a license for him or to pay his proxy: Dr. Raymond or the Rev. Mr. Forbes might be asked to check on Mr. Parvisol, the curate Lightburne on Mr. Proudfoot.

The land agent is prominently featured in the early Accounts of Livings, where his duties are shown to be extensive. His main concern was with tithes. He was responsible, first, for setting them; the income Swift was later to realize depended on the agent's knowledge and conscientiousness.[27] After he had set the tithes, the farmers gave him their bonds, and these were to be deposited with Swift or his receiver; but sometimes the bonds were not taken or could not be found at collection time (199, 200, 284). In due time the agent collected the tithes, dealing separately--and never too successfully--with those drawn in kind. But he had responsibilities unconnected with tithing. He paid ecclesiastical charges. He contracted for labor and, at least during Swift's absences in England, supervised work on his house, grounds, and church. At Laracor he saw to the grazing and care of the horses, and, when Swift was in residence, provided for his housekeeping needs.

For both setting and collecting Swift paid a fee of twelve pence in the pound. In addition, the agent received a setting fee--in Swift's opinion a valuable perquisite--but except for Rathbeggan, where Swift paid it, this was charged to the tenant. For travelling expenses the agent was reimbursed, as "travelling charges" allowed to Parvisol and "Journeys" in the "Tyths drawn" account indicate (32, 54). Swift was outraged by the amount Parvisol claimed in fees the first time he set deanery tithes, especially for his travels: "If he takes Journeyes are they above a dozen miles, and is he not pd for them by his Place" (Corres., II, 48).

Finally, after making permitted deductions, the agent turned over to Swift or his receiver the difference between collections and disbursements.

---

[27]Swift's complaints against Gillespy, 23 December 1716, show how tithes should not be set: "He hath set every Article but scurvily; His Method was to ask how it sett last year, & then without further examining to ask the same Rate, and so fall lower as they could agree."

Some agents were annoyingly dilatory in doing so, especially when Swift was abroad, as his letters to Stella and Walls attest. Some--Parvisol at least--turned money or bills directly over to MD or Mrs. Brent on Swift's direction.

Swift's first agent, as far as we know, was Isaiah Parvisol, a Frenchman. On 3 July 1714 Swift asserted that he had kept Parvisol "with his family a dozen years from starving," a figure corroborated by the account book record of his setting the tithes in the summer of 1702. The numerous references to the man in the Journal to Stella furnish details of his management, as well as his involvement in Swift's larger financial transactions, which are not recorded in the account books. From 1702 to 1713, in spite of Swift's occasional impatience with him ("I'll un-parvisol him" JS, p. 301), he seems to have served fairly well. Returning to Laracor after a three-year absence, Swift found his house habitable and his grounds "extremely pretty" and "in great beauty" (Corres., I, 373). However, when Parvisol undertook the management of deanery tithes, it was a different story. Even while he was still in London, Swift decided that Parvisol had taken advantage of him and wanted him dismissed, and on his return he found his house "gone to ruin" (Corres., II, 130).

We know from letters that in December 1714 a Mr. Gillespy was Swift's steward, resident in the deanery and managing the deanery tithes; early the next spring he was entrusted with tithes of the livings as well. But he lasted only two years. By May 1716 Swift suspected him of collusion with the farmers at Laracor, by December he had become "that Rascall Gillespy," and a week later he was discharged. He appears in the account books only in November 1717, when Swift paid him £7 3s for hay, a purchase Swift had authorized to Walls in August. Swift harbored no hostile feelings toward Gillespy: "I would rather he should have the money than another" (Corres., II, 283).

Parvisol was rehired, collecting the tithes from Laracor and Rathbeggan which Gillespy had set, and he continued during 1717, supervising the restoration of Swift's residence at Laracor and probably setting the tithes. He took no part, however, in collecting them the next year, no doubt for reasons of health, and his name occurs in the 1717-8 book only as the recipient of a gift in October. A month later "poor Parvisol" is dead (Corres., II, 302).

Two new land agents appear in the 1717-8 book: David Bourne and Proudfoot. Bourne, "of Trim gentleman" (Ball, IV, 459), is mentioned in Swift's letters soon after the dismissal of Gillespy, not only acting as agent but assisting Walls as receiver: according to the account book, he turns in collections from the deanery, Laracor, and Rathbeggan and is paid £10 for his work. He was clearly in Swift's confidence and might have served him well as chief land agent: Bourne witnessed the transfer deed of the tithes of Effernock from Raymond to Swift, 14 June 1718 (MS at St. Patrick's Hospital), and the deeds conveying Talbot's Castle and Dublin property from Esther Johnson to Swift, 20 May 1718 and 28 November 1721 (Ball, IV, 459). But after 1718, in neither account books nor correspondence is he again heard of.

Parvisol's successor instead was the other land agent named in the 1717-8 book: Proudfoot, possibly Robert. He had before this been mentioned by Swift to Walls in connection with deanery lands as "one whom I shall partly employ," (Corres., II, 242) and as working on deanery collections in the summer of 1717. The earlier account books show that a Proudfoot had for many years served Swift in his livings: he had assisted Parvisol with Laracor collections as early as 1704 and was still so employed in 1709. He appears in 1717-8 receiving the same salary as Davy Bourne, £10, with an added gift of 18s.[28] In 1725 Swift mentions "my Manager, Rob[t] Proudfoot" as concerned with deanery business and Laracor collections. Two years later, April 1727, he writes, "I have been plagued with the roguery of my deanry proctor, whom I have discharged. I believe I am worse for him, 600l., and his brother is not much better" (Corres., III, 205). If the reference is to Proudfoot, we may conclude that either Robert or his brother had been in Swift's service for over twenty years, the longest term of any land agent.

Swift's letter of December 1729 to Robert Percival names Daniel Griffin as his Laracor agent at that time, and a note to Swift's guardians (BL, Add. MSS. 38671, f. 18r) indicates that Griffin still served as Laracor agent at least as late as 1742. His name is not found in the account books.

The deanery tithe agent, who seems also to have been responsible for the living of Rathbeggan, was one Mr. Gorman. On 21 November 1730 Counsellor Lindsay rendered a mock-serious verdict "concerning Mr Gorman" in response to some queries Swift had submitted to him about stupid answers his land agent had given "J. S." Lindsay's opinion was that the agent "has not made one answer like a man of business, but has answered very much like a true agent" (Scott, XIX, 369, from Dr. Lyon's papers). But Gorman was still serving Swift in 1732-3, when the account book records his turning in large amounts of deanery tithes 9 November 1733; and it may well be he who deposits both deanery and livings tithes in February and again in March 1735. Both years he furnished Swift with alphabetical lists of deanery and Rathbeggan tithe-payers. But soon thereafter he proved intolerable, and on 17 July 1735 Swift wrote Orrery, "I have turned off a Worse-ham than Your Badham, Mine hath half ruined me, and I have still a worse." If the worse one is the Laracor agent, this may explain why the only Laracor entry in the later account book is under "Defalcations."

The deanery agent who succeeded Swift's "Worse-ham" was Dr. Francis Wilson, who indeed turned out to be worse. But in addition to being a prebendary of St. Patrick's, Wilson was rector of Clondalkin, near which most of the deanery tithelands lay, so that he had the sort of first-hand knowledge of a locality that Swift always valued. Soon after the previous agent's last submission of deanery tithes, 14 March 1735, Wilson is first mentioned; a lease was made to him 24 March 1735 (267). This may be the lease of the deanery tithes referred to in Swift's will as "now let to the Reverend Doctor Wilson" (PW, XIII, 154), although other deanery tithes, in Saggard and Rathcoole, were leased to Wilson by Swift in January 1739 (SPH MSS. 37A, 38A). In the summer of 1735 Wilson turned in his first tithe collections: arrears of 1732 tithes 28 June (227-38) and 1734 tithes in May, June, and December (287). Deane Swift impugns Wilson's honesty:

> It was notorious that so long as the Dean's memory and judgement were tolerable Wilson seldom or ever paid the Dean any money but in the presence of M[rs] Whiteway, and after the Dean's memory failed, he always paid the Dean in private; notwithstanding he was frequently

---

[28]There are no later account book entries of salaries to agents; they may be assumed to have been paid on settlement dates. The £20 18s paid this year was standard; Lyon records £20 for all charges on deanery tithes in 1742.

warned to the contrary (Corres., V, 210).

Deane Swift's words show that, in spite of Wilson's residence at the deanery and in spite of Swift's favorable allusions to him in letters and in his will, he never trusted Wilson, as he trusted Walls and Worrall, enough to let him hold tithe and rent money, but insisted that collections be turned in to him.

* * * *

Assisting Parvisol with tithe collections in 1703, in addition to Proudfoot, was one Cusack; he may be the R. Cusack who was Swift's tenant at Summerstown in 1708. Assisting Proudfoot and Bourne with deanery tithe collections in 1717-8 was Barnwell, who was paid £5 that year. Swift had proposed him to Walls as a helper on 19 December 1716, suggesting that his servant "find out old Barnwell," who will then order deanery farmers to pay up their current and past tithes. Wilson seems to have had a number of helpers, especially Roger Kendrick, who drew up the lease of tithes to Wilson, and who continued to assist him in 1735-6 (317) with tithe collections. Some others named are probably servants delivering the tithes or rent of their masters, like Dan Brown, who delivered Stopford's rent payment (288) and Vedel, "Parvisol's man" (JS, p. 140).

* * * *

Swift's financial manager not only received collections and kept records, he was expected to hold tithe bonds, to transfer as needed drafts of money in the form of bills, and often to supervise the discharge of Swift's ecclesiastical obligations. The correspondence proves how great was the authority vested in the surrogate. On 3 July 1714 Swift instructed Walls to turn Parvisol off and employ someone else, adding, "I believe the Power I left with you will suffice, for as I remember it was as large as I could make it." And to Lightburne on 22 April 1725 he said, "Mr Worrall has the remaining Bonds of Laracor, &c., and a Power from me to receive the money."

Letters to Walls are especially revealing as to the duties of the receiver. On 19 December 1716, even as Swift is reassuring Walls that he does not intend any longer "to constitute You my Receiver," he tells him to furnish Will Geddes with a list of the principal deanery farmers "both as to their Names & habitations," and asks that those farmers "who have their money ready would on the next Market day pay their money to You who have their Bonds, and can give them Receits on the back of them," adding a request that "with the Bills [bonds] of Laracor for this Year 1716, you would send me in a Paper separate, the Bills of Arrears for Laracor of which I find a list in y^{r} Book, from Parvisol."

According to account book records, Swift preferred to act as his own receiver. He does so in 1702-3, receiving collections directly from Parvisol "by coach," "in Dublin," "at Laracor" in twenty-three separate entries; he also seems for the first time to have been straightening out his business affairs, establishing his system of bookkeeping, and clearing old debts: charges are paid, for whatever reason, on the Rectory of Grenoge, and so is an ancient crown rent on Laracor, due since 1688. When Swift was out of the country in 1703-4, Parvisol turned over money "in absence, to Uncle." Possibly this uncle (William) had so acted during Swift's absences in 1701 and 1702. When in Ireland in 1704 and 1709, Swift is again in charge.

Two men who were authorized to act for Swift as receiver in his absences were both trusted colleagues in the chapter of St. Patrick's, Archdeacon Thomas Walls and Dean's Vicar John Worrall. In 1707-9 when Swift was in England, Walls was receiver. The 1708-9 account book lists six letters from him that year. In the letter Swift wrote him, 9 November 1708, he complained about Parvisol's failure to turn over to Walls collections of the previous year's tithes. Walls took prompt action, as account book entries show: a letter from him "with a bill" and a memo of the same date, "Dec^{br} 20. 1708 a Bill from Mr Walls" for £20. Twice again in the same account book Swift could record bills issued by Parvisol "to Mr Walls" in time to reach Swift in London (one of which, for £47 4s 7d½, tapped the resources of all three accounts, of Laracor, of Rathbeggan, and of Dunlavin). Two more bills to Mr. Walls, issued too late to have reached Swift in London, would have gone for the discharge of his Irish obligations. It is an instructive example of how Swift managed his affairs, through his receiver, while he was out of the country.

During Swift's three-year absence in England he again used Walls as receiver, although he wrote him no letters. As we learn from the Journal, his practice was to send messages or instructions through the ladies. At one point Swift even proposed that MD act as his receiver in place of Walls: "I am thinking, if either of you have heads to take his [Parvisol's] accounts it should be paid in to you; otherwise to Mr Walls" (JS, p. 220). After Swift became dean, Walls' duties naturally increased, involved now with receipt of rents as well as longer tithe lists, and during 1717, in accordance with his wishes, he was gradually relieved of his responsibilities. On 30 March Swift writes, "Mr Burn will be in Toun next Term to receive my Money and give you Ease." By 19 August Swift can say, "I know you have no Accounts by you of mine."

The 1717-8 account book shows Swift himself again taking up the duties of receiver. Having so recently lost Walls and working with two newly acquired agents, he clearly has many problems. Few tithes come in until September 1718: when they do come in, they are in driblets--twenty separate payments by deanery tithepayers between 5 and 24 September. Also, he lacks rent rolls of tithepayers and has to depend on tithe bonds, entering the payments chronologically as they happen to come in. There is evidence of confusion in deanery and Rathbeggan accounts. Yet more was eventually realized from deanery tithes this year than is recorded for any other: £458. There is no record of rent payments, although a page was left for receipt of rents.

In the absence of account books between 1718 and 1732 we have to rely on the correspondence to follow Worrall's career as Swift's receiver. In 1717-8 he is paid £3 in connection with some deanery service (192); by 1721 he is being entrusted with minor commissions. Swift's confidence in him was increased by his handling of the Pratt affair while Swift was at Quilca in 1725, and in the same year the letter to Lightburne already referred to shows Worrall with the full power of receiver. During Swift's absences in England in the summers of 1726 and 1727 his letters to Worrall make the requests formerly made of Walls: that he send bills, renew the license for absence, accept rent payments. "I leave my whole little affairs with you" (Corres., III, 238). As usual when about to leave England Swift is especially desirous of funds from his receiver: "Entreat the ladyes to speak to Worrall to send me a Bill of 100^{ll} not Irish but English. For I shall set out to Ireland in a month, I mean the middle of August, and I have not 10^{ll} left and I owe above 20^{ll}" (Paul V. Thompson, "An Unpublished Letter from Swift," The Library, 22, No. 1 (1967), 61). Letters written after Swift's return to Ireland show Worrall no longer employed as receiver, although he discharged many lesser commissions. Thereafter Swift acted as his own financial manager until the end.

* * * *

Swift often turned to clerical subordinates and neighbors for advice and sometimes for actual collection of arrears. He received help with Laracor tithes from his curates there, Thomas Warburton and Stafford Lightburne. He hoped in 1713 that Warburton might be placed "upon my Deanery" at Rathcoole and Saggart to assist him. Dr. Raymond of Trim is especially helpful: concerning his 1716 tithes, Swift understands "that Dr Raymd had taken care of all Laracor this year" (*Corres*., II, 229). So is Thomas Forbes, rector of Dunboyne, the parish between Dublin and Trim where Swift sometimes broke his journey. Swift refers to him as "my Commissioner" in the summer of 1714 and thanks Walls "for the Pains you and Mr Forbes are at about my rotten Affairs," leaving the question of Parvisol's dismissal "to you and Mr Forbes" (*Corres*., I, 387; II, 48, 90). Little of all this assistance appears in the account books, though that for 1717-8 does show Forbes receiving deanery rents (190).

Ready as Swift was to request assistance from others, he was very much in command of his own affairs. The account books document his presence at Laracor at those times when he could be most effective in bringing in his tithes: in mid-November, from late December through early January--he wrote Walls in December 1716, "now is my time of gathering money if I can"--in mid-March and early spring. From the time when he first held livings, he emphasized the importance of being "on the spot": to Winder, 1 April 1698; to Walls, 3 July 1714; to Sheridan, 28 June 1725. When he received his deanery, he would not allow Walls to accept rent payments from his Kilberry lands until he himself visited them, "which shall be as soon as I come over" (*Corres*., II, 30).

When Swift's attention to his livings flagged during his London years, he partly blamed himself: "I have made that Parvisol a Rogue by my own Carelessness, and trusting in his Accounts," and "Parvisol is playing the Rogue with me in my Accounts. . . . I shall be ruined with staying here" (*Corres*., II, 48, 61). Thereafter he kept a sharper eye on his agents. What he discovered from the farmers at Laracor caused him to dismiss Gillespy in December 1716. Years later he sadly gave to friends as one reason why he could not visit England that "most of my sorry revenues being of the Tyth-kind; I am forced to watch my Agents and farmers constantly; to get nothing" (*Corres*., III, 458), and "my ragged Church rents would never be payd in my absence" (*Corres*., IV, 184). Increasingly troubled as his mind was in later years, he continued to do as he had done in 1732-3, 1734-5, and 1735-6: receive collections from his agent and keep his own books, as Deane Swift's letter of 1742 shows, until the lunacy commission placed him under the protection of legal guardians.

24. Private Investments

The account books normally carry records of ecclesiastical income only. But even in the early books items point to Swift's broader financial concerns. After 1699 Swift was never without some private means. Deane Swift said that he was worth £500 in December 1699 when he offered to settle that sum on his sister if she would not marry Fenton (Deane Swift, p. 108). The sum would have included Swift's £100 legacy from Temple and the money paid him for the first two volumes of Temple's Letters published in 1700. His income was further supplemented by Tooke's payments for subsequent volumes of Temple's works: £30 on 29 July 1701, £50 on 3 September 1702, £40 in April 1709 (NYPL; Rothschild 2256, 2259).[29] The September 1702 payment would have tided him through his first full year on his Irish livings; the April 1709 payment would have been especially welcome just before he left England during a tight budget year. Private means kept Swift solvent in the years before the deanery. Never in the years covered by the account books does his ecclesiastical income cover his expenses.[30]

We can arrive at fairly exact figures for Swift's net annual income in each account book year by adding up funds actually received "in cash" or "in bills" and comparing the result with the total net expenses for the same year (adjusted for costs of housekeeping and horses). According to such a computation, in 1702-3 Swift had received by 1 November 1703 £114 in cash and bills. Arrears from previous years, judging by the average received in recorded years, might have brought the net income to £128; recorded expenses amounted to almost £143.

In 1703-4, a year divided between Ireland and England, the computing is more complicated, but net income by 1 November 1704 would at most have stood at something over £123 received in cash or bills. Swift's recorded expenses in England were heavy, including large amounts spent for clothing and gifts, and the total for the year is over £154.

In 1708-9, another year divided between England and Ireland, receipts in cash and bills by 1 November 1709 add up to £150 19s 1d½; total expenses to £150 8s 4d, a near thing indeed. Moreover, this tight budget balance was made possible only because Swift had received in the late autumn of 1708 some £30 from accumulated collections for 1707-8 which Parvisol had previously failed to turn over to Walls (Corres., I, 206).

Swift could sustain himself (and MC) only because he had supplementary private funds invested or held on deposit both in Ireland and England. (Since his sister refused his offer in 1699, one assumes as a matter of course that Swift, according to his custom, placed the money out at interest.) From early years Swift invested his private funds in Ireland: "money was then at ten per cent in Ireland" (PW, V, 228). "Coz Swift's Bond" on land near Castle Rickard commenced 22 February 1707 (72). When Swift invested in the South Sea stock in England in 1711, he took up "what I have in Ireland," £300 then on loan to Hawkshaw (JS, pp. 74, 87, 94, 313). He later confided to Walls that he would

---

[29]Account book records of meetings and correspondence with Tooke have been effectively used by Ehrenpreis in connection with the 1709 edition of the Tale of a Tub and with the Temple Memoirs (II, 326-49). We are here interested only in the Tooke payments as increments to Swift's subsistence.

[30]If Scott is approximately correct in the rounded figure of £100 he gives for Swift's expenses in 1700, he may have broken even this one year. Living at Dublin Castle, he bore no cost of lodgings, nor was MC in Ireland to receive an annual allowance. His income was also about £100; tithes were set at £230, but arrears were at least £10 (56), and charges amounted to £117.

be glad to get his money "returned to Ireld" (Corres., II, 31).

But he also maintained an English account, however modest, which he could tap when he was in England and which he could draw upon to discharge his obligations in England when he was back in Ireland. When he wrote Tisdall 3 February 1704 from London that he would "take up ten more" pounds here, it could have been from MD's limited English funds or from his own; and as he left for Ireland he recorded 19s "Left with Coz Swift at Chestr abt Engl acct (38). As late as October 1735 he maintained an arrangement with Motte for paying Mrs. Fenton in Surrey her allowance. Many of his letters of the time report his banking arrangements with Tooke and Barber during the 1710-4 years, and he lists to Walls in June 1714 the expedients at his disposal: "money I brought over with me," "a little Principall I melted," "Some Interest I receavd [South Sea stock dividends]," and "money I have borrowed [from Ford]"(Corres., II, 30).

One other expedient Swift clearly overstates to Walls, and it needs closer consideration. This is the second time Swift tells Walls that he has taken up revenues of Mrs. Johnson and Mrs. Dingley in England for his own use and repaid them by bills on Parvisol (Corres., I, 386; II, 49). These statements must have been screens to conceal from Walls (and Parvisol) the outright allowance he paid MC. It is true that to a certain extent Swift did make use of the device: "Tooke has just brought me Dingley's money. I will give you a note for it at the end of this letter. . . . I'll spend your money bravely here." The amount was £8 in funds at the Exchequer (JS, pp. 418, 449). It could be that she received that amount twice a year; references recur in April/May and November 1712 and in May 1713 (JS, pp. 530, 535, 575, 667); and Lyon speaks of £16 which she had in the Funds (Lyon, p. 57).[31]

As for Mrs. Johnson, she had £400 in annuities in England, held by Lady Giffard, which brought her 5% interest, or only £20 a year (JS, pp. 74, 428).[32] There is no mention in the Journal of a reciprocal arrangement with Stella's money--it is unlikely that Lady Giffard would have turned it over to Swift in any case after 1709--although there is a great deal of discussion of how MC's money was to reach them.

Yet Swift tells Walls in June 1714 that, in the ten months he has been in England, he has given Parvisol bills for the ladies amounting to nearly £100--interestingly enough, the new amount of the MC allowance now that Swift had become dean. It is not possible for the ladies' English revenues to have matched that. Account book records are of little help in clarifying the matter: the only statement that seems helpful--"p^{d} to May 1. by Accounts &c clearing from Eng^{d}" (66, 90)--does not really tell us anything except that Swift issued directions to Parvisol from England and had the amount deducted from tithe collections.

---

[31]There are differences in reported amounts of Mrs. Dingley's revenues. The annuity she inherited from her father in 1700 was just £14 (Margaret Toynbee, "The Two Sir John Dingleys," N. & Q. vol. 198, p. 417). She also received the interest on a £100 annuity from Lady Giffard (JS, p. 74, n 33). Hawkesworth says her whole fortune was £27, and Lyon, her executor, does not correct him (Lyon, p. 34). But in any case her revenues were very limited.

[32]The £100 "which I made over to you for Mariston" refers to Stella's inheritance of lands at Morristown, co Wicklow.

After 1714, of course, Swift's financial situation eased, although he was always to experience crises and temporary depletions--"I have within these ten days borrowed the very poor-money lodged in my hands" (Corres., III, 333). By September 1718 when he compiled "A State of my affairs" (316), his private investments amounted to at least £1000 (£1315 should the £315 due from Mrs. Benson be a private loan rather than deanery rents). In the spring and summer of 1718 he had bought property in Trim, as well as a part of the tithes of Effernock, both by arrangement with Raymond (Irvin Ehrenpreis, "Swift and Esther," TLS, 8 January 1954, p. 25). The document of the Effernock tithe transfer, now at St. Patrick's Hospital, shows that Staunton was assisting Swift with this year's transactions. All these matters appear in the 1718 list: securities in Staunton's hands; "three houses" in Trim. In addition there are the loan to Jo Beaumont made jointly with Bishop Stearne (Corres., IV, 236) and loans made by Swift alone to someone unnamed and to several persons in Trim.[33]

A similar memorandum is the "Debts and Mortgages due to me Munday Apr. 11, 1736" (310), except that here the investments are exclusively private. From subsequent entries it is clear that Swift should have written "1737," when 11 April did in fact fall on Monday. The memorandum contains the names of six interest payers, including the four given on the final page of the 1734-5 account book: George Nugent, Mrs. Throp, Alexander Lynch, and Robert Cope, adding, with many repetitions, details of date and amounts of interest due. The loans should have brought Swift £349 annually. This must have been a draft he was preparing for inclusion in the "Bound Paper-book in quarto wherein the Debts due to me . . . [are] entred to this present Month of April 1737" (Swift's letter of instructions to Mrs. Whiteway of 22 April 1737). The two records may be advantageously considered together, and the four account book entries will here first be taken up separately.

1. "Mar. 8th From Mr Nugent ½ a years Interest due July 11th, 1734 . . . 60 - 0 - 0."

George Nugent of Castle Rickard near Clonard Bridge, who, according to the 1737 record, "has a lease of lives renewable on Castle-Ricard," was a tenant of Deane Swift. Since May 1734 Nugent had been making interest payments on a £2000 mortgage which, a year earlier, Swift had granted at 6% to Deane Swift. On 7 April 1733 Swift had written Samuel Gerrard that he could not make a purchase Gerrard proposed because "there is one Mr Swift . . . whose estate is engaged to me for 2000l." Nugent made two more payments after the one noted in the account book. In April 1737 he would owe £180, £120 then due and £60 in arrears. In addition, Deane Swift, for the half year before Nugent entered and for other matters, would owe "near" £1000. Theophilus Swift reported to Scott that his father owed Swift "L. 2500, an immense sum in those days; his estates were mortgaged for it to the Dean," and complained that he himself was left with the mortgage (Deane Swift died in 1783) still "with a long arrear of interest upon it" (Scott, I, 449).

---

[33]The other items on the list are ecclesiastical concerns: rent due through Smith, Bishop of Down, on deanery land at Kilberry; money on Effernock tithes; money due from Mrs. Benson on deanery land at Deans Rath--a considerable accumulation of past rent, at £54 a year; and money to be spent on building at Nealstown.

2. "Apr. 17th 1735. From M[rs] Throp ½ a years Interest due Febr 3[d] last (abating 1[ll]-5[s]) . . . 13 - 15 - 0."

The 1737 list identifies Mrs. Throp's mortgage as £500 at 5% interest; it had been assigned to Swift by Mr. Reading on 16 June 1725 and was not in arrears. The lawyer Daniel Reading was the "useful and excellent" friend of the Temple family (Corres., III, 216). In June 1725 Swift was at Quilca, and Staunton and Worrall were finding ways to salvage the money (£1200) Swift had entrusted to John Pratt, Deputy Vice-Treasurer of Ireland, then in prison for fiscal deficiencies. Swift's taking over of Mrs. Throp's loan may have been part of a reassignment of his funds at that time (Corres., III, 64, 74). Mrs. Throp was the mother of Roger and Robert Throp. The former, rector of Kilcorman, co Limerick, was a litigant against Colonel John Waller. The case was heard (and decided in Throp's favor) in November 1735; Swift's "Great Gift" to "Mr. Throp" (265) the month before probably went to help him in his cause. The abatement of the mother's interest may be another instance of the kindness and friendship "shown to my mother and her family" for which Robert Throp thanked the dean on 10 December 1739.

3. "May 24th. 1735 (Date of Henry's bill.) from M[r] Lynch on Account Rx . . . 100 - 0 - 0."

Alexander Lynch's mortgage, dated 9 July 1732, was for £2000 at 5%. The history of this mortgage, as shown by documents at St. Patrick's Hospital, runs back to 1721 (SPH MSS. 16G, 18G, 19G). Lands in Rapheak and Killtee, co Roscommon, were mortgaged to Swift for £1000 24 June 1721 by William and Annabella Taylor. They were transferred in 1724 to Edmund Dowling of Rapheak, with adjustments "leading to uses of a fine" worked out among Staunton, Dowling, and Swift in May 1730, and were finally conveyed to Alexander Lynch 29 July 1732.[34] The 1737 list shows that, after the £100 interest recorded in the account book, Lynch made another payment of £80 on 20 September. On 9 April 1737 he owed £170, £100 then due and £70 in arrears.

4. "Jan[r]. 1735-6 Payd me 1 year and half Interest to Oc[tb]. 5th 1735. by M[r] Cope. Executor to S[r] Wm Fowns . . . 36 - 0 - 0."

The list in April 1737 shows Sir William Fownes' bond and warrant as a £400 loan at 6% interest, but does not give the date the bond commenced. Swift had been involved in financial transactions with him since 1725, the time of the Pratt affair (Corres., III, 74). The 1734-5 account book carries the record of payment to Mr. Hale for entering judgment "on S[r] W. Fowns Bond on Apr. 2[d]. 1735 in Exchek[r]" (267). Fowns died in April 1735. His executor and son-in-law, Robert Cope, paid off the loan: Swift acknowledges on 11 November 1737 "your note for thirty-six pounds, which was more by a third part than I desired, and for which I heartily thank you." The interest was not in arrears as of April 1737. As Fownes was a man of considerable wealth, the loan may have been a courtesy to Swift rather than a convenience to Fownes.

---

[34]All these transactions can be followed in Swift's correspondence: to Chetwode, 17 May 1729 ("engaged seven years in a lawsuit to recover"); to Pope, 26 February and 2 May 1730 ("my Creditor . . . hath levyed a fine and suffered a recovery") and 20 April 1731; to Wogan, 2 August 1732 ("a Lawsuit of ten Years standing, and I doubt very ill closed up"); and finally to Staunton, 4 August two days later ("about some defects in the Deeds of M[r] Lynch's affair."). None of the references except the last have been previously identified.

The 1737 list carries the names of two debtors who did not pay interest in 1734-5. One of them, a Mr. Cashor of Trim, on a loan of £100 at 6% had "long arrears." The other, John Putland, the stepson of Dr. Helsham, had had the loan only since 1735; it was for £1500 on which he was to pay £80 a year, as shown by Swift's letter to Gerrard, 20 February 1735:

> I have lately disposed of all my money, no less than 1500l., at interest, at L. 5, 6s. 8d. interest per hundred, which will yield me 80l. per annum. It is to the son-in-law of a friend, who hath a good fortune, and I think it safe.

But by August 1736 Putland had paid only £40, and by the following April he was one year and eight months in arrears.

With their discouraging tale of principal endangered and interest long overdue, the records here considered bear out Swift's frequent complaints in the thirties. "My temporal fortune," he tells Ford on 20 November 1733, "is in the utmost Confusion, and of 200ll a year that I ought to receive for interest, I never get one peny." The records also confirm and illuminate the statement he sent Faulkner on 13 July 1738 to be printed, in which he complains that, in spite of his desire for "a real estate in lands. . . his whole fortune consists in mortgages on lands, and other the like securities."

* * * *

Only in the earliest and latest of the account books is there a separate category for the law. In 1702-3 Swift enters expenses incurred in meeting with Delamer "for Answr" on 1 and 2 December 1702, and the attorney's (probably Delamer again) "bill of Cost" on 15 January following; he also had to pay Mr. Skelton on 16 March 1703 "for writts &c," possibly in the same affair. The matter, whatever it was, probably did not involve parochial concerns; Swift notes that this payment to Skelton is "Besides Parvisol's Account," where indeed Skelton again appears. In 1717-8, although there is no separate category for law, two payments are entered under "Deanry Charges"; the larger one--for £1 6s 8d--paid in the last week of May, may have had something to do with the lease of ground for Naboth's Vineyard on the 14th.

In 1734-5 law appears as "La Chicane," and again, as in 1702-3, the items listed under it have to do chiefly with private legal business rather than parochial. An attorney is paid £3 9s in February; a fee recorder, Hale, and Skelton are all paid on 16 March, very possibly in connection with Swift's loan to Sheridan--if so, this is the only account book reference to that financial venture. (When Hale is paid again two lines below, Swift mistakenly enters "Dr Sherid" and then crosses it out.)

Other professional help received by Swift is noted in "Febr. 1733. Payd Stoakes Survey for this May . . . 4 - 15 - 6." He also mentions the bankers, Burton and Henry, who remitted bills to him. But there is no reference in the books to the chief legal advisers to whom he turned: Thomas Staunton, Robert Lindsay, Eaton Stannard, Alexander Macaulay. One supposes they gave him friendly counsel and made no charge. This is certainly the implication of the letter to Stannard of 12 December 1733.

* * * *

Though Swift protested that he was "the greatest cully alive" in business matters, his accounts and his correspondence show him to have been sufficiently competent in the management of his own finances. He increased his private holdings from £500 in 1700 to £1000 in 1718 to £7500 in 1736; by 1738, according to the notice sent to Faulkner, he had a fortune of at least £8000; and by the time of his death, according to Orrery (p. 118) and Faulkner (p. 317), his investments amounted to nearly £11,000.

All this worldly substance which Swift had managed to accumulate went after his death, as he had intended it should, for a charitable use in the public interest. He was justifiably proud that at the same time he was accumulating it, "without any thoughts of hoarding," as he wrote Pope in 1733, he was able to bestow "every year at least one third" of his income on charity (Corres., IV, 154).

The account books, as repositories of daily expenses and ecclesiastical income, do not carry records of such large benefactions, but they are dotted with instances of Swift's small acts of generosity, which everyone who has read them has noticed. Scott stated flatly that more than one tenth of Swift's income went "in acts of liberality and benevolence" (I, 61). Scott's "Gifts and charity extraordinary" is probably the category "Gifts" in the 1702-3 account book. But whether so entered (3, 8, 13) or as "G" under daily expenses or "Extraordinaries" in later books, or under "Sm-- G--ts" in the deanery years (242-4), Gifts are mainly gratuities to servants or presents to close friends. Gratuities to servants were almost required of Swift for services received, whether in Dublin ("P^{vlls} C^{ochmn}," "Uncls mds") (3, 45) or London ("L^{d} T^{r}. Port^{r}") (155).

The gifts to close friends (MD, Mrs. Whiteway, Jackson, Webber) show liberality certainly, but are not quite the sort of charity meant by Hawkesworth and Lyon, who describe Swift's relief of misery as he walked Dublin streets, for which purpose "he constantly kept a Pocket full of all Sorts of Coin, from a Silver six pence or three pence when current to a Crown-piece" (Lyon, p. 151). And indeed many gifts of this kind can be found over the years in the account books, from "poor womn 2^{s} 8^{d}½ June 1703 (13) to "Old wom^{n} broke leg. 2^{s} 8^{d}½" in July 1735 (245), with many of the smaller denominations of coins scattered in between ("G. 3^{d}" and "G. 6^{d}," &c). "Sm-- G--ts," spread over three pages in 1734-5, are entered by months, and one can find "Sac^{rt} 1^{s} 1^{d}" (in a variety of abbreviations) or sometimes just "1^{s}. 1^{d}" recurring on days which turn out to be Sundays--"my usuall Shilling," as Swift says in the records of cathedral collections of money for the poor, records which carry other evidence of Swift's private charity (297). Lyon's final reckoning of cathedral money distributed to the poor from 1730 to 1742 shows the poor in debt to the dean £2 10s 8d (309).

The most remarkable and enlightened instances of Swift's benevolence, we might think today, would be his loans of money to people in need. The small amounts of "industrious money" to tradespeople at low rates of interest began early; a possible instance is on 23 May 1703: "Re^{cd} (and lent in part)"; the sums, under £10, are too small to have been more formal loans (28, 32). The system was still in operation in his last days (BL. Add. MSS 38671, f 18^{r}). When his income was larger, he was always willing to lend £50 to £1000 to friends in distress--Mr. Brent, Jo Beaumont, Stafford Lightburne, Thomas Sheridan--or an "immense" sum to his young cousin Deane Swift, never repaid in Swift's lifetime. Swift was able to encompass all this and still accomplish his greatest benefaction, the establishment after his death of St. Patrick's Hospital with money he had saved, the "little wealth he had."

25. The Ecclesiastical Landlord

"Although Tythes be of Divine institution they are of diabolical execution"

Perhaps the most striking evidence of Swift's financial competence is his management of the ecclesiastical holdings in his keeping. In spite of "the Miseryes of this Country," the steady decline in value of the tithes of his livings, and the fluctuations of deanery returns, he left his holdings in better condition than he found them.

The account books support Swift's frequent laments about the decline in value of his tithes and the increasing difficulty of collecting them. Though records are spotty, those we have show how much tithes of both livings and deanery diminished over the years and what proportion of them were actually paid, and they also show the improvements Swift brought about in his ecclesiastical earnings.[35]

During the first years of Swift's incumbency valuations stayed nearly the same: £230 for 1700 and 1701 according to Lyon and Scott; set at £231 for 1702-3 (Laracor/Agher £160 10s, tithes drawn £18 17s 11d, Rathbeggan £52 2s). In no year were all tithes paid. Of the £230 set in 1700 there were arrears of Rathbeggan tithes amounting to £9 15s 7d½ still unpaid as late as November 1704 (56); nor is there anything to show that they were ever paid.

In 1701-2, when Scott reports from the account book a tithe valuation of £230, many tithes went unpaid. Arrears of £10 15s 4d from Rathbeggan tithes, set for £50, were still due in 1704, a 20% default, and £1 8s 6d was owing from Laracor. As with the 1700 tithes, there is no reason to believe that these arrears were ever paid.[36]

The amount set for the three livings in 1702-3 comes to £231 10s 11d. This year, as in others, a portion of the tithes were never collected: Laracor/Agher had £7 18s 6d in arrears still outstanding as late as November 1704 (56); £17 due "in hay" was never accounted for; and tithes drawn from Readstown/Stokestown were not cleared until November 1709 (26, 30). During the current year, by 1 November 1703 77% of the tithes set were collected (£178; 26, 30, 32); ultimately 89% were. And yet this year, the first Swift had spent entirely in Ireland since receiving his livings, he was paying close attention to

---

[35] In the years before Swift received the livings, we know of two valuations of the worth of his union of parishes. In 1654 the Civil Survey valued Laracor at £210, Agher at £10, and Rathbeggan at around £10 for a total of just about £230, the amount set for the union in the early 1700's (Civil Survey, pp. 384, 386, 401). But Stearne in his 1697 revision of the State of the Diocese of Meath set the value of Rathbeggan at £20, Agher at £20, Laracor at £80, for a total of £120, far too low a total to be credible (ML, pp. 145, 146, 147).

[36] In every year, as valuation sank, ecclesiastical charges and maintenance costs remained constant and had to be met out of diminishing receipts. It is not surprising that, just as tithes were never all collected in a current year, so annual charges were never all paid in a current year. They were most fully met in 1708-9, but even then the curate's fourth quarter salary had not been fully paid by the close of the account book year.

his collections. Rathbeggan tithes were entirely cleared, with unusual promptness, by September 1704; deliveries in cash reached him twice and sometimes three times a month throughout the year.

In 1703-4 the valuation of Swift's livings shows the first decline. The setting of this year's tithes at £217 2s may have been realistic; arrears outstanding are lower than for any year of which we have record. By the end of 1704 90% had been collected (£194; 50, 52, 54); ultimately (April 1706) 97% was. Rathbeggan was completely cleared by 12 April 1705 (52); Laracor/ Agher was only £3 3s 4d in arrears on 22 December 1705; and tithes drawn were lacking only £3 11s by 18 April 1706 (54).

In 1708-9 tithes were set still lower: £204 5s 6d. The percentage of collections also declined: 73% collected in 1709 (£149; 90, 92); 80% by March 1710. The fifth still in arrears--£41 6s 4d--was probably never paid.

Between 1700 and 1708 we can see, then, that the value of Swift's tithes declined about 11% from £230, and the percentage of total collections decreased, also roughly 11%, from about 90% to 80%. We know from sources other than the account books that, in spite of some fluctuations, tithes continued to be valued at lower rates than over subsequent years. Parvisol set them for 1709-10 at £60 lower than for 1708-9 (£154). "Comfortable news that," Swift wrote Stella 26 October 1710. The agent was encouraged to set them higher in following years; in 1714 Swift hopes that he has set them at not less than £200 (Corres., II, 30).[37] Lyon, correcting Faulkner, set Swift's total ecclesiastical income in 1713 at £900 (Lyon, p. 317); he elsewhere values the deanery in 1713 at £700, making his valuation of the livings in 1713 £200.

Thereafter we know only that the Laracor as distinct from Rathbeggan lands were set at £82 in 1715, at £84 in 1716 (Corres., II, 230, 241, 242). The sketchy 1717-8 record of tithes from Laracor and Rathbeggan lands shows £113 realized in the current year and £15 subsequently for a total of £128. On 9 February 1717, when Swift purchased Nealstown glebeland, he valued Laracor union at £126 (Landa, pp. 36, 40). This means that the value of Laracor union tithes had dwindled from £230 in 1700 to £126 in 1717, a drop of 55%. From then on no records of tithe values from Swift's livings are available.

Swift set about reversing the sinking value of his Laracor union in 1717-8. We have already considered his purchase in 1717 of the 20 acres of Nealstown glebeland, with £200 First Fruits Fund money, and his improvement of the land with money out of his own pocket. The following year he purchased, with his private funds, the "impropriate tyths of the parish and rectory of Effernock" from the Rev. Dr. Anthony Raymond of Trim for £150, and £100 more in 1722 (SPH MSS 1F 3F). One would like to know how much these tithes increased the total returns from Laracor. In any case, in his customary way, Swift had strengthened the church property entrusted to him for the benefit of his successors.

---

[37] Swift's complaint to John Temple, 15 June 1706, "My little Revenue is sunk two Parts in three, and the third in Arrear," may not be as exaggerated as it at first appears. If Parvisol had set tithes as low in 1706 as he did in 1710, the proportion is accurate, as "two Parts in three" of £230 is £154.

* * * *

The value of deanery tithes fluctuated during Swift's time as Dean of St. Patrick's, with a marked drop in the thirties. In 1713 Parvisol set them for £430. Swift told Walls on 1 October that he had "hoped it would have amounted to near five hundred pounds." In 1717-8, when he was changing land agents and had no rent roll, the amount for which deanery tithes were set is never stated. But, acting as his own manager, he realized £393 15s 1d by mid-November, £440 11s by July 1719, and eventually £458 (199), the highest reported amount of deanery tithes set or collected.

The lowest setting of deanery tithes given is in 1732-3: they amount to about £375 (227-239), including names "Out of the Alphabet" and an estimated £5 for "Tyths drawn without notice." Collections were slow during the year: only £155 4s 6d½ by November 1733 (41%); a year later, by November 1734, £268 17s 5d (something over 71%); and by 28 June 1735 £311 12s 7d (83%). Ultimately, according to an undated entry (226), £353 15s had been received (94%).

Tithes were set somewhat higher in 1734-5: £396 10s, including "disputed" tithes and "Names that gave no Bonds" (270-84). Collection records, however, are scanty. Figures amounting to £223 are recorded by 7 February 1735 (284), but this includes an unspecified part of Rathbeggan collections; £40 more came in from the agent before his dismissal; thereafter £47 by December 1735, virtually within the current fiscal year. Thus something under £330 in deanery tithes was collected, the smallest amount recorded.

A scrappy listing for 1735-6 (317) shows that £315 12s was collected in deanery tithes during 1736, £343 6s 5d by 22 January 1737.

It is therefore understandable that Swift's complaints to his friends about deanery tithe collections should be most vociferous in the thirties. "All my revenues that depend on tythes are sunk almost to nothing," he writes to Gay, 3 October 1732, and to Ford on the 14th, "I can hardly get . . . a peny of Tythes." We have no record of the 1731-2 tithes, to which Swift would be referring at this time, but no collections of 1732-3 tithes came in until May 1733 and then only £35, no more thereafter until 9 November 1733; probably the situation had been no better in 1731-2. His despondency always seems to seize him in the autumn, when tithes of the current year should begin to come in but do not, and when he is closing the book on the shabby records of the year just ending. During the next three years, to separate correspondents--Ford, 20 November 1733; Arbuthnot, November 1734; and Oxford, 2 September 1735--he reiterates his lament that because of "the miserable oppressions of this Kingdom," his revenues from tithes and rents, but chiefly from tithes, are sunk £300.

In his letter to Oxford, Swift added, "yet with good Management I still make a shift to keep up; and am not poor, nor even moneyless." By good management he had indeed improved the state of his church economy. He left deanery tithes in nearly as healthy a state as he had received them. One means he used to strengthen the base of his deanery tithes is illustrated by his withholding some tithes from the lease of the lands of Deans Rath when he renewed it in 1720. The tithes Parvisol had rated at £430 in 1713 were valued by Swift and Lyon at £420 in 1742 (or £400 after £20 for charges had been deducted) (Landa, "Deanery," p. 164).

As to his deanery lands, Swift's problem was the low rate at which they had been leased when he received them rather than decline or fluctuation. He always considered deanery land rents a certain income, even though the account book record shows payments overdue by a year or more. He wrote Walls, 1 October 1713, "As to the land-rents, they are one hundred and seventy-four pounds a year in the country . . . and I am in no pain about them, because they are sure." Over the years he managed to increase the rent on his two properties whenever he renewed leases.

Swift's strong beliefs about leasing church lands for long periods or accepting fines without increasing rents, as the cost of living rose and the value of money declined, are well known; they are to be found in letters, in angry marginalia on deanery leases at St. Patrick's, in his writings, and in his will. The renewing of the leases of the Kildare and Dublin lands shows his principles in practice.

When Swift became dean, Mr. Deacon, then tenant of Kilberry near Athy in co Kildare, paid him "only £120," although, at Swift's estimate, the lands were worth £475 (Corres., II, 155). (When Lyon says that Swift "found ye lands let at 60 or 70£ a year only" [Lyon, p. 152], the reference must be to a semiannual rent.) The rent was paid through Edward Smith, Bishop of Down, formerly dean of St. Patrick's (1695-9), an inconvenience which is mentioned several times in Swift's business letters to Walls in 1715-7 (Corres., II, 172, 243, 263, 269, 270). Even after he increased Kilberry rent to £150 in 1717, Swift had to receive them through the Bishop, as the "State of my affairs" shows (316). Bishop Smith died in October 1720. Deacon the tenant was still in arrears with his rent in 1725, but at least he paid it directly to Swift (Corres., III, 238).

Leases at St. Patrick's Cathedral show that the rent in 1695 was £100, in 1710 £120. "After this," according to Mason, "Dean Swift encreased the rent as follows: in 1717 to 150£; in 1731 to 170£; and in 1741 to 200£" (Mason, p. 27, n h). J. Stopford, Esq. leased the land in 1731 at the higher rental: "a years rent for Michlmas 1735" was £170 (288). The lease was renewed in 1741.[38]

> The Lands & Tithes of ye Manor of Kilberry & Cloney near Athy in ye Co: of Kildare yield now p[er] Ann: £200--N: The Lease was renewed from March 25: 1741 to J: Stopford Esq And 400£ paid as a Fine. Mr Stopford owns these Lands to be worth to him 500£ p[er] Ann. (Landa, "Deanery," p. 163)

Swift was never able to get the annual rent of Kilberry up to the value of the £475 he had estimated it to be worth in 1714, although his estimate was quite accurate, as Stopford's admission proves. But in the course of twenty-eight years he had been able to raise the rent £80 and, according to Mason, from 1742 until 1820 it was increased only £10 more.

---

[38] Hawkesworth recounts that a "Tenant of one certain lease" urged Swift "a very short time before the Dean lost his Memory," to accept a large fine instead of raising the rent. But Swift was true to his principles and, Lyon noted, "did accordingly, in 1741 raise ye Rent of said lands near Athy in Co of Kildare from 170£ to 200£ a year" (Lyon, p. 152). Evidently the £400 Swift accepted was not considered "a large fine" by either Swift or Lyon.

The co Dublin lands of Deans Rath and Priestown, 357 acres near Clondalkin, which in 1713 Swift had found leased to Benson, Archdeacon of Kildare, at the shockingly low rental of £54 per annum, also had their lease renewed three times during Swift's incumbency, and each time the rent was raised. On 25 March 1720, when Swift leased the land to the Archdeacon's widow, Alice Benson, he raised the rent to £70 and was able to reserve, for the last eleven years of the lease, thirty-seven acres of Priestown "to be at the Dean's disposal" (Mason, p. 26, n d). In 1730 her rent was increased to £80 a year: Swift has slipped a reminder to himself in his 1737 list of private investments that "Mrs Bensons lease has seven years just expired Mar 25. 1737" (312). Alderman Pearson, the tenant in 1735, paid the increased rent, £40 for a half year to Michaelmas 1735 (288); he was still the tenant in 1742 and paid the £90 rent rate.

> The Lands of Dean Rath, Priest Town, Ballibane & Angerstown containing 357 Acres near Clondolkan yield p[er] Ann. £90. This Lease was renewed from 25: Decr 1740 And £ was paid by way of Fine. N: B: Mr Pearson the Tenant pays 20^s^ p[er] Acre for these Lands. (Landa, "Deanery," p. 164).

As with the deanery lands near Athy, Swift never got the rents on his Deans Rath land up to the value he had placed on them. But during his time as dean he did raise them from £54 to £90 and managed to retain for the use of the dean part of the acreage and tithes. From 1742 to 1820, Mason reports, the rent remained the same.

Deanery groundrents. "Rents adjoining to the deanery," like land-rents, are recorded only in the 1734-5 account book (288). Swift's problem with them when he assumed the deanery would seem to have been the scarcity of information. After he had examined cathedral records, he wrote Walls, 13 October 1713, that they were worth "about two pounds ten shillings . . . I forgot five pounds a-year for the verger's house."

The former sum is the modest rent Morgan was paying in 1734 and probably refers to his lease. The house may have been the "small Tenement somewhat ruinous now in Deanery Lane or Mitre Ally worth £3 p[er] Ann." listed by Lyon in 1742; if so, the rent had been slightly raised.

The "verger's house" was the Residentiary House, the lease of which Swift renewed in 1721 to the Chapter of St. Patrick's for £5 in return for a lease of chapter land near St. Kevin's Church which became Naboth's Vineyard. The exchange was beneficial to the deanery. Swift spent a considerable sum of his own money in developing it--the "cursed wall" alone cost him over £600. He paid £3 a year to the chapter for the ground; his trustees were able to lease Naboth's Vineyard in 1743 for four times that sum (Landa, "Deanery," p. 168). Swift included the lease of the "House now inhabited by Henry Land [sexton], in Deanry-Lane alias Mitre-alley" in his will (PW, XIII, 153), and Lyon noted in 1742 "The Residentiary House yields £5 which is paid by ye Proctor of ye Oeconomy."

Evidently no cathedral records were found by Swift in 1713 of the more substantial holdings leased to Goodman and Connly in 1735 for £10 and £9 per annum. The Goodman and Connly houses may not have been there in 1713; Swift's bequests of the leases of the holdings in his will says that the two houses of Goodman's are "lately built." Nor was there any record of another house mentioned by Lyon in 1742 in lease to Worrall at £5 per annum--no doubt the house where Bettesworth found Swift in 1732. The fact that Worrall's name does not appear among the 1734-5 payers of groundrent may mean that Swift forgave him his rent in return for extra services rendered by the Dean's Vicar, or Worrall may simply have been delinquent in his payment. From Swift's mention of length of leases in his will and Lyon's record of them in 1742 we know that the leases of Goodman, Connly, and Worrall had all run since 1732.

In any case the "Rents adjoining to the deanery," valued by Swift in 1713, according to records he then found, at £7 10s, were worth £32 by 1732; that is the sum Swift should have received in 1734-5. Not counting the benefit to the deanery after 1742 by Naboth's Vineyard, he left them in better order than he found them and at an increased figure.

Under Swift's management, then, deanery rents rose steadily as leases were renewed. Rents worth £174 in 1713 had increased nearly 45% when Swift wrote Pope, 2 May 1730, "All my comfort is, that I have 250. a year which I receive from lands of above three times the value"; the amount is made up of £170 for Kilberry lands from Stopford and £80 from Pearson for Deans Rath and is what Swift should have received in 1735. They were worth £290 in 1742. Groundrents had risen from a recorded £7 10s to £32. If the increases seem moderate, it was partly because Swift believed all such increases must be "by degrees"; as he wrote Barber, 30 March 1737, "Although my own Lands as Dean be let for four fifths under their Value, I have not raised them a sixth part in twenty three years, and took very moderate fines." Nevertheless, total deanery income, about which Swift had asked Stella 23 April 1713--"except the Deanry be worth more than 400<u>ll</u> a year; is it?"--had been brought up in value from the £700 it was then actually worth to £800 in spite of the misery of the country.

Account book records of deanery land rentals are scanty, limited as they are to the last page of the last book. Records of tithes received from livings and deanery are abundant and rich in detail. Both remind readers how much Swift drew on his own experience for the vivid detail he put into his writings from 1710 to 1735 in support of clerical income. He was proud of his knowledge of tithes and leases of church lands and readily shared that knowledge with other churchmen. By extension he used it to protect all Irish ecclesiastical landlords in their letting of leases and the management of their livings, arguing against their being forced to settle for a modus or to relinquish their tithes of pasturage. He wrote as a scholar of church history and a theoretical economist of leasing and tithing practices. But telling strokes in all such writings reveal the man drawing on personal experience of the delays, inconveniences, and injustices inevitable under the tithing system: "the whole System of <u>teazing</u>, <u>perplexing</u>, and <u>defrauding</u> the <u>Proctor</u>, or his <u>Master</u>, being as well known to every <u>Plowman</u>, as the reaping or sowing of his Corn, and much more artfully practised" (1723, <u>PW</u>, IX, 59); the bishop's "whole Business is once a Year to receive the Attendance, the Submission, and the Proxy-Money of all his Clergy, in whatever Part of the Diocese he shall please to think most convenient for himself" (1732, <u>PW</u>, XII, 192); the receipt by the clergy of "little more than one half of their legal Dues; not including the Charges they are at in collecting or bargaining for them . . . with great Defalcations, and in very bad Payments" (1734, <u>PW</u>, XIII, 100).

To such defrauding, inconvenience, and bad payments the account books bear discouraging witness.

26. Cathedral Records

The record of collections of "Poor money" covers a period of little more than three years, from February 1739 to April 1742 (295-305). Swift totalled the columns on the first three pages, and Lyon added up (not quite accurately) the column for the last half of 1740 and the figures on each of the pages for 1741-2. He entered his results along with Swift's totals on a blank page (300) and arrived at a grand total of £63 18s 11d. This he transferred to a small leaf of paper, Forster 512A (307), where he added it to a total of collections made between 1730 and February 1738, obviously taken from earlier collection records at the cathedral. The total came to £259 10s 8d½.

The collections for the poor at St. Patrick's were often disappointing, and Swift occasionally comments on them: "Poor Collection a Trifle," "Miserable doings," and, sarcastically, "A noble Collection." At certain times they improve, rising to above a pound on special ecclesiastical holidays, such as the Archbishop's Visitation, Whit Sunday, Ordination, Christmas, and Easter. Some signs of confusion appear--"I guess," "Some mistake," and entries on the wrong page--but the writing is strong and clear right through the final entry in April 1742 (305).

The record of disbursements to the poor of the Liberty covers just under three years, 25 March 1739 to 20 December 1741 (291-4). Nowhere are the distributions added up. Swift sometimes refers, pretending exasperation, to his assistants: "I was Worryed by Mr Lyon to give more," "by the pernicious vice and Advice of my daily Spunge and Inmate Will's Son," "<u>Hang</u> <u>Alba</u> <u>Via</u> for Blundring." A few notes about additional charities are entered on other pages, sometimes intruding into the collections: "Poor Mony to other Persons besides ye list," "Given to an honest Man one Luke," "Given at the Request of Mrs Ridgeway to a poor Family."

On another blank page (302) Lyon recorded considerable sums of money spent for Christmas clothing during seven years between 1729 and 1739; the information came from vouchers in the cathedral records and are not mentioned elsewhere in Swift's records. The sums amounted each year to ten or eleven pounds, all together totalling £68 14s 5d. Lyon added the clothing money to similar disbursements between 1739 and October 1742 and entered the total on the sheet of paper that is now Forster 512A, where other distributions of money to the poor are also added in. Part of the heading of the page has been torn off, but we can read that it included "Mony Disbursed" for "Cloathing" for "poor Boys" (308); it faced the page recording collections for 1730 to 1742.

Lyon was preparing a balance sheet, carrying the date "Octob^r^ 1742" (307), no doubt a part of the task, assigned to him by the Lunacy Commission in the autumn of 1742, of cataloguing all Swift's credits and debits. When he first subtracted the disbursement total from the collections total "Octob^r^ 1742," there seemed to be a "balance still due to ye Poor." But later, more "Vouchers being found," he added in money distributed by Kendrick and Worrall and an apprentice fee so that in the final balance the poor are in debt to the Dean £2 19s 8d. This amount must represent Swift's own contributions from his private purse. Other instances of his personal generosity appear: "I give 20 Shillings," "No Collection in the Church, but I gave" 2s 8d½, "10 Shillings more of my own," "I added my usuall Shilling."

PRINCIPLES OF EDITING

The transcripts of the account books are given as nearly as possible, except for the unavoidable differences between the typewriter and the pen, as they left Swift's hand. No editorial matter appears on any page. We have even made an effort to set the text on the page as Swift did, though he has often so crowded his entries and so huddled them at the top of the page that any rigid attempt at imitation would sacrifice readability.

As would be expected in a book of accounts, corrections are frequently made: entries crossed out and moved elsewhere, "not yet p^{d}" or "not settled" struck out, words rewritten for clarity, columns re-added. Swift draws lines through an original letter, digit, word, or phrase, once through an entire page (195); sometimes he draws loops over them or smudges them out. These scratchings out never indicate an attempt at concealment, as in the <u>Journal to Stella</u>; usually the cancelled word or phrase remains quite legible. Often a correction is written above or beside the cancellation; occasionally it is inked in directly over a word. Since it is not possible to reproduce any of Swift's means of cancellation, we have placed excised material in angle brackets, something Swift himself never used. Material included in these brackets is always to be understood as eliminated by Swift himself. Square brackets and parentheses, though not common, are Swift's own. Mere corrections of faulty arithmetic are not indicated.

When angle brackets enclose an empty space, it means that we have been unable to decipher the crossed-out material and have not attempted a guess. This usage occurs on pp. 2 (twice), 16, 32, 56, 103, 108 (twice), 132, 153, 155, 208, 263, 265 (twice), 287, 293, 317, and 318.

Swift's normal writing is large and easily legible, but in the account books he often saved space by abbreviating drastically, crowding entries against each other and using a tiny script. We have not always, in consequence, been able to read an entry. Rather than calling attention on the page to our difficulty, it has seemed wise to us to put down what the individual letters appear to be, though the resulting word may be nonsense. We have not pointed out such words, but the omission of them from the concordance will identify them.

For easier reading, Swift's practice of turning the books over to enter his Accounts of Livings has not been observed. The folio numbers at the bottom of the pages should make the original arrangement clear.

The account books, cathedral records, and statement of debts and mortgages are all in Swift's hand with the following exceptions:

35 - "Dean Swift's Memorandum Book"

85 - ("40 p.)" [probably not by Swift]

141 - "Mr Ridge dyed 8th. March 1709 of an Apoplexy. He left" [Lyon's hand]

290 - Note in Lyon's hand

294 - "Feb^{ry} 8 Ditto - - - 9 - 9 [Mrs. Whiteway's hand]

295 - "Entered by the Dean" [Lyon's hand]
300 - First line in Swift's hand; other figures by Lyon
302 - Whole page in Lyon's hand
303 - "6 - 5 - 7" [Lyon's hand]
304 - "5 - 19 - 11" [probably Lyon's hand]
305 - "6 - 7 - 8½" [Lyon's hand]
307 - Whole page in Lyon's hand
308 - Whole page in Lyon's hand
309 - Whole page in Lyon's hand

Account

From Nov^{br}. 1st. 1702

to

Nov^{br}. 1st. 1703

Law

ec br.. 1st. 1702. Delamer for Answr. & Clk - - -	0 - 14- 7
--2 Tavrn with Attorny, 1s. 6d. Coch. 9d - - -	0 - 2 - 3
Janry 15 Attorneys bill of Cost - - -	2 - 0 - 0
	2 - 16- 10
Mar. 16. 170$\frac{2}{3}$ to Mr Skelton for writts &c - - -	0 - 10- 2

Besides Parvisols Account

Lost		Won	
Since Novbr 1st abt 10s. - - -	0-10-0	Febr. 11. Ombre < > pd - -	2-10-0
Febr. 10. Pickt with Mr Percvl	0- 8-6	--12 Picket < > pd - -	0-16-6
May. 21. Pickt Percvll - - -	0- 4-0	Apr. 16. Ombr. at King's -	0- 2-8½
Novbr 29. Ombre B Cloghr - - -	0- 4-6	--17 Pickt wth Dr Strn - -	0- 1-9
	1- 7-0		3-10-11½

Mdm

Thursd. Novbr. 11 1703 ^1704 I went to sea, landed in Engld on < Saterd > 13. 1703

Tuesd. May. 29 I went to sea, landed in Ireld. on Thurd. Jun. 1. 1704

First Quarter

From Nov^{br}. 1st. 1702. to Febr. 1st. 170$\frac{2}{3}$.

JB

Dec^{br}. 31 Remains after clearing last year - - - 0-15-6

Servant.

Jan^{ry}. 14. A years wages & 10^{s} over to Rogue Jo^{n}. Kemp - - - 4-10-0
31st. 10 days wages . to J^{on} - tother Rogue - - - 0-2 -3
4-12-3

Cloaths.

Dec^{br}. ⟨17. A Rug 4^{s} 6^{d}⟩

Lodging.

A Quar^{tr} end Jan^{ry} 24. 170$\frac{2}{3}$. - - - 3-15-0

Gifts.

Nov^{br}
3 & 5. 6^{d}. - Charity 2^{s} 8^{d} -16. Bil. Sw^{ft}. 2^{s} 4^{d}½. Dec^{br} 3. bill Se^{vll} 1^{s} 1^{d} 0-6-1½
--21. P^{vlls} C^{ochmn} 1^{s}. ^{d}. Sm^{ll}. 6^{d}. 25. Sac^{rnt}. 2^{s}. 8^{d}½ - - - 0-4-2½
Jan^{r}. 4. P^{vlls} C^{omn}. 10^{d}. -14. Musik. 2^{s}. 8^{d}.½. -19. N. B^{rt}. 5^{d}. - - - 0-3-11½
--25. S^{t}. Pat^{rks} X^{mas} box. 2^{s}. 8^{d}.½ - - - 0-2-8½
0-17-0

Shoes. &c.

Nov^{br}. 14. 7 p^{r} Shoes. 1 p^{r} Galoshoes - - p^{d} in part - - 1-12-0

MC

Nov^{br}. 3^{ll}. 14. - - - 1^{ll} 17^{s}. -- 6^{s}. --14. 3^{s} 6-0-0
--20. 2^{ll} - - - 2-0-0
Dec^{br}. 17. 5^{ll} - - - 5-0-0
13-0-0

⟨Linnen⟩

⟨Besides 3 Pistoles for next q^{rtr}⟩

Expences. 1st Month.

Nov^{br}.

1. to 7.	1st Week.	
--2 C^{h}. 7^{d}. -6. Appls 1^{s}. 1^{d}. -Tavern. 1^{s}. 1^{d} - - -		0 -3 -0
--7 Jons bill 6^{s}-10^{d}. B^{d} wags. to -7. 5^{s}. - - -		0-11-10
		0-14-10
	2^{d} Week.	
7. to 14.		
--13. Wine. 1^{s}. J^{ns} bill. 5^{s}. 10^{d}. - - -		0 -6-10
--B^{d} wages. to 21st. 8^{s}. - - -		0 -8 -0
		0-14-10
	3^{d} Week.	
14. to 21.		
--19. Tav^{rn}. 2^{s}. 8^{d}. Sm^{ll}. 4^{d}. -20. C^{ch}, 1^{s}. 2^{d}. - - -		0 -4 -2
--20 J^{ns} bill. book, Coals, plush, penknife, &c Candles - - -		0 -9 -9½
		0-13-11½
	4th. Week.	
21. to 28.		
--21. Co^{ch}. 8^{d}. -22. Sr Cecil. 9^{s}. 3^{d}. - - -		0 -9-11
--28. Jon's bill. 2^{s}-3^{d}.½. - - -		0 -2 -3½
		0-12 -2½
	Rem^{dr}.	
28. to. D^{cr}. 1st.		
--Board wages. to De^{cbr}. 5th. 8^{s}. J^{ns} bill. 1^{s}. - - -		0 -9 -0

1st. - 0 - 14 - 10
2^{d}. - 0 - 14 - 10
3^{d}. - 0 - 13 - 11½
4th. - 0 - 12 - 2½
R^{dr}. - 0 - 9 - 0
3 - 4 - 10

Expences. 2^{d} Month.

Dec^{br}. Rem^{dr}.

1. to. 5.

--Jo^{ns} bill. 5^{s}. 2^{d}. - - -	0 - 5 - 2
	0 - 5 - 2

1st Week

--5. to. 12

--5. B^{d} wags. to -12. 4^{s}. -7. wine. 1^{s}. 1^{d}. - - -	0 - 5 - 1
--11. J^{ns} bill, Coals, Cord, Candles, &c 6^{s}. 4^{d} - - -	0 - 6 - 4
	0 - 11- 5

2^{d} Week.

12. to 19th

J. B^{s} bill. for wash. 10^{s}. - - -	0 - 10- 0
--16. wine. 7^{d}. J^{ns} bill. Coach Trim. Coals &c - - -	0 - 11- 9½
--B^{d} wages. to -19 - 4^{s}. - - -	0 - 4 - 0
	1 - 4 - 9½

3^{d} Week.

19. to 26.

⟨Coach. hire.⟩ At Trim

26 to ⟨31st.⟩ Jan^{r}. 1. Rem^{dr}.

26 Mr Parvis^{lls} bill

For a fortnights Vitt^{ls}, Ale. &c 17^{s}. 8^{d}.½ - - -	0 - 17- 8½

Re^{dr}.	-	0 - 5 - 2
1st	-	0 - 11- 5
2^{d}	-	1 - 4 - 9
Re^{dr}.	-	0 - 17- 8½
		2 - 19- 0½

⟨Memd. Jon's Horse to Trim⟩ --

Expences 3^{d} Month.

Jan^{ry}.	1st Week.	
1. to 9.		
Mr Parvis^{ll} bill for Ale, meat. &c - - -		0 - 9 - 0
--Washing for 3 weeks - - -		0 - 3 - 6
		0 - 12- 6
	2^{d} Week	
9 to 16.		
Jo^{ns} bill. Horses at Inn Candles. &c. 3^{s}. 7^{d}. - - -		0 - 3 - 7
13. Coals. 1^{s}. 5^{d}. s^{mll}. 2^{d}. - - -		0 - 1 - 7
--2 Horses hird frō Trim & man 7^{s}. [owd to Parvis^{ll}] - - -		0 - 7 - 0
--B^{ord} wags to 16. 4^{s}. - - -		0 - 4 - 0
		0 - 16- 2
	3^{d} Week.	
16. to 23.		
Bord wags. to 28. 4^{s}. Sm^{ll}. 6^{d}. Appl. 7^{d}.½ - - -		0 - 5 - 1½
	4th Week.	
23 to 30 & 31st.		
--26. Apples. 7^{d}.½. bord wags to 31. 2^{s}. 4^{d} - - -		0 - 2 -11½
Mans bill 1^{s}. 8^{d}. s^{mll}. 4^{d}. - - -		0 - 2 - 0
Mrs Brents bil, Wash, Lett^{rs}. Silv^{r} pencil: &c - - -		0 - 16- 4
		1 - 1 - 3½
Omitted, and allowd by Mr Parvis to clear debt &c		
Honey 27 quarts. - - -		1 - 3 -10
Wash - - -		0 - 3 - 6
Pages bill. 4^{s}-6^{d} Ale. 6^{s} - - -		0 - 10- 6
		1 - 17-10

1st Week.	0 - 12- 6		
2^{d} Week -	0 - 16- 2	Without the Horse	
3^{d} Week -	0 - 5 - 1½	in all - 4 - 12 - 11	
4th Week -	1 - 1 - 3½		
Omitt^{d} &c -	1 - 17-10		
A Horse -	4 - 5 - 0	A Horse Jan^{ry}. 30th.	4 - 5 - 0
	8 - 17-11		

[3v]

Totals of a Quarter From Nov[br] 1st. 1702
to Feb[r]. 1st $1703\frac{2}{}$

JB - - -	0 - 15- 6
Servant - - -	4 - 12- 3
Lodging - - -	3 - 15- 0
Gifts - - -	0 - 17- 0
Shoes &c. - - -	1 - 12- 0
MC - - -	13 - 0 - 0
Expences 1st Month - - -	3 - 4 -10
Expences 2[d] Month - - -	2 - 19- 0½
Expences 3[d] Month - - -	4 - 12-11
	35 - 8 - 6½
Jan[ry]. 30th. 1702. A Bay Nag bought	4 - 5 - 0
	39 - 13- 6½

⟨Goods⟩

Second Quarter.

From Febr. 1st. 170$\frac{2}{3}$ to May. 1st. 1703

JB

--Apr 30th. (p^{d} May. 7.) - - - 1 - 5 - 0

Servant.

Febr. 15. Shoes. 3^{s}. --13 Stockins. 10^{d}. Apr. 1. Part of wages. 1^{s}. - - 0 - 4 -10

Cloaths.

Febr. 4. Glovs. 1^{s}. 6^{d}. - - - 0 - 1 - 6

Lodging.

2 weeks to Febr. 6. 12^{s} --20. lodg. a week. 5^{s}-1^{d}. - - - 0 - 17- 1

Gifts.

Febr. 1st. M^{argt} 1^{s}. 2^{d}. boy. 4^{d}: --4 Hugh 1^{s} 1^{d} --5. C^{och}m^{n}. 1^{s}. 1^{d}.
--11. G^{rm}. 6^{d}. - - - 0 - 4 - 2
m^{ds} 2^{s}. 2^{d}. --25. God^{ws} man. 1^{s}. 1^{d}. Mar. 1. Un^{cls} 2 men, 2^{s}. 2^{d}.
--4. M^{ry}. 10^{d}. - - - 0 - 6 - 3
8. Pat. 6^{d}.½ --20. Pep^{rs} C^{och}m^{n}. 1^{s}. 1^{d}. --21 Pat. 1^{s}. 1^{d}. --27.
Com^{ns} Perc^{vll}. 9^{d}. Langl^{d} g^{rm}. 6^{d}.½ - - - 0 - 4 - 0
--28. Sac^{mt}. 2^{s}. 8^{d}½ ---31st. Uncle to Valent^{in}. 4^{s}. 3^{d}. Ap. 1. M^{rs}
Perc^{ll}. 4^{d}.½ --6 Coun^{tr}. 4^{d}.½ --MD-- 0 - 7 - 8½
--19. G^{rm}. 1^{s}. 1^{d}. --maid before. 1^{s}. 1^{d} --23. G^{rm}. 4^{d}. --27. N. d^{tr}.
2^{s} 8^{d}½. Pat. 1^{s}. 2^{d}. M^{d}. 2^{s} 8^{d}½ M^{d}. 6^{d}½ - - - 0 - 9 - 7½

1 - 11- 9

Shoes. &c

Apr. 9. Shoes 9^{s}. --old debt - 6^{d}

MC.

Febr. 1st. 3 Pist^{lls}. 2^{ll}-15^{s}-6^{d} --5. 17^{s}. 6^{d} --18. 7^{s}. - - - 4 - 0 - 0
Mar. 15th - 2^{ll} - --20. 17^{s}. 7^{d}½ - - - 2 - 17- 7½
--19 - to make up - - - 0 - 2 - 4½
--Apr. 2^{d}. 2^{ll} --10. 1^{ll}. --16. 1^{ll}-6^{s}-8^{d}. --18. from Mrs B. 13^{s}-4^{d}. - - 5 - 0 - 0

12 - 0 - 0

Horses.

Mar. 1. 6 loads of Hay.^{x} 2^{ll}.-8^{s}. --14. Lard &c 1^{s} 3^{d} mend saddl 9^{d} - - 2 - 10- 0
--18. Oats 1 bar^{ll}. 3^{s}-10^{d}. Straw a Load. 4^{s}. 6^{d}. --Apr. 14. Oats
1 bar. 4^{s}. 8^{d}. - - - 0 - 13- 0
--14. saddl & bridl mend. 1^{s}. 7^{d}. Parv^{lls} s^{mll} Acc^{t} to Apr. 21. 2^{s}. 4^{d} 0 - 3 -11
26 to May. 1. Hair cloth. 1^{s}. bran 4^{d} s^{mll}. 4^{d}½ - - - 0 - 1 - 8½

3 - 8 - 7½

Substract for Hay. 0 - 10- 0 2 - 18- 7½

Expences 1st Month.

Feb^{r}. 1st Week.

1st. to. 6th.

<Horse at Inn>-- brd wags. 1^{s}. 6^{d} --more. 1^{s}. - - - 0 - 2 - 6

6. to 13.

Coach 6^{s} Co^{ch}. 6^{d}½. Sm^{ll} 6^{d}. --9. Orang. cake. 1^{s}.1^{d}. Pats bill. 6^{d} 0 - 8 - 7½

13. to 20.

Hors hire. 3^{s}

--14 <Horse hire> & charges. & Pats batling 3^{s}-6^{d}. - - - 0 - 6 - 6

16. Co^{ch}. 6^{d}. sp^{t}. 6^{d}. - - - 0 - 1 - 0

Mrs Brents bill to --18.

--Dishes & plates. 9^{s}. Glass. 9^{s}. Currycomb. &c. 2^{s}.11^{d}. - - 1 - 0 -11

to Pat. for Sheath 2^{s}. Alm^{ds}. &c. 2^{s}. 1^{d} Lett^{rs}. 1^{s}.3^{d}. Ging^{rbrd}. 9^{d}. - - - 0 - 6 - 1

--Coffee. 7^{s}.6^{d}. Por^{tr}. 4^{d}. ros^{tr}. 3^{s}. sm^{ll}. 8^{d} - - - 0 -11 - 6

2 - 6 - 0

20 to 27.

--23. Co^{ch}. 1^{s}. 7^{d}½ 25. Ale &c. 1^{s}.½ --26. Treat MD. 3^{s}.9^{d} - 0 - 6 - 5

1st. Week	-	0 - 2 - 6
2^{d} Week	-	0 - 8 - 7½
2^{d} Week	-	2 - 6 - 0
4th Week	-	0 - 6 - 5
		3 - 3 - 6½

Mem^{d}. ? Apr 17. 1703.

Advanc^{d} to MC for next ½ y^{r}. 5^{ll}.

May. 4. Advanc^{d} more to MC - - 2^{ll}

Expences 2^{d} Month

March.

1st Week.

1. to 6.

--2. Tavern. 2^{s}.8^{d}½. --3. Co^{ch}. 1^{s}.6^{d}. --Dobson old debt. 9^{s}.6^{d} - -	0 - 13- 8½
--4. Co^{chn} Port^{r}. &c. 1^{s} - - -	0 - 1 - 0
	0 - 14- 8½

2^{d} Week.

6 to 13.

Bord - for Patt. and my own meat &c. from Febr. 4 to Parvis^{ll} to Mar. 14. -1^{ll} 3^{s}.5^{d}. Ale & beer the same 13-8	1 -17 - 1
--Candles 7^{ll} 2^{s}.7^{d}.½. sm^{ll} things. 3^{s}.11^{d}.½ Parvis^{ll} - - -	0 - 7 - 7
Wash - Parvis^{ll} to M^{ar}. 14 4^{s}9^{d} - - -	0 - 4 - 9
	2 - 9 - 5

3^{d} Week

13 to. 20. J B^{s} Bills from Febr. 20. to Mar. 18.

J B's bill. Lddright. 7^{s}. G. 1^{s}. Coals. 5^{s}6^{d}. sm^{ll} 7^{d} Sauce pan 3^{s}.	0 - 17- 1
Coff. pots 1^{s}.5^{d} sm^{ll}. 11^{d} Pou^{dr}. 1^{s}.9^{d} Cand^{l}. 10^{d}. Plates. 6^{s}. baskt. 1^{s}. sm^{ll}. 1^{s}.8^{d} - - -	0 - 13- 7
Sug^{r}. 2^{s}-2^{d} Cups. 4^{s}.8^{d}. sm^{ll}. 1^{s}-1^{d}. wash. 2^{s}-7^{d}.½ - - -	0 - 10- 6½

--15. Co^{ch}. 6^{d}. --18. Co^{ch}. 8^{d}. Co^{ch}. 2^{s}-2^{d} --19. win 1^{s}.1^{d} Co^{ch}. 1^{s}-1^{d} Orang. 4^{d} - - -	0 - 5 -10
--20. Co^{ch}. 6^{d}. sm^{ll}. 3^{d}. --Pats bill, sm^{ll}. 1^{s}.11^{d}. bord wag. 3^{s}.2^{d}.½ - - -	0 - 5 -10½

20 to 27.

Rem^{dr}.

27 to Apr. 1.

30. Pats bill, Inn, Balls, Lard, &c. 1^{s}-10^{d}.½, Oranges 6^{d}.½ - - -	0 - 2 - 5

1st Week	- 0 - 14- 8½
2^{d} Week	- 2 - 9 - 5
3^{d} Week	- 2 - 12-11
Rem^{dr}	- 0 - 2 - 5
	5 - 19- 5½

Mar. 16

A Horse chesn^{t}. - 3 - 15- 8

Expences. 3^{d} Month.

April.
1 to 3^{d}.

--Oranges 6^{d}½ Co^{ch}. 2^{s}.8^{d}.½. Treat 7^{s}.6^{d}.½ uncle L^{dys} &c - - - 0 - 10- 9½
--2. Oystrs 10^{d} -Pap^{r}. 8^{d}. Bord wages. 1^{s}-9^{d} - - - 0 - 3 - 3
0 - 14- 0½

3. to. 10.

--6. 2 Raz^{rs}. 10^{s}. Siz^{rs}. 3^{s}. blade. 1^{s}. with Jons. &c. 4^{s}. 6^{d} - - 0 - 18- 6
--7. Co^{ch}. 1^{s}.5^{d}½ sm^{ll}. 3^{d}. - - - 0 - 1 - 8½
1 - 0 - 2½

10 to 17

12. Pat's bill 2^{s}. ch^{r}. 1^{s}.1^{d}. wine &c. 1^{s}.9^{d}. --14 brush. 2^{d}.½ - - 0 - 5 - 0½
--15. Co^{ch}. 1^{s}-11^{d}. --Per^{wg} 1^{s}. --win. 1^{s}-4^{d} - 17. Brd. wags. 13 days 6^{s}.6^{d} - - - 0 - 10- 9
0 - 15- 9½

17 to 24.

Parvis^{lls} bill for meat &c from Mar. 14 to Apr. 21. - - - 0 - 16- 3½
--to Him for wash the same date - - - 0 - 4 - 6
--Oth^{r} sm^{ll} things. 10^{d}. - - - 0 - 0 -10
1 - 1 - 7½

24. to May. 1.

--29. Co^{ch}. 7^{d}.½. Co^{ch}. 1^{s}.2^{d} --Pats bill. wine. cap 3^{s}.2^{d} - - - 0 - 4 -11½

1st Week	0 - 14- 0½
2^{d} Week	- 1 - 0 - 2½
3^{d} Week	- 0 - 15- 9½
4th Week	- 1 - 1 - 7½
Rem^{dr}	- 0 - 4 -11½
	3 - 16- 7½

JB's bill to May. 1. Lett^{rs}. Cand^{l}. Ging^{rbrd}. sm^{ll} - &c - - - 0 - 8 -10

Mend. JBs bill here to be

Totals of a Quar^tr^. from Febr 1. 170$\frac{2}{3}$ to May. 1. 1703.

JB - - -	1 - 5 - 0
Servant - - -	0 - 4 -10
Cloaths - - -	0 - 1 - 6
Lodging - - -	0 - 17- 1
Gifts - - -	1 - 11- 9
Shoes &c - - -	0 - 9 - 6
MC - - -	12 - 0 - 0
⟨Horses⟩ - - -	
Mar. 16. a Chesnut Horse - - -	3 - 15- 8
Expences. 1st Month - - -	3 - 3 - 6½
Expences 2d Month - - -	5 - 19- 5½
Expences 3d Month - - -	3 - 16- 7½
JB's Bill to May. 1. - - -	0 - 8 -10
	33 - 13- 9½
Charge of Horses this Quartr	2 - 18- 7½
	36 - 12- 5

Third Quar^{tr}

From May. 1. to Aug. 1. 1703

JB

July. 31st - - - 1 - 10- 0

& Hatt. 6^{s} Servt.

May 8. . Wastcoat and Breeches for Patt - - - 1 - 2 - 0

Jun. 24. a Shirt for Patt - - - 0 - 2 - 7½

Wages for ½ year. end. Aug. 2^{d}. substract &c last Givn - - - 1 - 9 - 8½

2 - 14- 4

Cloaths

May--4: Glovs. 3^{s}-10^{d} --June - A Night gown cap & slipper 4^{ll}-12-6^{d} - - - 4 - 16- 4

July. 9th. a Shirt. 7^{s}. --31. Cloth for 4 Shirts & Hol^{d} 1^{ll}-10^{s} - - - 1 - 17- 0

6 - 13- 4

Lodging.

May. 22^{d}. For a q^{rts} Lodging then expired - - - 5 - 0 - 0

Gifts.

May--6 N. B^{rt}. 10^{d}. --16. Sac^{rmt} 2^{s}.8^{d}.½ --26 Tickl. Mn. 2^{s}.8^{d}.½ Jun. 5. 6^{d} --16 m^{d}. 1^{s}.1^{d} - - - 0 - 7 -10

--18. poor womn 2^{s}. 8^{d}.½ --22^{d}. Pat. 1^{s}-1^{d} --25. Dd^{s} box 6^{s} --29. JB 8^{s}.1^{d}.½ - - - 0 - 17-11

Jul. 10. M^{rgt}. 1^{s}-5^{d} --m^{d}. 6^{d}.½ --19. 10^{d} - - - 0 - 2 - 9½

1 - 8 - 6½

Shoes.

July. 1. Shoes a p^{r}. & clearg. 4^{s} & 6^{d}. old d^{bt}. 1^{s}-6^{d} - - - 0 - 6 - 0

MC.

〈Advanc^{d} (Apr. 17) 5^{ll}.〉 May. 4th. 1^{ll}. --8. 1^{ll}. --24. 2^{ll}. Jun. 5. 1^{ll} --12. 3^{ll} - - - 8 - 0 - 0

--25. 1^{ll}. Jul. 3. 1^{ll} --12. 2^{ll}. 24. 16^{s}, aftr. 4^{s} - - - 5 - 0 - 0

13 - 0 - 0

Horses.

to May. 8. 1^{s}-7^{d}. --28. Hay & grass 6^{s}-4^{d} Jun. 5. Grass 5^{s}-2^{d} --12. Grass. 5^{s}-2^{d} - - - 0 - 18- 3

--9. to King for shoing. 4^{s}-6^{d} --21. Grass. 7^{s}. Jul. 24. Grass. 13^{s}.4^{d} - 1 - 4 -10

2 - 3 - 1

Expences 1st Month.

May. 1st Week.

1. to 8.

--6. Co^{ch}. 10^{d}. Sm^{ll}. 2^{d}. Pat's bill 3^{s}. - - - 0 - 4 - 0

2^{d} and 3^{d} Weeks.

8. to 22^{d}.

--23^{d}.

P^{d} M^{r}. Parvis^{lls} fortnights Account ⟨f⟩ and 5 days, from Apr. 21.
to May. 21. for diet. 1^{ll}.2^{s}.6^{d}.½. & wash. 2^{s}-10^{d} - - - 1 - 5 - 4½

22. to 29.

25. Co^{ch}. 6^{d}½ --28. Sm^{ll}. 3^{d}. ⟨--Hay. 1^{s}-1^{d}.⟩ - - - 0 - 0 - 9½

Patts bill & bord wages 4^{s}-9^{d} - - - 0 - 4 - 9

0 - 5 - 6½

1st Week	-	0 - 4 - 0
2^{d} & 3^{d} weeks		1 - 5 - 4½
4th Week, &c	-	0 - 5 - 6½
		1 - 14-11

[7v]

Expences. 2^{d} Month.

June.

⟨1 - to 4⟩

⟨4 to 11⟩ 1 to 4

⟨5. Co^{ch} 6^{d}. Sm^{ll} 2^{d} --7. The Pace 1^{s}-11^{d} --8 Co^{ch}. 6^{d}½. Orang. 6^{d} - - - 0 - 3 - 7½⟩

Patts bill, win 9^{s}1^{d} bord wags 3^{s}. Sug^{r}. 1^{s}-1^{d} sm^{ll}. 3^{d}½ - - - 0 - 13- 8½

⟨11 to 18.⟩ 4 to 11

5. Co^{ch}. 6^{d}. Sm^{ll}. 2^{d}. 7. The Pace 1^{s}.11^{d}. --8. Co^{ch}. 6^{d}.½. Orang. 6^{d} - - 0 - 3 - 7½

Patts bill. Co^{ch}. 1^{s}. cand^{ls}. 10^{d}½ wine 3^{s}.6^{d} bord wag. 3^{s}. &c. in all - - 0 - 10- 1

0 - 13- 8½

11 to 18.

--15. win. 1^{s}-6^{d} - - - 0 - 1 - 6

Patts bill. bord wag. 3^{s}. Pap^{r}. 8^{d}. heel pecing. 4^{d}. &c in all - - - 0 - 4 - 6

0 - 6 - 0

18 to 25. sm^{ll}. 4^{d}. - - - 0 - 0 - 4

--Patts bill. bord wg. 3^{s}-6^{d} &c in all - - - 0 - 5 - 4½

0 - 5 - 8½

25 to 30

--sm^{ll}. 6^{d}.½. Goldsmith for Screw case. 6^{s} - - - 0 - 6 - 6½

Patts bill. Cand^{ls}. 10^{d}.½ &c in all - - - 0 - 2 -10

0 - 9 - 4½

1st Week	-	0 - 13- 8½
2^{d} Week	-	0 - 13- 8½
3^{d} Week	-	0 - 6 - 0
4th Week	-	0 - 5 - 8½
Rem^{dr}	-	0 - 9 - 4½
		2 - 8 - 6

Expences. 3^{d} Month

July.	
1. to 3	
--Win. 10^{d}. Cherrys. $1^{s}.6^{d}$. - - -	0 - 2 - 4
Patts bo^{rd} wags - 3^{s}-6^{d} - - -	0 - 3 - 6
	0 - 5 -10
3. to 10.	
--5. Co^{ch}. 1^{s}-1^{d} --6. $Cher^{ys}$. 1^{s}-1^{d} --7. Co^{ch}. 1^{s}-1^{d}. --8 $Cher^{ys}$. 11^{d} - -	0 - 4 - 2
--Patts bo^{rd} wages 3^{s}-6^{d}. Sm^{ll}. 1^{d} - - -	0 - 3 - 7
	0 - 7 - 9
10. to 17.	
--14. At Leslip - 11^{s} --15. Co^{ch}. 1^{s}-6^{d} --16 Tav^{rn}. 2^{s}-8^{d} - - -	0 - 15- 2
Patt B^{rd} wags. 3^{s}-6^{d} w^{n}. 1^{s}-7^{d} Sug^{r}. 9^{d}½ Co^{ch}. 1^{s}-6^{d} &c in all - - -	0 - 7 - 6
	1 - 2 - 8
17 to 24	
--Co^{ch}. 6^{d} --21. Co^{ch}. 1^{s}-3^{d} --22 At Ringsend. 8^{s}-1^{d} - - -	0 - 9 -10
Patts bill. $Cand^{l}$. 10^{d}.½ Co^{ch}. 1^{s}. B^{rd} wag^{s}. 3^{s} &c in all - - -	0 - 5 - 2½
	0 - 15- 0½
24. to 31.	
31. $Parvis^{lls}$ bill from May 21 to Aug. 1st. A week & odd days < > for Pat &c 4^{s} old debt Horse hire. 4^{s}-3^{d} wash. Ale. 2^{s}. $Lett^{rs}$ &c -	1 - 3 - 6
JB^{s} bill From May 1st to Aug. 1. Coffee, Combs, $Poud^{r}$, Hat mnd, basin &c - - -	1 - 13- 6
JB more for wash ugly Slutt to. Aug. 1 - - -	0 - 6 -11
	3 - 3 -11

Rem^{dr}	- 0 - 5 -10
1st Week	- 0 - 7 - 9
2^{d} Week	- 1 - 2 - 8
3^{d} Week	- 0 - 15- 0½
4th Week	- 3 - 3 -11
	5 - 15- 2½

Totals of a Quarter From May 1st
to Aug. 1st. 1703

JB - - -	1 - 10- 0
Servant - - -	2 - 14- 4
Cloaths - - -	6 - 13- 4
Lodging - - -	5 - 0 - 0
Gifts common - - -	1 - 8 - 6½
Shoes - - -	0 - 6 - 0
MC - - -	13 - 0 - 0
Horses - - -	2 - 3 - 1
Expences 1st Month - - -	1 - 4 -11
Expences 2d Month - - -	2 - 8 - 6
Expences 3d Month - - -	5 - 15- 2½
	42 - 3 -11

Fourth Quarter.

From Aug. 1st. 1703 to Nov^{br}. 1st. 1703

JB.

Octbr. 1^{s}. 18^{s}-6^{d}. Oct^{br}. 31st. --Cleard the year. 1-11^{s}-0   2 - 9 - 6

Servant.

Aug.
3^{d} --B^{d} w. 1^{s}. to 14. brd w. 3^{s}-6^{d}. - - -   0 - 4 - 6
Septr.1. p^{r} of Shoes for Hugh. 4^{s}. - - -   0 - 4 - 0
0 - 8 - 6

Cloaths, Shoes, Linnen, &c.

Aug. 26. 2 Colrd Hank^{fs}. 5^{s}. Sept. 28. mend Perewigs. 6^{s}-11^{d}. - - -   0 - 11-11
Oct^{br}. 16. Shoes, 2 p^{r}. 9^{s}. old debt. 2^{s}. Breeches. 11^{s}-5^{d}. Scald. 1^{s}-8^{d}.   1 - 4 - 1
1 - 16- 0

Lodging.

Aug. 24. To Mrs Fel^{tr} for a Qu^{r} end^{g}. Aug. 22. 1703 - - -   5 - 0 - 0
Lodg. at Fingl. 4^{s}. . Oct^{br}. 5. Lodg. 6^{s}. --18. 8^{s}. 3 weeks

MC.

Aug. 2. 1^{ll}. --9. 18^{s}-6^{d} --13. 18^{s}-6^{d}. --28. 18^{s}-6^{d} 3 - 15- 6
Sept^{br}. 13. 4^{ll}. --18. 6^{s}. Oct^{br}. 11. 18^{s}-6^{d}. --18. 1^{ll} < >   6 - 4 - 6
--28. 1^{ll} --1^{ll} - - -   2 - 0 - 0
12 - 0 - 0

Horses.

Horses.

Aug. 7. Grass. 5^{s}-3^{d}. Smith. 3^{d}. Grass. 9^{d} --12. mend. Brid^{ls}. 1^{s}-5^{d} <Grass>- - -   0 - 7 - 8
--28 Grass. 4^{s}-11^{d}: Sept^{br}. 18. Grass 4^{s}-9^{d}. mend. Sad^{l}. 2^{s}. being Geld. 2^{s}. - - -   0 - 13- 8
Pages. bill. from Febr. to. Aug. 16. 1^{ll}-0-2^{d}. Sept. 21. a bridle. 1^{s}-10^{d} 1 - 2 - 0
Octbr. 2. Grass. 5^{s}-2^{d} --14. mend saddl. 1^{s}8^{d} -a Coller. 1^{s}. - - -   0 - 7 -10
--24 Graz^{ng} at Laracor. in all. 1-2^{s}-4. Oats. 3 bush. 1^{s}-9^{d}. s^{mll}. 8^{d} -   1 - 4 - 9
3 - 15-11

Expences

1st Month

August.

1st Week.

1st to 7.

--2^{d}. Sp^{t}. 7^{d} G. 4^{d}. Sm^{ll}. 2^{d} --5. Sp^{t}. 3^{d} --Co^{ch} 6^{d} - - - 0 - 1 -10

--6 old debt for wine. 1^{s}-5^{d} - - - 0 - 1 - 5

0 - 3 - 3

7 to 14.

--Coffee. 1^{s}. ⟨B^{rd} wag. $3^{s}6^{d}$⟩ --11. $Powd^{r}$. ⟨potts⟩ 4^{d} - - - 0 - 1 - 4

14 to 21

--14. G. H. $6^{d}½$. - - - 0 - 0 - 6½

21. to 28.

--24. G. $Marg^{t}$. 10^{d}. Co^{ch}. 6^{d}.½. G. 2^{d} - - - 0 - 1 - 2½

--26 Sm^{ll}. 3^{d}. Tav^{rn}. 1^{s}-9^{d}. - - - 0 - 2 - 0

0 - 3 - 6½

28 to 31.

--Sm^{ll}. 6^{d}. --30 Co^{ch}. $6^{d}½$. Sm^{ll}. 2^{d}. - - - 0 - 1 - 2½

--31. Sp^{t}. 4^{d}. Sm^{ll} 1^{d} - - - 0 - 0 - 5

0 - 1 - 7½

1st Week	- 0 - 3 - 3
2^{d} Week	- 0 - 1 - 4
3^{d} Week	- 0 - 0 - 6½
4th Week	- 0 - 3 - 6½
$Remaind^{r}$	0 - 1 - 7½
	0 -10 - 3½

JB

JB

JB JB JB

JB

J J JB

B

Expences. 2^{d} Month

September.

1st Week.

1st to 4th.
--2. Tav^{rn}. 1^{s}-2^{d}. G. for Tettys table book. 12^{s}. - - - 0 - 13- 2

4. to 11. ----- -----
---- ----

11 to 18.
--13. G.$_{\wedge}$uncles m^{d}. 1^{s}-1^{d} Co^{ch}. 1^{s}-6^{d}. --16. treat MD. 2^{s}-8^{d}.½ sm^{ll}. 4^{d}. - - - 0 - 5 - 7½

18. to 25.
21. Mr Parvis^{lls} House bill, from Aug. 1. Hughs dyet 9^{s}.
wash. 4^{s}-8^{d} treating Mrs Wesly. &c. --and dyet &c - - - 1 - 17- 5½

<--28. G. 5^{d}.>

25. to 30.
--28. G. 5^{d}. . treat. 4^{s} - - - 0 - 4 - 5

Hughs bill. Brd wages 12 days. 6^{s} - &c - - - 0 - 10- 2½
0 - 14- 7½

1st Week	-	0 - 13- 2
2^{d} Week	-	0 - 0 - 0
3^{d} Week	-	0 - 5 - 7½
4th Week	-	1 - 17- 5½
Rem^{dr}	-	0 - 14- 7½
		3 - 10-10½

Expences 3rd Month

Octo^{br}.

1st Week.

1. to 9.
--Coach. 7^{d} G. 1^{s}-1^{d}. --5. Co^{ch}. 1^{s}-1^{d}. --8. Co^{ch}. 1^{s}-6^{d}. - - - 0 - 3 - 8
Hughs bill bord wages 3^{s}-6^{d} &c - - - 0 - 4 - 9
0 - 8 - 5

9. to 16.
11. Oys^{trs} 3^{d}. MD for Coffee. 1^{s}-9^{d}. - - - 0 - 2 - 0
Hughs bill - with bord wags - - - 0 - 3 - 5
0 - 5 - 5

16 to 23
18 Coffee. 4^{s}. Tav^{rn}. 1^{s}-1^{d} Co^{ch}. 1^{s}-1^{d}. --20. G. 1^{s}-1^{d}. - - - 0 - 7 - 3
--Sp^{t}. 2^{d} sm^{ll}. 6^{d} --22. Co^{ch}. 1^{s}-d - - - 0 - 1 - 8
0 - 8 -11

23 to 31st
sal prunll. 8^{d} Lett^{rs}.
P^{d} House bill from Sep^{tbr}. 21. incl. Joury.^ 3^{s}. Sm^{ll}. 1^{s}-3^{d} - - - 1 - 0 - 4½
Washing. to Parvis^{l} - - - 0 - 2 - 3
JB'^{s} bill to Nov^{b}. 1. Lett^{rs}, Mercuryes - &c. - - - 0 - 13- 6½
Washing the Qur^{tr} - - - 0 - 13- 0
G. JB Joury^{d} to Lara^{r} & Fingl - - - 0 - 12- 0
Hughs bill. b^{d} wages &c - - - 0 - 7 - 7
24. Co^{ch} 8^{d}. Inn. 3^{s}4^{d} --25. Co^{ch}. 6^{d}. --26. Co^{les}. 1^{s}-3^{d} - Co^{ch}. 1^{s}-6^{d} 0 - 7 - 3
27. Sp^{t}. 2^{s}-10^{d} --29. Co^{ch}. 1^{s}-8^{d}. Sp^{t} 1^{s}-1^{d}. - - - 0 - 5 - 7
4 - 1 - 7

1st Week.		0 - 8 - 5
2^{d} Week	-	0 - 5 - 5
3^{d} Week	-	0 - 8 -11
4th Week	-	4 - 1 - 7
		5 - 4 - 4

⟨Mem^{d}. JB's bill⟩

Totals of a Quar^{tr} from Aug. 1. to Nov^{br}. 1. 1703

JB - - -	2 - 9 - 6
Servant - - -	1 - 19- 0
Cloaths - - -	1 - 16- 0
Lodging - - -	5 - 18- 0
MC - - -	12 - 0 - 0
Horses - - -	3 - 15-11
Expences 1st Month - - -	0 - 10- 3½
Expences 2^{d} Month - - -	3 - 10-10½
Expences 3^{d} Month - - -	5 - 4 - 4

Memd' Remains to be putt here, Ms Felter, &c whip, Inn &c

Totals

Of a Year from No^br 1. 1702 to No^br. 1. 1703

First Quarter - - -	39 - 13- 6½
Second Quarter - - -	36 - 12- 5
Third Quarter - - -	42 - 3 -11
Fourth Quarter	

Axcount
Of my Livings
from
Nov^{br} 1st 1702
to
Nov^{br} 1st 1703

MC
MC

MC

25 -
- 8
16 - - 4
25 - 0 - 0 MC

MC

MC

Account
Of my Livings, from
Nov^{br}. 1st. 1702
to Nov^{br}. 1st. 1703.

132 - 8 - 0
122 - 4 -11
10 - 3 - 1
132 - 8 - 0

44 - 0 - 2
14 - 0 -10
4 - 5 - 0
3 -13 - 5
65 - -

48 - 8 - 0
47 - 8 - 1
0 -19 -11

50 - 0 - 0
39 - 6 - 8
10 -13 - 4
50 - 0 - 0

70 - 15 - 0
65 -19 -
4 -15 - 7
70 -15 - 0

If y fall don't stay to rise
Snap short makes look lean

Rec^d^ of Mr Parv^ll^

For the Tiths of Reads-Town and Stokes town,
drawn the Year 1702. all for thrash 1^ll^-3-11 in all - 18 - 17-11

Aug. 1. In money at Laracor - - -	1 - 10- 0
Sep^tbr^. 21. Allowed on House Acc^ts^ & Smith p^d^ &c - - -	3 - 9 -11½
Oc^tbr^. Allowed for Carriage of Turf - - -	1 - 17- 5
Allowed Oats for my Horses - - -	0 - 17- 6
Allowd 7^s^ for Rathbeggn Setting money of 1702 - - -	0 - 7 - 0
Allowd th Setting money of the Corn it self - - -	0 - 19- 0
Allowd the setting money of Rathbeggan for 1703 - - -	2 - 8 - 6
Nov^br^. 16 1705 Allowd in Thatching, & oth small Repairs - - -	0 - 17- 8
	12 - 7 - 0½

Nov^br^. 16. 1709 Remains due - - -

Allowd then to clear th Setting money of Rathbeggn for 1705 2^ll^-4^s^. for 1706. 1^ll^- 18. for 1707 1^ll^-11^s^-6 in all	5 - 13- 6
Th Rem^dr^ part of 1708 - 17^s^-4^d^½ - - -	0 - 17- 4½
	6 - 10-10

Annuall Charges for the Rectory of Grenoge

Crown rent - - -	5 - 8 - 0
Fees to the Receiver - - -	0 - 2 - 4
Proxyes - - -	0 - 12- 0
	6 - 2 - 4

[15v]

Rec^{d}

From the Parishes of Laracor and

Agher for the Year 1702.

Sett by M^{r} Is. Parvisol for 143^{ll} in money, besides Stokes-town and Readstown drawn, and Hay to value of 17^{ll}-10^{s} - in all 160-10-0

Dec^{br}. 2^{d}. From Mr Parvisol - - -	1 - 9 - 6
Jan^{ry}. 7 170$\frac{2}{3}$ Allowd on Acc^{t} then stated - - -	15 - 2 - 0
--more received - - -	5 - 0 - 0
--more allowd on Account - - -	0 - 13- 9
--8. Allowd to ballance the great Account - - -	1 - 9 - 5
--Received - - -	10 - 6 - 0
Febr. 2^{d} Allowd to clear Mr Smith - - -	14 - 5 - 0
--9 Rec^{d} - - -	0 - 13- 0
--17. Rec^{d} by the Coach - - -	4 - 3 - 1
--22. In milld Shill &c - - -	0 - 16-10
--Mar. 11 6 Pistolls. - - -	5 - 11- 0
--14 Rec^{d} - - -	2 - 8 - 6½
Apr. 21. ⟨Rec^{d}⟩ On Acc^{t} for Horse, Malaly, ^Skelton & Co^{ch} &c - - -	6 - 16- 4
--May. 17th. Rec^{d} Cash - - -	11 - 0 - 0
--23. Re^{cd} (and lent in part) - - -	2 - 18- 6
Jun 23 ⟨sent to me in Dublin⟩ by Coach - - -	2 - 18-10
⟨July 1st Rec^{d} in Dublin from Mr Par - - -	3 - 10- 0⟩
Aug.1. R^{cd} in money at Laracor - - -	2 - 11- 6
--8 In money at Laracor - - -	5 - 10- 0
	93 - 13- 3

^{pd}

Laracor & Agher

For Charges belonging to ^ <my Livings &c>

July 13. 1702	
Paid Mr Smith the remaind^r of	
a Quart^r ending. Jul. 12. 1702 - - -	<9 - 5 - 2>
Dec^{br}. 24th.	
p^d Mr Smith in part for a Quar^{tr}	
ending Oct^{br}. 12th. 1702. - - -	8 - 0 - 0
Febr. 2. P^d Mr Smith in full - - -	14 - 5 - 0
For Work done in the Garden below to	
Mar. 14. 170$\frac{2}{3}$ making Trenches & walks,	
and planting Sallyes - - -	1 - 12- 7
<--Horse hire and treating at Rathbeggan - - -	0 - 6 - 7>
<Setting money>	
Apr. 5. To And^r. Malaly for all acc^{ts}. - - -	1 - 10- 0
--May. 19. Proxyes, <School,> & BP^s. Clark. 1^s. - - -	2 - 7 - 9
--Schoolmast^r of Trim for the year 1703 - - -	0 - 10- 2
--Two Dinners at Visitation - - -	0 - 10- 9
--For making the westside Ditch, & other work, sallys, &c. - - -	0 - 13- 8
p^d in Dublin. Parvis^{ll} has his Acquittance	
--25. to Glascock ^ for 20 parts for 3 Parishes - - -	0 - 14- 3
<Jun. 2^d to Dean Read^r for a>	
May 28 to July. 31. Cleaning Sallyes 3 times & drawing Stone - - -	0 - 4 - 8
Jul. 31. 1703 For Hearth money p^d May. 28 - - -	0 - 4 - 0
--To Mr Smith for 2 Sermons - - -	1 - 3 - 0
	41 - 01- 0

Rec[d].
From the Parishes of Laracor and Agher for
the year 1702.

Brought over - - -	93 - 13 - 3
Aug. 5th. For the Queens Crown rent, being the old Arrear due by Dean Bolton, - - -	7 - 11 - 8
--22. In money - - -	5 - 0 - 0
Sep[tbr]. 12. In money - - -	4 - 11 - 10
--26. In money - - -	2 - 10 - 4
Oc[tbr]. 23. Overplus of Corn money allow[d] - - -	1 - 0 - 0½
--24. Allow[d] on House, Grazing, &c - - -	2 - 8 - 4½
-- In money at Laracor - - -	1 - 4 - 6
--30 In money sent me to Dublin - - -	4 - 1 - 6
	122 - 1 - 6
Sep[tbr]. 1. 1704. Allowd as p[d] me Substracted fr̄ grt Acct - - -	8 - 0 - 0
Allowd as receivd M[r] Perc[vlls] Tyths - - -	5 - 0 - 0
	135 - 1 - 6

M[r] Parvis[l] alledges the Tyths drawn for part
to be allowd. Some time when settl[d], thy are 17[ll]
Mights Arrear to place here - - -

P^{d} For An. 1702.	
For Charges belonging to Laracor and Agher	
Brought over - - -	41 - 1 - 0
Aug. 5. P^{d} an old Arrear of Crownrent for the Year 1688, due by Dean Bolton - - -	7 - 11- 8
P^{d} for setting money of the Corn, drawn - - -	0 - 19- 0

Re^{cd} out of the Parish of
Rathbeggan for the Year 1702.
Sett for 52^{ll}-2^{s}-0^{d}

Mar 13 Re^{cd} - - -	9 - 0 - 3
--14 Per Bill from Cusack on Th. Billing - - -	15 - 0 - 0
--More in Cash - - - < >	12 - 10- 5½
--More upon Allowance - - -	7 - 9 - 3½
Jul. 1 Rec^{d} in Dublin from Mr Par^{l} - - -	3 - 10- 0
	<47 - 10- 0>
Sepbr. 1. 1704. Allowd in Parvs^{ll} Account. 4^{ll}-12^{s}. - - -	4 - 12- 0
	52 - 2 - 0

Re^{cd} out of Donlaven. for the year .1702.

May. 22^{d}. (Allowd. and p^{rt} Lent) ---	9 - 0 - 0
--Aug. 1st Allowd, (For M^{r}. Smith, ^[2 Sern^{s}] House bill travell, &c) - - -	3 - 0 - 0
	12 - 0 - 0

Qu? what remains this year.

P^d.

Mar. 14

Horse hire and treating the People at their paying - - - 0 - 6 - 7

Setting money for 45[ll] receivd - - - 2 - 5 - 0

More for 7[ll] receivd - - - 7 - 0 - 0

P^d.

<--May. / Jun. 2 1703 To Dean Re[dr]. to Parv[ll] for a forfeiture - - - 1 - 0 - 0

--Jul. 31. Allow[d] for travelling charges: May 1st to 8 - - - 0 - 6 -10

Aug. 12 to My Vicar for a Year - - - 1 - 0 - 0

Dean Swifts Memorandum Book --

Account

Of Expences

From Nov^{br}. 1st. 1703

to No

Nov^{br}. 1st. 1704

John Cambell came Jul. 23. 1704

Took stable at 4^{ll} p^{r} an. Sep^{tbr}. 11. 1704

Came to Mrs Bradly 10^{ll} p^{r} an. Sep^{t}. 19. 1704

Came to Mr Close's May. 1. 1705

John Bunting came. De^{cbr}. 2^{d}. 1705

[1v]

Account.

Of Expences for a Year from.

Nov^{br}. 1 1703 to No^{br}. 1. 1704.

First⟨Quar^{tr}⟩ Half year.

JB.

Cloaths.

	ll	s	d
⟨Febr. 17. 6 Shirts. 4^{ll}-13-0. 6 Crav^{ts}. 12^{s}. M^{r}. 23 a Gwn &c 6^{ll}-6 - -	11 -	5 -	6⟩
⟨Shoes 14^{s}-6^{d}. Hank. 13^{s} thrd Stockins. 7^{s}-9^{d} Stock^{ns}. 2^{s}-4^{d} - - -	1 -	17-	7⟩

Lodging.

Recknd with my Expences.

MC

No^{br}. 1. 1^{ll}. --5. 3^{ll}-12^{s}-6^{d} -- in all -- - - - 26 - 0 - 0

Servant

Novbr. 9th. 1704. a Quartr - - - 0 - 18- 6

Exchange for 55^{ll} &

About - - - 5 - 0 - 0

Expences. 1st Month.

Nov^{br}.

1st Week.

1. to 6.	
--1. Sp^{t}. 6^{d} --2. Sp^{t}. 4^{s} --3^{d}. Sp^{t}. 1^{s}-6^{d}. --4. G. 6^{d}.½ - - -	0 - 6 - 9½
Hughs bill. 4^{s}-2^{d}.½ - - -	0 - 4 - 2½
6. to. 13.	
Spent, & given - & lodg. 16^{s}. - - -	1 - 9 - 3

England
Put to sea. Thurs^{d}. No^{br}. 11. 1703. landed
at Chestr. Sater^{d}. No^{br}. 13. 1703.

Expence of Journy from Dublin to London and stay at Leicestr. from Nov^{br}. 13 to 24. in all - - -	6 - 7 - 8
Sp^{t} to Dec^{br}. 1. - - -	0 - 1 - 0
P^{d} by Mrs Brent in my absence in Engld Mrs Felt^{r}. 1^{ll}-6^{d} Mrs Partigtn 16^{s}-5^{d} Shuttlecock 5^{s}-4 &c - - -	2 - 13- 6
Left with Coz Swift at Chestr abt Engl acct - - -	0 - 19- 0
	3 - 12- 6
	12 - 0 - 6

England.

1703.

Decemb^{r}. Sp^{t} - - -	1 - 18- 5
Jan^{ry}. Sp^{t} - - -	1 - 16- 0
February. Sp^{t} - - -	2 - 10- 2
March. Sp^{t} - - -	2 - 3 - 3
Apr. Sp^{t} - - -	2 - 17- 6
G. M^{rs} Da--s - - -	0 - 10- 0

& 4th
Third‸Quarter.

No^{br}
From May. 1. to ⟨Aug.⟩‸1. 1704

JB

P^{d} him at 8^{ll} p^{r} an? 4^{ll}. -8^{d}. & Jul. 26. 1^{ll}-15 - - -	⟨5 - 15- 8⟩
(G. him. 2^{ll}-6^{s}, not recknd) Sept. 8. 10^{s}-10^{d} - - 5^{s}5^{d}4 - - -	⟨0 - 16- 3⟩
Oct. 28. 1^{s}.2^{d}.½. No^{v}. 8. 5^{s}6^{d} Cleard. Jan^{r}. 10. 170$\frac{4}{5}$ - - -	8 - 0 - 0

Servt.

Octbr.1 Buttons. 1^{s}-6^{d}, a Hat before. Jun. 2^{s}-8^{d}.½ - - -	0 - 4 - 2½

Cloaths

Hank. 3^{s}. Shos. 5^{s}	
Hank 10^{s}. thrd Stock 4^{s}9 stock. 5^{s}4^{d} - Sho^{s}. 9^{s}-6^{d}. Crav. 12^{s}. - - -	2 - 1 - 7
Gown & Cass. 6-0-6.- 6 Shirts. 4 - 13 - 0 - - -	10 - 13- 6
May. 26. MD Stock. 5^{s}4^{d}. Perewig. 2^{ll}-7-6^{d}. Hat. 9^{s}. Scarf. 1^{ll}-6^{s} - -	4 - 7 -10
Crape Scarf. 15^{s}. Gl. 1^{s}-2^{d}. Muslin. 5^{s}. Camb. 2^{s}. Hank. 7^{s}-6^{d} Gard. 6^{s} -	1 - 16- 8
Jun. 2^{d}. Gl. 1^{s}.8^{d} --Jul. 27. Glvs. 1^{s}. Aug. 5. Bre^{chs}. 9^{s}-10^{d} - - -	0 - 12- 6
--8. Bre^{chs}. 11^{s}8^{d} --23 thrd Stock^{n} 4^{s}. Sep^{t}. 8. Shos. 9^{s} - - -	1 - 4 - 8
Jun. 28. Shoes forg^{t} 12^{s} Tayl. 1^{s}6^{d} - - -	0 - 13- 6
	21 - 10- 3

Lodg.

Lodg.

Jun. 4. 2^{s}8^{d}.½

MC

In all - - -	24 - 0 - 0

Lodging.

P^{d} Oc^{tbr}. 28. a Qua^{r} befor hand, to end de^{cbr}. 19. - - -	2 - 10- 0

Horses.

Aug. 17. Earnest for Stable 1^{s}-1^{d} Spurs 1^{s}. - - -	0 - 2 - 1
Sept. 20. 20 load of Hay. 6^{ll}. workmn 6^{s}-4^{d} workm^{n}. 8^{d}. - - -	6 - 7 - 0
--G. J^{n}. 1^{s}-1^{d}. Oc^{tbr}. 9. Straw & thatching 2^{s}-6^{d} - - -	0 - 3 - 7
Oc 20. Bridl. 1^{s}-2^{d} Curry comb & brush 2^{s}-6^{d} ⟨fork 8^{d}⟩- - -	0 - 3 - 8
box 3-8^{d} fork 8 - - -	0 - 4 - 4
--25. Bridle - 2^{s}-5^{d}, Oats 3^{s}-6^{d}, Comb, Sieve, &c 10^{d} - - -	0 - 6 - 9
30. bran 6^{d} - - -	0 - 0 - 6
	7 - 7 -11

Mem^{d}. Grass frg^{t}.

Expences. 1st Month.

May.

1\. to 22^{d}. --Spent G. at Cranfd, Lodg. &c --- 3 - 11- 5

22^{d} to June the 1st. Stayd at $Leicest^{r}$:

&c. G. &c - $Irel^{d}$. - - - 5 - 13- 9

Left $Leicest^{r}$. Mon^{d}. May. 29.

Mem^{dm}.

Left Neston. $Tues^{d}$. May. 30th.

1704. landed at Dublin, Thursday

morn. Jun. 1. 1704, being my 16th Voyage.

Expences on leaving London

for Things brought to $Irel^{d}$.

--20 Chocolate. 23^{ll} [in all 6^{ll} 10^{d} with tea &c]	4 - 0 - 0
--Bohe tea 1 Pound. 16^{s} p^{r} lb. - - -	0 - 16- 0
Green tea a Pound. Imper tea ½lb $Cani^{str}$ - - -	1 - 10- 0
Coffee 2 pounds - - -	0 - 6 - 4
Sug^{r} loaf & $Port^{r}$ 6^{d} - - -	0 - 6 - 6
Snuff and lead pots - - -	0 - 13- 0
Pills 3^{s}, Cards. 3^{s}. Pins 9^{s}-6^{d}. deal box, &c. 5^{s} - - -	1 - 0 - 6
	⟨12 - 7 - 6⟩
	17 - 17- 6

Expences. 2^{d} Month.

June.

1. to 10. At Larac^{r}. Jun. 3.

--Chair. 6^{d}. --3^{d}. Hors 6^{s}-6^{d}. G. 1^{s}-1^{d}. --4. Sac^{rt}. 2^{s}-8^{d}.½ - - - 0 - 11- 3½

--9. G. 6^{d}.½. Parvis^{ll} bill, dyet, wash, &c 12^{s}-5^{d}. - - - 0 - 12-11½

--12. Co^{ch}. 6^{d}½. G. 1^{s}-1^{d} --14. Sp^{t} 6^{d}. Paste 1^{s}. Co^{ch}. 1^{s}-1^{d}. Tav^{n} 3^{s}-1^{d} - - - 0 - 7 - 3½

--ch^{r}. 6^{d} --15. Co^{ch}. 1^{s}-1^{d} --16. Sm^{ll}. 4^{d}½ --19. Sp^{t}. 10^{d} --21. Co^{ch} 1^{s}-3^{d} - - - 0 - 4 - 0½

--22. Sp^{t} 1^{s}-6^{d}. G. 1^{s}-1^{d} to 24. 6^{s}-3^{d} --26. win 1^{s}1^{d} --27. Sp^{t} 6^{d} - - 0 - 10- 8

--28. Co^{ch} 1^{s}-6^{d} --30. Chair 10^{d}. frg^{t}. 1^{s}-8^{d}. Chwrf 1^{s}. - - - 0 - 5 - 0

2 - 11- 3

[4v]

<July.> Expences

July.

--3 Inn 3^s-6^d. Sm^{ll}. 6^d - - -	0 - 4 - 0
--13 G. 9^s-3^d, wash. 1^s. Inn. 1^s2^d - - -	0 - 11- 5
--14. J^n. 3^s-7^d - - -	0 - 3 - 7
--17. G. 1^s-6^d Co^{ch}. 10^d. G Coff MC. 3^s-**8^d** - - -	0 - 6 - 0
--19. Custom H. 19^s-6^d. --20 $Lett^{rs}$ 2^s3^d. Co^{ch} 1^s-6^d - - -	1 - 3 - 3
--21. Wages 7^s. --23 Sp^t. 1^s-3^d --24. Sp. 4^s-2^d - - -	0 - 12- 5
--25. JB's Bill, wash, mak Lin̄, Coffee &c 1^{ll}-5^s - - -	1 - 5 - 0
--Co^{ch} 1^s-1^d. 27. Sp^t. 7^d. 28. Sp^t. 1^s-1^d - - -	0 - 2 - 9
--30. Sp^t 4^d. Ball 1^s-3^d - - -	0 - 1 - 7
	4 - 10- 0
Joury to Cavan, & Servt b^d wags &c - - -	1 - 4 - 0
	5 - 14- 0

⟨August⟩ Expences

August

--2. Sp^{t} 6^{d} --5. Co^{h}. 6^{d}. Sp^{t}. 1^{s}. brd w. 3 weeks & - 12^{s} - - -	0 - 14- 0
--J^{ns} bill. 1^{s}-6^{d} --8. Sp^{t}. 8^{d}. G. 6^{d}. Coffee. 3^{s}-6^{d} - - -	0 - 5 - 9
--Brd w. &c. 4^{s}. Co^{ch}. 1^{s}-4^{d} --14. Sp^{t}. 2^{s}-9^{d} - - -	0 - 7 -10
--16. Lett^{rs}. 6^{d}. J^{ns} B^{ll}. 7^{d} G. 1^{s}-1^{d} --17 Sp^{t}. 2^{s}-1^{d} --18. Sp^{t} 1^{s}-3^{d} - - -	0 - 5 - 4
--J^{ns} B^{ll}. 1^{s}-8^{d}. Brd w. 4^{s} --23. w^{in} 1^{s}-6^{d} --25. Sp^{t} 2^{d} - - -	0 - 7 - 4
--W^{in}. 1^{s}-8^{d} -sp^{t}. 3^{s}-3^{d} Co^{ch}. 6^{d} - - -	0 - 5 - 5
	2 - 5 - 8

Expences

Sept^{br}.

Parvis$^{ll's}$ bil^{s} From Jun. 12. to Sep^{tr}. 1st. 1704

Horses sent 6^{s}, Tongues 5^{s}, mend saddles 3^{s}-9^{d} - - -	0 - 14- 9
Houskeeping - 10^{s}-8^{d}.½ - - -	0 - 10- 8½
For the use of his Horse - - -	0 - 7 - 0
--4. G -8^{d}.½ Sp^{t} 1^{s}. --5. brd wag. 2^{s}7^{d}. --6. Co^{ch}. 1^{s} --8. brd w. 4^{s} -	0 - 9 - 1½
--10. Sp^{t} 1^{s}-3^{d} --11. Sp^{t}. 9^{d}. --12. Sp^{t}. 8^{d} --14. Jns B^{ll} 6^{s}-1^{d} - - -	0 - 8 - 9
--16. G. 8^{d}.½ --18. B^{d} w. 4^{s}. G. Camp^{ll} 1^{s}.1^{d}. G. Bailf 5^{s}-5^{d} lett^{rs} 6^{d} - - -	0 - 11- 9½
--J^{ns} b^{ll} 4^{s}-6^{d} --20. Sp^{t}. 1^{s}-1^{d} --21. G. Uncls mds. 8^{s}-1^{d}½ J^{n}. 3^{s}7 - -	0 - 17- 3½
--G. 3^{d}. Parvis^{ll} bill for Elctn 16^{s}-9^{d} Ale 6^{s} Hors 3^{s}, wash - &c - - -	2 - 1 - 5½
forgot 2^{s} - - -	0 - 2 - 0
	6 - 2 -10½

Expences. 3^{d} Month

Octo^{br}, J^{ns} bill 3^{s}
--3^{d}. B^{d} w. 2^{s}-3^{d}. ⟨J^{ns} B^{ll} 2^{s}8^{d}⟩ G. 3^{d}. G. Nurse 2^{s}-8^{d}.½ - - - 0 - 8 - 2½
--4. Sp^{t} on MD 2^{s}-8^{d}.½ - - - 0 - 2 - 8½
--7 J^{ns} bill. 2^{s}-9^{d}.½, anoth. for book. 4^{s}-10^{d} lett^{rs}. 1^{s}-6^{d} - - - 0 - 9 - 1½
--9. G. 3^{d}. --11. G. 3^{d} --12. book bound 1^{s}1^{d}. - - - 0 - 1 - 7
--14. J^{ns} bill Co^{ch}. 1^{s}-6^{d}. book 1^{s}-3^{d} let^{rs}. 4^{d}. sm^{ll} 5^{d} - - - 0 - 3 - 6
brd w. 3^{s}-6^{d} - - - 1 - 8 - 7½

14 to 21.
B^{d} w. 3^{s}-6^{d}. Canvas. 1^{s}. 20 s^{mll}. 4^{d}. - - - 0 - 4 -10
J^{ns} b. Cand. 5^{d}.½ Cr^{m} Sug^{r}. 1^{s}-3^{d} pap^{r}. 7^{d}. powd^{r}. 4^{d}
Coals 1^{s}-6^{d} Lett^{r} 2^{d} nails 2^{d} s^{mll}. 1^{d}.½ - - - 0 - 4 - 7
0 - 9 - 4

21 to 28.
⟨J^{s} b. Candl. 5^{d}.½ Cr^{m} Sug^{r}. 1^{s}-3^{d}. pap^{r} 7^{d}. powd^{r}. 4^{d}⟩
⟨Coals 1^{s}-6^{d} lett^{r}. 2^{d}. nails. 2^{d} s^{mll} 1^{d}½⟩
--25. B^{dw}. 3^{s}-6^{d}. Sp^{t} 6^{d} book bound. 1^{s}-6^{d} - - - 0 - 5 - 6
J^{s} B. ⟨B^{d}⟩ Carp^{tr}. 3^{s}-5^{d}.½ Tind^{r} b. 9^{d}. Candl 8^{d}. . in all - - - 0 - 6 - 3
0 - 11- 9

28. to No^{vb}. 1.
Brd wg. -2^{s}.0. J^{s} B^{ll}. 1^{s}-2^{d} - - - 0 - 3 - 2

1st & 2^{d} weeks - 1 - 8 - 7½
3^{d} Week - - 0 - 9 - 4
4th Week - - 0 - 11- 9
Remd^{r} - - 0 - 3 - 2
⟨2 - 11-10½⟩
2 - 12-10½

Totalls

Of a Year. from No^{br}. 1st 1703. to No^{br}. 1. 1704

JB - - -	8 - 0 - 0
MC - - -	50 - 0 - 0
Servt - - -	1 - 2 - 8½
Cloaths - - -	21 - 10- 3
Lodg. 1 q^{rt} & week - - -	2 - 12- 8½
Horses - - -	7 - 7 -11
Exchange of money - - -	5 - 0 - 0
Exp. Nov^{br}. wth Journy - - -	12 - 0 - 6
Decbr - - -	1 - 18- 5
Jan^{r}. - - -	1 - 16- 0
Febr. - - -	2 - 10- 2
Mar - - -	2 - 3 - 3
Apr - - -	2 - 17- 6
G. M^{rs} D-- s - - -	0 - 10- 0
May, Journ. Choc^{l}. &c - - -	17 - 17- 6
June - - -	2 - 11- 3
July. Journ to Cavan &c - - -	5 - 14- 0
Aug. - - -	2 - 5 - 8
Sept. Elect^{n}, Parvs bils &c G. maids. - - -	6 - 2 -10½
Oc^{tbr} - - -	2 - 12-10½
	156 - 13- 7
J B's bill, part. 2^{s}. in all. 14^{s}.4^{d} - - -	0 - 16- 4
Wine forgot - - -	0 - 1 - 2
Brady for. meats. 1^{s}-9^{d} - - -	0 - 1 - 4

Account of my

Livings for

1703.

[19v]

Rec^{d}
From the Parishes of Laracor and Agher
for the Year 1703. Sett by M^{r}. Isay

Parvisol for 132 - 8 - 0	
Nov^{br}. 2. From Mr Burnford - - -	6 - 0 - 0
--5. From Mr Parv^{sll} in Dubl. - - -	4 - 0 - 6
(Sep^{tr}. 1. 1704) Allowd for what was p^{d} in absence, to Uncle, M^{rs}. B^{rt}, Crown rent, Curate ½ y^{r}	
⟨Proxyes, &c - - -	74 - 14- 9⟩
Proxyes &c - - -	67 - 4 - 9
To M^{r} Sm. a 4^{r} end. Aug. 7. 1704 - - -	10 - 0 - 0
½ years Crownrent due at Ester 1704 - - -	7 - 11- 8
Jul. 16. 1704. in Cash - - -	13 - 0 - 0
Sept^{br}. 3^{d}. - - -	3 - 0 - 0
--5. From Proudfoot in Dublin - - -	1 - 8 - 0
Oct^{br}. 1. From Parv^{sll} at Laracor - - -	2 - 10- 0
--Allowd for a Quart^{r} to M^{r}. Smith, end Novembr 7. 1704 - - -	7 - 10- 0
	122 - 4 -11

Arrears of this year not Adjusted Nov^{br}. 6. 1705	
Allowd to Mr Wesly for the Chancell, the 2^{d} Pay^{mt} of 10^{ll} - - -	5 - 0 - 0
Dec^{br}. 22. ⟨Cash 1^{s}⟩ 1705. Cash at Dublin - - -	2 - 0 - 9
	129 - 5 - 8
Arrear. adjusted. De^{cbr}. 22. 1705. (not p^{d}) - - -	3 - 3 - 4

	Pd
a Year ⟨& half⟩ Crownrent - - -	15 - 3 - 4
½ yr Arrear - - -	7 - 11 - 8
Mr Smith - - - 3 qrts - - -	30 - 0 - 0
Mr Smith ½ & yr - - -	7 - 10 - 0
Build. &c alld in Tyths drawn - - -	14 -
Proxyes	
Registr	

Rec^{d}

From Rathbeggan for the Year 1703

sett for 48^{ll} - 8 - 0 -

1703 Nov^{br}. 4th From Mr Parv^{sll} in Dublin.. - - -	4 - 2 - 1½
<--5 From Mr Parv^{sll} in Dublin - - -	4 - 0 - 6>
--More at sev^{rll} times in absence, allowd - - -	17 - 10-10½
June. 28. 1704. in Cash - - -	9 - 0 - 0
Aug. 10. 1704. in Cash - - -	7 - 0 - 0
Oc^{tb} 21. Rec^{d} in Dublin for Glebe - - -	1 - 0 - 1
--28. From Mr Cusack - - -	7 - 0 - 0
--No. more in dublin for the Glebe - - -	1 - 15- 0
Apr. 12. Arrear of Glebe (all p^{d}) - - -	1 - 0 - 0
Memd. overp^{d}. 1^{s}-3^{d}, charged - - - to next year	48 - 8 - 1

P^d

Allowd the setting money of Rathbeg^n - - - 2 - 8 - 6

in the old account of Tyths drawn 1702.

Rec^{d} 1703

The Prebend of Donlaven sett to severall	
Persons for 17^{ll} - 0^{s} - 0^{d}	
Sep^{br}. 1. Allowd for receivd in absence - - -	8 - 10- 0
Jan^{r}. 11. 170$\frac{4}{5}$ in Cash in dubl. from Parv^{sl} - - -	2 - 0 - 3
	10 - 10- 3

Rec^{d}

For Tyths drawn from Laracor. for 1703. Valu^{d}. 36-6-0	
Oct^{br}. 9 Barrell Beer - 5^{s}-6^{d} Bar^{ll}-- allowd for Carry &c - 1^{s}-3^{d} p^{r} Ba^{r} 2^{d} Custom - - -	1 - 18- 1
--12 Barrells and 1 Bush. the same rate - - -	2 - 11- 3½
--30th. 9 Barrells the same rate - - -	1 - 18- 1
June. 12. 1704. Allowd a week expence with Cydr. &c. 10-2, & wash, old arrear, 2^{s}-3^{d} - - -	0 - 12- 5
--Oats 4^{ll} barrell, & ½, for Horses in absence - - -	0 - 11- 3
Sep^{br}. 1. Allowd, Horse send, 6^{s}. Tongue 5^{s}. Houskeep, mend saddles &c, to Sep^{br}. 1. - - -	1 - 5 - 5¾
--Allowd for ridig his Horse &c - - -	0 - 7 - 0
Allowd for barn, stable, thatching, Sallyes, Journeys, Honey (drawing Qu?) Housebill, to May 31, 1704. Page's bill to May 30. 1704 - - -	14 - 7 - 6
Allowd Housbill &c from Septb. 2. to Oct.1. 1704 - - -	2 - 1 - 5
Jan^{r}. 1st. 170$\frac{4}{5}$ allowd a Housbill from Oct^{br} 2. to Jany 1st.	3 - 2 - 3
No^{vr}. 16. 1705. Allod setting Sallyes in Island, weeding setting Fruit trees &c from Febr. 19. 1704. to Oc^{tr}. 30. 1705 - - -	1 - 10- 3
--Apr. 18. 1706 Allowd the setting money of Rathb. 1704 - - -	2 - 10- 0
	32 - 15

P^d

A Tax for the Church 6 - 9 - 9

10 - 10- 3

17 - 0 - 0

P^d.

Out of Tyths drawn

Novr. 15. 1705

Allod a Bill for work. about Sallyes. &c - 1 - 10- 3

Due

Arrears of Laracor

Turle, Neal 1701	
Jonathan Ball 1701.	
R. Meight. 1701 - - -	0 - 14- 6
Nich. Dolan. 1701 - - -	0 - 14- 0
1702 Arrears - - - < >	7 - 18 - 6
1703. Arrears. - - -	10 - 3 - 1

Rathbeggan.

1700 <1699> Arrear due from Nichols - - -	9 - 15- 7½
1701. Arrear from Nich. sup. sett for. 50^{ll}. - - -	10 - 13- 4
<1703. Arrea> - - -	0 - 19-11

Dunlavan

1701. Arrear from Scot - - -	7 - 6 - 6
1702 Arrear From Fisher &c	
1703 - - -	6 - 9 - 9

P[d]

Arrears of Laracor & Agher.

Adjusted Dec[br]. 22. 1705. - - - 3 - 3 - 4

Account :

Of Expences

From Nov.^{br} 1. 1708

to

Nov.^{br} 1. 1709.

Won	ll s d
22 to 27. Picq^{t} at Cranfrd.	1-10-0
br. 2. Omb^{r} Ld B. & S^{r} A F.	0-16-6
pr. 6. Piqu^{t} Ld Berkly	0-8-0
Sep^{tbr} 3. Omb^{r}. A. BD. &c.	0-11-3
-26. Ombr. Walls. Stoit	0-2-0
Ombr. Morg^{n} before	0-1-1
-Oct^{br}. 5. Piqt. Perciv^{ll}	0-1-0
-7 Piq^{t}. Barry	0-10-0
-8 Piq^{ut} id.	0-4-3
-11 Piq^{t}. id	0-1-1
-15 Ombr. Barry's	0-5-7
-18. Tables Wesly	0-5-5
19. Piqt. Barry.	0-2-2
	4-18-4
	4-2-4
Won this year	0-16-0

Nov^{br}	Lost	
-5 L^{d} B & L^{dy} Tant. Omb^{r}. at Epsom		1-1-6
Dec^{br}. 4. Bartons. Ombre		0-2-0
-29. Piq^{t}. Mrs Finch		0-0-6
Jan^{r}.20. Omb^{r}. Long. Van Hom^{rs}.		0-0-6
Febr. 1. Omb^{r}. L^{dy} Lucy		0-2-0
Mar. 3. Piqut Ld Berk^{l}		0-3-6
-Jun. 20. at Chestr. Piqu^{t} Ld Meath, &c		0-8-0
Aug. 10. Piqut Keating		0-18-6
Aug. 27. Ombr.		0-2-0
<Sep^{t} 3^{d} Omb A. BD		0-11-0>
Sep. 8. Ombr. for Tpt		0-4-0
-9 Ombr. for Tpt		0-2-0
-16 Ombr. Walls, Den^{n} AD		0-0-8
-17 Ombr id		0-1-8
-20 mbr id		0-2-10
-24 Ombr. id. Stoit		0-1-8
28 Omb. Trim. Raym^{d}		0-1-10
Octr. 13 Piq^{ut} Barry		0-5-0
-24. Om^{b} Ray^{d}		0-0-8
-26. Piqt. Barry		0-2-2
31. Bass^{t} Raym^{d}		0-1-4
		4-2-4

[1v]

In suspense. Account England.

of Expences from Nov^{br}. 1. 1708 to Nov^{br}. 1. 1709

First Quarter.

from Novbr. 1st. 1708. to Feb^{r}. 1. 170$\frac{8}{9}$

JB.

July. 12. Allowd & p^{d}, & of this year p^{d} - - - 1 - 0 -10
--19 A Pistole - - - 0 - 18- 6

Cloaths.

Nov^{br}. 16. mend breeches 6^{d}. ^Scarf 19^{s}6^{d}^ Dec^{br}. 4. Cassock. 2^{ll}-6^{s} Shoes. 9^{s}. - - - 3 - 15- 0
Jan^{r}. 17. Glovs. 1^{s}-6^{d} --19. Tay^{lr}. 6^{d} - - - 0 - 2 - 0

3 - 17- 0

Servant.

MC.

Settled by Accounts &c - - - 11 - 0 - 0

Lodging.

From Nov^{br}. 8^{d} to De^{br}. 6. 4 weeks. 1^{ll}-2^{s} to Jan^{r} 3^{d}. 1^{ll}-2^{s} - - - 2 - 4 - 0
To Jan^{r}. 31 - 1^{ll}-2^{s} - - - 1 - 2 - 0

3 - 6 - 0

Extr^{dnys}.

Dec^{br}. 17. to Mrs Bartons Serv^{ts}. 7^{s}-6^{d} --25 Sac^{rt}. 2^{s}.6^{d}. G. Coff. by. 2^{s}-6^{d} - - - 0 - 12- 6
Jan^{r}. 6. Ld Berkely's Ser^{vts}. 10^{s} Pat Rolt. 10^{s}-9^{d} - - - 1 - 0 - 9

1 - 13- 3

Mrs Ann. Massy at Mrs Lenthall's ^a Cooper's^ in Sice Lane
near Queen street in Cheapside.

Ann Price, the Backside of Riders Court near Leicest^{r}
Fields. recomd to Dr Prat.
Thompson at the Wheat Sheaf Pate nost^{r} Row, Prenella's

Mem^{rdm}.

Hatter's Rule. Not leave a Hatt when dresst too long upon Basin, but as little as possible, and if possible, not at all, given me as a great Secret

From 6 to 16 often giddy G^{d} help me. so to 25th less

Expences. 1st Month

England.

ov^{br}.

1st Week.

to 6 13.

--4 M^{d}. 1^{s}. Co^{ch} 1^{s}-6^{d} --6. Eps^{m}. 6^{d} --8 Lett^{r} Col^{er}. 2^{d} Pat^{r}. 6^{d} - - -	0 - 3 - 8
--Coff. 4^{d} --9 Pat^{r}. 1^{s} Lett^{r} Patrk. 6^{d} Coff, & with Addis^{n} &c. 1^{s}-2^{d} - -	0 - 3 - 0
--10 Coff. 8^{d} Lett^{rs} Smth MD. Walls 1^{s}-6^{d} --11 Coff. 9^{d} G. 2^{d} - - -	0 - 3 - 1
--Sm^{ll}. 4^{d}. G. Maid. 10^{d} Cand^{ls} before. 4^{d} --12. Coff. 6^{d} Lett^{r} Rolt. 2^{d} -	0 - 2 - 2
	0 - 11-11

13 to 20. 2^{d} Week

Wash. 1^{s}. Pa^{tr}. 8^{d}. Coles 1^{s}-3^{d} Co^{ch} Addis^{n} 1^{s}. Tav^{rn} Adds^{n}. 1^{s}. - - -	0 - 4 -11
Coff. 4^{d}. --14. Coff. 6^{d}. --15 Coff. Sr A. F. 1^{s}-6^{d} Coff. 4^{d} - - -	0 - 2 - 8
--16 Brandy for Giddiness. 2^{s}. din^{r} Cran^{l} 2^{s}-6^{d} Br^{dy}. 3^{d}. Coff. 4^{d} - - -	0 - 5 - 1
<--mend breeches. 6^{d}> --17. Cand^{l}. 4^{d}.½ G. Maid 3^{d}. Sm^{ll}. 2^{d}. - - -	0 - 0 - 9½
--19 Tav^{rn} Addis^{n} 2^{s}-6^{d}. Coff. 4^{d} Lett^{r} MD 6^{d} - - -	0 - 3 - 4
	0 - 16- 9½

20 to 27. 3^{d} Week.

--Wash. 1^{s}. Coff. 6^{d} --21. din^{r} at home 8^{d} - - -	0 - 2 - 2
--22. G. maid cutt hair. 5^{d}- Coff. 7^{d} Raz^{rs} 4^{d} Lett R^{ding} & Rolt 8^{d}. - - -	0 - 2 - 0
--23 Coff. 8^{d} Co^{ch} Frankln 1^{s}. --24. Co^{ch}. 2^{s}. din^{r} Francklin 1^{s}-6^{d}. Coff. 6^{d}. - - -	0 - 5 - 8
--25. Coff. 4^{d}. --26. Sm^{ll} 4^{d} G. maid. 2^{d} Lett^{r} Bernage 6^{d} - - -	0 - 1 - 4
	0 - 11- 2

27 to Dec^{br}. 1. 4th Week

--wash. 1^{s}-4^{d} Coff. 4^{d} --28 Coff. 4^{d} G. 2^{d}. - - -	0 - 2 - 2
29 Co^{ch}. 1^{s}. Chair. 1^{s}. Coff. 4^{d}. --30 Din^{r}. 1^{s}. Coff. 4^{d}. Cand^{ls} 6^{d} -	0 - 4 - 2
	0 - 6 - 4

1st Week.	-	0 - 11-11
2^{d} Week.	-	0 - 16- 9½
3^{d} Week	-	0 - 11- 2
4th Week.	-	0 - 6 - 4
		2 - 6 - 2½

Dec^{br}. --5. Horrible sick. 12 much better. thank G^{d} & MD's Pray^{rs}

Expences.

(--16. bad fitt at Mrs Bartons 24. bettr, but-- dread a Fitt.)

2^{d} Month better still the End

1 to 11. 1st Week

--Coff. 5^{d} --2. Coff. 7^{d}. Co^{ch} Addis^{n} 1^{s}. --3. Coff. 2^{d}. Coles. 1^{s}-3^{d}. G mid 3^{d}. - - - 0 - 3 - 8
--4. Co^{ch}. 1^{s}. wash. 1^{s}-8^{d} --5. din^{r}. 8^{d} --6. din^{r} 8^{d} G ma^{d} 2^{d} - - - 0 - 4 - 2
--Sup^{r} Vomit 11^{d}. p^{d} Mrs Sall. Lett^{r} & G. 5^{s}. --7 Cand^{ls}. & G maid 7^{d} - - - 0 - 6 - 6
--8 Mutt^{n} broth. 9^{d} --9 Coals. 1^{s}-3^{d}. Cand^{l}. 4^{d} & G ma^{d} 2^{d} - - - 0 - 2 - 6
--10 Din^{r} 8^{d} - - - 0 - 0 - 8
0 -17 - 6

2^{d} Week

11 to. 18

--Din^{r}. 8^{d} --12. din^{r}. 8^{d}.½ Win d^{r} Prat. 2^{s}. - - - 0 - 3 - 4½
--13 Meat fr Broth. 10^{d}. Lett^{rs} 2 Walls 1^{s}. D Stearn. 6^{d}. Tav^{n} Add^{son} 1^{s}-6^{d} - - - 0 - 3 -10
--14. Din^{r} 8^{d}. G maid 2^{d}. Coff. 4^{d}. --15. Coff. 6. md^{r}fe Din^{r}. 1^{s}. - - - 0 - 2 - 8
--16. Din^{r} 8d. G. maid 2^{d}. Candl. 4^{d}.½. Chair sick Mrs Barton 1^{s}. Coles. 1^{s}-3^{d} - - - 0 - 3 - 5½
--17 Sm^{ll}. 6^{d}. Coff. 2^{d} - - - 0 - 0 - 8
0 -14 - 0

3^{d} Week.

18. to 25.

--Din^{r}. 8^{d}. --19. Din^{r}. 8^{d}. G. maid 2^{d}. wash. 11^{d} --20. Coff &c 3^{d} - - 0 - 2 - 8
--20. Lett^{rs} MD. 10. Mr Walls. 1^{s} --21. Por^{tr}. 3^{d} G. maid 3^{d}. Din^{r}. 7^{d} - 0 - 2 - 1
--23. Pa^{tr}. 1^{s}. Din^{r}. 6^{d} Coff. 4^{d} Lett^{r} Mrs Davis 3^{d}. --24 Din^{r} 8^{d} Coff. 4^{d} - - - 0 - 3 - 1
0 - 7 -10

4th Week.

25. to Jan^{r}. 1.

--Wash - 7^{d}. Raz^{r}. 2^{d}. Coffe 4^{d}. ⟨Sacr^{nt} 2^{s}-6^{d} G. Coff. boy 2^{s}-6^{d}.⟩- - - 0 - 1 - 1
--26 Lett^{r} Dr Raym^{d}. 8^{d}. Coff 4^{d}. --27. Coles 1^{s}-3^{d}. Cand^{l}. 5^{d}. Sm^{ll}. 3^{d} - - - 0 - 2 -11
--28. Chair 1^{s}. Coff. 8^{d}. sm^{ll}. 2^{d}. --30. Co^{ch}. L^{dy} Lucy. 1^{s}-6^{d} - - - 0 - 3 - 4
31. Lett^{r} MD. 6^{d}. Coff 4^{d} - - - 0 - 0 -10
0 - 8 - 2

First Week	-	0 -17 - 6
2^{d} Week	-	0 -14 - 0
3^{d} Week	-	0 - 7 -10
4th Week	-	0 - 8 - 2
		2 - 7 - 6

--21. an ill fitt but not to excess.
29. out of order.
31. not well at times
3^{d} Month

an^{ry}.

Expences.

1st Week.

1 to 8.

--Coff. 4^{d}. --2. Tav^{rn} Addis^{n}. 4^{s}-9^{d} - Wash - 1^{s} - - -	0 - 6 - 1
--Din^{r}. Addis^{n}. 2^{s}-6^{d}. Coff. 2^{d}. . 4 G. maid 1^{s}-6^{d}. din^{r} &c 11^{d} - - -	0 - 5 - 1
--6. Coles. 1^{s}-6^{d} Cand^{ls} 4^{d}½ Poud^{r}. &c 6^{d}. --7 Coff. 4^{d}. milk, 1^{s} - - -	0 - 3 - 8½
	0 - 14-10½

2^{d} Week.

8 to. 15

--Co^{ch} L^{dy} Lucy. 2^{s}. & wash. 1^{s}-9^{d}. --10. G. por. 4^{d}. - - -	0 - 4 - 1
--13 Lett^{rs} Freckl^{tn} ^ Moth. 9^{d}. Coff. 6^{d}. Chair. 1^{s}. --14. din^{r}. Took. 1^{s} -	0 - 3 - 3
	0 - 7 - 4

⟨15 to 22.⟩

3^{d} Week.

15 to 22

--Chair from Longs. 1^{s}. Coff. 3^{d}. --16. Chair 1^{s}. Co^{ch} Jacob Tonson. 1^{s} -	0 - 3 - 3
--17 Co^{ch} Seabright. 1^{s}. Coff. 4^{d} --18. Co^{ch}. 1^{s}. --19. G. maid. 6^{d} - - -	0 - 2 - 6
wash. 1^{s}-2^{d}. sm^{ll}. 3^{d} Coffe. 8^{d} Lett^{rs} Parvill; Ford. 1^{s}-2^{d} - - -	0 - 3 - 3
--21. Chair Addison & Trad's. 1^{s}. s^{mll}. 2^{d} - - -	0 - 1 - 2
	0 - 10- 2

4th Week.

22 to Febr. 1.

Powd^{r} Cand^{ls} &c before. 11^{d}. - - -	0 - 0 -11
At Cranford from --22 to 27. G. Mr Hickm^{n}. & Woman Cranford - - -	0 - 3 - 6
--28. Lett^{r}. Bp Cl. 6^{d}. Coff. 4^{d}. mend. Ham^{r}. 6^{d}. s^{mll}. 2^{d} - - -	0 - 1 - 6
Collectn at Cranford before. 1^{s}. --30 G. Mrs S. 2^{s}-6^{d}. Coff. &c. 6^{d} - - -	0 - 4 - 0
31. Wash. 2 weeks. 2^{s}-6^{d}. Coles, Cand^{ls}, & G. maid. 2^{s}-1^{d}.½ - - -	0 - 4 - 5½
	0 - 14- 4½

First Week.	-	0 - 14-10
Second. Week	-	0 - 7 - 4
3^{d} Week	-	0 - 10- 2
4th Week	-	0 - 14- 4½
		2 - 6 - 8½

Totalls

Of a Quar[tr] from Nov[br]. 1. 1708 to Feb. 1. 170$\frac{8}{9}$.

JB - - - ⟨(not sett[d])⟩ - - -	1 - 10 - 0
Cloaths - - -	3 - 17 - 0
MC - - -	11 - 0 - 0
Lodging - - -	3 - 6 - 0
Extr[dys] - - -	1 - 13 - 3
Expences 1st Month - - -	2 - 6 - 2½
Expences 2[d] Month - - -	2 - 7 - 6
Expences 3[d] Month - - -	2 - 6 - 8½
	28 - 6 - 8

Second Quarter.

From Feb^{r}. 1. 170$\frac{8}{9}$ to May 1. 1709.

JB.

Cloaths.

Fe^{br}. 1. Wastcoat. 1^{ll}-10^{s}. alter. Gown. 1^{ll}-3^{s}. G. Tayl^{rs} man 1^{s} - - -	2 - 14- 0
--15 A Beavr 1^{ll}-13^{s}. Glvs. 1^{s}-6^{d} Mar.2. Brechs. 1^{ll}. G man 6^{d} - - -	2 - 15- 0
--5 Knit Breches. 12^{s}. Ap^{r}. 2. Girdle 3^{s}-6^{d} Hank. 10^{s}-8^{d} 4 Cravts. 10^{s} - -	1 - 16- 2
--16. French. Gown & Cass. 4^{s}-6^{d} p^{r} yrd. 24 y^{rds} 5^{ll}-8^{s}. mak. 18^{s} - - -	6 - 6 - 0
Swap old gown. 12^{s}-6^{d} altr Cambt Gown. 12^{s} --29. Mrs S. mak night. Gown 2^{s} - - -	1 - 6 - 6
--30. Hatt. 1^{ll}-13^{s}. Box 1^{s}. old Gown. 15^{s}. mend. &c 3^{s}-6^{d} - - -	2 - 12- 6
	17 - 10- 2

⟨MC⟩

MC.

P^{d} to May 1. by Accounts &c. clearing from Eng^{d} - - -	11 - 0 - 0

Lodging.

to Febr. 27th - 1^{ll}-2^{s}. to Mar. 28. 1^{ll}-2^{s}. - - -	2 - 4 - 0
to Apr. 25 - 1^{ll}-2^{s}. - - -	1 - 2 - 0
	3 - 6 - 0

Extr^{drys}.

Febr. 3. Spir^{t} of Amb^{r}. 2^{s}-6^{d}. Mar. 30. Tav^{rn} Addis^{n} &c. 5^{s}.- - -	0 - 7 - 6
Apr. 2. Quack for Smuff &c. 3^{s}-6^{d}. 10 milk Porridge. 5^{s}. - - -	0 - 8 - 6
--14. Advertis^{mt} for Apr day, &c. 3^{s}. Corneiile & Moliere 1^{ll}-2^{s}-6^{d} - - -	1 - 5 - 6
--19 Theatr Ital. 5^{s}-6^{d} --24. Sac^{rt}. 2^{s}-6^{d}- - -	0 - 8 - 0
--27. Bohea. 1^{ll}-10^{s}. Green Tea. 1^{ll}-5^{s}. Canis^{tr}. 3^{s} 6 Cups 4^{s}-6^{d}. - - -	3 - 2 - 6
--Tea for Moth^{r}. 5^{s} - - -	0 - 5 - 0
	5 - 17- 0

Expences.

(--7 small fitt abroad
Pretty well to
th end, & bet^{r} still) 1st Month

Febr.

1st Week.

1 to 5.

--Lett^{r} MD. (12) 6^{d}. Coff. 4^{d}. sm^{ll}. 1^{d} --2. Coff. 4^{d}. --4. Coff. 6^{d}. - - 0 - 1 - 9
--Lett^{rs} Mr Walls, Mr Reeding. 1^{s} - - - 0 - 1 - 0
0 - 2 - 9

2^{d} Week.

5 to 12.

--Wash. 1^{s}-2^{d}. 6. Coff. 2^{d}. 7 Coff. 4^{d}. --8. Coff. 2^{d}. L^{tt} Bern^{ge}. 6^{d} - 0 - 2 - 4
candles & sm^{ll} before. 7^{d}. --9. Coff. 4^{d}. Chair. 1^{s}. --10. sm^{ll} 4^{d}. Coff. 2^{d} - - - 0 - 2 - 5
--11. Coff. 4^{d} sm^{ll}. 1^{s} - - - 0 - 0 - 5
0 - 5 - 2

3^{d} Week.

12 to 19.

--Coff. 4^{d}. sm^{ll} 1^{d} --13 Coff. 4^{d}. --15 Coff 2^{d} sm^{ll}. 1^{d}. Por^{tr} 6^{d} - - - 0 - 1 - 6
--16 sm^{ll}. 1^{d} wash. 1^{s}-2^{d}. --17. Coff. 4^{d} sm^{ll} 1^{d} - - - 0 - 1 - 8
--19 Coles 1^{s}-4^{d} Candles 5^{d}. G maid. 6^{d}. Co^{ch} Vanhom. 1^{s} - - - 0 - 3 - 3
0 - 6 - 5

4th Week.

19 to Mar. 1.

--Wash. 1^{s}-6^{d}. Din^{r} Addis^{n} 5^{s}. Coff. &c 3^{d}. Lett^{rs} MD (13, 14) 1^{s} - - - 0 - 7 - 9
--Let^{r} Mrs de Caudre. 6^{d}. Let^{tr}. A Bp D. 1^{s}. Coff 2^{d}. --20 Coff 6^{d} - - - 0 - 2 - 2
--21 Co^{ch}. Addison. 1^{s}. --22. Co^{ch}. 1^{s}. ∧ L^{dy} Lucy Chair Rolt. 1^{s}. Pap^{r}. 6^{d} - - - 0 - 3 - 6
--G Pat Rolt. 1^{s}-6^{d}. P^{d} old wash. &c. 2^{s}-6^{d} --23 Co^{ch} L^{dy} Lucy 1^{s}. sm^{ll}. 2^{d} - - - 0 - 5 - 2
--Din^{r} Mr Hughs. 1^{s}-6^{d}. Lett^{r} Wesly 1^{s}. Tav^{rn}. Addis^{n}. 2^{s}-6^{d} - - - 0 - 5 - 0
25. Din^{r} 8^{d} - Cand^{ls}, Powd^{r}. &c. 1^{s} --26 Coff. 6^{d}. sm^{ll}. 1^{d} - - - 0 - 2 - 3
27. Co^{ch} Addis^{n} 1. sm^{ll}. 1^{d} --28. Wash. 1^{s}-2^{d}. sm^{ll} 1^{d} - - - 0 - 2 - 4
1 - 8 - 2

1st Week	0 - 2 - 9
2^{d} Week	- 0 - 5 - 2
3^{d} Week	- 0 - 6 - 5
4th Week	- 1 - 8 - 2
	2 - 2 - 6

March. (Head ake frequent) Expences. (towards th end Cough a week, but end in a cold.) 2^{d} Month

1st Week

1 to 5

--Coff 4^{d} Sm^{ll}. 2^{d} por 2^{d}. --2. din^{r} S. Hughs. 1^{s}-9^{d} - - -	0 - 2 - 5
--3^{d} Coff 6^{d} Lett^{r} Mot^{hr}. 3^{d}. --4 Co^{ch} L^{dy} Lucy. 1^{s}. Coff. 2^{d} - - -	0 - 1 -11
	0 - 4 - 4

2^{d} Week

5 to 12

--Wash. 1^{s}-6^{d} --6 Coff 4^{d} --7 Sm^{ll} at Home 3^{d} <--8 Coles Cand^{ls}> - - -	0 - 2 - 1
--8. Coles 1^{s}-4^{d} Cand^{l} 4^{d}.½ G. maid 2^{d}.½ s^{mll} 2^{d} Coff 4^{d} - - -	0 - 2 - 5
--9 Co^{ch} to & from L^{dy} Lucy. 2^{s}. --10 Coff. 2^{d} Lett^{r} MD. 15. 6 - - -	0 - 2 - 8
	0 - 7 - 2

3^{d} Week

12 to 19

--Wash - 1^{s}-3^{d} Raz^{rs}. 2^{d}. s^{mll}. 2^{d}. Coff. 4^{d} --13. Chair 1^{s} - - -	0 - 3 - 1
--14 Co^{ch} Manly. 2^{s}. s^{mll} 2^{d} --15. Lett^{r} MD 16. 6^{d}. Coff. 6^{d} - - -	0 - 3 - 0
--17 Chair Pat Rolt. 1^{s}. Coff. 4^{d} --18 G. begg^{r} Pur^{nll} 6^{d} Coff. 4^{d} - - -	0 - 2 - 2
	0 - 8 - 3

4th Week

19 to 26.

--Coff 4^{d} Lett^{r} D. Stearn 6^{d} Lett^{r} A B D. 6^{d} --20. Coff. 4^{d} - - -	0 - 1 - 8
--21 Coffe. 4^{d} --22 Coffee. 4^{d} Chair Addis^{n} 1^{s} - - -	1 - 8
--23. Coff. 4^{d} Tav^{rn} Took. 1^{s}. --24. Coff. 4^{d} --25 Co^{ch} Henley. 1^{s} - - -	2 - 8
	0 - 6 - 0

26 to Apr. 1.

Rem^{dr}.

Wash. 2 weeks. 2^{s}. Coff. 4^{d} --27. Chair Ld Somm^{rs} ^& Wharton^ 1^{s}-6^{d} - - -	0 - 3 -10
--Buttrd ale 4^{d} G. maid 2^{d}. --28. Coff 6^{d} - - -	0 - 1 - 0
--30. Lett^{rs} Bp Clogh^{r}, Mr Walls, J B, 1^{s}-6^{d} - - -	0 - 1 - 6
--31. Coff. 4^{d} s^{ml} Cand^{l}, Poud^{r}, Cand^{ls}, G. maid 3^{d} in all - - -	0 - 2 - 4
	0 - 8 - 8

First week	-	0 - 4 - 4
2^{d} Week	-	0 - 7 - 2
3^{d} Week	-	0 - 8 - 3
4th Week	-	0 - 6 - 0
Rem^{dr}	-	0 - 8 - 8
		1 - 15- 5

April. Expences. (begins with Cough turn^{d} to Cold, well by th 6th) 3^{d} Month

1st Week

1 to 9

<--Coff. 4^{d} --Sm^{ll} 2^{d}. Por 2^{d}>
Co^{ch} Ld Hallifax. 1^{s}. Coff. 5^{d}. --2. Leq^{rice}. 6^{d}. Coff. 4^{d}. - - - 0 - 2 - 3
--Wash 1^{s}-6^{d} raz^{r} 2^{d}. G. Mrs S. 1^{s}. --4 Coff 4^{d} Lett^{r} Pat R. 2^{d} - - - 0 - 3 - 2
--5 G poor. 4^{d} --6. Coff. 4^{d}. --7 Coff. 4^{d}. --8 Lett^{r} MD. 17. 6^{d} <sm^{ll} Adis^{n}.> - - - 0 - 1 - 6
Small with Addis^{n}. 4^{d} - - - 0 - 0 - 4
0 - 7 - 3

2^{d} Week.

9 to 16.

--G. Addis^{ns} man. 2^{s}-6^{d}. Coff. 4^{d}. --10. Poor Ch. 6^{d}. Wash 1^{s} - - - 0 - 4 - 4
--12 Poud^{r}, Cand^{ls}, &c 1^{s}. --13 Coff. 4^{d} Tabac 3^{d} - - - 0 - 1 - 7
--15 Co^{ch} Henly - 1^{s}. Coff. 6^{d} - - - 0 - 1 - 6
0 - 7 - 5

3^{d} Week

16 to 23.

--17. Wash &c 1^{s}-5^{d} - Coff &c. 6^{d}. --18. Coff 4^{d} ^19 Chair Ld Berk. 1^{s} --20. Coff 4^{d} poor 2^{d} - 0 - 3 - 9
--Lett^{r} Pat Rolt 2^{d} --21. Coff. 4^{d} Chair Ld Treas^{r}. 1^{s}. --22 Coff. &c. 6^{d} - - - 0 - 2 - 0
0 - 5 - 9

4th Week.

23 to May. 1.

--Chop House Will Franck^{d}, Ld Petr. &c. 1^{s}. Tav^{n}. 1^{s}-6^{d}. Coff. 2^{d} - - - 0 - 2 - 8
--24. Coff 4^{d} sm^{ll} 2^{d}. --25 Coff. 6^{d}. Lett^{r} Mot^{h}. Bp Clogh^{r} 9^{d} - - - 0 - 1 - 9
--26. G. Ld Ranel. Gard^{n}. 1^{s}. Coff. 6^{d}. --27. Tav^{rn} Took 1^{s}-2^{d}. - - - 0 - 2 - 8
--Wash. 1^{s}-8^{d}. --28. Punch. Hughs &c. 1^{s}. Coff. 4^{d} - - - 0 - 3 - 0
--29. Co^{ch} Steel. 1^{s}. Tav^{rn} Steel. 1^{s}-6^{d}. --30. wash & G. 1^{s}-6^{d} Cha^{r} Ld Rad^{r} 1^{s} - - - 0 - 5 - 0
0 - 15- 1

1st Week.	0 - 7 - 3
2^{d} Week -	0 - 7 - 5
3^{d} Week -	0 - 5 - 9
4th Week -	0 - 15- 1
	1 - 15- 6

England

Totalls

of a Qua^{rtr} from Feb^{r}. 1st. 170$\frac{8}{9}$ to May. 1. 1709

JB - - - (not sett^{d}) - - -	1 - 10- 0
Cloaths - - -	17 - 10- 2
MC - - -	11 - 0 - 0
Lodging - - -	3 - 6 - 0
Extr^{drys} - - -	5 - 17- 0
Expences 1st Month - - -	2 - 2 - 6
Expences 2^{d} Month - - -	1 - 15- 5
Expences 3^{d} Month - - -	1 - 15- 6
	44 - 16- 7

Third Quarter.

From May 1st to Aug. 1. 1709.

JB.

--------- ---------- 1 - 10- 0

Cloaths

May. 1. Thrd Stock^{ns}. 7^{s} --21 a Perewig - 2^{ll}-10^{s}. Wastct & Brechs. 2^{ll}-3^{s} - - -	5 - 0 - 0
July. 25 Shoes 2 p^{r} 8^{s} (unp^{d} 11^{d}) - - -	0 - 8 - 0
	5 - 8 - 0

MC.

July. 25. 5^{ll} ⟨Sept 3^{d}. 1^{ll}-7^{d}.½ 9. 18^{s}.6^{d}⟩
Allwd of last qrtr overp^{d}. 2^{ll}-10
Sep^{br}. 3. 1^{ll}-7^{d}.½ --9. 18.6 --clear^{d} - - - 11 - 0 - 0

Lodging

Jul. 8th. a Week - 5^{s}
--Then came to Mrs Curry. th rest allowd next Qu^{rt} - - - 0 - 5 - 0

Extr^{drys}.

May. 3. A deal box &c. 5^{s} Lodging 1^{ll}-7^{s}-6^{d} - - -	1 - 12- 6
G. Mrs S. for MD. 10^{s}-9^{d}. --24 Plato. & Xephilin. 1^{ll}-10^{s} - - -	2 - 0 - 9
--Jun. 3^{d} 5 Books 1^{ll}-1^{s}-6^{d} --4. a Box 2^{s}-6^{d} - to Pat. G. 10^{s}-9^{d} - - -	1 - 14- 9
--9 G. Pat for Gown 2^{s}-6^{d} --13 Pothe^{ry}. 4^{s}-5^{d} - - -	0 - 6 -11
--to Mrs Worrall 1^{ll}-10^{s}. Horses 1^{ll} - - -	2 - 10- 0
Jul. 6 G. MD for Play. 1^{ll}-17^{s}- 9. Mrs Walls 1^{s}-1^{d} - - -	1 - 18- 1
--12 G. Chapt^{r} man. 3^{s}-4^{d}. Books. 10^{s}-10^{d}. - - -	0 - 14- 2
--19. G M^{r} Br. 5^{s}-5^{d}. Prison^{r}. 3^{s}-9^{d}½ --23. bind book. 5^{s}-5^{d} - - -	0 - 14- 7½
--25 G dd. 5^{s}-5^{d} --30. Dd old debt. 3^{ll}. - - -	3 - 5 - 5
	14 - 16- 2½

Left Lond. May. 5. ^1709^ on Thursd. came to Leicest^{r}. ^May. 7.^ on Saterd. following.

Left Leicest^{r}. Jun. 14th 1709. came to Chester. 15th on Wednesday.

Servt.

Ned came Jul. 15th. 1709.

Expences. Ubi. 8? Leicest^r. 7. 1st Month.

May.

1st Week

1 to 14

--Coffe. 6^d Let^r. MD. 6^d --3 G at Coffee H. 5^s G. m^rs S. 5^s - - -	0 - 11- 0
--Co^ch. 1^s G maid 2^s-6^d p^d Maid. 1^s-6^d --4. Co^ch 4^s-6^d Carr^ir &c 1^s - -	0 - 10- 6
5. Rose Inn. 5^s. St Albans. 5^s-6^d. Dunstab^l. 4^s-6 Newp^rt. 3^s - - -	0 - 17- 6
--Northampt^n. 5^s. Harborough. 2^s. G. Coachm^n. 1^s. Coach. 1^ll-2^s - - -	1 - 10- 0
At Leicest^r 9 Brief 1^s. Lett^rs MD & Bp Cl. 1^s-6^d. Cand^l &c. 1^s --11 a Book 1^s - - -	0 - 4 - 6
--sm^ll. 6^d --13 Thurmaston 4^s wash. 2^s - - -	0 - 6 - 6
	3 - 19- 0

2^d Week

14 to 21.

A Book. 1^s-6^d. old Bess. 1^s. Brief. 6^d Lett^rs & sm^ll. 1^s. - - -	0 - 4 - 0
--18. At Thurmaston Walls man. 1^s. maid. 1^s poor seaman 6^d - - -	0 - 2 - 0
Lett^r Sr A^d F. &c. 9^d - - -	0 - 0 - 9
	0 - 7 - 3

3^d Week.

21 to 28

--Wash. 1^s. Lett^r Mrs Bart. 6. s^mll. 5^d --25. G. old man 6^d - - -	0 - 2 - 5
--26. Coff Rost^r for Pat R. 3^s. Sr G. Beau^mnts Serv^ts. 3^s-6^d - - -	0 - 6 - 6
Letters Mrs Van Sr A. F. &c. 1^s. Wash. 1^s - - -	0 - 2 - 0
	0 - 10-11

Remain^dr.

28 to Jun. 1.

Lett^rs Bp Clogh^r. &c. 1^s --31 at Coleorton. 1^s. Sr G. B's man. 1^s-6^d - -	0 - 3 - 6
<--G. maid 6^d>	0 - 3 - 6

1st Week	3 - 19- 0
2^d Week	- 0 - 7 - 3
3^d Week	- 0 - 10-11
4th Week	- 0 - 3 - 6
	5 - 0 - 8

Memd. Coz Dean's Bond commences

Febr. 22^d. 170$\frac{6}{7}$

Expences. ubi, 12? Leicest^{r}. 8 Dublin. 30th 2^{d} Month.

June.

1st Week

1 to 11

--G. maid 6^{d}. 2. B. Airs maid. 1^{s}. --3^{d} Treat drabs. 1^{s}. Moth^{r} cand^{ls}. 1^{s}6^{d} - - - 0 - 4 - 0
--4 Pat -1^{s}. --5. Sac^{rt}. 1^{s} Wash. 2 weeks 1^{s} -7. Ale 3^{d}. Lett^{rs} &c 6.½ - 0 - 4 - 4½
--6 s^{mll}. Pat. 6^{d}. --7 Carrge 2^{s}-6^{d} Coff. 10^{d} --8 s^{mll}. 6^{d} - - - 0 - 4 - 4
--9 Ale & G. fish. 1^{s} - - - 0 - 1 - 0
0 - 13 - 8½

2^{d} Week.

11 to 18

P^{d} Pat. 1^{s}. wash. 6^{d} --12. Sac^{rnt}. 1^{s}.〈 〉--13. Moth^{r}. 1^{s}-6^{d} - - - 0 - 4 - 0
--Tav^{rn}. 2^{s} Wash 1^{s}., Coff. 6^{d}. left Moth^{r} 1^{s}-6^{d}. G. maid. 2^{s} - - - 0 - 7 - 0
--14. Journey to Chester
Dinn^{r}. &c. at Burton on th Hill. 2^{s}-10^{d} --15. Stone. 6^{s} - - - 0 - 8 - 10
--Nantwich. 3^{s}-9^{d} --Chest^{r}. Guide. 10^{s}. Hors. 2^{s}. - - - 0 - 15 - 9
At Ca^{mint} to 19. 12^{s}-6^{d}. Carriage 2 boxes - 14^{s}-6^{d} Coff 6^{d} - - - 1 - 7 - 6
3 - 3 - 1 2 - 7 - 4

3^{d} Week.

18 to -25.

--21. Books. 3^{s}-6^{d} s^{mll}. 6^{d}. --22. Coff. 6^{d} --24. Coff. 2^{d}. Wash. 1^{s} - 0 - 5 - 8
G Coz^{ns} maid. 1^{s} - - - 0 - 1 - 0
0 - 6 - 8

4th Week

25 to Jul. 1

--26 maid 1^{s} --board Mrs Kinas Inn. 10^{s} Coff. 1^{s} - - - 0 - 12 - 0
--27. Boxes carr^{d} to Parkgate. 2^{s} --Waiters there. 2^{s}-6^{d} G. maid. 1^{s} - - 0 - 5 - 6
0 - 17 - 6

〈Set Sail for Ireland on Jun. 29th 1709 at 3 a clock in the morning being Wednesday〉

Sett sail from Darpool for Ireland June. 29th. 1709 at 3 a cloack in the Morning being Wednesday, lay that night in the Bay of Dublin, and landed at - Ringsend the next day at 7 in the morning, - and went strait to Laracor without seing any - body and returnd to Dublin July 4. wch was Monday following

First Week	0 - 13 - 8½
2^{d} Week	- 3 - 3 - 1
3^{d} Week	- 0 - 6 - 8
4th Week	- 0 - 17 - 6
	〈 4 - 5 - 2½ 〉
	5 - 0 - 11½

3^d Month

Expences.

July. Laracor to. 4^t

Ireland.

1st Week

1 to 9

Jun. 30. Ringsend waiters 2^s-8^d.½ Co^ch. 1^s-1^d --s^mll. 6^d - - -	0 - 4 - 3½
Jul. 4. Co^ch 8^d --5 Custom H. 4^s-6^d - with Mr Addis^n 2^s. Co^ch. 1^s-1^d - -	0 - 8 - 3
--Chair 6^d.½ --6 G. MD. 2^s-8^d.½ --Co^ch 2^s-10^d Chair. 8^d - - -	0 - 6 - 9
--7 Co^ch 8^d. G MD 9^d --8^d G. maid 6^d -Co^ch 2^s-2^d to Sr T. Southw^lls - - -	0 - 4 - 1
	1 - 3 - 4½

2^d Week.

9 to 16.

--Forgot & lost account of all. 5^s. - - -	0 - 5 - 0

3^d Week.

16 to 23

Bo^rd wages 8 days, to th 24th. 4^s. Chair. 1^s-1^d - - -	0 - 5 - 1
--Din^r M^r Ad^sn. 2^s-8^d½ Tav^rn. Mr Add^sn. 2^s-2^d. Ch^r. 6^d.½ - - -	0 - 5 - 5
--19 Tav^rn Ford 2^s-2^d --20. Chair Ld Abercorn. 6^d.½ - - -	0 - 2 - 8½
--21. Co^ch MD. 1^s-7^d½ - - -	0 - 1 - 7½
	0 - 14-10

4th Week

23 to Aug. 1.

--Din^r Fingl^s. Mr Add^on. 2^s-8^d.½ G. Ned. 6. brd wages to Aug. 1 - 4^s - -	0 - 7 - 2½
Sm^ll 4^d --24 S^mll 3^d --25. G. MD. 2^s-8^d.½ - - -	0 - 3 - 3½
--Mrs Currys bill, Shdon 1^s Pat 9^d Cadl &c in all 3^s-4^d - - -	0 - 3 - 4
--Chair Mr Addis^n 6^d --26 s^mll 2^d --28. Wine Raym^d. 1^s-8^d. G. Patr. 1^s1^d	0 - 3 - 5
--29. G old wom^n. 6^d.½ G. I^ah Parvis^ll 1^s-1d. s^mll. 1^d - - -	0 - 1 - 8½
--30. Co^ch. Dr Stearn. 2^s-2^d. B^rd wags. 3^s-6^d Neds bill. 1^s-9^d s^mll 2^d -	0 - 6 -10
	1 - 5 - 9½

1st Week	- 1 - 3 - 4
2^d Week	- 0 - 5 - 0
3^d Week	- 0 - 14-10
4th Week	- 1 - 5 - 9½
	3 - 8 -11½

Totalls

Of a Quarter from May. 1. to Aug. 1. 1709.

JB - ⟨(not sett[d])⟩ sett[d] - - -	1 - 10- 0
Cloaths - - -	5 - 8 - 0
MC - - -	11 - 0 - 0
Lodging - - -	0 - 5 - 0
Extr[dys] - - -	14 - 16- 2½
Expences 1st Month - - -	5 - 0 - 8
Expences 2[d] Month - - -	5 - 0 -11½
Expences 3[d] Month - - -	3 - 8 -11½
	46 - 9 - 9½
Lodging a London a week forgot - - -	0 - 5 - 0
	46 - 14- 9½

Fourth Quarter

From Aug. 1. to Nov^{br}. 1. 1709.

JB.

24. 5^{s}-5^{d} Sept^{br}. 24 1^{ll}-7-9^{d} - - -	1 - 13 - 2
Jan^{r}. 5 - 1^{ll}-7-6^{d} - more 3^{s}-4^{d} -) - 16 - 8 - - -	2 - 7 - 6

Cloaths.

Aug. 20. Bands. 14^{s} Sep^{t}. Cleaning night gown 1^{s}-6^{d} - - -	0 - 15 - 6
--silk &c. 6^{d} - 14 Night gown. 14^{s}-9^{d}. Box for wigs. 10^{d} - - -	0 - 16 - 1
mend fust. wastcoat. & night gwn. 1^{s}-3^{d} - - -	0 - 1 - 3
	1 - 12 -10

MC.

⟨Sep^{t}. 3. 1^{ll}-7^{d}.½ --9. 18^{s}-6^{d}⟩
Sep^{br}. 13. 4^{ll}-0-1½ --26. 2 Pist (Qu? more) 1^{ll}17^{s}

Lodging.

Allow^{d} to 4 months of this year - - -	3 - 0 - 0

Servant.

Aug. 1. Boots. 3^{s}-2^{d}. Jul. 16. Hat. 2^{s}-8^{d}.½ --20. Shoes. 3^{s}-6^{d} - - -	0 - 9 - 4½
--Stick 4^{d} --27. Breeches. 4^{s}. Pat Wages. 9s4^{d} - - -	0 - 13 - 8
	1 - 3 - 0½

Extr^{drys}.

G. X church man. 2^{s}-2^{d} - - -	0 - 2 - 2
Aug. 19. P^{d} M^{r}. Grant money I lost by lending to Mr Brent, who faild and his Security - - -	4 - 0 - 0
--27 G. ⟨MD⟩- - 3^{s}-4^{d} --24⟨binding⟩Lettring book. 2^{s}-6^{d} - - -	0 - 5 +10
Sep^{br}. 20. Pills gilt. 5^{s}. --24 lett^{r} & bind books. 8^{s}-4^{d} - - -	0 - 13 - 4
	5 - 1 - 4

Wash

9 weeks to Sep^{br}. 12. 8^{s}-6^{d} to No^{vr}. 1. Larac^{r}. 9^{s}-5^{d} - - -	0 - 17 -11

Horses

Aug. 6. Sadd^{l} Brid^{l}. Housing, &c - 2^{ll}-10^{s}-1^{d} - - -	2 - 10 - 1

Horses

Sept. 15

Mend bridle - 5^{d} Levings^{tn} to Sep^{br}. 27. 8^{s}-8^{d}.½ - - -	0 - 8 - 8½
Snaffle &c 1^{s}6. Horses going & coming 17^{s}-2^{d} in all - - -	0 - 18 - 8
	1 - 7 - 4½

[9v]

August.	Expences.	1st Month.
	1st Week.	
1 to 6.		
--G. MD. 1^{s}-1^{d}. Coff. MD. 5^{d}. 2 lett^{rs} from S^{r}. A. F. 1^{s}. - - -		0 - 2 - 6
--Chair D. Stearn. 6^{d},½ brd wag. to 6. 3^{s}. - - -		0 - 3 - 6½
		0 - 6 - 0
	2^{d} Week. Laracor.	
6 to 13		
--6. at Mr Fords. 6^{d}.½ --10. G. at Ld Trimb^{stn}. 3^{d} s^{mll}. 4^{d} - - -		0 - 1 - 1½
Co^{ch} to Leving^{tn}. 6^{d}.½ - - -		0 - 0 - 6½
		0 - 1 - 8
	3^{d} Week.	
13 to 20		
--15 G at L^{dy} Shelb^{rns} 6^{d}.½ --16. G. at Mr Add^{ns}. 1^{s}-1^{d} - - -		0 - 1 - 7½
--Brd wag. to 20^{t}. 1^{s}-7^{d}.½ s^{mll} before. 3^{d}. --17. Chaise. 5^{d} - - -		0 - 2 - 3½
--G. 3^{d}. --18. Coff. 3^{d}. Tav^{rn} Raym^{d}. 1^{s}-4^{d}.½ Pap^{r}. 1^{s}-2^{d} - - -		0 - 3 - 0
--19. Chaise Fingl^{s}. 6^{d}.½ Fish. 3^{d}. Win. MD. 1^{s}-4^{d}.½ - - -		0 - 2 - 2
		0 - 9 - 1
	4th Week.	
20 to 27		
--Chair Mr Addis^{n}. 6^{d}.½ Coff. 3^{d}. s^{mll}. 1^{d} --21. Sac^{rnt} 1^{s}-1^{d} - - -		0 - 1 -11½
Brd W. 3^{s}-6^{d} --22. Din^{r}. 3^{d}.½. Neds bill Cand^{l} Bred, &c - - -		0 - 3 - 9½
Raz^{rs}. &c. 1^{s}-7^{d}.½ --23^{d}. Din^{r} MD - 1^{s}-4^{d}. Win. 1^{s}-4^{d} - - -		0 - 4 - 3½
--Wine. Raim^{d} - 1^{s}-4^{d}.½ Coff. Walls. 6^{d} - - -		0 - 1 -10½
--Dwarfs. 1^{s}-4^{d} Lett^{r} Sr A. F. 6^{d}.½ before) s^{mll}. 2^{d} - - -		0 - 2 - 0½
		0 - 13-11
	Rem^{dr}.	
27 to Sept. 1.		
G. Fingl^{s}. 1^{s}-7^{d} --G. Ned. 6^{d}.½ Co^{ch} MD. 1^{s}11^{d} s^{mll}. 2^{d} - - -		0 - 3 - 8½
JB's bill - Brandy 1^{s}-6 Sug^{r} 2^{s}-10^{d} Sage 1^{s}-6^{d} Coffee pot 10^{d} Sm^{ll}. 7^{d}.½ Mutt^{n} 8^{d}.½ in all		0 - 8 - 0
Neds bill Bread, Poud^{r}, Raz^{rs} Oyl, &c 1^{s}-4^{d}.½ - - -		0 - 1 - 4½
Brd wags to Sep^{tr}. 3^{d} 3^{s}-6^{d} - - -		0 - 3 - 6
		0 - 16- 7

1st Week -	0 - 6 - 0
2^{d} Week -	0 - 1 - 8
3^{d} Week -	0 - 9 - 1
4th Week -	0 - 13-11
Rem^{dr} -	0 - 16- 7
	2 - 7 - 3
Candles. forgt	0 - 1 - 0
	2 - 8 - 3

Expences 2^{d} Month

(JB)

Sept^{br}.

1st Week.

1 to 10.

--Brd wags. to 10th 3^{s}-6^{d}. Chair. 6^{d}.½ s^{mll} before. 4^{d} - - -	0 - 4 - 4½
--3. Win & Olives Mr Addis^{n}. 1^{s}-10^{d} s^{mll} 2^{d}.½ Co^{ch}. Fingl. 1^{s}-8^{d} - - -	0 - 3 - 8½
--5 Win Ad. 1^{s}-7^{d}.½ Co^{ch}. MD. 5^{d}.½ --8 Co^{ch} MD. 2^{s}-4^{d} G. Boy 5^{d}.½ - - -	0 - 4 -10½
--9 Snuff MD. 6^{d}.½ Co^{ch} MD. 6^{d}.½ - - -	0 - 1 - 1
	0 - 13-11½

2^{d} Week.

10 to 17.

12 ^ Neds bill Tobacco, Raz^{rs}, Lodg 6^{d} din^{r} J Beau^{mt} 2^{s}4^{d} - - -	0 - 2 - 4
Co^{ch} from Fingl. 1^{s}-1^{d} --13 Win MD. 1^{s}-4^{d} - - -	0 - 2 - 5
--15. Por Wom^{n}. 1^{s}-1^{d} Cakes 2^{d}. G. MD. 3^{d}. Chair 1^{s} - - -	0 - 2 - 6
--Wine. Walls, & MD. 1^{s}-4^{d}. Neds bill Bred butt^{r}. Poud^{r}. &c 2^{s}-7^{d}.½ - - -	0 - 3 -11½
Brd wages - 3^{s}-6^{d} --16. Co^{ch}. 3^{s}-1^{d} - - -	0 - 6 - 7
	0 - 17- 9½

3^{d} Week.

17 to 24

--Co^{ch} 6^{d}.½ --18 Win. Bern^{ge}. 1^{s}-4^{d} Pull^{t} &c 1^{s}-1^{d} - - -	0 - 2 -11½
--19. Coff. 6^{d} -s^{mll} 2^{d}. bor^{d} wages - 3^{s}-6^{d} - - -	0 - 4 - 2
--Neds bill Tob. 4^{d} Raz^{rs} Oyl. 4^{d} Brd butt^{r}. &c in all - - -	0 - 1 - 1½
--20. MD Coach. 1^{s}-1^{d} --Co^{ch} MD. 6^{d} s^{mll} 1^{d}½ - - -	0 - 1 - 8½
22 G. Finglas. 1^{s}-1^{d} Chaise 9^{d}.½ --23 Tav^{rn} Perc^{ll}. 1^{s}-7^{d} - - -	0 - 3 - 5½
	0 - 13- 5

4th Week.

24 to Oc^{tbr}. 1.

--JB's bill G old man. & lah 1^{s}½ Pull^{t}. 2^{s} (for MD before) Coff. &c in all - - -	0 - 4 - 6½
--Chair. 8^{d}. --25. din^{r} Jo. B. 1^{s}. - - -	0 - 1 - 8
--26. G. MD. 2^{s}-8^{d}.½ Co^{ch}. 1^{s}. win. MD. 1^{s}4^{d} - - -	0 - 5 - 0½
Laracor	
--27 --Co^{ch}. 10^{d} - --28. win. Dr R. 8^{d} G. Mr For^{bs}. man &c 1^{s} - - -	0 - 2 - 6
--sm^{ll} 3^{d} brd w. 1^{s}-6^{d} Neds bill Win. 8^{d}. Raz^{rs}. 3^{d}. sm^{ll}. 2^{d} - - -	0 - 2 -10
	0 - 16- 7

1st Week		0 - 13-11½
2^{d} Week	-	0 - 17- 9½
3^{d} Week	-	0 - 13- 5
4th Week	-	0 - 16- 7
		3 - 1 - 9

Expences 3d Month

Octobr.

1. to 8. 1st Week. Laracor

--2 Sacrmt. 2s-2d. -G. Ned 8d.½ --6 G at Prats. 3d - - -
Lettr Ldy G. inclosd 4d - - - 0 - 3 - 1½

8 to 15 2d Week. Laracor

G. 3d. Wine Raymd. 6d.½ - - - 0 - 0 - 9½
12 House bill for twice at Laracor to Septbr 27th for
eating &c. (too large a bill I think for only 12 days) - - - 1 - 7 - 0½
--G. smll. 3d. --14. Dinr Raymd. 5s - - - 0 - 5 - 3
1 - 13- 0½

15 to 22. 3d Week Laracor

--16. G. por mad girl. 3d. --17 G. workmn 6d.½ --18. por. 2d - - - 0 - 0 -11½
--19. Doubl. Lettr. MD. 4d. G. 2d Punch, before (18th) Forbs. 3s - - - 0 - 3 - 6
0 - 4 - 5½

22d to No. 1. 4th Week. Laracor

--23 Lettr D. Ash. 2d. 24 win. Rayd &c. 1s-6d - - - 0 - 1 - 8
25. G. workmn. 6d.½ Neds bill. 6d.½. smll 2d. - - - 0 - 1 - 3
--30. Lettrs. Mr Add. Sr A. F. Mr PhilP. &c. 1s-6d G. Ned. 2d - - - 0 - 1 - 8
31. Punch Rayd. 2s-2d G. his man &c 8d G Ned 4d - - - 0 - 3 - 2
0 - 7 - 9

Part of a House bill ^of 1ll-10-9d½^ at Laracor from Septr. 27
to Novbr. 1. th rest allwd next year - - - 1ll-0 - 0

<Washing allowd at Laracor to Novbr. 1. - - - 0 - 9 - 5>

1st Week	-	0 - 3 - 1½
2d Week	-	1 - 13- 0½
3d Week	-	0 - 4 - 5½
4th Week	-	0 - 7 - 9
Remdr	-	1 - 0 - 0
		2 - 8 - 4½

Totalls

Of a Quarter from August. 1. to Nov^{br}. 1. 1709

JB ⟨(not sett^{d})⟩ sett^{d} - - -	1 - 10- 0
Cloaths - - -	1 - 12-10
MC - - -	11 - 0 - 0
Lodging - - -	3 - 0 - 0
Servant - - -	1 - 3 - 0½
Extr^{dys} - - -	5 - 1 - 4
Wash - - -	0 - 17-11
Horses & Saddle &c - - -	3 - 17- 5
Expences 1st Month - - -	2 - 8 - 3
Expences 2^{d} Month - - -	3 - 1 - 9
Expences 3^{d} Month - - -	2 - 8 - 4½
	36 - 0 -11

[11v]

Totalls

Of a Year from Nov^{br}. 1. 1708 to Nov^{br}. 1. 1709

JB - - - Settled - - -	6 - 0 - 0
Cloaths - - -	28 - 8 - 0
MC - - -	44 - 0 - 0
Lodging - - -	10 - 2 - 0
Servant - - -	1 - 3 - 0½
Extraord^{rys} - - -	27 - 7 - 9½
Washing. part (the rest with Expences) - - -	0 - 17-11
Horses, &c - - -	3 - 17- 5
Expences 1st Quarter - - -	7 - 0 - 5
Expences 2^{d} Quarter - - -	5 - 13- 5
Expences 3^{d} Quarter (Travelling) - - -	13 - 10- 7
Expences 4th Quarter (Ireland) - - -	7 - 18- 4½
	155 - 18-11½
Allwd JB. more for New Years gift - - -	0 - 8 - 1½
	156 - 7 - 1
Washing rem^{dr} forgot - - -	0 - 4 - 2
	156 - 11- 3
Grazing Horses from Jun. to Oc^{tbr}. 1709 - - -	0 - 18- 0

Lett^{rs} to

Nov^{br}. 9.

A. B. Dublin.
Bp Clogher.
Dr Raimond.
Mr Henly.
Mr Walls
Mr Percivall.
--12 MD 10
Mrs Davis.
--18. Mr Crow.
--20 Dr Smith.
--23 MD. 11
--Pat Rolt
--27 Moth^{r}
--30 Dean of St Patricks
--A. Bp Dublin inclosd.
Dec^{br}. 2. Mr Domvile.
--14. MD. 12.
--30 MD. 13.
Jan^{r}. 4. Bp of Clogher.
--6 A. Bp of Dublin.
--Mother
--MD. 14.
--13 MD. 15.
--Govern^{r} of Virginia
--22^{d}. MD. 16.
--29 MD. 17
Febr. 4th. Ld Sommers.
--Tom Ash.
--12 MD 18
--Bp of Clogh^{r}
--24 Mother
--26 MD. 19.

Letters from.

fro' Nov^{br}. 1 to 10.

Bp Clogh^{r}
Mr Walls
Dr Smith
Mr Crow
Mr Domvil.
Mr Henly.
--19 MD. 9.
Mrs Davis.
--22 Pat Rolt
--Mr Reeding.
Pat Rolt before
Dec^{br}. 4. A. Bp of Dublin
--6 Earl of Abercorn.
--8 Mother.
--13 Mr Walls
Mr Walls anoth^{r}
--Dean of St Patricks
<--14. MD. 12>
--20 MD. 10
--Mr Walls (with a Bill).
--23 Mrs Davys.
--26 Dr Raymond
--30. MD. 11.
Jan^{r}. 7. Bp of Clogh^{r} (by Mr Read)
--unknown hand with a Slur.
--Govern^{r} of Virginia from Paris.
--13 Freckleton.
--Mother
--19 Parvisol.
--Mr Ford
--28. Bp of Clogher.
Sr Mathew Dudley.
Sr Mat. Dudly.
Feb^{r}. 1. MD. 12.
--4 Mr Walls.
--Mr Reading.
--8 Mr Bernege
--12 Mr Domvil from Geneva
--19 MD 13
--MD 14.
--Mrs de Caudre
--A. Bp of Dublin

Letters to

Mar. 5. Dean of St Patricks
--8 Mr Ford.
Govern^{r} of Virginia.
--15 MD. 20.
--Mr Philips at Copenhagen.
--24 Ld Primate with Ld Whart^{n} inclosd.
--26 A. Bp Dublin. inclosd
--Dean of St Patricks.
--31. Mr Domvile at Geneva.
--Bp of Clogher.
--JB & Parvisol inclosed.
Apr. 2. MD. 21.
--9. Bp of Clogh^{r} by Mr Addison.
--15 Mr Addison.
--19 Mother.
--MD. 22.
--21. Pat Rolt.
--23. E. of Berkeley
--24 Mr Dubois
28. Mr Ford.
May. 9. MD 23. from Leicester
--Bp of Clogh^{r}.
--Mr Addison.
--Mr Took.
--Ld Mountjoy
--11 Mr Steel
--Mrs Barton
--Sr Andr Fountain
--16 Lady Lucy
--Mrs Vanhomrigh.
--21 Ld Mountjoy
26 S^{r} G Beaumont
--Sr And^{r} Fountain
--Mr Steel.
--Will Franckland.
--Mrs Barton
--30 Ld Mountjoy.
Jun. 1. Mr Took.
--Ld Mountjoy
--Sr And^{r}. Fountain.
--Mr Franckland.
--4 Govrn^{r} of Virginia
--Harry Coot.

Lett^{rs} from

Feb^{r}.
--19. Mr Gordon. (the 18th.).
--22 Mr Philips from Copenhagen.
--24 Mr Wesly. (Bill for Watch)
Mar. 10 MD. 15.
--15 MD 16
--19 Dean of St Patricks
--A. Bp of Dublin.
--30. Bp of Clogh^{r}.
--Mr Walls.
--J B.
Ap^{r}. 4. M^{rs} B---n
--Pat Rolt
--8 MD. 17.
--20 Pat Rolt
--23 E. of Berkeley
24 Bp of Clogh^{r}
--Mr Ford
--Mother
May. 1. MD. 18.
--Mr Addison. (from Irel^{d})
--9 Bp Clogh^{r} to Leicester
--MD. 19.
--14 Ld Mountjoy
--Mr Steel.
16 Sr And^{r} Fountain.
--21 Mrs Barton
--26 Mrs Vanhomrigh
--Sr And^{r}. Fountain
--28 Bp of Clogher
--Mr Addison.
Ld Mountjoy (before)
Mrs Armstrong & lady Lucy
Mr Philips from Copenhagen
Jun. 6. Will Franckland
--Sr And^{r}. Fountain.

(receivd a little before)

Letters to.

Jun.
--6. Mrs Armstrong
--Ben Tooke.
--13. Ld High Admirall
--Ld President
--E. of Berkeley
--Ld Mountjoy
--Ld Hallifax
--Mr Steel.
--Mrs Vanhomrigh
--MD 24 inclos^d to Reading.
--Mr Took.
to 30. at Chester.
--Mother
Mr Addison.
Bp Clogher.
Irel^d.
July. 8. Mother
--18 Mrs Barton
--Sr A. Fountain
Aug. Sr A. Fountain.
Mrs Barton
--27 L^dy Giffr^d
Sept^br. 13. Mother.
--Mr Took.
--Parvisol
Octr. 20. Mr Addison
--H. Coote.
--30 Mr Addison
--Mr Steel.
--Mr Philips
--Sr And^r Fountain
--Bp Clogh^r

Letters from

Ireland.

Jul. 1. Mrs Barton
--Sr And^r Fountain.
Mishessy.
Mr Addison, return^d me from Chester
Ld Mountjoy.
Aug. 6. Sr A. Fountain.
--L^dy Giff^rd
--Mother.
--16 Mr Philips. Copenhagen
--Mr Took.
--24 Sr A. Fountain
Octr. 23. Sr A. Fountain
--Ld Hallifax
--Mr Steel
--30 Mr Addison
--Mr Philips from Lond^n
Sr And^r Fountain
--Mother

Account

Of my Livings

For the Year

1708.

I was all this Year in England

(40 p.)

[20v]

Bills

	ll s d
ec^{br}. 20. 1708 a Bill from Mr Walls - - -	20 - 0 - 0

Laracor & Agher Sett. 1708.

Proudfoot & Shore, Tyth of Wool & Lamb - - -		1 - 0 - 0
Mr Melthrop, his own Tyth. & Keatings Wint^r^ Corn - - -		8 - 15- 0
Mic. Heaps &c. their own Tyths. Somerstown - - -		1 - 10- 0
R. Cusack. his Wint^r^ Corn. Sum^r^. town - - -		4 - 0 - 0
M^rs^. Prat. Her Tyth & th Gleab - - -		16 - 0 - 0
Mr Burnford - - -		7 - 0 - 0
Mr Jones his own Remd^r^. & little Fressons - - -		19 - 10- 0
Alvin & Airy Tyths of Umberstown - - -	10 - 10- 0	10 - 10- 0
Alvin. John Mahon's Tyths at Dangan - - -		1 - 0 - 0
To Mr Jones, great Fressons - - -		7 - 0 - 0
Jams Daniel. Balintogh^r^, & some part of Agher - - -		6 - 10- 0
Mr Percivall - - for Coliers town - - -		5 - 10- 0
Jam. Soogan. Twenty Acres - - -		2 - 5 - 0
Wat. Carly. Clondogan - - -		15 - 0 - 0
Jo^n^. Fagan. his Tyths at Somerhill - - -		2 - 10- 0
Mr Dennis his own Tyth & wood hay (5^s^) - - -		8 - 15- 0
Nic. Dolan. Knockbeg - - -		10 - 10- 0
Mic. Heaps &c. Tyth Corn at Laracor - - -		14 - 0 - 0
H^y^. Burn. part of Agher - - -		0 - 16- 0
Mr Wesly His own Tyths & wall Stock & Reads town - - -		6 - 10- 0
		148 - 11- 0
Browns town not returned - - -		0 - 18- 6
Tyths drawn.		149 - 9 - 6
Neals town & Steacum - - -		3 - 10- 0

Rathbeggan Sett. 1708.

Clynch, his Holding in Rathbeggan - - -	8 - 0 - 0
Jo^{n}. Hartford his holding in Rathbeggan	8 - 15- 0
Chris. Lewis Part of Parsonstown - - -	4 - 0 - 0
Ric. Andros. Rainstown - - -	9 - 0 - 0
Jon Martin. Tyth of Mill Land - - -	1 - 5 - 0
Tom Clynch, Comorinrs part Rathbeggan - - -	3 - 0 - 0
Mr Bushfield his Tyth in Pouderlagh - - -	0 - 16- 0
Wat. Clynch. Tyth of R. Andros in Pouderlagh - - -	11 - 0 - 0
Mr Shelly. Small Tyth. of Impropriation - - -	2 - 15- 0
Glebe Rent, end May 1. 1709 to Ed^{md} McKenna - - -	2 - 15- 0
	51 - 6 - 0

Donlavan

Sett. 1708 - - -	14 - 8 - 0

[18v]

Received

From the Parishes of Laracor and Agher

for the Year. 1708. Sett by Mr Parvisol for

149^{ll}-9-6, & Tyth drawn 3^{ll}-10-0

Nov^{br}. 9. 1708. Crown Rent. for Mich^{lm}. 1708. - - -	7 - 11- 8
Febr. 11. 170$\frac{8}{9}$ a Bill to MC. (cheat 6^s-6^d) - - -	11 - 6 - 6
--Allowd Patrick for Wages in absence - - -	0 - 13- 0
Mar. 3. 170$^8_9$ Mr Warb^{tn}. Qu^{rtr}. end. Febr. 19 - - -	7 - 10- 0
Apr. 15. 1709. to Mrs Brent by a Bill from me - - -	3 - 0 - 0
May. 31. Mr Warb^{tn}. Qu^{rtr}. end. --19. - - -	7 - 10- 0
June. 10 to Mr Walls - - -	18 - 0 - 0
--16 Crown rent due Eastr. last - - -	7 - 11- 8
--17. Visitation. Proxys. 2^{ll}-7-9. 20th Parts - 14^s-9^{d}½ Para^{tr}. 9^d (Reg^{sr}. not pd) - - -	3 - 3 - 3½
Mar. 25. 1709. Part of a bill to Mr Walls. of 49-4^s-7^{d}½ - - -	9 - 19- 4½
Stated thus far. Oct^{br}. 12. 1709. J. S.	76 - 5 - 6
Refer what follows to my Table book	
July. 5. 1709. Cash at Dublin - - -	12 - 0 - 0
--7 Cash at Dublin - - -	4 - 0 - 0
Aug. 15. at Laracor - - -	10 - 0 - 0
Oct^{br}. 12. Allowd for saddle &c 2^{ll} 10^s-1^d. Horses sent &c & a House bill to Sept. 27th, & Hearth money &c in all - - -	4 - 19- 9½
Nov^{br}. 16. 1709. Allwd for work & thatching from Dec^{br}. 13 1707 to Sept. 1. 1709 - - -	1 - 9 - 0
Nov^{br}. 16. House bill from Septr. 27th to Nov^{br}. 16,--- 1^{ll}. 10^s. 9^d.½. & wash 10 weeks 13^s-11^d in all - - -	2 - 4 - 8½
--A Qua End. Aug. 19. half cleard, & 10^s more allwd (to Mr Warb^{tn}) - - -	6 - 15- 0
	41 - 8 - 6
Settld - - Novr. 16. 1709. J. S.	117 - 14- 0

P^d

Smoak money due Jan[r]. 170$\frac{8}{9}$. - - -	0 - 4 - 0
Work done in th Garden from Dec[br]. 13 1707 to Sep[t]. 1. 1709. & thatch; &c - - -	1 - 9 - 0
Nov[br]. 9. 1708 Crown[rt] to Mich[lmas] - - -	7 - 11- 8
Mar. 3 170$\frac{9}{8}$ Qu[rtr] to M[r] Warburton - - -	7 - 10- 0
May. 31. 1709 Qu[rtr] to M[r] Warburton - - -	7 - 10- 0
Jun. 16. 1709 Crownrent due Easter 1709 - - -	7 - 11- 8
--17 Visitation, &c - - -	3 - 3 - 3

Received

From Rathbeggan for 1708. Sett for	51 : 6 : 0
Febr. 11. 170$\frac{8}{9}$ to Mr Walls - - -	13 - 8 - 0
Mar. 25. 1709. to Mr Walls, part of a bill. 49^ll-4^s-7^d.½	18 - 0 - 0
	31 - 8 - 0
Jan^r. 3^d. 17$\frac{10}{09}$. Cash at ⟨the Pace⟩ Rathbeggan - - -	2 - 10- 0
--20 Cash at Dublin - - -	7 - 0 - 0

Received

From Donlavan for 1708 part of the Bill to Mr Walls of 49^ll-4^s-7^d½ - - -	13 - 5 - 3

P[d]

Jan[r]. 3[d] $17\frac{10}{09}$ At the Pace Spent wth Parvis[1] - - - 0 - 3 -10

July. 26.

P[d] to my Vicar in Dublin for 2 Years.

for him & late M[r] Buck[n] to lady day.

1709. - - - 1 - 0 - 0

Arrears

of Laracor. of the Year 1708

Settld & remains Nov^br^. 16. 1709 - - -	31 - 15 - 6
Febr. 4 From Mr Vedel in Dublin - - -	5 - 0 - 0
Mar. 20. Allow^d^ for Schoolmas^tr^ of Trim to end Mich^l^. 1709 - - -	0 - 10 - 2
	37 - 5 - 8
Rem.	26 - 5 - 4

Account

Of Expences

From Nov^{br}. 1. 1709

to

Nov^{br}. 1. 1710

At Mrs Frances's old Pallas yard. West^{nr}. M^{rs} S.

Vandrheyden & Drummod Amsterdam Donvill

Won	
Nov^{br}. 2. Omb^{r}. Perci^{vll} Barry - -	0-6-10
--4 Piq^{t} Barry - - -	0-2-2
--9 Omb^{r} & Piq^{t}. Perc^{vl} & Barry -	0-10-10
From Nov^{b}. 22^{d} to Dec^{br}. 20 at Clogh^{r} with Bp & Dilly & Cards & tables in all	0-16-0
Dec^{br}. 26. Tables Wesley - - -	0-6-6
--27 Ombre. Ray^{md}. Morg^{n} - - -	0-1-1
Jan^{r}. 3 Omb^{r}. D Stern - - -	0 2-5
Mar. 6. Basset L^{dy} Tint &c - - -	0-2-0
--14 Basst Perc^{vlls} - - -	0-0-6
--21 Ombre Raynd. Tpt - - -	0-4-4
--22 Omb^{r}. Mrs Walls - - -	0-5-6
Apr. 6. Omb^{r}. Manly, Walls* - - -	0-3-2
Jun. 13. Omb^{r}. Mrs Tigh, Ba^{ry} - - -	0-6-6
--21--Omb^{r}. D. St^{n} Walls. - - -	0-3-4
Jul. 27. Omb^{r}. Manl. Pratt - - -	0-4-11
Aug. 5. Ombre. Walls Tpt - - -	0-1-4

Lost.	
Nov^{b}. 7. Omb^{r}. Raynd &c - - -	0-2-7
--8 Omb^{r} Perci^{vl} Barry - - -	0-5-8
11. Omb^{r}. & whisk. Ray^{md}. Morg^{n}	0-2-4
Dec^{b}. 28. Tables Wesly - - -	0-4-4
--31. Omb^{r}. Raynd Morgan - - -	0-2-2
Jan^{r}. 24. Omb^{r}. Tpt & Lee - - -	0-1-4
--26. Piq^{t}. Bp. Cl. - - -	0-0-6
Feb. 3. Ombre Mrs Manly - - -	0-2-9
--6 Ombre Mrs Manly - - -	0-1-1
7 Omb^{r}. Walls* - - -	0-2-10
--13 in all & allw^{d} - - -	0-0-4
--18 Omb^{r} Tpt - - -	0-0-11
Mar. 15 Tables Wesly - - -	0-3-3
--24 Basset Walls Tpt - - -	0-0-8
--27 Lost for Tpt. th & asiline Esh - - -	Q-2-7
--30 Lost for Tpt. tep md crt	0-0-8
Apr. 5. Omb^{r}. Stoit Walls - - -	0-0-5
May. 18. Omb^{r}. Barry Perci^{vll} -	0-2-6
--20. Ombre Barry, Perci^{vll}. [the last]	0-9-2
Jun. 8. Omb^{r}. Walls D^{r} St^{rn} - -	0-4-0
--26 Omb^{r}. Walls Manly - - -	0-3-11
Jul. 22. Omb^{r} Punch. Jo. War^{br}	0-1-9
Aug. 1. Omb^{r}. Walls Stoit - - -	0-0-9
--7 P^{d} for Tpt Walls Ombre - -	0-1-1
--23 Omb^{r}. Walls Stoit - - -	0-1-4

Account

Of Expences from Nov^{br}. 1st. 1709 to Nov^{br}. 1st. 1710.

First Quart^{r}.

From Nov^{br}. 1. 1709 to Febr. 1. $17\frac{10}{09}$

JB.

In p^{rt}. 5^{s}-5^{d} Mar. 23. sett^{d} - - -	1 - 10- 0

Cloaths.

Jan^{r}. 3^{d}. making Ind. Nightgown. 3^{s}-4^{d} --18. Bar^{br} advan^{cd}. 5^{s}-5^{d}	0 - 8 - 9
Silk for nightgown. 7^{s}. Silk for outside. 1^{ll}-14^{s} - - -	1 - 19- 0
	2 - 9 - 9

Servt.

shoes about Oct^{br}. 3^{s}-6^{d}

Jan^{r}. 17. Part. wages. 18^{s}-6^{d} Stock^{ns}. 10^{d}.½ Shoes 2^{s}-6^{d}

MC.

Jan^{r}. 22^{d}. 5^{ll}

Lodging.

Jan^{r}. 3^{d}. $17\frac{10}{09}$ P^{d} to. Jan^{r}. 9th. for ½ a year 5^{ll} place to this year	2 - 0 - 0

Extr^{drys}.

Dec^{br}. 15. G. for find. Screw. 2^{s}-8^{d}.½ - - -	0 - 2 - 8½
--Jan^{ry}. 4th. $17\frac{10}{09}$ to Henry Brent for Purse G - - -	0 - 18- 6
G. Freckl^{tn}. 2^{s}-8^{d}.½ --7 Book for Mr Deering 6^{s} --13. G. MDs maid 1^{s}-1^{d}.	0 - 9 - 9½
--14 G. MD. 2^{s}-8^{d}.½ --20 Teakettle. 3^{s}. Herbs. 2^{s}-1^{d} --26 Books 1^{ll}-6^{d}	1 - 8 - 3½
	2 - 19- 3½

Horses.

Dec^{br}. 16. Smith Clogh^{r}. 1^{s}-1^{d} on road 6^{d}.½ Jan^{r}. 27. Whip. 10^{d} - - -	0 - 2 - 5½
A Horse bought abut Oct^{br} th end - - -	6 - 5 - 0
	6 - 7 - 5½

Washing

3 weeks at Laracor. 4^{s}-6^{d} --4 weeks at Clogh^{r}. 3^{s}-4^{d}.½. to Febr.
to Febr. 6. 4^{s}-9^{d}

Expences. 1st Month

Nov^{br}.

First Week. Laracor.

1. to 5

—

2^{d} Week. Laracor

5 to 12.

--Punch, Ray^{md} Barry &c. 2^{s}. --7. Punch at Raym^{ds}. 10^{d} s^{mll} 2^{d} - - -	0 - 3 - 0
--Win. Ray^{md} - 9^{d} - - -	0 - 0 - 9
	0 - 3 - 9

3^{d} Week Laracor.

12 to 19

--G. Ned. 3^{d}. G. workm^{n}. 3^{d}. --13 Wine Ray^{md} &c 1^{s}-6^{d} - - -	0 - 2 - 0
--14. Punch at home 6^{d}. - - -	0 - 0 - 6
Part of a Hous Bill of 1^{ll}-10-9^{d}½ the rest charg^{d} to th last year, this from Nov^{br}. 1st to 16 - - -	0 - 10- 9½
Washing at Laracor 3 weeks to No^{br}. 16 - - -	0 - 4 - 6
--16. Win. Raym^{d}. 11^{d} --19. G. Ray^{mds} maid 1^{s}-1^{d} - - -	0 - 2 - 0
	0 - 15- 3½

4th Week. Going to Clogh^{r}. 19.

19 to 26

--Oats at Trim 6^{d} --20. Bill at Virginia 8^{s}-7^{d} - - -	0 - 9 - 1
--21 Bill at Cavan 5^{s}-10^{d} --22 G. at Nixons 3^{s}. G. sm^{ll}. 4^{d} - - -	0 - 9 - 2
	0 - 18- 0

Rem^{dr} Clogh^{r}.

26 to Dec. 1.

--G. poor. 6^{d} - - -	0 - 0 - 6
Lett^{r} Miss hessy. 6^{d} - - -	0 - 0 - 6
	0 - 1 - 0
Lett^{r} Mr Morgan - 6^{d} - - -	0 - 0 - 6
	0 - 1 - 6

1st Week	-	0 - 3 - 9
2^{d} Week	-	0 - 15- 3½
3^{d} Week	-	0 - 18- 3
Rem^{dr}	-	0 - 1 - 6
		1 - 18- 9½

Expences. 2d Month

Decbr.

1st Week Clogher.

1 to 10.

Lettr E. Berkly 8d --12. Lettr. MD. 5d - - -	0 - 1 - 1

2d Week

10 to 17

--Brandy. 10d. Neds bill. Poudr & shot. 1s-3d Tobac. 2d.½ - - -	0 - 2 - 3½

3d Week.

17 to 24

--19. <Wash> Neds lodg. 2s Allwd him 1s-1d - - -	0 - 3 - 1
--G at Cloghr. 8s-1d.½ --20 at Mr Willouhby. 2s-6d - - -	0 - 10- 7½
--21 At Mr Parnel's 2s-11d - on road 1s-6d. --22 At Navan 7s-1d - - -	0 - 11- 6
--smll. 2d G. Shan o Teague 10d - - -	0 - 1 - 0
	1 - 6 - 2½

4th Week. Laracor.

24 to Janr. 1.

--G. Wesly's Butlr. 10d -Groom 3d --25 Sacrt. 2s-8d.½ Smll 2d - - -	0 - 3 -11½
--26. G. Iah Parvsll 10d --27. G. Ned. 10d. smll. 2d - - -	0 - 1 -10
--27. G Mumrs. 6d.½ --28. G. Isay Parvisll. 5d. - - -	0 - 0 -11½

1st Week	-	0 - 1 - 1
2d Week	-	0 - 2 - 3½
3d Week	-	0 - 6 - 2½
4th Week	-	0 - 6 - 9
		1 - 16- 4

Jan^{ry}. Expences 3^{d} Month

1st Week

1 to 7.

--2. G. Coz deans man 5^{d} --3. G. Post an Express 1^{s}-1^{d} - - -	0 - 1 - 6
--4 Co^{ch} MD 1^{s}-1^{d}. G Mrs Walls 1^{s}-1^{d} --5 Chair 6^{d}. Sm^{ll} 3^{d} - - -	0 - 2 -11
6. G. MD 6^{d}.½ Neds bill. Raz^{rs} 9^{d} Candl. 3^{d}.½ Toba^{co} 2^{d}. &c in all 1^{s}-4^{d}½	0 - 2 -11
Board wages 3 days. 1^{s}-6^{d} - - -	0 - 1 - 6
	0 - 8 -10

2^{d} Week

7 to 14

All^{d} Ned 3^{d}½ --7 Co^{ch} MD. 6^{d}.½ --8 Sug^{r}. 5^{d} Cakes wine MD 1^{s}-1^{d} - - -	0 - 2 - 4
--Sm^{ll} 2^{d} --9 Sug^{r} drabs. 1^{s}-3^{d} rolls 1^{d} Co^{ch} MD 1^{s}. - - -	0 - 2 - 6
--10. Din^{r} Tav^{rn} Manly. 3^{s}-8^{d}.½ sm^{ll} 2^{d} Co^{h} & Chair 10^{d} - - -	0 - 4 - 6½
12 Co^{ch} MD 3^{s}-3^{d} --13 brd wags 3^{s}-6^{d} Neds bill Cand^{l} &c. 1^{s}-2d.½ - - -	0 - 7 -11½
	0 - 17- 4

3^{d} Week

14 to 21

P^{d} MD 6^{d}.½ G. old Marg^{t}. 6^{d}½ --15 sm^{ll}. 2^{d} - - -	0 - 1 - 3
--17 Co^{ch} MD. 1^{s}-8^{d} --18 Chair. & sm^{ll} 8^{d} Coals, [16] 2^{s}-9^{d} - - -	0 - 5 - 1
Neds bill. Tobac. 2^{d}. Cakes & Cand^{ls} 3^{d}½ in all 11^{d}. - - -	0 - 0 -11
Brd wags 3^{s}-6^{d} sm^{ll}. 1^{d} - - -	0 - 3 - 7
	0 - 10-10

4th Week

21 to Febr. 1.

--Co^{ch}. MD 1^{s}-1^{d} --22 Win MD din^{r}. ciz me 9^{d} - Sm^{ll} 2^{d} - - -	0 - 2 - 0
--24. MD. 6^{d} Sm^{ll} 1^{d}. --26. G. Tpt. 1^{s}-1^{d} Co^{ch}. MD. 7^{d} - - -	0 - 2 - 3
Brd wags. 3^{s}-6^{d} Mrs Currys bill during absence - - -	0 - 3 - 6
For Lett^{rs}, Coles, &c - - -	0 - 8 - 5
Neds bill Ca^{dls}. 3^{d}.½ Raz^{rs} 3^{d} Tobac. 2^{d} Powd^{r} 3^{d} in all - 1^{s} - - -	0 - 1 - 0
	0 - 17- 2
--30 Bread. 1^{s} Bord w. 2^{s} - Cand^{l}. 3^{d}.½ Co^{ch} MD. 6^{d} - - -	0 - 3 - 9½
31 Din^{r} at home Mr Forbes. 1^{s}-7^{d}.½ Tobac. 2^{d} - - -	0 - 1 - 9½
	0 - 5 - 7
	1 - 2 - 9

1st Week	-	0 - 8 -10
2^{d} Week	-	0 - 17- 4
3^{d} Week	-	0 - 10-10
4th Week	-	1 - 2 - 9
		2 - 19- 9

Totals

Of a Quar[tr] for Nov[br]. 1. 1709 to Fe[br]. 1. $17\frac{10}{09}$

JB ⟨(not sett[d])⟩ Settl[d] - - -	1 - 10- 0
Cloaths - - -	2 - 9 - 9
Servant - - -	
MC - - - not sett[d] - - -	11 - 0 - 0
Lodging - - -	2 - 0 - 0
Extr[dys] - - -	2 - 19- 3½
Horses - - -	6 - 7 - 5½
Washing - - -	
Expences 1st Month - - -	1 - 18- 9½
Expences 2[d] Month - - -	1 - 16- 4
Expences 3[d] Month - - -	2 - 19- 9
Drugs & forgot & sug[r] - - - in all - - -	0 - 4 - 4
Jan[ry]. G. D. Stearn for a poor Clergyman - - -	0 - 5 - 5

Second Quarter

From Febr. 1. 17$\frac{10}{09}$ to May. 1. 1710

JB

Mar. 30. ⟨3s-6d⟩ 4s. Jun. 5. 1s --16 -5s --17. 10s10d cld - - - 1 - 10- 0

MC

Settd - - - 11 - 0 - 0

Cloaths.

Febr. 5. 2 pr shoes 1 pr Slipprs, (1s unpd) 10s-10d more 4s-5d ⟨so but 7d unpd⟩ - - - 0 - 15- 3
--16. mend Shirts, 1s-1d mend Cra. 2d Febr. 25. ridg Coat. 11l-3s - - - 1 - 4 - 3
Mar. 23. Bands 10s --27. Shoes 2 pr. 8s-2d thrd Stocks 2 pr. 4s-6d - - - 1 - 2 - 8
--29 dress hat. 9d½ Apr. 14. mend Gown Mrs Parvisll. 1s-1d ⟨G⟩ - - 0 - 1 -10½
3 - 4 - ½

Servant.

Febr. 4
Rendr wages & G. 15s. Hat bought of Ned. 2s-2d - - - 0 - 17- 2
Mar. 27. Shoes for Patr. 4s. Apr. 6 Hat Patr. 4s-6d - - - 0 - 8 - 6
1 - 5 - 8

Lodging

Extrdys.

Febr. 3. Cards MD. 4s --4 Coffee pots. 1s-10d. strap 1s. --7 Potcary 18s-6d 1 - 5 - 4
--8. Book bind - 10s-3d½ --13 G. dd. 2s-8d½ --15. G. Sextn St Patr. 1s-1d 0 - 14- 1
Mar. 21 2 Books 2s-2d --25 G MD treat Manly. 3s-9d½. --28. Book. 1s-1d - 0 - 7 - 0½
Apr. 22. G. MD at Trim. 5s-5d. G dd. Apr. 8. 5s-5d - - - 0 - 10-10
2 - 17- 3½

Horses

Febr. 4. Oyl. 2d mend boots 2d Spur. 2d 25 prt of bill Levingstn. 6s-9d -0 - 7 - 3
Mar. 24. mend. whip. 4d Apr. 7. Whips. 2s-6d. mend boots. 8d - - - 0 - 3 - 6
--8. Pd Levingstn arrears 4s. more then. 4s-6d - - - 0 - 8 - 6
0 - 19- 3

Washing

To Mar. 30. 5s-2d

Patrick came to me the 2d time, Febr. 9. 17$\frac{10}{09}$

[5v]

Expences. 1st Month

February

1st Week.

1 to 11.

--Co^{ch}. 6^{d}. sm^{ll} 2^{d} --2. Co^{ch}. 10^{d}. --3^{d} Coles 2^{s}-7^{d} - - -	0 - 4 - 1
--3 G. MD. 7^{d}. sm^{ll} 1^{d} G. 2^{d}. --4 G. Man 2^{d} brd w. 3 days 1^{s}-6 - - -	0 - 2 - 6
Brd & butt^{r}. 1^{d}½ --4. sm^{ll} 2^{d}. Co^{ch} MD. 6^{d} --5 Raz^{rs}. 3^{d}. G. MD. 7^{d}. -	0 - 1 - 6½
--sm^{ll} 2^{d} Bred 2^{d} --6. G MD. 6^{d}.½ Chair 6^{d}½ - - -	0 - 1 - 5
--8. Din. Tav^{rn} D. Ash. 1^{s}-1^{d} --9 sm^{ll}. 2^{d} Brd wags 2 days 1^{s} - - -	0 - 2 - 3
	0 - 11- 9½

2^{d} Week.

11 to 18.

--Parvis^{ll} chaise to Fingl. 6^{d}.½ --12. por. 3^{d}. --13 Co^{ch} MD 1^{s} - - -	0 - 1 - 9½
Pat's bill Cand^{l}. Poud^{r} Oyl &c. 11^{d}. --15 Chair 6^{d}.½ sm^{ll} 2^{d}. Co^{ch}.1-6^{d} -	0 - 2 - 1½
Brd wag. 3^{s}-6^{d} --16. G Por Wom^{n} 6^{d}½ G MD. 7^{d} G. Man Parvi^{ll} 2^{d} - - -	0 - 4 - 9½
17--G. MD. 6.½ - - -	0 - 0 - 6½
	0 - 9 - 3

3^{d} Week.

18 to 25

--Co^{ch} & G. MD. 1^{s}-1^{d} --20 Co^{ch} MD 1^{s}. --22 Win MD. 1^{s}-4^{d}. Co^{ch}. 6^{d} - -	0 - 3 -11
--23 G. MDs boy 1^{s}-1^{d}. sm^{ll}. 2^{d} Tav^{rn} Dearing Roch^{ft} &c. 3^{s}-1^{d}. - - -	0 - 4 - 4
24 G. MD. 1^{s}-1^{d} Sug^{r} 4^{d}. Brd wag. ⟨(not sett^{d})⟩ 3^{s}-6^{d} - - -	0 - 4 -11
	0 - 13- 4

4th Week. Laracor.

25 to Mar. 1.

--G. ⟨md⟩ maid at Currys 1^{s}-1^{d}. Co^{ch} 6^{d}.½ Sug^{r} 5^{d} Coff. 4^{s}-8^{d} - - -	0 - 6 - 8½
Bord wag. in absence 3^{s} - - -	0 - 3 - 0
	0 - 9 - 8½

1st Week	-	0 - 11- 9½
2^{d} Week	-	0 - 9 - 3
3^{d} Week	-	0 - 13- 4
4th Week	-	0 - 9 - 8½
		2 - 4 - 1

March. Expences 2^{d} Month

1 to 11 1st Week. Laracor.

--G J. Beau^{nts} boy. 5^{d}. 2^{d} Punch Raynd. 6^{d}.½ --6 Treat Trim Peopl. 5^{s}-7^{d} - - - 0 - 6 - 6½
--7 Sm^{ll} & G. 6^{d} - - - 0 - 0 - 6
0 - 7 - 0½

11 to 18 2^{d} Week Laracor

12 Sm^{ll} 2^{d} --13 G at Dick Ash. 2^{s}-8^{d}.½ Punch Ray^{md}. 7^{d} - - - 0 - 3 - 5½
--14 Punch Raynd. 7^{d} --15 G. Dick Ashs man Plov^{rs} Eggs. 1^{s}-1^{d} - - - 0 - 1 - 8
0 - 5 - 1½

18 to 25 3^{d} Week.

--19 Sm^{ll} 1^{d} --20 The Pace. 1s-1d - Co^{ch} 1^{s}-1^{d} - - - 0 - 2 - 3
--21 G. MD. 1^{s}-1^{d} - Tav^{rn} T. Ash Raynd. 1^{s}-7^{d} - - - 0 - 2 - 8
--22. G. MD. 1^{s}-1^{d}. Cand^{l}. 10^{d}.½ Washb. Poud^{r}. 7^{d} Coals. 1^{s}-4^{d}½ - - - 0 - 3 -11
Brd wag. 4 days. 2^{s} G. MD. 1^{s}-1^{d} - - - 0 - 3 - 1
0 - 11-11

25 to Apr. 1. 4th Week.

--Lett^{r} Rec^{d} Puppy. 2^{s}. --26. Wine treat MD. 1^{s}-6. Sm^{ll} 2^{d} - - - 0 - 3 - 8
Brd w. 3^{s}-6^{d} --30. G. 3 old Wom^{n} 11^{d}. Coff. 2^{d} Co^{ch}. MD. 6^{d} - - - 0 - 5 - 1
31 Pats bill Candles Raz^{rs}. &c. 6^{d}.½ - - - 0 - 0 - 6½
0 - 9 - 3½

1st Week	-	0 - 7 - 0½
2^{d} Week	-	0 - 5 - 1½
3^{d} Week	-	0 - 11-11
4th Week	-	0 - 9 - 3½
		1 - 13- 4½

Expences. 3d Month

April.

1st Week

1 to 8.

A Pot & Glass. 1s-1d Lettrs. 8d. Lettr Ldy Berkl. 6d. Lettr Sr A. F. 6d- 0 - 2 - 9
--4. Poudr. 1d½ Bread. 10d --5. Snuff. MD. 3d. Treat Breakfst Drbs 1s-11d - - - 0 - 3 - 1½
--6 G. MD. 9d.½. Coch. MD & to Manly. 4s Brd wag. 3s6d - - - 0 - 8 - 3½

0 - 14- 2

2d Week Laracor.

8. to 15.

--Coch. 6d. Oyl & Tobac. 1d.½ --13. Punch treat Forbs. 1s-8d - - - 0 - 2 - 3½
8. Coffee $\frac{1}{4}$ lb. bought from MD - - - 0 - 1 - 2

0 - 3 - 5½

3d Week. Laracor MD

15 to 22

--16 G. Pat. 1s-1d G. & smll 9d --21 G. Pat treat Margt. 1s-1d. - - - 0 - 2 -11
--Punch Raymd 6d - - - smll 2d - - - 0 - 0 - 8

0 - 3 - 7

4th Week. Laracor. MD

22 to May. 1.

Pd MD. for Coff & Sugr. 4s-5d --28. Ale & smll 6d - - - 0 - 4 -11
--29. Wine MD. 1s-10d G. smll. 2d - - - 0 - 2 - 0

0 - 6 -11

First Week -	0 - 14- 2
2d Week -	0 - 3 - 5
3d Week -	0 - 3 - 7
4th Week -	0 - 6 -11
	1 - 8 - 1

Third Quart^{r}.

From May. 1. to Aug. 1. 1710.

Totalls

Of a Quart^{r} from Febr. 1. 17$\frac{10}{09}$. to May. 1. 1710.

JB - - - (not sett^{d}) - - -	1 - 10- 0
MC - - - sett^{d} - - -	11 - 0 - 0
Cloaths - - -	3 - 4 - 0½
Servant - - -	1 - 5 - 8
Lodging - - -	0 - 0 - 0
Extr^{drys} - - -	2 - 17- 3½
Horses - - -	0 - 19- 3
Washing - - -	
Expences 1st Month - - -	2 - 4 - 1
Expences 2^{d} Month - - -	1 - 13- 4½
Expences 3^{d} Month - - -	1 - 8 - 1

JB

MC

Cloaths.

Servant.

Lodging

Extr^{dr}.

Horses.

Washing.

Expences. 2^{d} Month.

June.

1st Week. Laracor.

1 to 10.

<--Punch Ray^{md} 1^{s}-1^{d} >
--P^{d} a large House Bill from Nov^{br} 16. 1709 which was in all
7^{ll}-17^{s}-4^{d} but Substract for Horses, & Charge to my Livings, remains
as House Charges in all (MD being at Trim 7 weeks) - - - 4 - 10- 0
--4 G. 2^{d}. Punch Raynd. 1^{s}-1^{d} - - - 0 - 1 - 3

Dublin

--5 G. maid at Parvs^{ls}. 5^{d} --Pace 2^{s}-7 Co^{ch} to Town 2^{s}-6^{d} - - - 0 - 4 - 6
--6. Co^{ch} & Chair. 1^{s}-1^{d} Coff. 6 - - - 0 - 1 - 7
7 Tea Mr Addis^{n}. 9^{d} Sug^{r} 4^{d} --8. old Marg^{t}. 4^{d} Co^{ch} Mrs F. 1^{s}-8^{d} - - - 3 - 1
--Raz^{rs}. 3^{d} Brd w. 4 days. 2^{s}-2^{d} --9 Tav^{rn}. 1^{s}-6^{d} - - - 0 - 3 -11
Pats bill. Cand^{l}. 7^{d} Pod^{r}. Oyl. Brd & Butt^{r} in all - - - 0 - 1 - 4

5 - 5 - 8

2^{d} Week.

10 to 17.

--11 Co^{ch}. 6^{d}. Brd w. 3^{s}-6^{d} Sm^{ll} 4^{d}
Lett^{r} old 4^{d}

3^{d} Week

17 to 24

Co^{ch}. Ray^{d}. 6^{d}.½ -sm^{ll} 4^{d} Brd w. 3^{s}-6^{d} - - - 0 - 4 - 4½
23. G. JB. 6^{d}.½ Co^{ch}< > Adds^{n} 6^{d}.½ --24 Co^{ch} Mr Add. 6^{d} - - - 0 - 1 - 7
Sm^{ll}. 2^{d} Pats bill a fortnight sug^{r}. bread butt^{r} &c. 2^{s}-4^{d} - - - 0 - 2 - 6

0 - 8 - 5½

4th Week

24 to Jul. 1.

--Brd wag. 3^{s}-6^{d} --25 Sac^{rt}. 1^{s}-1^{d} Sm^{ll} 4^{d} --26. Co^{ch} J. 6^{d}½ - - - 0 - 5 - 5½

Expences. 3^{d} Month

July.

1st Week.

--1 to 8

--MD come home. Cherys Coffee. Walls &c. 1^{s}-2^{d} Mutt^{n} pys. 4^{d} - - - 0 - 1 - 6
--Co^{ch} MD. 6^{d}½ Coff. 3^{d} -Brd w. 3^{s}-6^{d}. 4 Co^{ch} MD. 6^{d}.½. Coff. 2^{d} - - - 0 - 5 - 0
Pats bill. 2 weeks Brd butt^{r}. Cand^{ls} &c. 2^{s}-2^{d} - - - 0 - 2 - 2
--5 Dunlary. Mr Addis. &c. 2^{s}-10^{d} Sug^{r} Cand^{l} &c 8^{d}.½ - - - 0 - 3 - 6
--6 Lett^{r} Domv^{ll} & Dr R. 1^{s}-6^{d} --Pyes & Coff. Mr Lee. 1^{s} - - - 0 - 2 - 6
--7 Co^{ch} MD to donibrook 2^{s}-2^{d} - - - 0 - 2 - 2
0 - 16-10½

2^{d} Week.

8 to 15

--old bill for Lett^{rs} Mrs Curry. 4^{s}-9^{d}. Co^{ch}. MD. 1^{s}-1^{d}. Win MD. 9^{d} - - - 0
Brd w. 3^{s}-6^{d} Pats bill, 6^{d} --14. Din^{r} Addsn. 5^{s} Chair 6^{d}.½
JB 6^{d}.½ Coff. 3^{d} G. Mr Prats man 1^{s}-1^{d} JB before 6^{d}½

3^{d} Week Laracor. 17

15 to 22

--16. Chair 1^{s}-1^{d} --17 Co^{ch}. 6^{d} 20 G. poor boy 6^{d}.½ more 1^{d} - - - 0 - 2 - 2½
<--bor^{d} w. 2 days>

4th Week.

22 to Aug. 1.

--Win of Jo 9^{d} --24 Win. MD. 10^{d} <--25. din^{r} & Co^{ch} Mr Addis^{n}>
--25. Din^{r} & Co^{ch} Fingls. Mr Addis^{n}. &c. 4^{s}-4^{d}
27. Co^{ch} MD to Manlys - 1^{s}-7^{d}.½ sm^{ll} 2^{d} --28. Din^{r} MD. 2^{s}-10^{d}
29. Co^{ch} Fingl Baligenly. 1^{s}-8^{d} Brd w. 3^{s}
Pat old Bills - 0 - 1 - 4 new bill 1^{s}-1^{d}.½

Totalls

Of a Quart[r] from May. 1. to Aug. 1. 1710

Fourth Quarter.

JB.

MC

Cloaths

Aug. 4. Glovs. 2^s-8^d.½ --6 dress hat. 6^d.½. Sep^{br}. 22^d. Hat. $1^{ll}13^s$, Oc^{tr} 20. Glovs. 2^s. --28 Shoes 2 p^r. 10^s.

Servt.

Sep^{br}. 5. Boots. 2^s6^d

Lodging

Sep^{br}. 7 to 21. 10^s. to Oc^{br} 12. $1^{ll}4^s$ to No^{br}. 2. 1^{ll}-4^s

Extrd.

Aug. 16. treat drabs at MD's 7^s. --22. G. Ppt.^for^ cocking letter man 11^s-6^d
Oct^{br}. 8. Tav^{rn}. Sr A. F. fool. 7^s --13 Tav^{rn} & din^r Sr A. F. fool ag^n. 7 0 - 14- 0
16 Mr Harlys $Port^r$. 2^s-6^d $Chocl^t$. ppt. 15^s

Horses

Shoing Horse old bill to Clergy, alld. Aug. 1703 - - - 0 - 17- 0

Washing.

to Sep^{br}. 23 2 weeks. 2^s-9^d --Oc^{br}. 1. 2^s --8. 2^s --14. 1^s-6^d --21. 1^s-3^d --28. 1^s-6^d

Expences. 1st Month

August

1st Week.

1 to 12.

--Co^{ch} MD. Donybrook. 1^{s}-7^{d}.½ G. 2^{d} Sage p^{d} JB. 1^{s}-6^{d} - - -	0 - 3 - 3½
JB. 2 weeks 1^{s}-1^{d} --2^{d} Co^{ch}. Mr Addis^{n} Chapt^{r} 3^{d}. 1^{s}-8^{d} - - -	0 - 2 - 9
--4 Chair. Mr Addis^{n}. 6^{d}.½ G. MD. 1^{s}-1^{d} Cand^{ls}. 3^{d}.½ JB 1 week 6^{d}½ - - -	0 - 2 - 5½
Brd w. 3^{s}-6^{d} --5. Co^{ch} MD. 6^{d}.½ --7 Win & Co^{ch} MD 2^{s}-2^{d} Sm^{ll} 4^{d} - - -	0 - 6 - 6½
--8 Din^{r} Mr Addis^{n}. 3^{s}-3^{d}. Co^{ch}. 6^{d}½ --9. Co^{ch}. 1^{s}-1^{d}. Coff dd. 3^{d} - - -	0 - 5 - 1½
--10 Co^{ch} & Chair. 1^{s}-7^{d} Brd wag. 3^{s}-6^{d} - - -	0 - 5 - 1
--11 Co^{ch}. 1^{s}-1^{d} JB 1 week 6^{d}.½ Lett^{r} old. 6^{d} Pat's bill 6^{d}.½ - - -	0 - 2 - 2
	1 - 7 - 5

2^{d} Week.

12 to 19.

--Win & Ale MD 9^{d}. G. old Marg^{t}. 4^{d}. Brd w. 3^{s}-6^{d} - - -	0 - 4 - 7

3^{d} Week.

19 to 26

--Pap^{r}. 8^{d} --20 Co^{ch} MD Balig^{ll}. 2^{s}. Brd w. 3^{s}-6^{d} - - -	0 - 6 - 2
--22 Sm^{ll} 4^{d}. 23. Co^{ch} MD. Donibk. 1^{s}1^{d} --24. Ale & Py att MD 4^{d}½ - - -	0 - 1 - 9½
--25 Tav^{rn}. Mr Ford &c 2^{s}-4^{d}½ Pats bill. 1^{s} - - -	0 - 3 - 4½
	0 - 11- 4

26 to Septr. 1.

--28. Win. Coff. ch. MD. 1^{s}-7^{d} --31. Co^{ch} 1^{s}-7^{d}.½ Pats bill -1^{s}
--Brd w. 2^{s}-8^{d} Boat to ship. 10^{s}-10^{d}
Jo 5^{s}-5^{d} --a Gun. 1^{ll}

Sett out for Engl^{d} Aug. 31st on Thursday, 10 at night: landed at Parkgate Friday 1. at noon. Sep^{tbr}. 1st. 1710. came to London. Thursday at noon. Sep^{br}. 7th. with Ld Mountjoy &c

England.

Sept^{br}. Expences. 2^{d} Month

1st Week.

1 to 9

--Boat to Ship 10^{s}-10^{d}. Brchault. 1^{ll}-1^{s}-6^{d} Custom. 2^{s}-6^{d} - - -	1 - 4 - 0
--3^{d} Chest^{r}. 2^{s}-8^{d} WhitChurch. 6^{d} --4 New^{p}rt. 6^{d} --5 Coventry. 6^{d} - - -	0 - 4 - 2
--to Patr. 3^{s}-6^{d} --Torcest^{r}. 6^{d} --Dunstab^{l}. Musick & G. 1^{s}-6^{d} - - -	0 - 5 - 6
--7. Horses hired. 2^{ll}-18^{s}. Din^{r} Lond^{n}. & Co^{ch}. 3^{s}. Brd w. to 9. 1^{s}-6^{d} -	3 - 2 - 6
Coff. 10^{d}. [Mem^{d}. Ld Mountjoy bore my Expences from Chest^{r} to London] - -	0 - 0 -10
Ld Mount. man - - 2^{s}-6^{d} - -	4 - 19- 6

2^{d} Week.

9 to 16.

Coffee 5 days. 2^{s}. Pats bill. Candl. 1^{s}. Oyl Poud^{r}. &c in all 1^{s}-11^{d} - -	0 - 3 -11
--13. Co^{ch}. M^{r}. Bull. 1^{s}-6^{d} --14 Coff. Orang. 8^{d} --15. Coff. Let^{t} Dr R. 7^{d} - - -	0 - 2 - 9
Brd wages 5^{s} - - -	0 - 5 - 0
	0 - 11- 8

3^{d} Week.

16 to 23

--Raz^{rs} 9^{d} Ink &c 3^{d}. --17 Co^{ch} Stratford to Pates. 2^{s}-6^{d} - - -	0 - 3 - 6
--to 20 Coffe 6^{d}. brd wag. 3^{s}-6^{d} --21. Coffee 2^{d} (Pats bill 1^{s}) - - -	0 - 4 - 2
--22 Coff. 4^{d} Lett^{r} MD & Beau^{nt} 1^{s}-2^{d} G. maid 1^{s}. - - -	0 - 2 - 6
--Co^{ch} to L^{dy} Lucy, wth Mrs Armstrong. 4^{s} - - -	0 - 4 - 0
	0 - 14- 2

4th Week.

23 to Oct. 1.

--Brd w. 5^{s} Coff. 4^{d} --24. Co^{ch} Franck^{l}. 1^{s}. Coff. 4^{d} - - -	0 - 6 - 8
25. Lett^{r} Morg^{n}. 6^{d}. Coff. 2^{d} --26 Lett^{r} MD 6^{d}. --A. B^{P}. 1^{s}-6^{d} - - -	0 - 2 - 8
--28 Coff. 6^{d} Sm^{ll}. 2^{d} Co^{ch} Stratf^{d}. 1^{s} Pats bill 1^{s}-6 Coff 6^{d} - - -	0 - 3 - 8
	0 - 13- 0

Expences. 31 a small giddy fitt & swoon MD G^{d} help me. 3^{d} Month

Octo^{br}.

1st Week

1 to 7

--
Coff. 2^{d} -3 Brd w. 5^{s} -Coff. 2^{d}. --3. Let^{r} Prat. 6^{d}. Coff. 6^{d} - - - 0 - 6 - 2
--to 7. Coff. 8^{d}. Pats bill 4^{d}.½ Sm^{ll} 1^{d}½ - - - 0 - 1 - 2
0 - 7 - 4

2^{d} Week.

7 to 14

--Coff. 2^{d}. --8 Coff. 4^{d} --9 Coff. 2^{d} --10 Coff 4^{d} Chair Mr Harly. 1^{s} - 0 - 2 - 0
--11 Coff 2^{d}. --12 Coff 2^{d} --13 Coff 4^{d} - - - 0 - 0 - 8
Pats bill Cand^{ls}. 1^{s} Pap^{r} 1^{s}-3^{d} Coles. 7^{d}.½ Oyl 3^{d} - - - 0 - 3 - 1½
Brd wages. 5^{s} - - - 0 - 5 - 0
0 - 10- 9½

3^{d} Week.

14 to 21.

--Coffe. 4^{d} --15 Coff. 2^{d} sm^{ll}. 2^{d}. --16. Chair Mr Harley. 1^{s}. Coffe 4^{d} - - - 0 - 2 - 0
--17 Coff. 4^{d} --18 Coff. 8^{d}. --19 Co^{ch} Mr Addis^{n} 2^{s}. Coff. 4^{d} - - - 0 - 3 - 4
--20. Coff. 4^{d} Brd w. 5^{s}. Pats bill 1^{s} - - - 0 - 6 - 4
0 - 11- 8

4th Week.

21. to Nov^{br}. 1. 28 N. 4

--Chair Mr Lewis. 2^{s}. Lett^{r} MD. 6^{d}. Co^{ch} Mr Harley, 1^{s} Coff. 2^{d} - - - 0 - 3 - 8
--22 Coff. 2^{d}. --23. Coff. &c. 6^{d}. --24. Coff. 6^{d} --25 Coff. 4^{d} - - - 0 - 1 - 6
26. Coach Pat Rolt 2^{s}-6^{d}. Lett^{rs} Morgan, Parvis^{ll}. 1^{s}-2^{d} Coff. 2^{d} - - - 0 - 3 -10
--27. Row, Congreve, Sr R. Temple &c. 1^{s}. Pats bill. 1^{s}-8^{d} Brd w 5^{s} - - - 0 - 7 - 8
0 - 16- 8

Rem^{dr}.

28. Din^{r}. Adds^{n}, Garth. 2^{s}-6^{d}. Coff. 4^{d}. --29. Coffe 2^{d}. sm^{ll}. 2^{d} - - - 0 - 3 - 2
Brd w. 4 days. 2^{s}-10^{d} Coff. 2^{d} - - - 0 - 3 - 0
0 - 6 - 2

Account

Of Expences

From Nov^{br}. 1. 1711

to

Nov^{br} 1. 1712.

Won

3. Piqu^{t} Mr Van - - -	0-1-0
--19 Piqu^{t} Mr Van - - -	0-6-0
Mar. 8. L^{dy} Masham. Picqu^{t} - - -	0-5-0
--10. at B--s whisk - - -	0-3-0
--22. L^{dy} Masham	
May. 12. L^{dy} Masham Picq^{t} - - -	0-3-0
--14 L^{dy} Masham - - -	0-7-6
Jun. abut. 16. Tables Lewis - - -	0-7-6
--24 Picquet Lewis - - -	0-2-0
July. 8. Haz^{d} Bar^{br} - - -	0-2-0
--14. Picq^{t}. Van - - -	0-3-0
Aug. 15. Haz^{d}. L^{d} Tr - - -	0-18-6
--28. Omb^{r}. D^{s}. Shr^{s}. D^{r}. Arbth - -	1-16-0
Sep^{t}. 3^{d}. Piqu^{t}, & before - - -	0-5-6
--15. Piq^{t}. Lewis - - -	0-6-0
--17. Piq^{t} Lewis - - -	0-3-0
--18 Piq^{t} Lewis, Ford - - -	0-3-0
--20 Omb^{r}. Van & Hess - - -	0-15-0
23. Piq^{t}. L^{dy} Mash^{m}. - - -	0-15-0
--24 Piqu^{t} Van - - -	0-5-0
--27. Ombr. Lewis, Disny - - -	0-3-6
Oct^{br}, 17. Haz^{d} &c - - -	0-7-0
--30. Piqu^{t} - - -	0-1-0
	7-18-6

Lost.

Nov^{b}. 26. Piqu^{t} Mr Van - - -	0-7-0
Dec^{br}. 28. Hazrd - - - in all - - -	0-0-6
Mar 22 L^{dy} Masham. Picquet - - -	0-5-0
Jun. 27. Hazrd M--y - - -	0-0-6
Jul. 28 Piqu^{t}. Wind^{r}. Mrs Hils - -	0-17-6
--29. Piqu^{t} Idm - - -	1-1-6
Aug. 1. Van Lewis Piq^{t}. - - -	0-12-0
--2. Idem Piq^{t} - - -	0-7-0
--9 Duk. & Dutch^{s} Shrws^{b}. Ombre - -	0-16-6
18. Lewis Piqu^{t} - - -	0-8-0
22. Mrs Hill Piqu^{t} - - -	0-10-0
--29. Picq^{t}. Lewis - - -	0-10-0
Sep^{tr} 1. Piqu^{t} Lewis - - -	0-8-0
--10. Piq^{t}. L^{dy} Masham - - -	0-12-6
--11 Ombr. Lewis Mishess - - -	0-6-0
--26. Piqu^{t} - - -	0-5-0
Oct^{br}. 11. Piq^{t} Coll Van - - -	0-7-0
--23 -Piqu^{t} Van - - -	0-3-6
--27. Omb^{r}. L^{dy} Orkny - - -	0-12-6
--31. Omb. Lewis, Ford - - -	0-11-0
	9 1-0

⟨No^{br}. 2. Sa^{ct} 2^{s}-6. G. L^{dy} Ork. 2^{s}-6. at Took. 1^{s}. --6 at Rumnr. 1^{s}.⟩
⟨--8. Co^{ch} 2^{s}. --9 Coach 1^{s} Will. 6^{d}⟩

Dec^br^. 22. 1711

On Saterday, at 4 in the morn. dyed M[rs] Ann. Long at Lynn in Norfolk, where she had retired about 2 Years before, and lived under the Name of Smyth. The News of it came to Town on Monday night following, w[ch] was Xmas Eve and I heard it on Xmas day at Noon, w[ch] was Tuesday. She was the most beautifull Person of the Age, she lived in, of great Hon[r] and Virtue, infinite Sweetness and generosity of Temper, and true good Sense. J Swift.

Came to St Martin's Street Oct^{br}. 11 1711 on

Thursday. at 10^{s} p^{r} week.

Left St Martin's Street Thursday. Nov^{br}. 29 1711, came then

to little Panton Street. at 10^{s} p^{r} week.

Jun. 5. 1712. left Mrs Crane. & remov^{d} to Kensington.

Jul. 19. left Kensington. went to Winds^{r}.

Sep^{tr}. left Windsor. came to Mrs Hubbots in Rider Street.

Apr. 8. 1712. Patrick left me

--11 William came

Xmas Gifts. Pat. 2^{s}-6. Maid. 1^{s} Mr St J^{ns} Port^{r} 2^{s}-6^{d}

Jan^{r} 5. Ld Tr^{srs} Port^{r} 5^{s}. --7. D. Or^{mds} Port^{r}. 2^{s}-6^{d}

Account

Of Expences from Nov^{br}. 1. 1711 to Nov^{br}. 1. 1712.

First Quarter.

From Nov^{br}. 1. 1711 to Feb^{r}. 1. $17\frac{12}{11}$

JB.

Cloaths.

Jan^{r}. 1. Caps. 5^{s}. --7 Gloves. 1^{s}-3^{d}. - - - 0 - 6 - 3

Servt.

MC.

Lodging.

to Nov^{br}. 22^{d} 3 weeks. 1^{ll}-10^{s} to 29th -10^{s}. - - - 2 - 0 - 0
to Dec^{br}. 27th 2^{ll} to Jan^{ry} 24. 2^{ll} To Febr. 1. 10^{s} - - - 4 - 10 - 0

6 - 10 - 0

Extra^{dr}.

--Nov^{br}. 12. Spectacles dd. 6^{s}. Dec^{br}. 24. G. ⟨Patr. 2^{s}-6^{d} [no ▦ more. 13^{s}-6^{d}]⟩ X^{mas} Gifts - - - 0 - 19 - 6
Dec^{br}. 27. Treat Society. 7^{ll}-5^{s}-6^{d} - - - 7 - 5 - 6

8 - 5 - 0

Washing.

to No^{br}. 10. 1^{s}-8^{d} to 17. 1^{s}-5^{d}.½ to 24 1^{s}-9^{d} to De^{br}. 1. 1^{s}-5^{d}.½ - - - 0 - 6 - 4
to 8. 1^{s}-8^{d}½. to 15. 1^{s}-4^{d}. to 22 1^{s}-8^{d}.½ to 29 1^{s}-4^{d}.½ - - - 0 - 6 - 1½
to Jan^{r}. 5. 2^{s}. to 12. 1^{s}-6^{d} to 19. 1^{s}-8^{d}.½ to 26. 1^{s}-5^{d}.½ - - - 0 - 6 - 8
to Febr. 1st. 1^{s}-9^{d} - - - 0 - 1 - 9

1 - 0 - 10½

Expences

Nov^br^. 1st Month

1st Week.

1 to 10.

--2. Chair Van. 1^s^. B^d^ w. 1^s^-6^d^. Pats bill Coals Cand^ls^. &c. 2^s^-2^d^	0 - 4 - 8
--4. G. 3^d^. B^rd^ w. 5^s^. Pats bill. 7^d^. --9. Lett^rs^. A Bp D. 4^s^. G maid 1^s^ - - -	0 - 10-10
	0 - 15- 6

2^d^ Week.

10 to 17.

--12. Co^ch^ to & from Strat^fd^. 3^s^. --13. Wine. Van's 1^s^-6^d^. ⟨16⟩- - -	0 - 4 - 6
--16 Chair Van's. 1^s^ Pats bill Coles, Cand^ls^, Brush, &c. 1^s^-11^d^. - - -	0 - 2 -11
B^rd^. w. 5^s^. sm^ll^ 4^d^ Sm^ll^ 2^d^ - - -	0 - 5 - 6
	0 - 12-11

3^d^ Week

17. to 24.

--18. Chair to Church. 1^s^. Sm^ll^ 2^d^ Pats bill. Coals Cand^ls^. G. &c 1-11^d^.½ - - -	0 - 3 - 1½
--22. G. Pat. 6^d^ B^rd^ w. 5^s^ - - -	0 - 5 - 6
	0 - 8 - 7½

4th Week

24 to Dec^br^. 1.

B^rd^ w. 5^s^ Lett^rs^ 4^d^ sm^ll^ 4^d^. --29. G maid. 1^s^. sm^ll^ 2^d^ - - -	0 - 6 -10
Pats bill Cand^l^ 1^s^-2^d^ w. ball 5. Coals 7^d^ carrying 1^s^ Liq^rce^. 6^d^ in all - - -	0 - 4 - 2½
	0 - 11- 0½

1st Week	-	0 - 15- 6
2^d^ Week	-	0 - 12-11
3^d^ Week	-	0 - 8 - 7½
4th Week	-	0 - 11- 0½
		2 - 8 - 1

Dec^{br}.

Expences.

2^{d} Month

1st Week.

1 to 8

--1. Chair Vans. 1^{s}. --4. Carrg Picture for Ppt. 1^{s}. sm^{ll} 2^{d} - - -	0 - 2 - 2
--6. Co^{ch}. Harcourt. 1^{s}. G. there. 1^{s}. Brd w. 5^{s} - - -	0 - 7 - 0
Pats bill. Coff. Cols. Brlkls &c. 2^{s}-1^{d} - - -	0 - 2 - 1
	0 - 11- 3

2^{d} Week.

8 to. 15.

--10 Co^{ch} Bar^{br}. 1^{s}. Punch. Bar^{br}. 4^{s} --14 Co^{ch}. Van. 1^{s} Brd w. 5^{s} -	0 - 11- 0
Pats bill Coles Candles, Coffee &c. 2^{s}-9^{d}.½ - - -	0 - 2 - 9½
	0 - 13- 9½

3^{d} Week.

15 to 22.

--18. Co^{ch} Mr Harc^{rt} & Bar^{br}. 3^{s}. --19 G Pat for bur^{ll}. 1^{s} - - -	0 - 4 - 0
--Patr. 6^{d}. brd w. 5^{s} Pats bill Ca^{dl} 1^{s}-2^{d} Cols 6^{d}½ &c in all 2^{s}-5^{d} -	0 - 7 - 5
	0 - 11- 5

4th Week

22 to Jan^{r}. 1.

--24. Choco^{lt}. Bar^{br} &c. 2^{s}. Wine Bar^{br}. 1^{s}. Brd w. 5^{s}. blind man 6^{d}-	0 - 8 - 6
--29. Pats bill. Coles, &c. 1^{s}-11^{d}.½ --30. Chair. Mrs Wesly. 1^{s} - - -	0 - 2 -11½
Penknife. before. 1^{s}. sm^{ll} 4^{d} wine Bar^{br}. Sug^{r}. 6^{d} Brd w 2^{s} - - -	0 - 3 -10
	0 - 15- 3½

1st Week	-	0 - 11- 3
2^{d} Week	-	0 - 13- 9½
3^{d} Week	-	0 - 11- 5
4th Week	-	0 - 15- 3½
		2 - 11- 6

Expences.

Jan^{ry}. 3^{d} Month

1st Week.

1 to 12.

Brd w. 8^{s}. --5. Pats bill. 1^{s}-10^{d}. --6. Co^{ch} ⟨Ld Riv^{s}⟩ Nuttle. 1^{s} - - - 0 - 10-10

--6. Co^{ch} Ld Riv^{s}. 2^{s}. --Ch^{r} Ld Mash^{m}. 1^{s}. sm^{ll}. 4^{d}. - - - 0 - 3 - 4

--9. Co^{ch} Cunyhm. 1^{s}. Pats bill. Cols 1^{s}-2^{d}. Cand^{l}. 1^{s}-2^{d} &c in all 2^{s}-11^{d} 0 - 3 -11

2^{d} Week

12 to 19

--sm^{ll}. 3^{d} --14. Ch^{r} Ld Mash^{m}. 1^{s}. Brd. w. 5^{s} Pats bill. 1^{s}-5^{d} - - - 0 - 7 - 8

3^{d} Week

19 to 26

--21. Chair Ld Masham 1^{s}. --24 Tav^{rn} Domvil. Vezy. 3^{s}-6^{d} - - - 0 - 4 - 6

brd w 5^{s} Pats bill. Cols. 7^{d} Cand^{l}. 7^{d} Poud^{r}. 6^{d} &c. 2^{s}-3^{d}.½ - - - 0 - 7 - 3½

small 2^{d} - - - 0 - 0 - 2½

0 - 12- 0

4th Week.

26 to Febr. 1.

--30. G. old woman 6^{d}. sm^{ll} 2^{d}. Pats bill. Coles 1^{s}-2^{d}. &c. 1^{s}-8^{d} - - - 0 - 2 - 4

Brd w- 5^{s} - - - 0 - 5 - 0

0 - 7 - 4

1st Week	-	0 - 18- 1
2^{d} Week	-	0 - 7 - 8
3^{d} Week	-	0 - 12- 0
4th Week	-	0 - 7 - 4
		2 - 5 - 1

Totalls

Of a Quarter from Nov^{br}. 1. 1711 to Febr. 1. 17$\frac{12}{11}$.

Second Quarter.

From Febr^{y} 1. 17$\frac{12}{11}$ to May. 1. 1712.

JB.

Cloaths

Febr. 16. Gwn & Cass^{ck}. 24 y^{rds} 4^{s} 2^{d} pr yard. 5^{ll}. making. 18^{s}. - - - 5 - 18 - 0
--18. 4 Hankrfs 14^{s}. mend old gown. 3^{s}-6^{d} --23 Gloves. 1^{s}-3^{d} - - - 0 - 18 - 9
--29 Ristband 2 Sh^{rts} 1^{s} Mar. 29. mend Brchs. 1^{s}-4^{d}

Servt

Apr. 8. Cleard off. Patr. 3^{ll}-10^{s}

MC.

Lodging.

To Febr. 21. 3 weks. 1^{ll}- 10^{s}. to Mar. 20. 2^{ll}. to Apr. 17. 2^{ll}

Extr^{dys}

Febr. 13. a Key broke. 1^{s}. --28 a Box 5^{s}. --29 2 old Boks 1^{s}
May
Sickness Mrs Cranes bill. 1^{ll}-12^{s}-2^{d}.½ G. Mrs Crane 1^{ll}-1^{s}-6^{d}
Jun. 30. At Pontacks. 8^{s}.

Washing.

To Febr. 9 1^{s}-5^{d} to 16. 1^{s}-8^{d} to 23 1^{s} 5^{d} to Mar. 1st 2^{s}. to 8. 1^{s}-5^{d}
to 15 1^{s}-9^{d} to 22. 1^{s} 5^{d}.½ to 29 1^{s}-8^{d}.½ to Apr. 5. 1^{s}-4^{d}.½
to 12. 11^{d}.½ to 19. 3^{d} to 26. 10^{d}.½ to May 3 1^{s}-8^{d} to -10. 1^{s} 5^{d}.½
to 17. 1^{s}-8^{d}.½ to 24. 1^{s}-5^{d} to 31. 1^{s}-11^{d}½

Expences.

Feb^{ry}. 1st Month

1st Week

1 to 9.

--5. Tavern Domvile &c. 3^{s}. Pats bill. Cand^{l}. 1^{s}-2^{d} Cols 7^{d} &c. 2^{s}-5^{d}.½ - 0 - 5 - 5½

--Brd w. 5^{s}. Sm^{ll} 1^{d}.½ - - - 0 - 5 - 1½

0 - 10- 7

2^{d} Week.

9 to 16.

--11 sm^{ll}. 3^{d} Brd w. 5^{s}. Pats bill Coles 1^{s}-9^{d}. Liq^{ris} 6^{d} &c. in all 3^{s}-4^{d} - - - 0 - 8 - 7

3^{d} Week.

16 to 23

G. Patr. 6^{d}. G 3^{d} --22. Chair. 1^{s}. Pats bill Cols 1^{s}-2^{d}. Cand^{l}. 7^{d}. 2^{s}-6^{d}.½ - - - 0 - 4 - 3½

Brd w. 5^{s}. - - - 0 - 5 - 0

0 - 9 - 3½

4th Week

23 to Mar. 1.

--Co^{ch} M^{r} S^{cty}. 1^{s}. --27. G. Misess. 4^{d}. --29. G. Misess, maid. 1^{s} - - - 0 - 2 - 4

Brd w. 5^{s}. Pats bill Coles 7^{d} Candle 7^{d}. in all 1^{s}-10^{d}½ <Sm^{l} 4^{d}> - - - 0 - 6 -10½

Oranges 7^{d} sm^{ll} 4^{d}. - - - 0 - 0 -11

0 - 10- 1½

1st Week	-	0 - 10- 7
2^{d} Week	-	0 - 8 - 7
3^{d} Week	-	0 - 9 - 3½
4th Week	-	0 - 10- 1½
		1 - 18- 7

Expences

March. 2d Month

1st Week

1 to 8

--Coff. 3d. --2. Chair 1s. Smll 1d. --3 G. 2 maids at Barbrs. 2s - - -	0 - 3 - 4
Pats bill Coles 1s-2d. Candl. 7d. in all 2s-4d. Brd w. 5s. smll. 6d - -	0 - 7 -10
	0 - 11- 2

2d Week

8 to 15.

--12 Chair Ld Mashm. 1s. Bp Cloyn Lettr. 6d G. maid. 1s - - -	0 - 2 - 6
Lettrs 6d. Pats bill 1s-6d. Brd w. 5s - - -	0 - 7 - 0

3d Week

15 to 22.

--17. Coch. Barbr Sachvll. 1s. --19. Kensington. 5s-6d. smll 3d - - -	0 - 6 - 9
Brd w. 5s. Pats bill. Coff. 1s sugr 2d Poudr oyl. 6d &c in all 2s-9d.½	0 - 7 - 9½
--21 Chair to Mr Sommers 1s - - -	0 - 1 - 0
	0 - 15- 6½

4th Week.

22 to Apr. 1.

--Wine. Barbr. 1s-6d --24 Coch. 1s. --25. Coch 2s brd w. 5s - - -	0 - 9 - 6
Pats bill Razrs sett Candls 7d Coles 6d &c in all 2s-2d - - -	0 - 2 - 2
	⟨0 - 11- 8⟩

--30. Chr. Van's. 1s. Brd w. 3 days. 2s.

April.	Shingles begun Mar. 27 Sick all this Month	Expences.	3^d Month
⟨1 to 12⟩		1st Week.	

During sickness

16, 17, 18. Chair. 4s. --21. George Scrty St J. 5s. - - -	0 - 9 - 0
G. Will. 6d Chair 2s. Lettr 6d. Lettr Dr Prat 6d - - -	0 - 3 - 6
Will's bill. 1s 4d½. G. W. 6d - - -	0 - 1 -10½
Brd w -- 1ll-1s-6d 4 6 pences 2s - - -	1 - 3 - 6
	1 - 17-10½

To George for th Chest of Florence - - -	0 - 5 - 0
For Lock &c to th Chest - - -	0 - 2 - 6
Wills bill - - -	0 - 3 - 9½
Wills bills - - -	0 - 1 - 8

Totals

Of a Quarter from Feb[r]. 1. 17$\frac{12}{11}$ to May. 1. 1712.

Third Quarter.

From May. 1. to August. 1. 1712

JB.

Cloaths

May. 17. mend Shirts. 1^{s}. Jun. 2. Gloves. 1^{s}-3^{d}
--27 Shoes 2 p^{r}. 11^{s}. Aug. 8. Gloves. 1^{s}-10^{d}
Scarf . 1^{ll}-1^{s}-6^{d}

Servant.

May. 10. Breches 4^{s}-6^{d} Jun. 27. Shoes 4^{s}-6^{d}
Jun. 15 Coat

MC

Lodging

To May. 15. 2^{ll}. to Jun. 5. (then left Mrs Crane's) 1^{ll}-10^{s}
to July. 19. (at Kensington) 3^{ll} L^{nd}. . 1 week. 5^{s}
Sep^{t}. 27. Woman at Wi^{dr}. 10^{s}

$Extr^{dys}$

Jun. 5. Drugs for dyet drink. &c 17^{s}. Pothcaryes bill. 1^{ll}-4^{s}-6^{d}

Washing.

To Jun. 7. 1^{s}-2^{d}½ to 14 1^{s}-9^{d} to 21 1^{s}-5^{d} to 28. 1^{s}-6^{d}
to Jul. 5 1^{s}-4^{d}½ to 12 1^{s}-7^{d}½ to 19 1^{s}-1^{d}½ to 26. 1^{s}-8^{d}.½
to Aug. 2. 1^{s}-9^{d} <to 9. 1^{s}-4^{d}.½ to 16. 1^{s}-5^{d}½ to 23 1^{s}-8^{d}½
to 30. 1^{s}-6^{d} to Sept. 6. 1^{s}-9^{d}½ to 13. 1^{s}-9^{d} to 20 1^{s}-6^{d}
to 27 1^{s}-6^{d}½ to Oct^{br}. 4th 1^{s}-9^{d} to 11. 1^{s}..6^{d} to 17 1^{s}-7^{d}>

Expences

May. 1st Month

1st Week.

1 to 10 -	
--Brd w 7^{s}-6^{d} Will's 6^{d} - - -	0 - 8 - 0
--9. Co^{ch} &c Vans. 3^{s}-6^{d} - - -	0 - 3 - 6
Wills bill - 5^{d} - - -	0 - 0 - 5
	0 - 11-11

2^{d} Week.

10 to 17	
--Boat Bar^{br}. 6^{d} ⟨G Will⟩ --12 G. Will. 6^{d} - - -	0 - 1 - 0
--14. Co^{ch} L^{dy} Masham. 2^{s}. Wills bill 6^{d}. Brd w. 5^{s}-6^{d} - - -	0 - 8 - 0
	0 - 9 - 0

3^{d} Week

17 to 24	
19. ⟨Boat Bar^{br} 6⟩ Co^{ch} 1^{s}. G Mr Lewis man 2^{s}-6^{d} - - -	0 - 3 - 6
--20. Boat Bar^{br}. 6^{d} Brd w. 5^{s}. Wills bill - 2^{s}-1^{d} Will 6^{d} - - -	0 - 8 - 1
	0 - 11- 7

4th Week

24 to. Jun. 1.	
--Boat Bar^{br}. &c 8^{d}. G Will. 6^{d}. --26. G. Ld Riv^{rs} Co^{chmn} 2^{s}-6^{d} - - -	0 - 3 - 8
⟨--27. Ld Riv^{rs} Co^{chmn} 2^{s}-6^{d}.⟩ Conduct French. 1^{s}. - - -	0 - 1 - 0
Brd w 5^{s}. Will's 6^{d} Wills bill - 1^{s}-5^{d} - - -	0 - 6 -11
	0 - 11- 7

Expences

June | --8 Colick ⟨ ⟩sadly for a day. | 2^d Month

1st Week.

1 to 7. ⟨--3 Boat 1^s⟩ Co^{ch} 1^s	
--sm^{ll}. 4^d. --5 For removing Boxes &c 3^s-9^d. - - -	0 - 4 - 1
--G Mrs Cranes maid. 2^s B^{rd} w. 5^s. Will, 6^d Wills bill 1^s-7^d.½ - - -	0 - 9 - 1½
	0 - 13- 2½

2^d Week.

7 to 14.	
--Boat to & from B-- 1^s. to Miss hess for Coach 2^s. - - -	0 - 3 - 0
--Maid 1^s. --13. Boat Bar^{br}. 1^s. B^{rd} w. & 6^d. 5^s-6^d - - -	0 - 7 - 6
Maid at B-- before 1^s. a Hone. 2^s. Wills bill. 1⟨0⟩^{d} - - -	0 - 3 - 1
	0 - 13- 7

3^d Week.

14 to 21.	
--Boat D. Or^{md}. 2^s-6^d. --19. G. por girl. 6^d. at Society. 1^s. - - -	0 - 4 - 0
--20. G. C. Hills man 2^s. a Coach before. 1^s. boat. 1^s. - - -	0 - 4 - 0
B^{rd} w. & 6^d. 5^s-6^d Wills bill 10^d - - -	0 - 6 - 4
	0 - 14- 4

4th Week.

21 to July. 1.	
G. 4^d. 24. Co^{ch}.^Hessy^ 2^s --26. Co^{ch} L^d $Mans^l$. 1^s. 27. Boat. 6^d. - - -	0 - 3 -10
G. Will. 6^d Wills bill. 3^s-6^d.½ B^{rd} w. 6^s-6^d - - -	0 - 10- 6½
Sm^{ll}. 2^d. --30. Boat 6^d. Coach. 2^s	

Expences

July. 3d Month.

1st Week

1 to 5

Brd w. 3s-6d --Boat. 6d --2. Coch Lod. 6d. -Coch Ld Tr. 1s. - - - 0 - 5 - 6

Wills bill. 8d.½ G. Will a book. 6d Wills 6d smll. 1d ⟨G. 6d⟩ - - - 0 - 1 - 9½

0 - 7 - 3½

2d Week

5 to 12

Smll. 2d. --6 Coch. 2s-6d --7. Boat 1s. G. boy. 6d - - - 0 - 4 - 8

Brd w. 5s. Will 6d Wills bill. 9d.½ - - - 0 - 6 - 3½

0 - 10-11½

3d Week

12 to 19

--smll. 2d --15 boat 1s. Brd w. 5s. Will 6d - - - 0 - 6 - 8

Wills bill Candl. &c. 1s-2d - - - 0 - 1 - 2

0 - 7 -10

4th Week. Windsor ⟨ ⟩ 26. a week

19 to 26.

--20. Coach 3s. G. Vans man 1s. --22. Boat. 1s. - - - 0 - 5 - 0

--23 Boat Bp Cl. 6d. 24. Coch. 1s-6d. boat. 1s - - - 0 - 3 - 0

Wills bill Candl. &c. 1s-7d½ Brd w. 5s Will 6d - - - 0 - 7 - 1½

G. at Mrs Van. 4s-6d - - - 0 - 4 - 6

0 - 19- 7½

Remdr. Windsr.

26 to Aug. 1.

--27. G. poor man. 6d Brd w. 6s. Wills bill. 1s-4d - - - 0 - 7 -10

Fourth Quarter

From. Aug. 1st to Nov^{br} 1st 1712

JB.

Cloaths

Sep^{br}. 28. Shirts brought from Hol^{d}. 5^{s}. for th Shirts bought there.
Oct^{br}. 16. mend. Bre^{chs}. 1^{s}. --Gloves 1^{s}-10^{d} --24 mend Brec^{h}. 1^{s}

Servt

MC

Lodging

A Month at 6^{s} p^{r} week to Nov^{b}. 1. - - - 1 - 4 - 0

Extr^{dys}

Abot Oc^{tr}. 4. G. Printer. 10^{s}-9^{d} Sep^{tb}. 28. Poth^{y}. Wind^{sr}. 11^{s} - - - 1 - 1 - 9
G at Wind^{sr} to old woman - 10^{s}

Washing

to Aug. 9. 1^{s}-4^{d}.½ to 16. 1^{s}-5^{d}½ to 23 1^{s}-8^{d}½ to 30. 1^{s}-6^{d}
to Sep^{t}. 6^{d} 1^{s}-9^{d}½ to 13. 1^{s}-6^{d} to 20 1^{s}-6^{d}½ to 27 1^{s}-9^{d}
to Oct^{br}. 4th 1^{s}-6^{d} to 11. 1^{s}-7^{d}½ to 18 1^{s}-5^{d} to 25. 1^{s}-7^{d}½
to Nov^{b}. 1st. 1^{s}-5^{d}

Expences. Sick with Giddyness much. 1st Month

August.

1st Week

1 to -9

--4. Co^{ch} from Wind^{sr}. 7^{s}-6^{d} --5. G. 2 Voices. 1^{s}. - - - 0 - 8 - 6

Wills bill. Lodg. 2^{s}-3^{d}. Candles Raz^{rs}. &c. in all 3^{s}-9^{d} - - - 0 - 3 - 9

Brd w & 6^{d}. 5^{s}-6^{d} - - - 0 - 5 - 6

0 - 17- 9

2^{d} Week. Windsor

9 to 16

Wills Coach 3^{s}-6^{d} Wills bill. 2^{s}. 11. brd w. 6^{s} - - - 0 - 12- 5

Coff. 6^{d} - - - 0 - 0 - 6

3^{d} Week Wind^{sr}.

16 to 23

--20. Coff. 1^{s}. sm^{ll}. 6^{d}. brd w. 6^{s}. - - - 0 - 7 - 6

Wills bill 1^{s}-9^{d}½

4th Week. Wind^{sr}.

23 to Sep^{br}. 1. Brd w. 6^{s}. Wills bill. 2^{s}-10^{d} Coff. 6^{d}.

--3. G. L^{dy} Mash^{ms} man for Venson. 2^{s}-6^{d}

Septbr. Expences 2d Month.

1st Week Windr

1 to 6.

--Horse-hire to Ldy Orkney's. 2s-6d Wills Bill. 1s-9d½ Bd w. 6s - - - 0 - 8 - 6

2d Week. Windsr

6 to 13.

G. Vensn & Carrg. 3s-6d. Brd w. 6s. Wills bill 1s-9d½ - - - 0 - 11- 3½
sm11. 6d - - - 0 - 0 - 6
0 - 11- 9½

3d Week. Windsr

13 to 20

G. 6d. Wills bill 2s-1d.½ Brd w. 6s. G. Will+. 1s-6d - - - 0 - 9 - 7½
G Gate man 6d - - - 0 - 0 - 6
0 - 10- 1½

4th Week Windsr to 29th

20 to Octbr. 1.

--Wills bill. lodg. 1s. &c. in all. 2s-6d G. black. 1s. - - - 0 - 3 - 6
Brd w. 6s. --30. Coch. to Ld Tr. 1s. Brd w. 3s. - - - 0 - 10- 0
Wills Coach 3s-6d Bill. 1s-10d½ - - - 0 - 5 - 4½
0 - 18-10½

Expences.

October. 3^{d} Month

1st Week

1 to 4

--at Cue. &c. 3^{s}-6^{d} Brd w. 2^{s}-6^{d}. G. Will. 6^{d} - - - 0 - 6 - 6

2^{d} Week.

5 Co^{ch}. 1^{s}-6^{d}

4 to 11th. Brd w. 5^{s}-6^{d}. --9. Co^{ch}. 2^{s}-6^{d}. --10 Chair L^{dy} Or^{k}. 1^{s}. - - - 0 - 9 - 0

Wills bill 2^{s}-3^{d}. - - - 0 - 2 - 3

3^{d} Week.

11 to 18.

G. Will. 6^{d} --12. Sac^{rt}. 1^{s}. Sm^{ll}. 2^{d}. Glasses 1^{s}-6^{d} - - - 0 - 3 - 2

Wills bill. Coals 8^{d}. Cand^{l}. &c. in all - 2^{s}-4^{d}.½ Brd w. 5^{s}-6 - - - 0 - 7 -10½

G Miss hessy - - - 0 - 2 - 6

0 - 13- 6½

4th Week (17 to 24)

17-to-25

G. W. 6^{d} --23. G. por &c 3^{s}-6^{d} Wills bill. 1^{s}-8^{d} brd w. 5^{s}-6^{d} - - - 0 - 11- 2

Rem^{dr}

25 to Novr. 1.

--29. G. W^{ll}. 6^{d} --30. G. Treat. Van - 1^{s}. --27 Chair L^{dy} Ork. 1^{s} - - - 0 - 2 - 6

Brd w. 5^{s}-6^{d}. sm^{ll}. 6^{d} - - - 0 - 6 - 0

Wills bill Coals. 1^{s}-4^{d}. Ca^{dl}. 1^{s}-4 in all. - - - 0 - 3 - 2

A shill. melt. 1^{s}

Letters to.

No^{vbr}. 1. Lady Oglethorp
--Mrs Masham.
--3 MD. 33.
--7 Mrs Long.
--17. MD. 34.
--Mr Lewis.
Dec^{br}. 1. MD. 35
--14. MD. 36.
Bp Clogher.
--19 --Mrs Long.
--29 MD. 37
--Dean of St Patricks
Jan^{r}. 8. A. Bp. Dublin.
--12. MD. 38
--19. Bp of Clogher.
--26. MD. 39.
Febr. 1. Dr Sacheverell.
--9. MD. 40.
--23 MD. 41.
--28. Dr Prat.
--Mr Harrison.
Mar. 8. MD. 42
--Mr Harrison
⟨--Jo Beau^{nt}. & a bit from ppt.⟩
Bp Cloyn
--20 Ld Lansdown.
--22. MD 43
--Bp Clogher.
--29. A. Bp Dublin.
--Coz Dean Swift.
Ap^{r}. 10. MD. 44
--22. Mrs Wesly
--25. MD. 45. short
May. 10. MD. 46. short.
--M^{rs} W
--20 A. Bp Dublin.
--Pat Rolt
--24 M^{rs} W--
--29. MD. 47

Letters from

No^{br}. 3. Mr Masham
--9. A. B Dublin. 3 Pacquets.
--15 Mr Sec^{rty} S^{t} Jn
--17 Ar. Bp Dublin
--21. MD. 23 Mrs Long
--Mr Lewis. Mr Warburton
--Dec^{br}. 20. Bp Clogh^{r}.
--Couzn Dean Swift.
--27 MD. 24
--Jo Beau^{mt}
Jan^{r}. 11 MD. 25
--29. MD. 26.
Bp of Cloyn.
--31. Dr Sacheverell.
Febr. 6th. Pat Rolt.
--11 Bp Clogh^{r}.
--Mr Walls
--13 Dr Prat.
18 Bp. Cloyn. A Bp Dublin
Mar. 9. Mr Harrison
⟨Bp Cloyn⟩ Jo B. & a Bitt from ppt.
--19. Feherston.
--Ld Abercorn.
--MD. 27.
Bp Clogh^{r}
Ap^{r}. 10 A. B Dublin
--Dr Tisdel
Bp Cloyne.
Mrs Wesly.
--21. MD. 28.
--26. M^{rs} W--
--28. Bp Clogh^{r}
--Dr Prat
May. 9. MD. 29
--16. Pat Rolt

Letters to

Jun. 17. MD. 48
--Bishop of Clogher.
20 ⟨Mrs Wesly⟩
--26 A. Bp Dublin
Jul. 3. MD. 49
--7 ⟨Mrs Wesly⟩
--19. MD. 50
Aug. 7 MD. 51.
Sept^{br}. 20. 52
Oct^{br}. 9. MD. 53
--20. Ar^{ch} B Dublin
--Bp Cloyn
--D. Ormond.
--31. -54

Letters from

Jun. 2^{d}. M^{rs} W--
--Mr Geree
--13. MD 30.
--27. Jo Beau^{mt}
--Dr Ray^{md}
⟨--30 Mrs Wesly⟩
July. 4. MD 31.
--29. MD. 32
Sep^{br}. 23 MD. 33
Oct^{br}. 22. MD. 34

[13v]

Me^{md}. A large Bible for ppt.

Account

From Nov^{br}. 1. 1712 to Nov^{br}. 1. 1713.

Mr Ridge dyed 8th. March 1709 of an Apoplexy. He left

Won.

De^{br}. 13. Piq^{t}. Van - - -	0-3-0
--Jan^{r} 23. Omb^{r}. Bp Cl. - - -	0-4-6
Feb. 23. Omb^{r}. Sr A. F. D^{r} P^{rt} - - -	1-5-6
Mar. 7. Hazrd Vans S^{r}. A. - - -	0-2-0
--Small at sev^{ll} times - - -	0-2-0
--25. Omb^{r}. S^{r}. A. F^{n} Prvost - - -	0-6-0
--26. Sr T. Cl. S^{r} An^{d}. F^{n}. Omb^{r}. - -	0-10-6
Apr. 28. Piq^{t}. Provst - - -	0-7-6
May. 15. Omb^{r}. Provst. Ford - - -	0-2-6

Lost.

De^{br}. 19. Whisk. Took &c. - - -	0-1-6
Fe^{br}. 9. Omb^{r}. S^{r}. Fount^{n} - - -	0-11-6
--16. Omb^{r}. L^{dy} Clarges - - -	0-10-0
--20. Omb^{r}. Sr A. Foun^{tn} - - -	0-6-6
--26. Haz^{d}. M. V. - - -	0-1-0
Mar. 7. Omb^{r}. Dis^{ny}. M^{rs} Y^{ng} - -	0-3-6
--9. Omb^{r}. D^{r} P^{rt}. Mr Ford - - -	0-16-0
--11 Omb^{r} S^{r} A F. Dr Prat. - - -	0-14-6
Apr. 10. Omb^{r}. D^{r} P^{rt}. Lewis - -	0-11-6
--16. Piq^{ut}. Lewis - - -	0-2-0
May. 4. Omb^{r}. Lew^{s}. Provst - - -	0-4-6
--7. Piq^{ut} Provst - - -	0-1-0
--13. Omb^{r}. Lee Ford - - -	1-7-0
--18. Omb^{r}. Provst. Dr Lee - - -	0-10-6
--19. Omb^{r}. Provst Ford - - -	0-5-0

Ireld.

Jul. 17. Piq^{et} Mrs W. - - -	0.3-9^{d}.
--24. Piq^{t} M^{rs} W-- - - -	0-5-5
Aug. 1. Omb^{r}. Raynd. Tpt. - - -	0-2-0
--3. Omb^{r}. Mrs Wes^{l}. Mrs Barry - - -	0-8-0
--17 Omb^{r}. Walls. - - -	0-2-7

to Jul. 12. - - -	0-7-0
more - - -	0-3-3
to Aug. 14 Omb^{r} - - -	0-2-9
--22. Omb^{r}. Wal^{s} Tpt - - -	0-1-11
--25. Omb^{r}. Tpt Walls - - -	0-1-4
--27. Omb^{r}. Tpt. Walls - - -	0-3-6

Me^{md}--

Mund. Apr. 12. ^1713 at^ 10 in the morning. M^{r} L came to me & showed me the Order from L^{d} D-- for a Warrant for the 3 Deanryes.

May. 19. A deal box. 4^{s}-6^{d}

Knives & Forks. - - 3^{ll}-1^{s}.

--30. A saddle - &c - - 4-3^{s}-6^{d}

Account

Of Expences from Nov^{br}. 1. 1712 to No^{br}. 1. 1713

First Quar^{tr}.

From No^{br}. 1. 1712. to Febr. 1. 17$\frac{13}{12}$

JB.

Cloaths.

No^{br}. 20. 6 Hank^{rcfs}. 16^{s}-6^{d}. --22. Raz^{rs}. 5^{s}. --24. Stock^{s}. 2 p^{r}. 9^{s}.
Jan^{r}. 26. Wastcoat & Breeches
⟨Febr. 1. Shoes 2 p^{r}. 11^{s}.⟩

Servt.

MC.

Lodging

for 13 weeks - - - 3 - 18- 0

Extr^{ds}.

De^{br}. 11. a Book 6^{d} --18. Tav^{rn} Ld Bol. &c 19^{s}. Jan^{r}. 3. Pat Rolt. 1^{ll}-1^{s}-6d - - - 2 - 1 - 0
Jan^{ry}. 10. Books. 3^{ll}-12^{s}-6^{d} --26. G. poor Greek. 5^{s} - - - 3 - 17- 6

Washing

N^{br}. 8. 1^{s}-8^{d} --15. 1^{s}-6^{d}.½ --22. 1^{s}-8^{d}.½ 29. 1^{s}-5^{d}.½ - - - 0 - 6 - 4½
De^{br}. 6. 1^{s}-9^{d} --13. 1^{s}-4^{d}.½ --20. 1^{s}-8^{d}.½ --27. 1^{s}-5^{d}.½ - - - 0 - 6 - 3½
to Jan^{r}. 3^{d} 1^{s}-8^{d} to 10. 1^{s}-5^{d}.½ to 17. 1^{s}-9^{d}.½ to 24. 1^{s}-5^{d} - - - 0 - 6 - 3
to Febr. 1. 1^{s}-9^{d} ⟨to 8. 1^{s}-5^{d}.½ to 15. 1^{s}-6^{d}⟩

Expences.

Nov^{br}. 1st Month

1st Week.

1 to 8 - Brd w. 5^{s}-6^{d}. Wills bill. 3^{s}-6^{d}.½ --2^{d}. Sac^{rnt}. 2^{s}-6^{d}
Ld Ork^{nys} man. for Spaw water. 2^{s}-6^{d} at Tooks. 1^{s}. --6. at Rum^{mnr}. 1^{s}

2^{d} Week

8 to 15
Brd w. 5^{s}-6^{d}. Wills bill 3^{s}-6^{d}.½ -Co^{ch} 2^{s}. --9. Coach. 1^{s}. ^G Will, 6^{d}. - 0 - 12- 6½

3^{d} Week

15 to 22.
--17. Chair L^{d} T^{r}. 1^{s}. --18. Chair L^{d} T^{r}. 2^{s}. G. Will. 6^{d}.
Brd w. 5^{s}-6^{d} Wills bill. 3^{s}-10^{d}.½

4th Week

22 to 29.
--26. Co^{ch} Ld Trea^{r}. with Prior. 1^{s}. Wills bill. 4^{s}.

Expences.

Dec^{br}. 2^{d} Month

1st Week

1 to 6

--Co^{ch}. 1^{s}. G. Will. 6^{d} Brd w. 5^{s}-6^{d} - - - 0 - 7 - 0
Wills bill. Co^{ls}. 2^{s}-4^{d}. Ca^{dl}. 1^{s}-2^{d} - in all. 5^{s}-3^{d} - - - 0 - 5 - 3

2^{d} Week.

6 to. 13.

--8. Co^{ch} Ld Dupl. 1^{s}. --10. Chair L^{dy} Ork^{ny}. 1^{s}. - - - 0 - 2 - 0
--12. G. D. Or^{nds} Ser^{vt} for Choco^{lt}. 2^{s}-6^{d} - - - 0 - 2 - 6
--G. L^{dy} Ork^{ys} Ser^{vt} that brought Table. Nov^{br}. 21. 5^{s} - - - 0 - 5 - 0
Brd w. 5^{s}-6^{d}. Wills bill. Coals. 2^{s}. Co^{ch}. 1^{s}. Ca^{dls}. 1^{s}-2^{d} - 5^{s}-10^{d}.½ -0 - 11- 4½
G Mr Reed 2^{s}-6^{d} - - - 0 - 2 - 6

1 - 3 - 4

3^{d} Week.

13 to 20.

G blind m^{n}. 6^{d}. G. por. 6^{d}. Brd w. 5^{s}-6^{d} - - - 0 - 6 - 6
Wills bill. Tea - 10^{d}. Coals. 2^{s}-4^{d} &c in all. 4^{s}-2^{d}

4th Week.

20 to 27.
21
--Co^{ch} to L^{d} T^{r} & hom 2^{s}. Mr Reed for Lett^{rs}. 1^{s}
--23. Sm^{ll}. 3^{d}. P^{d} Diapres Co^{ch}. 1^{s}. G. maid. 1^{s}.
--25. Co^{ch} Ld Bol. Wills bill - 4^{s}-10^{d}

Rem^{dr}.

27 to Jan^{r}. 1.

Brd w. 3^{s}. --31. Co^{ch}. Bol - 1^{s} Wills Bill - 4^{d}.½

Expences. Giddy ⟨about⟩ 27th ⟨26th⟩

Jan^ry.

3^d Month

1st Week.

1 to 10.

B^rd w. 8^s. --8. Co^h L^d T^r. 1^s - - -	0 - 9 - 0
Wills bill. Co^ls 2^s. &c. 3^s-3^d.½ ⟨B^rd w.⟩ - - -	0 - 3 - 3½
	0 - 12- 3½

2^d Week.

10 to 17.

--12. din^r. 1^s-3^d. Co^ch. 6^d. --13. G. poor wom^n - 1^s. - - -	0 - 2 - 9
--14. Co^ch Cesar. 2^s. B^rd w. 5^s-6^d G. Will. 6^d. - - -	0 - 8 - 0
W's bill. Co^ls. 2^s. Cand^l. 1^s-2^d - in all - - -	0 - 4 - 3
	0 - 15- 0

3^d Week

17 to 24

--G. 3^d. --23. Ch^r. Bp Cl. 1^s. B^rd w. 5^s-6^d - - -	0 - 6 - 9
W's bill. Coles - 2^s 6^d Cand^ls 7^d Powd^r 6^d - in all - - -	0 - 3 - 7
	0 - 10- 4

4th Week

24 to Feb. 1.

--25. Chair L^d T^r. 1^s. --27. Co^ch Ld Dupplin. 1^s. - - - 0 - 2 - 0

--Lett^r Tisdel &c. 1^s-1^d G. 4^d. --29. at Society. 2^s-6^d

--31. Co^ch. with D^r Fr^nd. 6^d G. Van's boy. 1^s.

Wills bill. 3^s-10^d.½

Totalls

Of a Quar^{tr} from Nov^{br}. 1. 1712 to Febr. 1. 1712-13.

JB - - -

Cloaths - - -

Servant - - -

MC - - -

Lodging - - -

Extraord^{ys} - - -

Washing - - -

Expences 1st Month. - - -

Expences 2^{d} Month - - -

Expences 3^{d} Month - - -

⟨Expences⟩

Second Quarter

From Fe^{br}. 1. 1712-13. to May. 1. 1713

JB.

Cloaths

Feb^{r}. 1. mend Cassock. 6^{d} --Shoes. 2 p^{r}. 11^{s}. Hat. 1^{ll}-13.
Mar. 29. Gown & Cass. 6^{ll}-7^{s}-6^{d}. mend Cass^{k}. 4^{d}.
Apr. 11. Gloves. 1^{s}-10^{d} --18. Towells. 4^{s}

Servt.

MC

Lodging

to May. 1. - - - 3 - 18- 0

Extr^{dys}.

Feb. 18. Wine Ld Bol. Ser^{vts}. 7^{s}-6^{d} Mar. 3^{d}. Picture. 2^{ll}-5^{s}.
--8. Pict^{r}. 14^{s}. Apr. 20. Books 1^{ll}-2^{s} Raz^{rs} before & G. Will. 6^{s}

Washing

to Feb. 7. 1^{s}-5^{d}.½ to 14. 1^{s}-6^{d} to 21. 1^{s}-9^{d} to 28 1^{s}-6^{d}
to Mar. 7. 1^{s}-9^{d} to 14. 1^{s}-5^{d}.½ to 21. 1^{s}-8^{d}½ Wastct. 3^{d}
to -28. 1^{s}-6^{d} to Apr. 4. 1^{s}-8^{d}.½ to 11. 1^{s}-6^{d} to 18. 1^{s}-8^{d}½
to 25. 1^{s}-5^{d}.½ to May. 2^{d}. 1^{s}-9^{d}.½

[6v]

Expences.

Febru^{ry}. 1st Month

1st Week.

1 to 7.

--2. Coffee 6^{d}. --6. Co^{ch} Ld Keep^{r}. 1^{s}. 7 Co^{ch}. L^{d} T^{r}. 1^{s}.
Brd w. 5^{s}-6^{d}. Wills bill. ⟨3^{s}-10^{d}.½⟩ 2^{s}-8^{d}

2^{d} Week.

7 to. 14.

Wills bill. 2^{s}-8^{d}½ 3^{s}-1^{d}½ B^{d} w. 5^{s}-6^{d}

3^{d} Week.

14 to 21.

--20th. Co^{ch} Ld Bol. 1^{s} --15. Chair. Fun^{rll}. 1^{s}.
Wills bill. 4^{s}-5^{d}½ Brd w. 5^{s}-6^{d}

4th Week.

21 to Mar. 1.

--25. S^{m} - 8^{d}. --27. G. Vann 1^{s}. M^{rs} M^{ary} 2^{s}-6^{d}.
Wills bill. 2^{s}-10^{d} Brd w. 5^{s}-6^{d}

Expences

March. 2^{d} Month

1st Week.

1 to 7. Sm^{ll}. 6^{d}. Wills bill. 2^{s}-9^{d}. Brd w. 5^{s}-6^{d}.

2^{d} Week.

7 to 14

--9. Coach 6^{d}. Wills bill 3^{s}-7^{d} B^{d} w. 5^{s}-6^{d} - - - 0 - 9 - 7

3^{d} Week.

14 to 21.

Wills bill. 3^{s} ⟨2^{d}.½⟩ Brd w. 5^{s}-6^{d} - - - 0 - 8 - 6
--22 Chair L^{d} St^{wd}. 1^{s}. 23. Co^{ch}. 4^{s}. 24. Co^{ch}. 1^{s} - - - 0 - 5 - 0
0 - 13- 6

4th Week.

21 to 28.

--22. Chair Ld Stewrd. 1^{s}. --23. Co^{ch}. 4^{s}. --24 Co^{ch}. 1^{s}. - - - 0 - 6 - 0
27 Seeing moving picture 2^{s}. 28. Co^{ch} & Chair L^{d} T^{r}. 2^{s}. - - - 0 - 4 - 0
Wills bill. 2^{s}-4^{d}. Brd w. 5^{s}-6^{d} - - - 0 - 7 -10
0 - 17-10

Rem^{dr}.

28. to Apr. 1.

Brd w. 2^{s}-6^{d} Wills bill. 1^{s}-2^{d}.

April. Expences. ubi nunc? --23^{d}. Warrant sign^{d}, sent 25th. 3^{d} Month

1st Week.

1 to 11.

--5. Sacr^{mt} 2^{s}-6^{d} --6. Coff. 1^{s}. Co^{ch}. L^{d} T^{r}. 1^{s}-6^{d}. ⟨Brd w. 5^{s}-6^{d}⟩ - - - 0 - 5 - 0

--8. Chair. 1^{s}. --9. Co^{ch} L^{dy} Jersys Son. to L^{d} T^{r}. 3^{s} --10. G. Pat Rolt. 1^{s}-6^{d} - - - 0 - 5 - 6

Wills bill. 11 days, Sug^{r}, &c. 5^{s}-2^{d}.½ Brd w. 8^{s}-6^{d} - - - 0 - 13- 8½

1 - 4 - 8½

2^{d} Week.

11 to 18.

--13. Chair. D. Orm^{d}. 1^{s}. --14. G. at Barb^{rs}. 1^{s}. Co^{ch}. 1^{s}. - - - 0 - 3 - 0

--15. G. po^{r}. 7^{d}. ⟨Miss⟩ Coach. 1^{s}. ⟨Wills bill. 3^{s}-7^{d}.½⟩ Cand^{ls} 1^{s}-2^{d} - - - 0 - 1 - 7

⟨Coles⟩ Wills bill. Cand^{l}. 1^{s}-2^{d}. Coles 1^{s}-6^{d} &c. in all 3^{s}-7^{d}.½ Brd w. 5^{s}-6^{d} - - - 0 - 9 - 1½

3^{d} Week.

18 to 25.

--18. Chair & Coach. --21. Din^{r}. Parn^{ll} Berkly 2^{s}.

--23. Dinn^{r} Prat. Parn^{ll}. 2^{s}-6^{d}. Wills bill. 1^{s}-10^{d}.½

Brd w. 5^{s}-6^{d}

4th Week.

25 to 30

--28. Din^{r}. Provst. &c. 1^{s}-6^{d}. --29 Coff. 6^{d}.

Brd w. 5^{s}-6^{d}. Wills bill. 2^{s}-3^{d}.½

Third Quarter.

From May. 1. to Aug. 1. 1713.

JB.

Jun. 27. 2^{ll}-6^{d} --more 3^{ll} --clear to ⟨this time⟩ Aug. 1.

Cloaths.

May
--15 P Rogue Tayl[r] old debt. 17^{s}-6^{d} Jun. 1. A Cap. 10^{s}.
Jun. 24. Night gown. Jul Jul. 27. Gloves. 1^{s}-7^{d}.½
Riding coat Gloves. 1^{s} mend. Gown. 6^{d}½

Serv[t].

Jun. 15. P[d]- Will ⟨5 over 4⟩^{ll}-- --Jul. 30 allod Tom 3^{s}-7^{d}.½

MC.

Lodging

A Fortnight in Dublin to Jun. 25. 12^{s}. G. Maid - 2^{s}-2^{d} - - -	0 - 14- 2
To Jun. 1. in London. - - -	1 - 4 - 0
Bar[brs] bill for Chocolate &c. 16^{ll}-	

Extr[dys].

May. 7. treat Brats at Ogres. 7^{s}-6^{d}. Box. 4^{s}-6. Knivs. 3^{ll}-1^{s} - - -	3 - 13- 0

Jun. 14. to dd. 2^{ll}-6^{s} --25.⟨Wine Laracor.⟩
Custom House. 1^{ll}-13^{s}-4^{d}. Wills g[ods] 1^{s}-7^{d}.½ M[rs] Kena - 2^{ll}-6^{s}
Plan to M[r] Might. 9^{s}-3^{d} Jun. 6. Poth[crys] Bill 16^{s}-11^{d}
--Chocolate (each) 3^{ll}-11-[3]

Washing

To May. 9. 1^{s}-6^{d} to 16 1^{s}-10^{d} to 23 1^{s}-6^{d}
to Aug. 8. 8^{s}-9^{d}

Horses

Jun. 1. A saddle &c. 4^{ll}-3^{s}. A Horse to Ches[tr]. 1^{ll}-4 - - -	5 - 7 - 0

Horse brought over & G. 15^{s}. Jo's Horses. Dub[l]. 3^{s}
Shoes & Oyl. 9^{d} Girth &c. 2^{s}-3^{d} Saddle mend. 1^{s}-8^{d}

Expences

May. 1st Month

1st Week: ubi nunc? --6. ibid sed dubius. ob Red sing. --16. heard I dont prst.

1 to 9.

--6. G. Will. 6^{d} --7 Wills bill. 11^{d}. Brd w. 5^{s}-3^{d}
Lett^{r}. 1^{s}-8^{d}

2^{d} Week

9 to 16
Boat & Coach
--sm^{ll}. 6^{d} --11. ⟨Chair.⟩ 2^{s}. 12 Glass. 1^{s}. Chair. 2^{s}.
--14 Sm^{ll}. 6^{d}. ⟨Coff⟩ Boat. 6^{d} Wills bill. 2^{s}-1^{d}.½ Brd w. 5^{s}-6^{d}

3^{d} Week.

16 to 23

--G Mrs Hills man. 2^{s}-6^{d}. Carp^{tr}. 6^{d}. Boat & Port^{r} 1^{s}-2^{d} - - -	0 - 4 - 2
G. Will. 6^{d} Coach. & Port^{r}. 1^{s}-4^{d} --18. Ch^{r}. 1^{s}. sm^{ll}. 2^{d} - - -	0 - 3 - 0
--19 G Will. 9^{d} ⟨Box. 4^{s}-6^{d}⟩ 21. G. maid. at Van. 3^{s}-6^{d} - - -	0 - 4 - 3
--22. Boat 6^{d}. G. Pat R. before. 3^{s}. G. old wom^{n}. 1^{s}. - - -	0 - 4 - 6
Wills bil 1^{s}-2^{d}. Brd w. 5^{s}-6^{d} Barb^{rs} maid. 1^{s} - - -	0 - 7 - 2
	1 - 3 - 1

4th Week.

23. to Jun. 1.

--Chair L^{d} T^{r}. 1^{s}. --28. to Mr Law^{lss} man. 2^{s}-6^{d} - - -	0 - 3 - 6
G. Ld Tyr^{ls} Port^{r}. 2^{s}-6^{d}. G. Mr Silvest^{r}. 5^{s}. poor 6^{d}. Boat. 6^{d} - - -	0 - 8 - 0
--29. G. Ld Bol's Groom. 5^{s} Ld Orknys Port^{r}. 2^{s}-6^{d} - - -	0 - 7 - 6
--30. Boat. 6^{d}. Co^{ch}. 1^{s}. G. L^{d} T^{r}. Port^{r}. 5^{s} --31. G. sad^{l}. boy 1^{s} - -	0 - 7 - 6
D. Orm^{ds} Port^{r}. 5^{s}. Ld Mashams Man 5^{s} - - -	0 - 10 - 0
Vans man 2^{s}. Co^{ch} Kensig^{tn} 2^{s}. Co^{ch} Barb^{r}. 2^{s}. - - -	0 - 6 - 0
Jun 1. Co^{ch} to ⟨ ⟩Horses. 2^{s}. Brd w. 5^{s}-6^{d} - - -	0 - 7 - 6
Din^{r} & Coach before - 3^{s}-6^{d} - - -	0 - 3 - 6
	2 - 13 - 6

Expences.

June. 2^{d} Month.

sed ubi nunc?

1st Week.

Left London. 1.

Left London. Jun. 1. Monday to Chest^{r}. 6. to Holyhe^{d}. 10th.

Landed in Dublin Jun. 10. Wednesday at 9 at Night.

Spent in travelling &c. to Jun. 10 - - -		12 - 18^{s}-0
Install^{d} Sate^{dy}. 13th. [Ire^{ld}]	⟨A Horse to Chest^{r} - - -	1 - 4 - 0⟩
Ireland.	At Mr Barbers - - -	0 - 5 - 0
		13 - 3 - 0

Left Dublin for Laracor. Jun. 25. Thursd.

G. MD. at sv^{ll} times. 10^{s}. at Walls. 2^{s}-2^{d}. - - - 0 - 12- 2

G. I. Parv^{sl}. 1^{s}. Ned. 1^{s}. Drabs 1^{s}

Tavern Raynd. 2^{s}-8^{d}. Coach hire - - - 10^{s}.

G. at Sac^{rnt} &c 10^{s}-10^{d} MD's maid 2^{s}-8^{d}.½

Laracor.

25. to Jul. 1.

Din^{r}. MD &c. G. por Boy. 6^{d}.½

G. at Gelbrins. 1^{s}. Sm^{ll}. 1^{s}-6^{d}. Prison. 1^{s}-1^{d}

Expences

July. 3d Month

1 to 11 — 1st Week — Laracor

G. Jo. 2s-2d. G. Esay. 1s-1d Wine Trim. 1s-6d. - - -	0 - 4 - 9
Dinner. MD &c 2s-8d. G. Venison. 1s-1d - - -	0 - 3 - 9
Tom's bill Carg. Tobac. &c 4s-1d - - -	0 - 4 - 1
	0 - 12 - 7

11 to 18. — 2d Week — Laracr

--13. G. Tom. 1s-1d. --16. Wine. Trim 1s-6d. - - -	0 - 1 - 7
--18 Win Trim. 1s-6d. ⟨--19 G. 6d½. Win Trim. 1s-1d⟩ - - -	0 - 1 - 6
Win. Jo. 5s-2d. Dinr. MD. &c 2s-8d Ale. 1s-8d. - - -	0 - 9 - 6
	0 - 12 - 0

18 to ⟨26⟩ 25 — 3d Week. — Laracor

--G. 6d½. Win. Trim 1s-1d --20. Win. Trim. 7d.½ - - -	0 - 1 - 8½
--21. Dinr. Win. Ale, &c. MD. 6s-6d. G. Tom. 1s-1d. --22 Langlds 1s-1d-	0 - 8 - 8
Smll. 3d. - - -	0 - 0 - 3
	0 - 10 - 7½

25 to Aug. 1. — 4th Week. — Laracor

--Win. Raynd. 1s-7d.½. --26. Smll. 2d. - - -	0 - 1 - 9½
--27 Win. Raynd. 1s-5d --28th Win Jo. 2s-6d Dinr 3s. - - -	0 - 6 - 11
--Ale 3s --29. dinr Coz. 1s-2d --Win Raynd. 8d. - - -	0 - 4 - 10
--30. Toms bill 1s-5d. Win. Raynd. 1s-1d - - -	0 - 2 - 6
--31. G. Esay. 1s-1d Portr 4d - - - Smll. 3d - - -	0 - 1 - 8
	0 - 17 - 8½

Fourth Quarter

From Aug. 1. to Nov^{br}. 1. 1713.

JB.

Cloaths.

Aug. 20
mend Sh^{rt}. 1^{s}-1^{d} --28. Glovs. 4^{s}.
Shoes 2 p^{r} & Slipp^{r}. 12^{s}. Shoes 1 p^{r}. & G. 5^{s}. Hat dressd. 1^{s}.
Sept^{br}. 26th Risband. Shirts 9^{d}. me^{d} Brechs. 15^{s}. For Linnen Mrs Manly. 3^{ll}-9^{s}

Servt.

Aug. 21. p^{d} a Coachm^{n}. 1^{s}-1^{d} --26. Brec^{hs}. 9^{s}-4^{d}
Cloaths. 2^{ll}-15^{s}-6^{d} Boots & Shoes. 11^{s} Sep^{t}. 11th. Hat. 9^{s}-6^{d}
Gloves. 1^{s}. a whip. 2^{s} Sep^{t} 25. Stockins. 6^{s}

MC

Extr^{dys}.

Aug. 12. X^{ng} Mrs Walls. 2^{ll}-2^{s}-5^{d} --19. ppts Cloak Castan 5^{ll}-15^{s}.
Car. Customs &c of Books & allowd Jo. -5^{ll} Aug. 20. G. Jo. 10^{s}-10^{d}
Chocolate Tpt --Sep^{tr}. 12. Books. 17^{s}-6^{d}. --15 Plautus. 1^{ll}-10^{s}.
25. Pools Synops. 4^{ll}. Appian &c 12^{s}. Pray^{r} book. 2^{s}-6^{d} Oct^{br}. 6. Book 6^{d}
Oct^{br}. 9. G. boy Books. 5^{s}.

Washing.

Aug. 22. M^{rs} Br. old Acc^{t}. 5^{s}. new Accn^{t}. 4^{s}-4^{d}½
Aug. 12. to 24. ⟨5^{s}-6^{d}⟩ 4^{s}-9^{d} at Sr G. D. 1^{s}-1^{d}.
Sep^{tr}. 14. 1^{s}-4½ to 22. 3^{s}-2^{d} to Oct^{br}. 10. 6^{s}-11^{d}.½
at Winds^{r} before 1^{s}-6^{d} to 17. 2^{s}-6^{d}. to 24. 2^{s}-6^{d} to Dec^{br}. 1. 2^{s}-7^{d}.

Lodging

Sep^{br}. 9th to ⟨Dec^{br} 17⟩ Nov^{br}. 1. - - - 2 - 2 - 0

Horses

Horse forg^{t}. 1^{s}-11^{d}

[11v]

August. Expences Irel^{d} 1st Month

1st Week Laracor

1 to 8.

Wax & Pap^{r} Jo. 6^{d}½ forget 3^{d} - - -	0 - 0 - 9½
5. and 6 at Trim. G. & wine &c 4^{s} - - -	0 - 4 - 0
House Bill at Laracor. from Jun. 25 to Aug. 8, including. wine. 1^{ll}-6-8. Tom 1 week. 7^{s}. ⟨Post Lett^{rs} 5^{s}-5^{d}⟩ Poud^{r} & Shot. 1^{s}-8^{d} - - -	2 - 16-10
Post Lett^{rs} to the same date - - -	0 - 5 - 7
	3 - 7 - 2½

2^{d} Week. Laracor to 11th

8 to 15.

--Wesly's Keep^{r}. 2^{s}-8^{d}½. --9. Jo. 4^{s}. G. Jo. 1^{s}-1^{d}. - - -	0 - 7 - 9½
--G Wesly's Groom. 1^{s}-1^{d}. --11. G. maid at Larac^{r}. 1^{s}-1^{d} - - -	0 - 2 - 2
--Co^{ch}. 1^{s}. Win. &c 1^{s}-6^{d}. - - -	0 - 2 - 6

3^{d} Week.

15 to 22

Co^{ch} &c. 3^{s}. Co^{ch} to Chapl^{d}. 3^{s}-3^{d} --18. Co^{ch}. 6^{d}.½ - - -	0 - 6 - 9½
--19. Co^{ch}. 6^{d}.½ --20. Win. 1^{s}-7^{d} Co^{ch}. 2^{s}-2^{d} - - -	0 - 4 - 4½
--21. Co^{ch}. 5^{s}-5^{d}. Lobstr. 1^{s}-1^{d}. Ale. 6^{d}.½ --M^{rs} Br. acc^{t} 2^{s}.	

4th Week.

22. to Sep^{t}. 1.

--Win. MD. 1^{s}-11^{d} --23. Win. MD. 11^{d}. Sac^{rt}. 1^{s}-1^{d} --24. Win. MD. 1^{s}-2^{d}. Toms bill. Tobac. Car^{aws}. Raz^{rs} ground. &c. for 2 week & Lett^{rs} - - -	0 - 6 - 5
--25. Co^{ch}. 24. MD. & Walls 2^{s}-2^{d}. Chair. 6^{d}.½ - - - --26 Co^{ch}. 6^{d}.½	0 - 5 - 0½
27. G. MD. 2^{s}-8^{d}.½ Co^{ch}. 3^{s} - - -	0 - 5 - 8
--28 Chair. 6^{d}½ Tom's bill - 1^{s}-5^{d}	
--29 Bp Drom^{r}. Serv^{ts}. 9^{s}-2^{d}.½ Co^{ch}. 2^{s}-8^{d}½ Rings^{d} 7^{s}. Boats. 5^{s}-5^{d} - - -	1 - 4 - 4
poor. 1^{s} - - -	0 - 1 - 1

Sett Sayl. Sated. Aug. 29. landed at Parkgate Monday the 31st. Set out to London. Sep^{br}. 1st.

Engl^{d}

Expences.

Sept^{br}. 2^{d} Month

1st Week. Engl^{d}. Aug. 31. Mond.

1 to 12.

--Aug. 31. to Brisco. 1^{ll}-1^{s}-6^{d} Crew 6^{s}. Survy^{r}. 2^{s}-6^{d} - - -	1 - 10- 0
Horses. 4^{s}-6^{d}. Parkgate. 2^{s}-6^{d} more there 7^{d} - - -	0 - 7 - 7
Chest^{r}. & G. 5^{s}-6^{d} --Whitchurch. 4^{s}-11^{d} G. &c. 1^{s}-6^{d}. ⟨Whip 2^{s}.⟩- - -	0 - 11-11
--2. Nieuport. 8^{s}-6^{d}. four Crosses. 3^{s}-10^{d} --3. Welch harp. 12^{s} - - -	1 - 4 - 4
--Coventry & G. 5^{s}-6^{d} --Dunchurch - about 6^{s} ⟨G. 8^{d}⟩- - -	0 - 11- 6
--4. G. at Northamp^{tn} 1^{s}. --8. G. at Sr G. Dolbens 1^{ll}-7^{s}. --Inn. 5^{s}-6^{d} -	1 - 13- 6
--9. Market street. 7^{s}. ⟨Barnet.⟩ Tom's bill. 2^{s}-5^{d}. Barnet. 4^{s}. forg^{t}. 1^{s}. - - -	0 - 14- 5
Horse Hire from Chest^{r} to London - - -	2 - 10- 0
--Porter 1^{s}. --10. Boat 6^{d}. Co^{ch} L^{d} T^{r}. 1^{s}. - - -	0 - 2 - 6
	9 - 05- 9

2^{d} Week.

12 to 19.

--14. Co^{ch}. 1^{s}. --16. gl. Cochm. 6^{d} --18. Din^{r}. Provst. 3^{s}-6^{d} - - -	0 - 5 - 0
Brd w. 6^{s} Brd w. forgot. 2^{s}-6^{d} Toms bill Cand^{ls} &c. 1^{s}-8^{d} - - -	0 - 10- 2

3^{d} Week

19 to. 26

--20. sm^{ll}. 4^{d}. 21. Milk wat^{r}. 1^{s}. --22. Choc^{lt}. 2^{s}. - - -	0 - 3 - 4
--24 Tav^{rn}. 1^{s}. --24 sm^{ll}. 6^{d} --25 Din^{r}. 1^{s}-1^{d}. sm^{ll}. 1^{d} - - -	0 - 2 - 8
Toms bill 1^{s}-1^{d}. Brd w. 6^{s}. - - -	0 - 7 - 1

4th Week. Windsor

26 to Oct^{br}. 1.

--Toms Coach. 3^{s}-6^{d}. Co^{ch} L^{dy} Orky. 5^{s}. Win Cl. Godfry. 2^{s}-6^{d} - - -	0 - 11- 0
Brd w. 6^{s}. Steels Pamplt. 1^{s}. - - -	0 - 7 - 0

Oct^{br}. Expences 3^{d} Month

Wind^{sr}. to 5th

1st Week.

1 to 10.

Sm^{ll}. 1^{s}-6^{d}. Toms Co^{ch}. 3^{s}-6^{d} Ld Mashms man. 2^{s}. G. 6^{d}. - - -	0 - 7 - 6
--6. Din^{r}. 1^{s}. wine. 2^{s}. --8 Co^{ch} L^{d} T^{r}. 1^{s}. - - -	0 - 4 - 0
Toms bill Co^{ch}. 3^{s}-6^{d}. lodg. 3^{s}. &c 1^{s}. - - -	0 - 7 - 6
--9. Chair. 1^{s}. G. maid. 1^{s}. Brd w. 6^{s}. - - -	0 - 8 - 0
	1 - 7 - 0

2^{d} Week. Winds^{r}. 2 days.

10 to 17.

Coffee Hos. &c. 1^{s}. --12 Ch^{r} L^{d} T^{r}. 1^{s}. Sm^{ll}. 6^{d}. - - -	0 - 2 - 6
Toms Co^{ch}. 3^{s}-6^{d} Brd w. 6^{s}. - - -	0 - 9 - 6
Toms Coach. 3^{s}-6^{d} - - -	0 - 3 - 6
	0 - 15- 6

3^{d} Week. Windsor. 2 days

17 to 24

Co^{ch}. Tom. 7^{s}. G. woman. 2^{s}-6^{d}. --20. Co^{ch}. 2^{s}-6^{d}. Din^{r} Pope 5^{s}. - - -	0 - 17- 0
--21. Chair. D. Orm^{d}. 1^{s}. Toms bill, lodg^{ng}. Coles. Raz^{rs}. Brush &c. 2^{s}-10^{d} - - -	0 - 3 -10
Brd w. 6^{s}. --22. Straps 6^{d}. Ivory stick. 7c 8^{d}. deaf girl. 6^{d} - - -	0 - 7 - 8
--sm^{ll}. 9^{d}. Co^{ch} L^{d} T^{r}. 1^{s}. - - -	0 - 1 - 9
	1 - 10- 3

4th Week Winds^{r}. 2 days.

24 to Nov^{b}. 1.

Toms bill. Tobac. 5^{d} Pict^{r}. 6^{d} Coles 1^{s}-2^{d} Cand^{l}. 7^{d}. Poud^{r} 5^{d} &c - - -	0 - 3 - 2
Toms Coach 7^{s}. Brd w. 6^{s}. --27. Din^{r} Pope. 2^{s}. --28. Co^{ch} L^{d} T^{r} 1^{s} - - -	0 - 16- 0
Coff & G. 1^{s}. G. landlady. 1^{s}. - - -	0 - 2 - 0
	1 - 1 - 2

Letters to.

Nov^{br}.
--18. MD. --55
Dec^{br}. 13 MD. 56.
Jan^{r}. 3. MD. 57.
--8. A. Bp. Dublin.
--23. ⟨MD⟩ about. -58.
Feb. 14. MD. 59
--28. MD. 60.
Mar. 21. MD. 61
Apr. 7. MD. 62
--28. MD. 63
May. 16. MD. 64

Letters from.

No^{br}. 10. Ar-Bp Dublin
Dec^{br}. 2. MD. 35.
--11. MD. 36.
Jan^{r}. 23. MD. 37
Febr. ab^{t}. 18. MD. 38.
Apr. 24. MD. 39.
May. 8. Bp Dromore
--Dr Coghill
--Id.
Dr Ray^{md}
Mr Walls
Bp Killdare.
M^{r} Wo^{ll}
Mr Diaper.

Sept^{br}. 1st. MD. 1.
--17. MD. 2.
-- MD. 3.
Oct^{b}. 22. MD. 4.
-- A. B Dubl
-- Bp Clogh^{r}
-- Mr Walls

Charges of the Dean^{ry}

Sept^{br}. 15 1713 Licence for Engl^{d} - - - 5 - 19- 1

Commissions for MD. &c

6 blew & white Coffe cups with handles. for dd.

A quarto Bible for Tpt.

Charges on entring the Dean^{ry}.

The Patent - - -	19 - 19- 7
Severall incidents, Fees for install^{mt}. to the Quire, Drums, Sexton &c - - -	8 - 1 - 5
To Harris for othr Fees of the Quire (a^{bt} 3^{ll})	
Aug. ⟨20⟩ 19. Treat Chapt^{r} - - -	1 - 0 - 0

Received from

Parvisol since I came over Jun. 10. 1713

Account

Of Expences from

Nov^{br}. 1st 1717 to Nov^{br}. 1st 1718

Lost - 8 - 2 - 3½

Won - -6 - 3 - 1½

Rem. lost. 1 19- 2

Account

Of Expences from Nov^{br} 1st 1717 to Nov^{br}. 1st 1718

First Quarter

From Nov^{br}. 1st 1717 to Febr. 1st $\frac{18}{1717}$

Cloaths

Nov^{br}. 16 Scouring old night gown 2^{s}-8^{d}½ Sm^{ll} 6^{d}½ - - -	0 - 3 - 3
Jan^{ry} Silk 1^{s} Serge 7^{d} thr^{d} 6^{d} Fust^{n} 1^{s}-10^{d} Lin^{n}. 5^{s} Cam^{bt}. 1^{s}-6^{d} - - -	0 - 10- 5
butt^{ns} 4^{d} mend Brechs 1^{s}. Jan^{r}. 18. Wast^{ct} (with 1^{s}-7^{d} to JB) 1^{ll}-18-3^{d}	- 1 - 19- 7
	2 - 13- 3

Serv^{ts} Cloaths.

Nov^{br}. 19 altering hughs Cloaths 4^{s}-6^{d} Stockins for him 3^{s}-6^{d} - - -	0 - 8 - 0
Shoes for him 3^{s}-9^{d} sm^{ll} 6^{d} Jan^{r}. 17. G. Sand^{rs} Shoes 4^{s}. - - -	0 - 8 - 3
Hughs Brechs 7^{s} - - -	0 - 7 - 0
	1 - 3 - 3

Extr^{dys}.

Jan^{r}. 8th wash. at Larac^{r}. 2^{s}-4^{d} Nov^{br}. 30 Livrs 10^{d} - - -	0 - 3 - 2

Horses.

Nov^{br}. 28th. Sad^{lrs} bill in part 2^{ll}-15-6^{d} in all p^{d} - - -	3 - 8 - 7
--30 Oats 5^{s}. Bran 1^{s}-6^{d} a Sieve 5^{d} Dec^{br}. 6. Bran 1^{s}-6^{d} - - -	0 - 3 - 5
Dec^{br}. 12 Physick 3 times 1^{s} Hughs old Bill 1^{s}-3^{d} - - -	0 - 2 - 3
--1 a Purge 1^{s} --18 a Purge 1^{s} --Straw 5^{s}-8^{d} - - -	0 - 7 - 8
--21. Oats 4^{s}-10^{d} --26 at th Pace 3^{s}-1^{d}½ - - -	0 - 7 -11½
Jan^{r}.24 Bran 1^{s}-6^{d} --25 Oats 5^{s} - - -	0 - 6 - 6
	4 - 16- 4½

Hay to Gillespy - - -	7 - 3 - 0
	11- 19- 4½

Expences

Nov^{br}. 1st Month.

1st Week.

1 to 9	
MD 4^{s}-10^{d}.½ Brd w. 12^{s}-6^{d}. --2. Din^{r} MD. 2^{s} Ale &c. 1^{s}-7^{d}½ - - -	1 - 1 - 0
--3. Din^{r}. 2^{s}-3^{d} 4. Din^{r}. 9^{d}.½ - - -	0 - 3 - 0½
7 MD. 6^{d}½ Chair. 1^{s}-1^{d} Co^{ch}. 8^{d} 5. Lett^{r}. 6^{d} - - -	0 - 2 - 9½
sm^{ll}. 2^{d} - - -	0 - 0 - 2
	1 - 7 - 0

2^{d} Week.

9 to 16.	
--Brd w. 11^{s}. --Din^{r} MD Walls &c 5^{s}-7^{d}. . . Ale. 1^{s}-8^{d}½ - - -	0 - 18- 3½
11. Din^{r}. Cusack. Grah^{m}. 2^{s}-8^{d}½. . Ale. 5^{d}. . Lett^{r} 6^{d} - - -	0 - 3 - 7½
--13. Co^{ch}. 7^{d} --14 MD. 2^{s}. --15. Din^{r}. 2^{s}-2^{d} MD. 6^{d} - - -	0 - 5 - 3
Raz^{rs} 6^{d} sm^{ll} 1^{d} - - -	0 - 0 - 7
	1 - 7 - 8½

3^{d} Week.

16 to 23	
⟨--Brd w.⟩ --Din^{r} MD &c. 6^{s}. . Ale &c 2^{s}-6^{d}. - - -	0 - 8 - 6
--17 Co^{ch}. 4^{d}½ MD 8^{d}½ MD 3^{d} Brd w 11^{s}. - - -	0 - 12- 4
--20. Din^{r}. Gratt^{ns}. 12^{s}-10^{d} Ale. 1^{s}-10^{d} 21. Din^{r} Ld Trmblston 15^{s}-3^{d} Ale 2^{s}-8^{d} -	1 - 12- 7
--22. Chair 6^{d}½ Poud^{r} 3^{d}. sm^{ll} 5^{d} - - -	0 - 1 - 2
	2 - 14- 7

4th Week.

23 to Dec^{br}. 1.	
--Brd w. 11^{s}. Co^{ch}. 1^{s}-4^{d} MD 1^{s}-1^{d} - - -	0 - 13- 5
--26. Din^{r} Chapt^{r}. 10^{s}-10^{d}.½ ⟨Ale⟩- - -	0 - 10-10½
--Din^{r} MD at home 5^{d}.½. . . 29. din^{r} MD 1^{s}-8^{d} Co^{ch} 10^{d} - - -	0 - 2 -11½
Ginger brd. 1^{s}-6^{d} - - -	0 - 1 - 6
	1 - 8 - 9
30.	
Birth day dinn^{r} MD &c 10^{s}-6^{d} - - -	0 - 10- 6
	1 - 19- 3
more Birthday - - -	0 - 4 - 8½
	2 - 3 -11½

1st Week -	1 - 7 - 0
2^{d} Week -	1 - 7 - 8½
3^{d} Week -	2 - 14- 7
4th Week -	1 - 19- 3
	7 - 8 - 6½
	4 - 8
	7 - 13- 2½

Expences

Dec^{br}. 2^{d} Month

1st Week

1 to 7

Brd w. 11^{s}. -din^{r} at home. 3^{d} --2. MD. 1^{s}-1^{d} - - -	0 - 12- 4
4 MD 8^{d} --5 MD 2^{s}-2^{d} - - -	0 - 2 -10
Lett^{r} 2^{d} sm^{ll} 2^{d} Washb^{ll} oyl &c 1^{s}-8^{d}½ Tobac. 1^{s}-7^{d} --1^{d} - - -	0 - 3 - 8½
	0 - 18-10½

2^{d} Week.

7 to 14

MD 10^{d} Sm^{ll} 1^{d} Brd w 11^{s}. --10 din^{r} at home 5^{d}½ - - -	0 - 12- 4½
--before to MD 1^{s}-1^{d} --12 MD 1^{s}-1^{d} - - -	0 - 2 - 2
13 Din^{r} MD. Grat^{n}. Holt &c in all 7^{s}-1^{d} Small 8^{d} - - -	0 - 7 - 9
	1 - 2 - 3½

3^{d} Week.

14 to 21

Brd w. 11^{s}. Co^{ch} 1^{s}-1^{d} --16 MD 1^{s}-7^{d}½ Co^{ch}. 6^{d}½ - - -	0 - 14- 3
--17. Din^{r} at home Jo. 1^{s}-3^{d}. before 14. Din^{r} &c 1^{s}-10^{d} - - -	0 - 3 - 1
Lett^{rs} 1^{s}. sm^{ll} 3^{d} - - -	0 - 1 - 3
	0 - 18- 7

4th Week. Larac^{r}. 27th

21 to 28

--Brd w 11^{s} --23. MD 2^{s}-10^{d}½ --24 din^{r} at Bott^{lg}. 1^{s}-6^{d} - - -	0 - 15- 4½
--27. din at home to Sa^{le} 6^{d} Lett^{r} 1^{s} Brd c^{h} &c 1^{s}½	0 - 2 - 6½
Sm^{ll} 2^{d} - - -	0 - 0 - 2
	0 - 18- 1

1st Week -	0 - 18-10½
2^{d} Week -	1 - 2 - 3½
3^{d} Week -	0 - 18- 7
4th Week -	0 - 18- 1
	3 - 17-10
Ging^{rbd} -	0 - 1 - 6
Coffee -	0 - 3 - 3
Starch blue	0 - 1 - 9
	4 - 2 - 7

From 3^{d} to 9th
at Ludlows. Expences

Jan^{ry}. Dubl. 10th 3^{d} Month

1st Week

1 to 11 Brd w. 16^{s}-5^{d} --2. Hare 1^{s}-2^{d} Din^{r}. 6^{s}-6^{d} - - -	1 - 4 - 1
more spent at Trim 2^{s}-2^{d} --10 MD 2^{s}-2^{d} light 2^{d} - - -	0 - 4 - 6
--13. Chair 6^{d}½ --15 Din^{r} Hog^{shd} MD. 5^{s}-11^{d}½ Ale 1^{s}-9^{d} - - -	0 - 8 - 3
sm^{ll} 1^{d} Tobac. 1^{s}-4^{d} Shot 2^{d}. - - -	0 - 1 - 6
	2 - 9 - 4

2 Weeks by mistake

2^{d} Week
⟨Brd w. 11^{s}⟩

⟨11⟩ 18 to ⟨18⟩ 25

--Brd w. 11^{s}. Din^{r} L^{dy} B^{ty} Copes &c. 18^{s}-2^{d}½ Ale &c 1^{s}-8^{d} - - -	1 - 10-10½
Ging^{r} br^{d} 1^{s}-6^{d} --21 MD 1^{s}-4^{d} --22. MD 2^{s}-2^{d} Candle 1^{d}½ - - -	0 - 5 - 1½
Ging^{rbd} at Trim hugh 1^{s}-7^{d}. Sm^{ll} 5^{d} --24 MD 5^{d} sm^{ll} 2^{d} - - -	0 - 2 - 7
Poud^{r} &c 5^{d}½ - - -	0 - 0 - 5½
	1 - 19- 0½

4th Week.

25 to Febr. 1st

--Brd w 11^{s}. MD 6^{d}½ --26. Din^{r} at home 4^{d}.½ - - -	0 - 11-11
--28. MD 1^{s}-1^{d} 29 Co^{ch}. 6^{d}½ MD. 1^{s}-1^{d} - - -	0 - 2 - 8½
--30 Din^{r} Ray^{mds} MD Prcv^{l}. Grattans. meat 8^{s} Ale Oyst^{rs} &c 3^{s}-9^{d}½ - - -	0 - 11- 9½
	1 - 6 - 5

2 - 9 - 4
1 - 19- 0½
1 - 6 - 5
5 - 14- 9½

[3v]

Totalls

Of a Quarter from No^{vbr}. 1st 1717. to Feb. 1. 17$\frac{18}{17}$

Cloaths - - -	2 - 13 - 3
Servants Cloaths - - -	1 - 3 - 3
Ex^{trd} - - -	0 - 3 - 2
Horses - - -	11 - 19 - 4½
Expences first Month - - -	7 - 13 - 2½
Exp. 2^{d} Month - - -	4 - 2 - 7
Exp. 3^{d} Month - - -	5 - 14 - 9½
⟨Exp⟩	33 - 9 - 7½

Account

Of Expences from Febr. 1st $\frac{18}{1717}$ to May. 1st 1718

Second Quarter

⟨From Febr. 1⟩ Cloaths.

--Jan^r. 1st Cap. Loop, lace. 2^s-9^d Mar. 1. Stockins 3 p^r. 17^s-4^d - - -	1 - 0 - 1
--Muslin 2^s-9^d $Wors^{td}$ 4^d. Mar. 22. Caps & mend. 3^s-3^d - - -	0 - 6 - 4
Mar. 14 th^{rd} Stockins 6^s-6^d. $wors^{td}$ Stockins & dying 5^s - - -	0 - 11- 6
Feriting 1^s sm^{ll} 1^s-3^d½ - - -	0 - 2 - 3½
	2 - 0 - 2½

$Serv^{ts}$ Cloaths

Mar. 19. Boots mend. 1^s-4^d - - -	0 - 1 - 4

$Extr^{dys}$

Sand 3^d. Febr. 15 Livers 2^s-8^d Wash at $Lara^{cr}$. 7^s-7^d - - -	0 - 10- 6
Apr. 4 Matts 2^s --24. Livers 3^s-10^d - - -	0 - 5 -10
	0 - 16- 4

Horses.

Febr. 20th Smith at $Lara^{cr}$. 7^s-6^d - - -	0 - 7 - 6
Mar. 3 Smiths bill from Mar. 1716. to this day - - -	1 - 0 - 5½
--⟨8⟩Oats 5^s-3^d work at hay. 1^s a Girth $butt^r$ & Tar. 1^s-5^d Oyl 6^d - - -	0 - 8 - 2
--8 Straw 5^s-8^d --19 Oats 5^s-2^d Bran 1^s-6^d - - -	0 - 12- 4
--Currycomb & brush. 2^s-6^d --30 Stable at Jo 1^s-4^d - - -	0 - 3 -10
--28.Oyl. 6^d --27 at th Pace. 9^d - - -	0 - 1 - 3
Apr. 12. Horses shod 6^s $Butt^r$ 5^d. to 15. at Trim. 1^s-3^d - - -	0 - 9 - 1
--16. Honey 6^d - - -	0 - 0 - 6
	3 - 3 - 1½

[4v]

April | Expences. | 3^{d} Month

1st Week. Lud^{l}

1 to 5

Brd w (6^{s}) 3^{s} all^{ed} - at Ludlows - - - 0 - 3 - 0

2^{d} Week Lara^{cr}. 7th

5 to 12

Brd w. 11^{s}. --7. at Trim 3^{s}-9^{d}. - - -	0 - 14- 9
--Plovs eggs. 9^{d}. Lamb, Bred. &c. 11^{d} --9 Plovrs eggs. 3^{d} - - -	0 - 1 -11
Gingr^{bd}. 2^{s}-4^{d} Lett^{r} 2^{d}. Car^{g}. 4^{d}. Lett^{r} 2^{d} - - -	0 - 3 - 0
--11. Din^{r} Lar^{acr}. 1^{s}-8^{d} - - -	0 - 1 - 8
	1 - 1 - 4

3^{d} Week. Larac^{r}.

12 to 19

--wine Trim. 2^{s}-2^{d} --Brd w. 11^{s}. - - -	0 - 13- 2
--14 Din^{r} Lar^{cr}. Wes. Perc^{ll}. &c. 12^{s}-6^{d}½ - - -	0 - 12- 6½
Plovrs Eggs. 1^{s}-2^{d} --15 Win Trim 2^{s}-5^{d} sm^{ll} 6^{d} - - -	0 - 4 - 1
--17. Win &c Trim 6^{s}-6^{d} --18 Co^{ch}. 6^{d}½ - - -	0 - 7 - 0½
Sand^{rs} Bill. 1^{s}-6^{d}½ Lett^{r} 4^{d} - - -	0 - 1 -10½
	1 - 18- 8½

4th Week. Dubl. 18.

19 to 26

--Brd w. 11^{s}. MD. 1^{s}-7^{d}½ sm^{ll} 2^{d} sand &c. 1^{s}-1^{d} - - -	0 - 13-10½
A Hare 4^{d}½ --23 MD 1^{s}-7^{d}½ --Portr. 6^{d} sm^{ll} 2^{d}½ - - -	0 - 2 - 8½
25. Tobac. 1^{s}-4^{d} - - -	0 - 1 - 4
	0 - 17-11

Rem^{dr}. S^{r} W^{m}. Fowns 28th.

26 to May. 1.

Brd w 5 days. 7^{s}-10^{d} Lett^{r} 1^{d} - - - 0 - 7 - 4

1st Week	-	0 - 3 - 0
2^{d} Week	-	1 - 1 - 4
3^{d} Week	-	1 - 18- 8½
4th Week	-	0 - 17-11
Rem^{dr}	-	0 - 7 - 4
		4 - 8 - 3½

Totalls

Of a Quarter from ⟨May⟩ Febr. 1st 1717-18

to May 1st 1718.

Cloaths - - -	2 - 0 - 2½
Servts Cloaths - - -	0 - 1 - 4
Extrd - - -	0 - 16- 4
Horses - - -	3 - 3 - 1
Expences 1st Month - - -	4 - 16-11
Expences 2d Month - - -	6 - 14- 8½
Exp. 3d Month - - -	4 - 8 - 3½
	22 - 0 -10½

Account

Of Expences from May. 1st 1718 to Aug. 1st 1718

Third Quarter

Cloaths.

May. 4. Breches. 15^{s}-$2^{d}\frac{1}{2}$ Caps & mend. 2^{s}-10^{d} - - -	0 - 18- 0½
Gloves. 1^{s}-2^{d} Ferriting. 6^{d} --Jun 5. Tay^{lr}. 1^{s}-6^{d} - - -	0 - 3 - 2
Silk &c 2^{s}-8^{d} Stockins 4^{s}-4^{d} Jul. 5th R^{d} gown 1^{ll}-19^{s}-10^{d} - - -	2 - 6 -10
Lutstring 9^{s}-2^{d} - - -	0 - 9 - 2
	3 - 17- 2½

$Serv^{ts}$ Cloaths.

May 30. $Saund^{rs}$ $Leath^{r}$ Breeches 7^{s} - - -	0 - 7 - 0

$Extr^{ds}$

Lost by Gold. 5^{s} May. 17. $Phys^{k}$. 1^{s}-6^{d} Livers 2^{s} Coff. 3^{s}-2^{d} - - -	0 - 11- 9
May. 16. Watch. MD. 4^{s}-6^{d}. Livers 6^{d} --31. Snuff box. 11^{d} - - -	0 - 5 -11
Jul. 17th. wash at Laracor. 6^{s}-6^{d} $Bitt^{rs}$ 1^{s}-6^{d} - - -	0 - 8 - 0
Jun. 17th Sug^{r}. 8^{s}-8^{d} $Bitt^{rs}$ 1^{s}-6^{d} Snuff & $Canis^{tr}$ 1^{s}-9^{d} - - -	0 - 11-11
	1 - 17- 7

Horses.

May. 7. Oats 5^{s}-1^{d}. Bran. 1^{s}-6^{d} --14. Oyl & Tar &c 1^{s}-$2^{d}\frac{1}{2}$ - - -	0 - 7 - 9½
--28. Sad^{lr}. 6^{s}-11^{d} --31. Sad^{lr}. 3^{s}-6^{d}. Jun. 14. Shoes. 1^{s}-4^{d} - - -	0 - 8 - 9
Sm^{ll}. 8^{d} July. 14. Shoes. 6^{s}-8^{d} Stabl. Jo. 1^{s}-3^{d} - - -	0 - 8 - 3
	1 - 4 - 9½

3^{d}. -terrible Fall G^{d} knows what may be th Event. bettr twards th End.

1st Mo

Expences

May. D bl. 3^{d}

1st Week

1 to 10

Brdw. 14^{s}. 2^{d}. 3^{d}. at Bray 5^{s} 7^{d} -Sup^{r} MD. 2^{s} 9^{d}½ - - -	1 - 2 - 6½
--6. Chair -6^{d}½. sm^{ll}. 3^{d} Poud^{r} 1^{d}½ sm^{ll}½ - - -	0 - 0 - 11½
--8..Din^{r}. Irvins Copes &c. 8^{s} 2^{d}.½ ⟨Ale &c⟩ - - -	0 - 8 - 2½
--9. MD 1^{s} 7^{d}½ Coch. 6^{d}½ blue 5^{d} seeds & Brand. 1^{s} 8^{d} - - -	0 - 4 - 3
Lett^{rs}. 1^{s} 6^{d}	1 - 15- 11½

2^{d} Week.

10 to 17

--Brd w. 11^{s}. Din^{r} MD Grat^{ns}. &c. 4^{s}.6^{d}. Bief Ale. 4^{s} 8^{d}½ - - -	1 - 0 - 2½
--14 MD 2^{s} 8^{d}½ --16. MD. 2^{s} 8^{d}½. Coch. 6^{d}½ Let^{tr} 2^{d} - - -	0 - 6 - 1
	1 - 6 - 3½

3^{d} Week.

17 to 24

Brd w. (all^{d} maid) 12^{s}. Ging^{r} bd. 2^{s} 2^{d} - - -	0 - 14- 2
--Dinr Jarv^{s} MD. Grat. Sherid^{n} 7^{s} 8^{d}½ Bief ale &c. 4^{s} 5^{d}½ - - -	0 - 12- 2
--19th MD 8^{d}. 18 a Glass 1^{s} 7^{d}½ Worr^{ll}. - - -	0 - 2 - 3½
⟨--19 MD [ ] 8^{d}.⟩ --20. MD. 1^{s} 1^{d} --22^{d} Din^{r} Grah^{m} 3^{s} 8^{d}½ Bief Ale 3^{s} 2^{d}	-0 - 7 - 11½
--23 MD. Botling. Din^{r}. 4^{s}. 6^{d}. Ale &c 2^{s} 8^{d}½ Lett^{r} 2^{d} sm^{ll} 1^{d} - - -	0 - 7 - 5
	2 - 4 - 0

4th Week

24 to Jun. 1.

Brd w. 12^{s}. --27 MD 1^{s} 7^{d}½ --28. MD. 2^{s} 4^{d} - - -	0 - 15- 11½
Bief 10^{d} Brd ale. 4^{d}. Lett^{r} 2^{d} Oyl. 4^{d}½ wash balls 4^{d}½ - - -	0 - 2 - 1
Tobac. 2^{s} 8^{d}½ Furses 8^{d} --29 din^{r} MD. 5^{s} 1^{d}½ ale &c 1^{s} 8^{d} - - -	0 - 10- 2
Lett^{r} 2^{d} - - -	0 - 0 - 2
	1 - 8 - 4½

First Week	-	1 - 15- 11½
2^{d} Week	-	1 - 6 - 3½
3^{d} Week	-	2 - 4 - 0
4th Week	-	1 - 8 - 4½
		6 - 14- 7½

Expences

June		2d Month
	1st Week Laracr. 2d	
1 to 7.		
--Brd w 11s sand 3d Coffee 3s-2d - - -		0 - 14- 5
at Trim &c 5 & 6. abt 1ll. - - -		1 - 0 - 0
Horse to Dublin 2s. ⟨Gingr br⟩- - -		0 - 2 - 0
Saundrs bill - - -		0 - 1 - 3½
		1 - 17- 8½
	2d Week. Laracr 9d	
7 to 14		
--1- at Laracor & before &c 6s-10d Gingrbrd. 1s-7d - - -		0 - 8 - 5
Brd w 11s Sandr bill Tobac. 1s-4d &c. 1s. road to Laracr. 2s - - -		0 - 16- 4
		1 - 4 - 9
	3d Week Ludl. 19th	
14 to 21		
Brd w. 11s Lettr 6d Freestone 2d Lettr 2d - - -		0 - 11-10
Lettr 4d		0 - 0 - 4
		0 - 12- 2
	4th Week Ludlows	
21 to July. 1st		
--27 Win &c. 5s Brd w 3s - - -		0 - 8 - 0

1st Week	-	1 - 17- 8½
2d Week	-	1 - 4 - 9
3d Week	-	0 - 12- 2
4th Week	-	0 - 8 - 0
		4 - 2 - 7½

Expences

July. 3^{d} Month

1st Week Lud^{l}.

1 to 5. Brd w 3^{s} - - - 0 - 3 - 0

2^{d} Week Ludlows.

5 to 12.
Lett^{r} 2^{d} Brd w 3^{s} - - - 0 - 3 - 2

3^{d} Week. Lara^{cr}. 14th.

12 to 19th
Brd w 11^{s}. --15 din^{r} Lar^{cor}. 5^{s}. Trim 6^{d} - - - 0 - 16- 6
Sand^{rs} Bill 11^{d}½ - - - 0 - 0 -11½
0 - 17- 5½

4th Week. Rochforts 1⟨8⟩9th

19 to 26th.
Brd w 3^{s} - - - 0 - 3 - 0

1st Week	0 - 3 - 0
2^{d} Week	0 - 3 - 0
3^{d} Week	0 - 17- 5½
4th Week	0 - 3 - 0
	1 - 6 -⟨0½⟩ 5½

Totals

Of a Quarter from May the 1st to Aug. 1st 1718

Cloaths - - -	3 - 17- 2½
Servts Cloaths - - -	0 - 7 - 0
Extrd - - -	1 - 17- 7
Horses - - -	1 - 4 - 9½
Expences 1st Month - - -	6 - 14- 7½
Exp. 2d Month - - -	4 - 2 - 7½
Exp. 3d Month - - -	1 - 6 - 5½
	19 - 10- 3½

Account

Of Expences from Aug. 1^{s} to Nov^{br}. 1st 1718

Fourth Quar^{tr}

Cloaths

Sep^{tr}. 13 tow^{ds} mend. Per^{wg}. 15^{s}-2^{d} --19. Shoes & old debt for Shoes. 19^{s}-6^{d} - - -	1 - 14- 8
--24 mend. Cloath. &c. 2^{s}-2^{d} Buttons. 1^{s}. --Oc^{tb}. 31st Shoes. 9^{s}-6^{d}. - - -	0 - 12- 8
--Oc^{tr}. 31st⟨3^{ll}⟩ a Perewig 3^{ll} - - -	3 - 0 - 0
	5 - 7 - 4

Ser^{ts} Cloaths &c

Sep^{t} to Sand^{rs} in Cons^{d}. of Cloath. 10^{s} - - -	0 - 10- 0
To him for washing 5^{s}-5^{d} - - -	0 - 5 - 5
Oc^{tbr}. 14. Saund^{rs} Cloaths in all Hat Shoes &c - - -	4 - 4 - 8
Wills frock then - - -	0 - 17- 9
Hatts then 13^{s}.	5 - 17-10

Extr^{ds}

Aug. 25. Wash at Galstown. 5^{s}-10^{d} Phisick 7^{d} - - -	0 - 6 - 5
mend draw^{r}. 6^{d} Liv^{rs} from May to Sep^{tb}. 25. 5^{s}-10^{d}	0 - 6 - 4
Oc^{tb}. 4. Messge Parvis^{ll}. 1^{s}-7^{d}½ Coff. 7^{ll} (Oc^{tb} 22^{d}) 1^{ll}-2^{s}. - - -	1 - 3 - 7½
	1 - 16- 4½

Horses.

Aug. 19 Smith 2^{s}-6^{d} Hors standing. 1^{s}-2^{d} Sm^{ll} 4^{d} - - -	0 - 4 - 0
--29. Bran. 1^{s}-6^{d} 30 Oats 4^{s}-3^{d} Straw 4^{s}-4^{d} sm^{ll} 1^{d} - - -	0 - 10- 2
clean yrd 6^{d}. Hay put up. 8^{s}. Butt^{r} 3^{d} mend whelbarrw 1^{s}-4^{d} - - -	0 - 10- 1
Sep^{t}. 29. sm^{ll}. 3^{d}½ Oct^{br}. 2^{d}. Bran 1^{s}-4^{d} - - -	0 - 1 - 9½
Hay 11^{ll}-5^{s}-6^{d} Turpent &c 1^{s}. Oct. 11. Oats 4^{s}-10^{d} - - -	11 - 11- 4
25. Arrear Sadler. 2^{s}. Oyl. 5^{d} - - -	0 - 2 - 5
To Rob Grattan for grazing mare &c - - -	1 - 12- 0
G. a Jocky 1^{s}-1^{d} Medicus 6^{d} - - -	0 - 1 - 7
	14 - 13 4½

Expences.

August. 1st Month

1st Week. Gaulstown

1 to 9

Lett^{r} 6^{d} Lett^{r} 1^{s}-6^{d} Brd w 6^{s} - - - 0 - 8 - 0

2d Week. Gallstown

9 to 16

Brd w 3^{s} - - - 0 - 3 - 0

3d Week. Trim 19.

16 to 23.

Brd w 8^{s}. Win &c. 1^{11} --Brd w 3^{s} - - - 1 - 11- 0

4th Week. Lud^{l}. 23^{d} Dubl. 28^{d}

23 to Sep^{br}. 1.

Brd w 5^{s}. ⟨Din^{r} MD. Sherd^{n}.⟩ --29. Co^{ch}. 1^{s} Din^{r} 1^{s}-1^{d} - - -	0 - 7 - 1
--30 din^{r} MD. Sherid^{n}. 5^{s}. Ale. &c. . . 2^{s}-11^{d} - - -	0 - 7 -11
MD 2^{s}. Co^{ch}. 6^{d}½ Ging^{r} bd 2^{s}-2^{d} Powd^{r} 3^{d} - - -	0 - 4 -11
Lett^{rs} 1^{s} - - -	0 - 1 - 0
	1 - 0 -11

1st Week		0 - 8 - 0
2d Week	-	0 - 3 - 0
3d Week	-	1 - 11- 0
4th Week	-	1 - 0 -11
		3 - 2 -11

Expences.

Sept^{br}. 2^{d} Month.

1st Week

1. to 6.	
Brd w. 11^{s}-6^{d} --3 Co^{ch}. &c 8^{d} Coff. 6^{d}½ Sm^{ll} 2^{d} - - -	0 - 12-10½
--5. Din^{r} MD Eust. Jax^{ns}. 5^{s}-5^{d}.½ Ale &c. 3^{s}-10^{d}½ - - -	0 - 9 - 4
	1 - 1 - 2½

2^{d} Week.

6. to 13	
--Coff. 3^{d} Win 1^{s}-1^{d} Sm^{ll} 2^{d}. --8. MD. 1^{s}-9^{d}½ - - -	0 - 3 - 3½
--10 Sm^{ll} 3^{d}. --9. Din^{r} Dr Hamilt^{n}. 6^{s}-4^{d}½ Ale. 1^{s}. - - -	0 - 10- 4
--Co^{ch}. 2^{s}-8^{d}½ Sm^{ll} 2^{d} Cans. 8^{d} Tobac. 1^{s}-4^{d} - - -	0 - 4 -10½
Wash balls 1^{s}. Brd w 7^{s}-6^{d} - - -	0 - 8 - 6
	1 - 7 - 0

3^{d} Week

13 to -20.	
--14 Din^{r} Dr Hamil^{tn} J. Jacks^{n} 2^{s}-4^{d}. 2^{s}½ 15. MD. 1^{s}-1^{d} - - -	0 - 5 - 5½
--16 Din^{r} Warrens. 1^{s}-4^{d}. Brd w 7^{s}-6^{d} - - -	0 - 8 -10
17. Co^{ch}. 6^{d}- Ale &c Ld Angl. 6^{d}.½ - - -	0 - 1 - 0½
--19. Sm^{ll} 1^{d} sm^{ll} 2^{d} Lett^{r} 1^{s} - - -	0 - 1 - 3
	0 - 16- 7

4th Week

20 to 27	
--Brd w. 7^{s}-6^{d}. Din^{r} MD. Grattn. 4^{s}-9^{d}½. Ale. &. bief 3^{s}-6^{d} - - -	0 - 15- 9½
--23. Din^{r} Cap^{n} Echlin Grimes. Jim 2^{s}-10^{d}½ Ale, bief. 2^{s}-4^{d}½ - - -	0 - 5 - 3
Co^{ch}. before. 6^{d}½ --26. MD. 9^{d}½ sm^{ll} 2^{d} Ging^{r} bd 2^{s}-2^{d} - - -	0 - 3 - 8
sm^{ll}. 5^{d}½ sm^{ll} 2^{d}½	
	1 - 4 - 8½

Remd^{r}

27 to Oc^{tb}. 1.	
--Brd w 7^{s}-6^{d} Din^{r} MD. Sher^{dn}. Gratt^{ns}. Jacks^{ns}. 5^{s}-10^{d} Ale. 2^{s}-8^{d} - - -	0 - 16- 0
Co^{ch} 6^{d}½ - - -	0 - 0 - 6½
	0 - 16- 6½

1st Week.	-	1 - 1 - 2½
2^{d}	-	1 - 7 - 0
3^{d}	-	0 - 16- 7
4th	-	1 - 4 - 8½
Remd^{r}	-	0 - 16- 6½
		5 - 6 - ½

Expences.

Oct^{br}. 1 to 11. — 3^{d} Month

1st Week.

Brd w ⟨5^{d}⟩ 3 days. 3^{s}-6^{d}. MD. 1^{s}-9^{d}½ Co^{ch}. 10^{d} - - -	0 - 6 - 1½
--3. Co^{ch} 6^{d}½ Din^{r} -1^{s} ⟨6^{s}-4^{d}⟩ Ale. mutt^{n}. &c 3^{s}-5^{d} - - -	0 - 4 -11
Sm^{ll} 1^{d} Oct^{b}. 1. Din^{r} MD. Grat^{ns} &c 3^{s}-10^{d} Ale. &c. 2^{s} - - -	0 - 5 -11
sm^{ll} 1^{d}½ Lett^{r}. 6^{d} Brd w. 7^{s}-6^{d} - - -	0 - 8 - 1½
--4. Din^{r} MDs landing. Gratt^{n} Jacks^{ns} &c. 6^{s}-11^{d} Ale &c 4^{s}-1^{d} - - -	0 - 11- 0
--6 at Jacks^{ns} 1^{s}-1^{d} Win 1^{s}-1^{d} Co^{ch} & lanth^{n}.10^{d} - - -	0 - 3 - 0
--8 MD. 1^{s}-2^{d}. Co^{ch}. 6^{d}½ --10. Co^{ch}. 6^{d}½ MD 1^{s}-1^{d} - - -	0 - 3 - 4
Lett^{r} 6^{d} pigtail 6^{d} Tobac. 1^{s}-4^{d}½ Lett^{r} 2^{d} - - -	0 - 2 - 6½
	2 - 4 -11½

2^{d} Week.

11 to 18.

--Brd w. 11^{s}-6^{d} --14 Din^{r} Rochft. Smith. 3^{s}-2^{d}. Ale &c 1^{s}-4^{d} - - -	0 - 16- 0
--MD. 2^{s}-8^{d}½ --17. din^{r} MD. Rice 3^{s}-7^{d}. Bief ale &c. 4^{s}-7^{d} - - -	0 - 10-10½
Lett^{r} 2^{d} Lett^{r} 2^{d} - - -	0 - 0 - 4
	1 - 7 - 2½

3^{d} Week

18 to 25

--Brd w 11^{s}-6^{d} MD 1^{s}-1^{d} ⟨Bief ale &c⟩ - - -	0 - 12- 7
--20 Chair 1^{s}-1^{d} --21 Co^{ch}. 6^{d}½ Lett^{rs} 4^{d} - - -	0 - 1 -11½
24 Lett^{rs}. 4^{d} Raz^{rs} 6^{d} Fens mate 7^{d}½ - - -	0 - 1 - 5½
23^{d}. Din^{r} MD. Gratt^{ns}, Jacksons 6^{s}-5^{d}. Bief, ale &c. 4^{s}-1^{d}½ - - -	0 - 10- 6½
Oyl. 6^{d}. ⟨--29. MD. 4^{s}. Din^{r} Clos^{t}. Gratt^{n}.⟩- - -	0 - 0 - 6
Ging^{r} br^{d} 4^{s}-4^{d} JBs old sham debt 8^{d}½ - - -	0 - 5 - 0½
Rice, Olivs &c -10^{d} 2 Lett^{rs} 2^{s}. Lett^{rs} 1^{s} - - -	0 - 3 -10
Pap^{r}. 1^{s} - - -	0 - 1 - 0
	1 - 16-11

4th Week.

25 to Nov^{b}. 1.

Brd w. 11^{s}-6^{d} --29. MD 4^{s} 31. din^{r} Clos^{t} Gr^{ttn}. 11^{d} - - -	0 - 16- 5
--Mutt^{n} &c at night Chapt^{r}. 1^{s}-2^{d} sm^{ll} 2^{d} - - -	0 - 1 - 4
	0 - 17- 9

1st Week.	2 - 4 -11½
2^{d}	- 1 - 7 - 2½
3^{d}	- 1 - 16-11
4th	- 0 - 17- 9
	6 - 6 -10

Totals

Of a Quar^{tr} from Aug. 1st. to Nov^{br}. 1st 1718

Cloaths - - -	5 - 7 - 4
Servants Cloaths - - -	5 - 17-10
Extrd. - - -	1 - 16- 4½
Horses - - -	14 - 13- 4½
Expences 1st Month - - -	3 - 2 -11
Exp. 2^{d} Month - - -	5 - 6 - 0½
Exp. 3^{d} Month - - -	6 - 6 -10
	42 - 7 - 8½
Linnen for Shirts Aug -- from Rook --	4 - 8 - 0

Totalls

of a Year from Nov^{br} 1st 1717 to Nov^{br}. 1st. 1718.

Cloaths - - -	13 - 18- 0
Servants Cloaths - - -	7 - 9 - 5
Ext^{rds}. - - -	4 - 13- 5½
Horses - - -	31 - 0 - 7
Horse bought - - -	10 - 10- 0
Shirts to Rook - - -	4 - 8 - 0
Expences 1st Month Nov^{br} - - -	7 - 13- 2½
2^{d} Month - Decemb^{r}. - - -	4 - 2 - 7
Jan^{ry} - - -	5 - 14- 9½
Feb - - -	4 - 6 -11
March - - -	6 - 14- 8½
April - - -	4 - 8 - 3½
May - - -	6 - 14- 7½
June - - -	4 - 2 - 7½
July - - -	1 - 6 - 5½
Aug - - -	3 - 2 -11
Sep^{tbr}. - - -	5 - 6 - 0½
Oct^{br} - - -	6 - 6 -10
	132 - 9 - 5

W
H

Brought over - - -	389 - 6 - 4
To M F - - -	11 - 0 - 0
Layd out at Neals Town - - -	100 - 0 - 0
Houshold goods - - -	30 - 0 - 6
Plate - - -	36 - 1 - 8
	566 - 7 - 6

MC &c &c &c

Clear^{d} at Sev^{ll} times - - -	100 - 0 - 0

JB.

P^{d} to Feb^{r}. 1st - - -	3 - 0 - 0
To JB G 2^{s}, & tow^{rds} a Qu^{tr} 1^{ll}-10^{s}. p^{d} - - - Qu? - - -	1 - 12- 0
Feb. 28 G. JB. 5^{s}-5^{d} Weeks 3^{s}-4^{d} weeks. 1^{s}-3^{d} - - -	0 - 10- 0
to May 24. 2^{s}-1^{d} --26 p^{d} th rest of Qua^{tr} to May. 1st abt. - - -	1 - 12- 1
(JB)'s weeks 5^{s}-10^{d} --P^{d} to Aug. 1 3^{ll} & for &c 8^{s}-1^{d}½ &c - - -	3 - 14- 0
Coles 1^{ll}. Cheese. 2^{s}-6^{d} G. 2^{s}-8^{d}½ p^{d} last Qu^{tr}. 3^{ll} - - -	4 - 5 - 2½
JB's weeks 4^{s}. - - -	0 - 4 - 0
	14 - 17- 3½

M F.

Sm. Ch.

Nov^{br} - - -	0 - 15- 5
Dec^{br} - - -	1 - 2 - 7
Jan^{r} - - -	1 - 2 -10½
Febr.- - -	0 - 17- 5
March - - -	1 - 0 - 8
Aprill - - -	1 - 3 -11½
May - - -	1 - 2 - 6½
Jun about - - -	0 - 12- 0
(July & August mixt with gr G--ts) - - -	0 - 0 - 0
Sep^{tbr} - - -	1 - 13- 4½
Oct^{br} - - -	1 - 1 - 6½
	10 - 11- 4½

Gr. -G--ts.

Nov^{br}.	
13. G Mr Tooly. 5^{s}-5^{d} --30. G JB. birth day 5^{s}-5^{d} - - -	0 - 10-10
Dec^{br}. 11th at the Greek play 5^{s}-5^{d} --12 to Cap^{tn} Tooly 5^{s}-5^{d} - - -	0 - 10-10
Christmas Gifts with Ludl^{ws} &c to Jan^{ry} 11 - - -	4 - 2 - 5½
Then to MD. G - - -	0 - 18- 6
Then to the Smith in Dublin - - -	0 - 2 - 8½
Mar. 18 to Will 5^{s}-5^{d} --Apr. 7. at Ludlows. --12^{s} - - -	0 - 17- 5
Apr. 14. to Kelly of Car^{brys} To^{n}, House burn^{d}. 5^{s}-5^{d}. - - -	0 - 5 - 5
May. 3. Sr Wm Fowns. 10^{s}-3^{d}½ 11 JB 4^{ll} - - -	4 - 10- 3½
--14 Sent to M^{rs} D- in Eng^{d} 5^{ll}-12^{s}. - - -	5 - 12- 0
--23. JB. 5^{s}-5^{d} Jun. 25 at Mr Gran^{thams} 6^{s}-6^{d} - - -	0 - 11-11
--27 to G. Rochforts Man with th Horse 9^{s}-2^{d}½ - - -	0 - 9 - 2½
July. 14 at Mr Ludl^{ws}. 1^{ll}-4^{s}-4^{d}½ - - -	1 - 4 - 4½
Aug. 19 at Mr Rochf^{ts}. 1^{ll}-10^{s} sm^{ll} there 6^{d} - - -	1 - 16- 0
--28. at Mr Ludl^{ws}. 15^{s}. - - - forgot 5^{s} - - -	1 - 0 - 0
Aug. 21. Mrs Bensons Son (not p^{d} to Forbes yet) - - -	2 - 0 - 0
Sept. 15. G. Mrs Hewton 11^{s}-6^{d} --Oct^{br}. G. ϕ1^{ll}-10^{d} - - -	2 - 1 - 6
--G ppt 5^{s}-5^{d} --18. G. Nurses daught. 5^{s}-5^{d} - - -	0 - 10-10
	27 - 4 - 3½
Small G - - - -	10 - 11- 4½
	37 - 15- 8
To Nan Halswall	0 - 2 - 8½
	37 - 18- 4

Wine, Coals, Candles. Soap. 1718.

Nov^{b}. 3 & 6. Candles 9^{d} --to 12 Candl. 9^{d} Cand^{l}. 9^{d}½ - - -	0 - 5 - 9½
--28. Candl. 4^{d}½ Dec^{br}. 27 Cand^{ls}. at Trim 9^{d}½ - - -	0 - 1 - 2
Jan^{ry} 15. Corks 2^{s}. Corks 4 gross 6^{s} Cand^{ls} before 1^{s} - - -	0 - 9 - 0
Eggs for wine 8^{d}½ Starch 1^{s}-9^{d}. Dec^{br}. 21. Soap 8^{s}. Cand^{l}. 1^{s} - - -	0 - 11- 5½
--Dec^{br}. 10 Cand^{ls} from Jo 1^{ll}-2^{s}-0 - - -	0 - 1 - 2
⟨--Febr⟩ Jan^{r}. 1. fining white wine 5^{s}-5^{d} Febr. 10 Candles Lara^{cr}. 1^{s}-1^{d}½ -	0 - 6 - 6½
Cand^{l}. 9^{d} Mar. 25 Corks 3^{s} -Corks. 2^{s}-8^{d} - - -	0 - 6 - 5
--27 Cand^{l}. 10^{d} Apr. 10 Cand^{l}. 10^{d} Cand^{l}. 5^{d} - - -	0 - 2 - 1
Mar. 18. Cand^{l} 4^{s}-2^{d} Apr. 16 Coals 1^{s}-6^{d} - - -	0 - 5 - 8
--Apr. 24 Wine (⟨not yet p^{d}.⟩) 2 Hog^{sds} 14^{ll} & 10^{ll} - - -	24 - 0 - 0
Wine porters 3^{s}-3^{d} --May 16. Bottles 2 gross. 2^{ll}-4^{s} - - -	2 - 7 - 3
--17 Soap. 1^{s}-4^{d}½ May 20. old Arrear, Wine copr. 5^{s}-5^{d} - - -	0 - 7 - 0½
--21. Win. (not p^{d}) 10^{ll}. bring. 1^{s}-1^{d} --19 Candles. 1^{s}-1^{d} - - -	10 - 2 - 2
--22. Coals 4^{s}-9^{d} Jun. 6. Candles 10^{d} to Jul. 15 Cand^{ls}. 1^{s}-3^{d} - - -	0 - 6 -10
Jun. 17. Sope 1^{s}-1^{d} Cand^{l} 2^{s} Sope 1^{s} Cand^{l}. 1^{s} Cand^{l}. 9^{d} - - -	0 - 5 -10
Sep^{tr}. 25 Soap & Cand^{l}. 2^{s} - - -	0 - 2 - 0
Forgt. Jun. 9 Coals & Carriage - - -	9 - 0 - 0
	49- 0 - 0
Substract 1 Hogshd sold to Jo - - -	10 - 0 - 0
	39 - 0 - 0

Dean^{ry} Charges and Repairs. 1718.

Nov^{br}. 28th Soyl for the Garden - - -	0 - 17- 6
--A workman 7^{s}-6^{d}. anoth^{r} in part 6^{s} - - -	0 - 13- 6
Dec^{br}. 3. Glazier 12^{s}. (p^{d} but 10^{d} 10^{d} at present) - - -	0 - 12- 0
--18 the Plummer. 15^{s}. ⟨Gard^{nr} (in part of 4^{ll}-5^{s}-6^{d}) 3^{ll}-18-6^{d} - - -	4 - 13- 6⟩ 0 - 15- 0
⟨--anoth^{r} Gardner. - - -	0 - 9 - 0⟩
Jan^{r}. 13. Visitation dinner. in all malchm 1^{ll}-16^{s}-7^{d} Ale 2^{s}-2^{d} - - -	1 - 18- 9
--20 P^{d} French Gard^{nr} - - -	4 - 5 - 6
Jan^{r}. 24 P^{d} the Gardn^{r} ½ Year. end Jan^{r}. 10 - - -	1 - 5 - 0
P^{d} then an arrear of work. to him - - -	0 - 4 - 0
Febr. 27th. 1717-18. for a Pannel. 1^{s}-0^{d} Chim. sweep^{r}. 1^{s} - - -	0 - 2 - 0
Mar. 4 bringing Trees 9^{d}½ 2 keys 5^{d}½ Mar. 22 G Gard^{nr} 1^{s}-1^{d} - - -	0 - 2 - 4
May. 7 Roberts Bill 1^{ll}-12^{s}-3^{d} --14. Gard^{nr} Trees. 6^{s} - - -	1 - 18- 3
--23 mend gard^{n} lock 6^{d} - - -	0 - 0 - 6
Law --1 - 6 - 8^{d}. Brady. 2^{s}-2^{d} - - -	1 - 8 -10
Old Barwell - 5^{ll} May-- G to Prodfut 5^{ll} - - -	10 - 0 - 0
For Scales & Wights 7^{s}-8^{d}. all^{d}. light mny 2^{s} - - -	0 - 9 - 8
May. 29. Hinges 1^{s}-2^{d} Carpent^{r}. 4^{s}-4^{d} - - -	0 - 5 - 6
⟨G. to Mr Proudfoot. 5^{ll}⟩ Sep^{tr}. 1. Paint^{r} 1^{s}-1^{d} - - -	0 - 1 - 1
About Jul. 1718 Paviers bill 16^{s}-3^{d} - - -	0 - 16- 3
...... To Mr Bourne Sallery - - -	10 - 0 - 0
Hinge &c. 1^{s}-6^{d}. Sep^{t}. 29. Carpen^{tr}. 1^{s}-5^{d}½ - - -	0 - 2 -11½
Gard^{nr} clear^{d} to Oct^{b}. 10th 1718 - - -	1 - 17- 6
⟨To Mr Proudfoot - - -	5 - 0 - 0⟩
Oct^{b}. 4th mend lock. 1^{s} a Bolt 4^{d} - - -	0 - 0 - 8
--G to Mr Proudfoot - - -	5 - 0 - 0
--Oct^{b}. 25th G Mr Proudfoot - - -	0 - 18- 6
--Carpen^{tr} work in leading - - -	0 - 5 - 4
⟨Old⟩ To Mr Worrall (not p^{d} Nov^{b}. 1st) - - -	3 - 0 - 0
	46 - 19-11

Law. 4^{s}-4^{d}

Painting Rails &c - - -	6 - 6 - 0
Mending th Leads - - -	4 - 7 - 6
Jun. 27. Barwell -1^{ll}-16 more No^{br}. 29. 10^{s} - - -	2 - 6 - 0
--more 18^{s}-6^{d}. more & cle^{d}. 1^{ll}-14-6 - - -	2 - 13- 0
	15 - 12- 6

Taxes and Cesses. 1718.

Jan^{ry} 15. Kilmain^{hm} Cess 9^{d} --23 Orphans 2^{s}-2^{d} - - -	0 - 2 -11
May. 10. Lights due Mar. 25th. 1718. 3^{s}. - - -	0 - 3 - 0
--22 Cess for Orphans 3^{s}. - - -	0 - 3 - 0
Sep^{tr}. 2^{d}. Watch 4^{s}. --Cess 2^{s}-6^{d} - - -	0 - 6 - 6
--16 Chim^{y} mony. 1^{ll}-10^{s}. - - -	1 - 10- 0
Oct^{b}. 4. Kilmain^{m} Cess 1^{s}-4^{d} - - -	0 - 1 - 4
--25 Tax for Orphans 3^{s}. - - -	0 - 3 - 0
	2 - 9 - 9

Proxyes & other Charges for Laracor. 1718

Mar. 7th. Crownrent - - -	7 - 11 - 0
To Mr Warren Sallary to Mar. 25th 1718 - - -	20 - 0 - 0
Quit rent for Michlms 1718 - - -	7 - 11 - 8

<Jo's Account

Debtor

To Wine - - -	13 - 0 - 0
To Annuall Paym^{t} to Bp Cl. & my self - - -	20 - 0 - 0
To a Hogs^{hd} of Graves - - -	10 - 0 - 0
To 2 Hogs^{hds} of Greaves. 9^{ll} p hog^{d} - - -	18 - 0 - 0
	61 - 0 - 0

Creditor

Apr 23 <For Wine ^Wine^ tow^{rds} Bp Clogh^{r}> - - -	1 - 10- 0
--For towards annuall Paym^{t} - - -	1 - 10- 0
Jun. 12 From Jo to Wine debt - - -	5 - 0 - 0
Jan^{r}. 30th 1718-19 For Wine - - -	16 - 0 - 0
<A Quart^{r} rent due ^for his House^ Jun. 25. 1718 - - -	1 - 10- 0>
A Bill discounted dated May 6.	24 - 10- 0
1719. for Neelstown - - -	18 - 0 - 0
Settled & transfer^{d} to new	42 - 10- 0
Book. Aug. 5th. 1719 JS.>	

Account

Of Receits from the Deanry &c.

For the Year 1717

And for Rents for the Year 1718.

[19v]

Mem^{d}. Rece^{id} Sep^{br}. 3^{d}. ^1718 the Tythes
of this Year for the Deanry from
Mr Falkner - - - 3 - 0 - 0

<Then received from Mr Proudfoot, for
which he has <no> a receit. ((<but lost it>) - - - 2 - 11- 2>

Me^{d}. Sep^{br}. 20 Mr Prodfoot sent me by Saund^{rs} - - - 1 - 10- 0

Received

R^d from the $Dean^{ry}$ for 1717. 458 - 4 - 0

Mar. 12th. 1717-18 From Mrs Allison in part - - -	1 - 10- 0
May. 28. From Wm Dodd for Coldrino His Bond.- - -	9 - 0 - 0
Sep^{br}. 5 From Magran by Barnwell on Acct, for wch he has my Receit.- - -	10 - 13- 4
--From Caffre by Barnwell on Acc^t for wch he has my Receit - - -	8 - 3 - 0
--3 From Th. Funt a small Bond p^d - - -	2 - 10- 0
--8 From Rich Keating in part - - -	2 - 11- 6
--From Wm Carney of Tallow his Bond - - -	1 - 2 - 0
--Edm^d Moran his Bond - - -	1 - 0 - 0
--Wm Sennet his Bond - - -	1 - 6 - 0
--Pat^r. ⟨Regan⟩ Egar of Job's Town ⟨(Bond not found)⟩ - - -	0 - 18- 0
--13. Thom Hoyle on Account - - -	3 - 0 - 0
--Pat^r. Donnelly - - -	0 - 6 - 0
--From Mr Ord - - -	8 - 0 - 0
--16. From M^r $Faulkn^r$ by Barnwell - - -	5 - 0 - 7
John Ransford - 1 bond p^d before - - -	3 - 0 - 0
--24 Owen Smith in part - - -	1 - 10- 0
--Franc. Maccartys Bond - - -	5 - 0 - 0
--p^d Simon Farrells bond p^d before-time, $forg^t$ - - -	1 - 4 - 6
--27 p^d John Browns bond - - -	1 - 0 - 0
--Hugh Masterson's bond - - -	1 - 5 - 0
--Coghlen & Galvan - - -	1 - 10- 0
--Nic Hoy - - -	3 - 15- 0
⟨--John Brown - - -	1 - 0 - 0⟩
Oct^{br}. 1st Th. Hoyle in part - - -	3 - 0 - 0
--Ed. Bermingham Rem^{dr} - - -	3 - 0 - 0
--J^n $Will^{ms}$ in part - - -	2 - 0 - 0
--Ralph Jackson's bond - - -	3 - 5 - 0
Oc^{tb}. 4th p^d J^{on} Mathews bond - - -	1 - 5 - 0
--Wm Barry in part - - -	2 - 15- 0
87 - 19 - 11	87 - 19-11

Brought over - - -	87 - 19-11
Oc^{tb}. 4. Rec^{d} long before in Part of Hawkins - - -	5 - 0 - 7
--8 Mr Hawkins Remai^{dr} - - -	5 - 9 - 5
--11. Pat^{r}. Coyle his bond - - -	0 - 13- 0
--J^{n}. Mullaly in part - - -	1 - 10-10
--Mat. Lawler his bond - - -	0 - 12- 0
--J^{n} Tarl his bond - - -	0 - 12- 0
Wm Barry in part - - -	1 - 15- 0
--16. Ben Ransford in part - - -	1 - 0 - 0
--Mollolly Remd^{r} - - -	0 - 9 - 0
--Brian Doyle his bond - - -	1 - 5 - 0
--Dan Haggarty in full - - -	1 - 5 - 0
--18. Robinson in full - - -	0 - 17- 0
--16. Simon Farrell in full. (misplac^{d}) - - -	1 - 4 - 6
--J^{n} Ransford in part Qu? (misplac^{d}) - - -	2 - 0 - 0
--Before. Wm Strong in part - - -	1 - 10- 0
Before-- Wm Dry in part - - -	0 - 10- 0
Before. Wm Brown his bond - - -	0 - 15- 0
Jam. Allen in part - - -	2 - 18-10
Edm Knolls his bond - - -	0 - 15- 0
Nov^{br}. 1st Wm Rose his Bond - - -	3 - 5 - 0
--8 Wm Barry to compleat one bond - - -	1 - 0 - 0
--8. J^{n} Lyon in part - - -	1 - 16- 0
--Wm Strong in part - - -	1 - 9 -10
--15 Mr Rich. Powers bond - - -	1 - 13- 0
	127 - 5 -11
Nov^{br}. 19. 1718 Account for with Mr Bourne - - -	266 - 9 - 2
--23 Christ^{phr} Conrows Bond in full - - -	8 - 5 - 0
--25 J^{n} Will^{ms} in part - - -	3 - 0 - 0
--29. Math Bellew in full (10^{s} to Barnwell) - - -	1 - 15- 0
--Dempsy. (no bond) 10^{s} Hay & Colcot. (no Bond) 10^{s} - - -	1 - 0 - 0
--J^{n} Purcell - - -	0 - 7 - 0
Dec^{br}. 19. J^{n} Williams Remai^{dr} - - -	4 - 0 - 0
--24. Peter Cavan in part - - -	1 - 9 - 8
Jan^{r}. 3. Wm Dry his Remain^{dr} - - -	0 - 14- 0
--Rich Keating in part - - -	2 - 4 - 8
in all 416 - 10 - 7.	289 - 4 - 6

Receiv^{d}

For Laracor for 1717

Nov^{br}. 19. 171⟨7⟩8. Account^{d} for wth Mr Bourne. - - -	76 - 15- 0

Dean^{ry}.

Brought over - - -	416 - 10- 7
	⟨289 - 4 - 6⟩

Dean^{ry}.

H. Cavanagh. 6^{s}. Th. Kendel^{n}. 6^{s}. both in full - - -	0 - 12- 0
Richd Keating in part - - -	1 - 14- 5
Th. Hoyle in part - - -	1 - 9 - 8
--16. Th. Mulva in full (vide old book) - - -	0 - 10- 0
--John Hylan - - -	0 - 6 - 0
Apr. 4th 1719 J^{n} Lyon his Arrear - - -	0 - 19- 0
--22. Mr Preston in part - - -	7 - 4 - 0
Forg^{t}. Owin Smith Remd^{r} - - -	0 - 8 - 0
Wm Quin (p^{d} in my absence) in full - - -	0 - 6 - 0
	13 - 9 - 1
In all - - -	429 - 19- 8
Peter Cavan. Jul. 4th. 1719. - - -	0 - 6 - 4
--Th. Preston his Arrear - - -	9 - 6 - 4

Receiv^d

From Rathbeggan for the Year 1717

Oc^tbr 18. Pat^r Maddin in part - - -	6 - 0 - 0
--29. Richd And^r Arrear - - -	7 - 10- 0
--30 Pat^r Whites Arrear - - -	8 - 18-10
	21 - 8 -10
(Some mistake in Mr Bourne)	
Account to Me by Mr Bourne - - -	26 - 6 -10
⟨Richd And^rews Arrear	8 - 18-10⟩
Richd Andrews Arrear	7 - 10- 0
⟨Pat^r Whites Arrear - - -	8 - 18-10⟩
Thom Clinch in part - - -	2 - 10- 0
	⟨67 - 17- 6
Jan^r. 10th. Mr Shelly in full - - -	4 - 0 - 0
Nov^br. 2^d 1719 John Martin his Arrear which with his ⟨Arrear⟩ form^r Paym^t (that I do not rememb^r makes I found it - - -	3 - 10- 0
Madden and Carnell. Jun. 13. 1719. (I absent	4 - 10- 0
John Baily in full p^d long ago - - -	2 - 0 - 0
Th. Clinch Rend^r in full, p^d long ago - - -	1 - 5 - 0

Dean^ry. 1717.

Jul. 25 1719. Jan Greyburn in full - - -	0 - 5 - 0
--John Grindon. (all but 6^d) - - -	0 - 4 - 6
--Richd Carick - - in full - - -	0 - 4 - 0
--Tho. Hoyl in full - - -	0 - 5 - 4

Received

For Customs, Dutyes &c for the Dean^{ry} for. 1718.

Dec^{br}. 2^{d} 1717 For the Fun^{rll} of Mr Cuft - - -	4 - 0 - 0
Jan^{r}. 13th 1717 For the Fun^{rll} of Mrs Delaune - - -	4 - 0 - 0
Feb^{r}. 8th For 1717-18 Fun^{rll} of Ld Powerscourt - - -	4 - 0 - 0
Mar. 17th. 1717-18. For a Lease - - -	0 - 11- 8
--27 Funer^{ll} of Merediths Child (1^{s}-1^{d} cheated) - - -	1 - 18-11
May. 6. Ld Blessingtons Funerall - - -	4 - 0 - 0
--28. L^{dy} Cavans Child - - -	4 - 0 - 0
Aug. 30. For a Licence (half given Wor^{ll})- - -	0 - 4 -10
Sep^{tr}. 10 For signing a Lease to Dr Traverse - - -	0 - 11- 8
--16 Simon Farrels Bond full - - -	1 - 4 - 6
--John Ransford in part - - -	2 - 0 - 0
Oct^{br}. 31st a Lease of Dr Bouhereau - - -	0 - 11- 8.

Received

Rents of Lands and Houses for 1718.

A

Rent Roll for the Year 1717 for Tythes,

and the Year 1718 for Lands &c.

Account

Of Expences from

Nov^{br}. 1st 1732 to Nov^{br}. 1st 1733.

Account

Of Expences From Novr. 1. 1732 to Novr. 1st. 1733

First Quar^{tr}

From Novr. 1st 1732 to Febr. 1st. 1732-3.

Cloaths

Wig block. 8^{d} 2 Perewigs &c 5 5^{s}-6^{d} Cloath mend. 3^{s}-3^{d} - - -	5 - 9 - 5
Jan^{r}. 23^{d}. Square cap 6^{s} - - -	0 - 6 - 0
	5 - 15- 5

Serv^{ts} Cloaths

Jan. Cloth for big coats 2^{ll}-8^{s}-6^{d}. mak^{g}. - - -

Extr^{dys}

No^{r}. 4. Ink. 6^{d}½ Dogs. 1^{s} Dogs 6^{d} Nov. 18. Usqub. 5^{s}. Dogs 7^{d} - - -	0 - 7 - 0½
Novr. 23. Tobac. 2^{s}. Dogs. 6^{d} Dog. 7^{d} Dogs 6^{d} Sc^{t}. 12^{s}. Usq. 5^{s} - -	?1 -?0 - 7
--9. Tobac. 1^{s} Dog. 6^{d}½ Box M^{rs} < May > 1^{s} - - -	0 - 2 - 6½
	1 - 10- 2

Horses.

Novr. 11. Smith 6^{d} Turnp. 2^{d} Sm^{ll} 6^{d} Honey 4^{d} sm^{ll} 2^{d} - - -	0 - 1 - 8
sm^{ll}. 1^{s}-1^{d}. Decr. 20. Straw 3^{s}-6^{d}. Smith. 6^{s} sm^{ll} 4^{d} - - -	0 - 11- 2
Jan^{r}. 17. Girth 1^{s}-8^{d} sm^{ll} 4^{d}½ 24. G. 4^{d} 1^{s}-8^{d}½ 26. sm^{ll}. 6^{d} - - -	0 - 4 - 8
	0 - 17- 7

Novr. Expences. 1st Month

1 to 4 1st Week.

--Brd w 07^{s}. --2^{d}. Wor^{ll}. 1^{s}-4^{d}½ Sm^{ll} -1^{d}. --2. Worr^{ll} 1^{s}-4^{d}½ - - - 0 - 15-10
H. bill. 1^{s}-6^{d}½ ⟨H. bill 3^{s} H. bill. 3^{s}⟩- - - 0 - 1 - 6½
0 - 17- 4½

2^{d} Week

4 to 11.

Brd w 12^{s}. D^{r}. White - 2^{s}-2^{d} --5. Worr^{ll}. 2^{s}-2^{d}. --H. bill. 8^{s}. - - - 1 - 4 - 4

3^{d} Week

11 to 18

Brd w 12^{s}. --14. Co^{ch} 6^{d}½ Lemons. 8^{d} --15. Cha^{r}. 8^{d}. - - - 0 - 13-10½
--H. bill. 0 - 7^{s}-4. Lett^{r}. 6^{d} - - - 0 - 7 -10
1 - 1 - 8½

4th Week

18 to 25.

Lett^{r} 6^{d} ⟨Tobac. 2^{s}⟩- - - 0 - 0 - 6
Brd w 12^{s}. --22. Ma^{d}. 2^{s}-2^{d}. --23. Whitwy. 2^{s}-2^{d} Chair. 8^{d} - - - 0 - 17- 0
sm^{ll}. 1^{d} Lett^{r} 6^{d}. ⟨s^{ll} 2^{d} Balibck.⟩H. Bill 8^{s}-4 - - - 0 - 8 -11
1 - 6 - 5

Dec^{b}. Remd^{r}.

25 to. ⟨Nov.⟩1st 27. Ma^{d}. 2^{s}-2^{d}. Ch^{r}. 8^{d} Sm^{ll}. 4^{d} - - - 0 - 3 - 2
Brd. w- 12^{s}. H. bill 8^{s}-9^{d} - - - 1 - 0 - 9
1 - 3 -11

⟨Mrs Worrall⟩

1st Week	- -	0 - 17- 4½
2^{d}	- -	1 - 4 - 4
3^{d}	- -	1 - 1 - 8½
4th	- -	1 - 6 - 5
Remd^{r}.	- -	1 - 3 -11
Mrs Worr^{ll}	- -	0 - 17- 0
		6 - 10- 9
more Mrs Worr^{ll}		0 - 5 - 4
Totall		6 - 16- 1

Expences.

Decb^{r}. | 2^{d} Month

1st Week.

1st to. 9.

Brd. w. 12^{s} 2. Ma^{d}. 2^{s}-2^{d}. Chair. 8^{d} --3. Wor^{ll}. 3^{s}-3^{d} - - -	0 - 18- 1
--4. Chair &c 9^{d}½ Ch^{r}. 8^{d} W^{r}. 8^{d} 7. Ch^{r} 8^{d} --8. Wor^{ll}. 2^{s}-2^{d} - - -	0 - 4 -11
Lett^{r} 6^{d} H. bill. 9^{s}-9^{d} - - -	0 - 10- 3
	1 - 13- 3

2^{d} Week.

9 to. 16

Brd w 12^{s}. -Ch^{r}. 8^{d} C^{r}. 10^{d} Sm^{ll}. 10^{d} --15. Co^{ch}. 1^{s}-1^{d} - - -	0 - 15- 5
H. bill. 7^{s}-9^{d} - - -	0 - 7 - 9
	1 - 3 - 2

3^{d} Week.

16 to 23.

Brd w. 12^{s} 18. Ch^{r}. 10^{d} --17. Wor^{ll}. 2^{s}-2^{d}. Co^{ch}. 1^{s}-1^{d}½ - - -	0 - 16- 1½
26. Co^{ch}. 2^{s}. 27. Ch^{r}. 8^{d} --28 Ch^{r}. 8^{d} H. bill. 7^{s}-8^{d}½ - - -	0 - 11- 0½
--29. Ch^{r}. (glass broke) 1^{s}-7^{d}½ Ale. 4^{s}-8^{d} H bill. 8^{s}-8^{d} - - -	0 - 15- 0
	2 - 2 - 2

4th Week

23 to Jan^{r}. 1

Brd w. 12^{s} Worr^{ll} 2^{s}-2^{d} forgot - 2^{s} - - -	0 - 16- 2

1st week -	1 - 13- 3
2^{d} week -	1 - 3 - 2
3^{d} -	2 - 2 - 2
4th -	0 - 16- 2
Mrs Wor^{ll} -	1 - 12- 3
<More Mrs W.	0 - 5 -10½ >
	< 16- 8½ >
Mrs Wor^{ll} mor	0 - 5 -10½
	7 - 12-10½
Mor Wor^{ll}	2 - 3 - 1
	9 - 5 -11½
<Mor. Wor^{ll}	0 - 5 -10½ >

Jan^{r}. Expences. 3^{d} Month

1st Week

1 to 6

B^{r} w. 12^{s}. 2. Co^{ch} &c. 1^{s}-2^{d} --3. Ch^{r}. 1^{s}-2^{d}½ --4. Ch^{r}. 8^{d} - - -	0 - 15- 0 -1
H. bill. 13^{s} --2 more 1^{s}-7^{d} - - -	0 - 14- 7
	1 - 9 - 7½

2^{d} Week

6 to. 13

Brd w. 12^{s}-7^{d}. Worr^{ll} 3^{s}-3^{d}. Co^{ch}. 6^{d}½ --9 Chair 1^{s}-1^{d} - - -	0 - 16-10½
--11. [Ma^{d} 1^{s}-4^{d} Wine] H. bill 2^{s}-7^{d}. more Lett^{r}. 6^{d}. - - -	0 - 4 - 5
	1 - 1 - 3½

3^{d} Week

13 to 20.

Brd w 12^{s}. ⟨to Deal^{r}.⟩ 2^{s} --14 Worr^{ll}. 2^{s}-6^{d}. Coal. 1^{s}-4^{d} - - -	0 - 16-10
--15 Cha^{r}. 8^{d} sm^{ll}. 4^{d}½ --17. Ch^{r}. 6^{d}½ H. Bill 4^{s}-5 - - -	0 - 6 - 0
	1 - 2 -10

4th. Week

20 to 27.

Brd w 12^{s} . . . Co^{ch}. 1^{s}-1^{d} sm^{ll}. 6^{d} --21. Worr^{ll}. 2^{s}-2^{d} - - -	0 - 15- 9
H. ⟨bill 4^{s}-5^{d}⟩ --23. Mrs Whit^{wy}. 2^{s}-2^{d}. Ma^{d} din^{r} 1^{s}-1^{d} Co^{ch} 1^{s}-1^{d} - - -	0 - 4 - 4
H. Bill 13-5^{d} - - -	0 - 13- 5
	1 - 12- 6

Remd^{r}.

Brd w . . . . Co^{ch}. 1^{s}-11^{d} 28. Wor^{l}. 2^{s}-2^{d} To. Wr^{ll}. 10^{d}	0-3-0	0 - 3 - 0
⟨JB^{s}⟩H bill. 7^{s}-1^{d}. Worr^{ll}. 2^{s}-2^{d}	0-9-3	0 - 9 - 3
--29. Mav &c din^{r} 1^{ll}-16 more. - - -	1-16-0	1 - 16- 0
		0 - 14- 4
		3 - 2 - 6

Mrs Wor^{ll}. 0 - 14- 4
⟨More 0 - 11- 7⟩
⟨ 1 - 5 -11 ⟩

1st Week.	- 1 - 9 - 7½
2^{d}	- 1 - 1 - 3½
3^{d}	- 1 - 2 -10
4th	- 1 - 12- 6
Mrs Worr^{ll} -&c - - -	- 3 - 2 - 6
Brd w. forgot - - -	- 0 - 12- 0
	9 - 0 - 9

Totals

Of a Quar^{tr} from Novr. 1st. 1732 To Febr. 1st. 1732/3

Account.

Of Expences from Feb^{r}. 1st 1732/3 to May. 1st 1733

Second Quar^{tr}

Cloaths.

⟨Sm^{ll} 4^{d}⟩

sm^{ll} 4^{d}. Boot irons 8^{d} Sm^{ll} 8^{d} --Mar. Wastcoat & risb. 4^{ll}-12^{s}-4. - - - 4 - 14- 0
Ap^{r}. 25. Mrs Tool. Jobbs. 3^{s}-9^{d}½ Ap^{r}. 9. Hat dresst. 2^{s}-6^{d} Ap^{r}. 4th.
Stocks. 1^{ll}-9^{s} - - - 1 - 15- 3½

Servants Cloaths

Extraord^{rys}

Dogs 7^{d} --17. Seal. wax 3^{s} Dogs. 6^{d} Ma^{r}. 3. Orangs ^preserv^{d} 30. 17^{s}-8^{d}½
Mar. 7. Usque^{b}. 5^{s} Dogs 6^{d} Ma^{r}. 19 Snuff. 1^{s}-7^{d}½
Feb. 27. Sican bill Sug^{r} &c. 1^{ll}-1^{s}-9^{d} Dogs 6^{d}½ ⟨Mour^{s} wine 6^{s}⟩
Pap^{r}. 1^{s} Dogs. 1^{s}-2^{d} Ap^{r}. 23^{d} mend screw 1^{s}-6^{d} Tobac. 2^{s} Dgs 6^{d}½
Apr. 14. Usqu^{b}. 5^{s} --Hopps 3^{s}-6^{d} Dogs 6^{d}½ Lett^{rs}. 10^{d} Dogs 6^{d}½
--27. Country. Usqu^{b}. 6^{s}. dogs 7^{d}

Horses

Donkey 6^{d}½ Mar. 7. Straw 3^{s}-6^{d} June. 6^{d}½ 1^{s}. Hors, 4^{d}-9^{d}
Mar. 27. Smith. 6^{s}-9^{d}½. --8^{d} Hors. 1^{s}

[4v]

Expences

Febr. 1st Month

1st Week

1 to 10.

Brd w 12^{s}. -Co^{ch} &c. 1^{s}-4^{d}½. 3. Ch^{r}. 8^{d} --4. Sheil. 1^{s}-1^{d} - - -	0 - 15- 1½
--Worr^{ll} 9^{d}½ Worr^{ll} before. 2^{s}-8^{d}½ --9. Ma^{r}. 2^{s}-2^{d} H. Bill 7^{s}-11^{d} - -	0 - 13- 7
	1 - 8 - 8½

2^{d} Week.

10 to. 17

B^{d} w. 12^{s} 11. Wor^{ll}. 3^{s}-3^{d} --14. Wor^{ll}. 2^{s}-6^{d} H bill. 2^{s}-5^{d} - - -	1 - 0 - 2
Lett^{rs}. 1^{s}-2^{d} - - -	0 - 1 - 2
	1 - 1 - 4

3^{d} Week

17 to 24

Brd w. 12^{s}. Ch^{r}. 8^{d}. Ma^{d}. 2^{s}-2^{d}. 19. Ch^{r}. 8^{d} --22. Ch^{r}. 1^{s}-3^{d} - - -	0 - 16- 9
Charwoman arrear 3^{s}-3^{d} - - -	0 - 3 - 3
	1 - 0 - 0

4th Week.

24 to Mar. 1.

--Brd w. 12^{s}. Wor^{ll}. 2^{s}-2^{d}. --24. Wor^{ll}. 6^{d}½ Ch^{r}. 8^{d} - - -	0 - 15- 4½
H. bill	

Mrs Wor^{ll} - - - - 0 - 14- 4
Mrs Worr^{ll} - - - - 1 - 15- 7
For Char^{w}. & wash. 0 - 11- 4
⟨Mrs Wor^{ll} more⟩

Expences — Giddy from 4th --14. very ill

March. — 2^d Month

1st Week

1 to 10

B^{rd} w. 12^s. Cha^r. 8^d --2. Whitway. 2^s-4^d $Worr^{ll}$. 2^s-2^d - - - 0 - 16-10

Wor^{ll}. 1^s-8^d --8. Chair. 8^d --House bill Cha^r 8^d H. bill. 11^s-3^d - - - 0 - 14- 5

1 - 11- 3

2^d Week

10 to 17.

B^{rd} w. 12^s. --14. Co^{ch} 8^d½ H. bill. 11^s-3^d½ Lett. 6^d $Char^w$. 1^s-4^d - - 1 - 5 -10

3^d Week.

17 to 24

B^{rd} w 12^s. 22. Whitway. 2^s-2^d 23. Orangs. 1^s-1^d H. bill. 4^s-5^d - - - 0 - 19- 9

4th Week.

24 to Apr. 1st

B^{rd} w. 12^s $Worr^{ll}$ 8^d. H. Bill. 11^s-4^d - - - 1 - 4 - 0

M^{rs} $Worr^{ll}$ - - - 1 - 10- 3

More - - - 0 - 11- 7

2 - 1 -10

Expences

Apr. 3^{d} Month

1st Week.

1 to 7.

Brd w. 12^{s} Wor^{ll}. 2^{s}-2^{d}. 3^{d}. Co^{ch} 1^{s}-1^{d} cha^{r}. 8^{d} - - -	0 - 15- 9
8. Wor^{ll}. 2^{s}-2^{d} H. bill 13^{s}-2^{d}½ - - -	0 - 15- 4½
	1 - 11- 1½

2^{d} Week. Castle Rick^{d}

7 to 14 From th 8th to the 11th day

Brd w. 12^{s} Wor^{ll}. 2^{s}-2^{d} H. bill 6^{s}-3^{d} - - -	1 - 0 - 5
Charwom^{n} 1^{s}-4^{d} - - -	0 - 1 - 4
	1 - 1 - 9

3^{d} Week

14 to 21.

Brd w. 12^{s} Wor^{ll}. 3^{s}-3^{d} 19. Ch^{r}. 8^{d} H bill 9^{s}-11 - - -	1 - 5 -10
Char.w^{n}. 1^{s}-4^{d} - - -	0 - 1 - 4
	1 - 7 - 2

4th Week.

21. to ⟨29.⟩ 28

Brd w. . . . 24. Din^{r}. Sherd^{n}. 1^{s}-7^{d}½ --25 Ma^{d}. 1^{s}-9^{d}
Char^{w}. 8^{d} H. bill. ⟨5^{s}⟩ 4^{s}-4^{d}

Mrs Worrall 1 - 2 - 11½

Totals

Of a Qu^{tr}. from Febr. 1. 1732. to May 1st. 1733

[6v]

Account

Of Expences from Febr. 1. 1733. to ⟨May.⟩ Aug 1. 1733 [May interlined above Febr.; Aug interlined above May]

Third Quar^{tr}

Cloaths.

Boots 2^{d} Aug. 10. Linnen cheated by Mad^{m} Worrall for 7 Shirts

Serv^{ts} Cloaths

May. 19. Boots 1^{ll}-1^{s}. (not allow^{g} but charg^{d} to them tho payd) vide Servants

	1 - 1 - 0

Extr^{dys}

Dogs. 7^{d} Dog. 7^{d} seeds 7^{d} Dogs. 6^{d}½ Dogs 6^{d}½ ⟨Jun. 9. Usq 5⟩ Jun. 9. Usque 5^{s}. - - -	0 - 7 - 7
Honey & Rozin 8^{d}. Dog. 7^{d} Jun. 9. Tobac. 5^{s} Dogs. 7^{d} Dogs 7^{d} - - -	0 - 7 - 5
Dogs. 7^{d} ⟨Lett^{r}. 1⟩ small 2^{d}½ Dogs 7^{d}. Dogs 7^{d} Jul. 12th Usqu^{b}. 5^{s} - -	0 - 7 - 0
Jul. 12th. Raz^{rs} Set. 1^{s} Dogs 7^{d} Dogs 7^{d} dogs. 4^{d} Dogs 7^{d} - - -	0 - 3 - 0
Febr. 1733. Payd Stoakes Survey for this May - - -	4 - 15 - 6
	6 - 0 - 6

Horses.

May 15. Oats &c. 2^{s}-9^{d}½ Jun. 9. Smith 6^{s} - - -	0 - 8 - 9½
Jun. 16. Oats. 5^{s}-8^{d} Mare cold. 1^{s}-9^{d}½. Jun. 20. Straw 3^{s}-4^{d} - - -	0 - 10 - 9½
Jul. 8th. Saddle. 7^{d}½. Whip. &c 5^{d}½ July. 26. Smith. 6^{s} - - -	0 - 7 - 1
	1 - 6 - 8

Expences

May. 1st Month

1st Week

1 to 5th

Brd w. 12s. 4th Dinr. Whitwy. 2s-8d½ Lettrs 0d 1s. 0 - 15- 8½
H, bill ---17s-2d½ - - - 0 - 17- 2½
1 - 12-10½

2d Week.

5 to 12.

Brd w. 12s 5. Dunlary Chir. 6d½ --12th. Chair. 8d - - - 0 - 13- 2½
Char. 8d H. bill. 11s-6d½ - - - 0 - 12- 2½
1 - 5 - 5

3d Week at Trim ⟨from⟩ &c from 15 to 19 Visitation.

12 to 19--

Brd w 4s. 13. Dinr Worll. 2s-2d. 14. Dinr. bought of Servt. 6d½ - - - 0 - 6 - 8½
--Lettrs. 1s-2d H. bill 4s-6d - - - 0 - 5 - 8
0 - 12- 4½

4th Week.

19 to. 26

Brd w 12s. Char. 1s-4d Dogs 6d H. bill. 4s-10d½ - - - 0 - 18- 8½

Redr

26 to Jun. 1.

Brd w 12s 29. Leslip. 5s-5d. Coch. 8d. Char 8d - - - 0 - 18- 9
House bill. 1ll-11d - - - 1 - 0 -11
1 - 19- 8

Mrs Worrall. - - -	1 - 15-10½
For an arrear - - -	0 - 12- 0
	2 - 7 -10½

1st Week	- -	1 - 12-10½
2d	- -	1 - 5 - 5
3d	- -	0 - 12- 4½
4th	- -	0 - 18- 8½
Remdr	- -	1 - 19- 8
		8 - 15-11½

Jun. Expences. 2^{d} Month

1st Week

1st to 9th

Brd w. 12^{s}. Lett^{r}. 4^{s}-4^{d}. 3^{d}. Wor^{ll}. 2^{s}-2^{d}. 4. Ch^{r}. 8^{d} - - -	0 - 19- 5
Charw^{n}. 1^{s}-4^{d} Lett^{rs}. 1^{s}-4^{d} H. Bill 4^{s}-10^{d} - - -	0 - 7 - 6
	1 - 6 -11

2^{d}. Week.

9 to 16.

Brd w 12^{s}. Chair. 8^{d}: 10 Wor^{ll}. 3^{s}-3^{d}. 12. D^{r}. Sher^{dn}. 1^{s}-4^{d}½ - - -	0 - 17- 4½
Sm^{ll}. 2^{d} ⟨Lett^{r}⟩ Q. H. bill 3^{s}-2^{d} - - -	0 - 3 - 4
	1 - 0 - 8½

3^{d} Week.

16. to 23

Brd w 12^{s}. 18. Wor^{ll}. 2^{s}-2^{d}. Cha^{r}. 8^{d} Tobac. 6^{d} - - -	0 - 15- 4
Wash ball. 2^{d} --22. White^{w}. 1^{s}. H. Bill 8^{s}-9^{d}½ Cha^{r}. 8^{d} - - -	0 - 10- 7
Lett^{r}. 6^{d} ⟨--17 Win 4^{s}-6^{d}⟩- - -	0 - 0 - 6
	1 - 6 - 5

4th Week

23. to ⟨Jul. 30th.⟩ Jul. 30th

Brd w 12^{s}. Chair. 6^{d}½ --24. Wor^{ll}. 2^{s}-2^{d}. 28. Co^{ch}. 1^{s}-1^{d} - - -	0 - 15- 9½
⟨--30.⟩ 30. Din^{r} Barb^{r}. 2^{s}-2^{d} W^{oll}. 9^{d} Lett. 1^{s} - - -	0 - 3 -11
Char - 1^{s}-4^{d}. H bill 7^{s} - - -	0 - 8 - 4
	1 - 8 - 0½

Mrs Worr^{ll}		2 - 12-11
1st W	-	- 1 - 16-11
2^{d}	-	- 1 - 0 - 8½
3^{d}	-	- 1 - 6 - 5
4th	-	- 1 - 8 - 0½
		7 - 15- 0

July. Expences 3d Month

1st to 7th. 1st Week.

Brd w. 12s Dinr Worll. 2s-2d Smll. 3d. Coch. 8d - - -
--10. Chr. 8d ⟨--13. Coch⟩ Char. 1s-8d smll 2d Lettr 4d - - -
House bill 9s-9d.½ - - -

0 - 15- 1
0 - 2 -10
0 - 9 - 9½
1 - 7 - 8½

7 to 14. 2d Week

Brd w 12s 13th Coch. 6d½ Char. 8d H. bill. 14s-1d - - - 1 - 7 - 3½

3d Week

⟨15⟩ 14 to ⟨22⟩ 21.

Brd w. . . 17. Dinr. Whitew. 1s. Worrll 1s-1d. Coch. 9d½
19. at Howth. 11s-6d --16 Lettr Ldy B. 1s-6d Char. 8d
H. bill. 6s-6d. H. bill. 6s-6d

21 to 28 4th Week 25 to 28. at Belcamp.

Brd w . . . . --Coch. 6d½ --24 Chr (Walk] 6d½ ⟨--29. Lett Pends.⟩
⟨--29. Lettr. (Pendarvis.)⟩ 1s-8d. Letters be Lettr. 2d H. Bill. 5s-6d½

28. to Aug 4. Remdr.

--Lettr. (Pendarvis) 1s-8d --Worll. 2s-2d --Char. 1s-4d
⟨Lettr 6d⟩ Chair. 8d H. Bill. 3s-10½

Mrs Worll - 0 - 12- 2½

[8v]

Totals.

Account

Of Expences

4th Quarter

Cloaths

Aug. Shoes. 5^{s}. mend & make Towells &c 4^{s}. Wig mend. 2^{s}-8^{d}½ - - - 0 - 11- 8½
Aug. 27. Shoes Cobbl^{d} 1^{s}-9^{d}½ Aug. 29. make 7 Shirts 13^{s}-2^{d}½ - - - 0 - 15- 0
Stockins sm^{ll}. 3^{d}. Oc^{tbr}. 15th. Muslin. 5^{s}-7^{d} Sep^{b}. 24 Wig mend. 1^{s}-1^{d}

Serv^{ts} Cloths

Oct^{br}. 15. 2 - 16- 2
Oct^{b}. Cloth Making and Trim. Liveryes & Frocks
Mrs Ton Stockins. 7^{s}

Extr^{dyes}

Dogs 7^{d}. Aug. 4th. Usq^{b}. 5^{s}. Aug. 6. Ging^{r} ^{br} 2^{s}-2^{d} - - - 0 - 7 - 9
Dogs. 6^{d}½. Dogs 7^{d} Ras^{bry} & Sug^{r} by Mrs Wor^{ll}, 12^{s}-2^{d} - - - 0 - 13- 3
Aug. 25. gilt Pap^{r}. 1^{s}. Dog. 7^{d} Ging^{r} ^{bd}. 4^{s}. Snuff⟨1 8⟩1^{s}-8^{d}
Carriage. 1^{s}-6^{d} Dog. 6^{d} --28. Smith. 6^{s} Aug 29. Snuff 10^{d}
Sep^{b}. 14. Ging^{r}. 2^{s}-2^{d} Sep^{b}. 2. Tobac. 2^{s}. --2. Usqu^{b}. 5^{s} Dog. 7^{d}
Wafers 2^{d}½ Tape. 8^{d} Wash balls⟨1^{s}-2^{d}⟩Sep^{tb}. 15. 1^{s}-2^{d} Dog 6^{d}
Sep^{b}. 15. Sug^{r}. 6^{s}-8^{d} Dogs 6^{d}½ sm^{ll} 1^{d} Sep^{br}. 24 Ging^{r} 1^{s} Dog. 7^{d}
Pap^{r}. 8^{d} Dog. 7^{d} Oc^{tb}. 18. Sug^{r}. 7^{s}-7 Dog. 6^{d}½ Dog 7^{d}

Horses.

Turn p. 1^{d}½ Aug. 16. Hay 30 loads. ^8^{ll}-5^{s} Work. 1^{s}-4^{d} Ale 4^{s}-5^{d}.
G. Charles at Grange for his care 11^{s}-1^{d} Turn. p. 3^{d}½ -1^{d}½
Sm^{ll} 2^{d}½ Sep^{b}. 15 --Oats. 8^{s}-4^{d} sm^{ll} 2^{d} Oct^{br}. 12. Smith. 6^{s}.

Account

Of Receits from the Deanry &c

for 1732

And of Rents, dutyes &c for

1733.

[18v]

L.

Memorandum

Novr. 9th. 177

Gave Mr Gorman a Receit for 95^{ll}-16^{s}-4½ for money received Sev^{rll} times, and likewise for Bills on Sam Burton for 66^{ll}-10^{s}-8^{d} -- deposited with me (not as a Receit for the money) but to answer for them <when> till he pay me the money. both sums make - - - 95 - 16- 4½

First	
Burtons bill - - -	66 - 10- 8
	162 - 7 0½

Dean^{ry} this year - M^{r} Go

353 - 15- 0

⟨Account⟩

Deanry Set for 1732

N^r. 1.	Andrews John.	4^{ll}	
	Novr. 9th. 1733. Rx full - - -		4 - 0 - 0
--2	Ascun Jo^n.	15^{ll}	
--3.	Brown. Hen^r.	1^{ll}	
	Novr. 9th. 1733. Rx full - - -		1 - 0 - 0
4.	Brown. Olv^r.	2^s-6^d	
	Jun. 28 1735. P^d by Dr W. full - - -		0 - 2 - 6
5.	Brooks W^m.	2^{ll}-15^s.	
	Febr. 9th. 1733-4. P^d full - - -		2 - 15- 0
6	Byrn. Jam.	2^s-2^d	
	Jun. 28th. 1732 P^d by Dr W. full - - -		0 - 2 - 2
7.	Bellew. Chr^{str}.	2^{ll}-12^s	
	Rx May. 19. 1732 - full - - -		2 - 12- 0
8.	Bellew. Tho.	25^{ll}	
	Dec^{br}. 20th. 1733. Rx full - - -		25 - 0 - 0
9.	Bellew Jam	5^s	
	Febr. 9th. 1733-4. P^d full - - -		0 - 5 - 0

N^r			
10	Bottom John.	4^{ll}	
	⟨No^v. 9th.⟩ Mar. 14th. 1734 - Rx full - - -		4 - 0 - 0
11.	Byrn Garrat -	2^{ll}	
	May. 3^d. 1733. Rx full - - -		2 - 0 - 0
12	Byrn Bryan -	4^s	
13.	$Berming^{hm}$. Edw	2^{ll}-15^s	
	Mar. ⟨Edw⟩ 14th. 1734 Rx on account - - -		1 - 3 - 0
14.	Bottom. Tho^m -	4^{ll}	
	Novr. 9th. 1733 Rx full - - -		4 - 0 - 0
15.	Byrn Ed^m. -	2^s-8^d½	
	May. 19th. 1734 Rx full - - -		0 - 2 - 8½
16.	Byrn Edm. -	2^s-8^d½	
	Novr. 9. Rx full - - -		0 - 2 - 8½
17.	Byrn. Pat^r -	8^s-6	
	Novr. 9th. Rx - - -		0 - 8 - 6
18.	Byrn Ed^m	2^s-8^d½	
19	Barefoot. Tho. -	1^{ll}-10^s	
	\Jun 28th. 1735 P^d by D^r W on Account - - -		1 - 8 - 1½
20.	Coleman. Jo^n -	10^s-2^d	
	Novr. 9th. 1733. Rx full - - -		0 - 10- 2
21.	Cavan Pet^r. -	1^{ll}-10^s	
	Mar. 14th 1734 On account - - -		0 - 15- 0
	⟨Cook Jo^n. For Pearson Tho. $Rath^b$⟩	point troveè	
	⟨Novr. 9th 1733 P^d Qu? --en acompt - - -		4 - 10- 0⟩

N^r			
22.	Coghlan Ed^w. -	0 - 5 - 0	
	Febr. 9th. 1733-4 - Rx full - - -		0 - 5 - 0
	for. Jo^n Chester		
23.	Coghlan Edw -	0 - 4 - 4	
	Febr. 9th. 1733-4. Rx full - - -		0 - 4 - 4
24.	Conolly Rich^d -	o - 11- 6	
	Jun 28th. 1735 P^d by D^r W on Account - - -		0 - 9 - 2
25.	Colcot S^al. for J. Price -	3^ll	
	Rx full - - -		3 - 0 - 0
26.	Clinton Al^xdr -	4^s	
	May. 3d. 1733 Rx full - - -		0 - 4 - 0
27.	Carol for Kensel^gh -	12^s	
	Novr. 9th. 1733. Rx full - - -		0 - 12- 0
28.	Colcot Sam -	8^ll	
	Rx full - - -		8 - 0 - 0
29.	Clifton Jo^n -	2^ll-10^s	
	Novr. 9. 1733 Rx full - - -		2 - 10- 0
30.	Coyl Pat^r -	10^s	
	May. 3d. 1733 Rx full - - -		0 - 10- 0
31.	Dillon Cath^r -	10^ll.	
	Rx full - - -		10 - 0 - 0

N^{r}.			
32	Dod. W^{m} -	3^{11}	
33.	Doyl Jam - Novr. 9th. 1733. Rx full - - -	11^{s}-6^{d}	0 - 11- 6
34.	Donnahu Pat^{r}. & Hugh. Mar. 14th. 1734 Rx full - - -	9^{s}	0 - 9 - 0
35	Den Phil - Novr. 9th. Rx full - - -	6^{11}	6 - 0 - 0
36	Eustace, Hugh & Chris^{t} - Novr. 9th. 1733. Rx full - - -	11^{s}	0 - 11- 0
37	Emmerson. Jo^{n} - Novr. 9th. 1733. Rx full - - -	4^{11}	4 - 0 - 0
38.	Ellis Pat^{r}. - Novr. 9th. 1733. Rx full - - -	5^{s}	0 - 5 - 0
39.	Espinas for Wm Dry - May. 3^{d}. 1733. Rx full - - -	3^{11}-10^{s}	3 - 10- 0
40.	Eager. James - Rx full - - -	4^{s}	0 - 4 - 0
41.	Fitzimons Cha^{l} - Novr. 9th. 1733. Rx full - - -	15^{s}	0 - 15- 0

N^{r}

42. Farrall Jam. & Robt - 10^{s}
Novr. 9th. 1733. Rx full - - - 0 - 10- 0

43. Font Thom - 8^{s}
Novr. 9th. Rx full - - - 0 - 8 - 0

⟨44.⟩ Faulk^{nr}. Jo^{n} Esqr - 2^{ll}-6^{s}
Novr. 9th. 1733. Rx full fallen - - - 2 - 6 - 0

45. Farrell Sim. - 16^{s}-3^{d}
Mar. 14th 1734. Rx full - - - 0 - 16- 3

46 Fullham Hugh - 16^{s}
Novr. 9th. Rx full - - - 0 - 16- 0

47. Fagan Tho - 2^{ll}-10^{s}
Novr. 9th Rx full - - - 2 - 10- 0

48 Fagan T. for Hefernan - 16^{s}-3^{d}
Novr. 9th. Rx full - - - 0 - 16- 3

49 Gibton. W^{m} - 5^{ll}
Novr. 9th. 1733. Rx full - - - 5 - 0 - 0

50. Gibton Mic^{h} - 2^{ll}
Novr. 9. 1733. Rx full - - - 2 - 0 - 0

51. Grumly Pat^{r} - 3^{s}
Rx full - - - 0 - 3 - 0

52. Hiland Th. & Parh^{rs} 14^{s}

[14v]

N^{r}.			
53	Hoyl. Barth	10^{s}	
54	Harny Hugh -	1^{11}	
	╲Jun. 28th 1735. P^{d} by Dr W. full - - -		1 - 0 - 0
55	Hyland Luke -	2^{s}-2^{d}	
	Febr. 9th. 1733-4. Rx full - - -		0 - 2 - 2
56.	Hewson W^{m} -	5^{11}-10^{s}	
	Novr. 9th. 1733. Rx full - - -		5 - 10- 0
57.	Hill Tho' -	10^{s}	
	Novr. 9th. 1733. Rx full - - -		0 - 10- 0
58	Hudson Edm. -	2^{11}-10^{s}	
	May. 3^{d}. 1733 Rx full - - -		2 - 10- 0
59	Hudson Ed^{m} -	16^{s}-3^{d}	
	May. 3^{d}. 1733. Rx full - - -		0 - 16- 3
60.	Hoy Nich -	16^{s}	
	╲Jun. 28th. 1735. P^{d}by Dr W. full - - -		0 - 16- 0
61	Hart Andrew -	4^{11}	
	Febr. 9th. 1733-4. Rx full - - -		4 - 0 - 0
62	Jackson W^{m} -	8^{s}	
	May. 3^{d}. 1733. Rx full - - -		0 - 8 - 0
63.	Johnson. Joseph ^ due stll	1^{11}-3^{s}	⟨0 - 8 - 0⟩

N^r.			
64.	Jackson Charles - Novr. 9th. 1733. Rx full - - -	8^s	0 - 8 - 0
65	Kerney W^m - Novr 9. 1733. Rx full - - -	8^s	0 - 8 - 0
66	Kegan, Marg^t - Novr. 9th. 1733. Rx full - - -	11^s	0 - 11 - 0
67.	Kering Morgan - Novr. 9th. 1733. Rx full - - -	2^{ll}-10^s	2 - 10 - 0
68	Kenselagh Jo^n - Novr. 9th. 1733. Rx full - - -	18^s	0 - 18 - 0
69.	King Pat^r - Novr. 9th Rx full - - -	4^s-6	0 - 4 - 6
70	Keating Jam - May. 3^d. 1733 - - -	7^{ll}-10^s	7 - 10 - 0
71.	Lusk Jam. For Dan Reddi Es^q Novr. 9th. 1733. Rx full - - -	15^{ll}-0	15 - 0 - 0
72	Levi Chris^{tr} - Febr. 9th. 1733-4. Rx full	5^s	0 - 5 - 0
X	⟨Leacy Pierce (oux nomme)⟩ Mistak^n. Rathbeg ⟨Novr. 9th. 1733. Rx full - - -		0 - 12 - 0⟩

N^{r}			
73.	Lyons. Jo^{n} -	2^{ll}-10^{s}	
	Novr. 9. 1733. Rx full - - -		2 - 10- 0
74.	Lenon Ter -	0-8^{s}	
	Novr. 9. 1733. Rx full - - -		0 - 8 - 0
75	Lawler Math -	1^{ll}-5^{s}	
	May. 3^{d}. 1733. Rx full - - -		1 - 5 - 0
76.	Masterson W^{m} -	2^{s}-2^{d}	
77.	Martin Pat^{r} -	7^{ll}	
	Novr. 9th. 1733. Rx full - - -		7 - 0 - 0
78	Moorhouse Robt -	1^{ll}-10^{s}	
	Rx full - - -		1 - 10- 0
79	Murry Jam -	5^{s}	
	Jun. 28th. 1735 P^{d} by Dr W. full - - -		0 - 5 - 0
80	Mullconro Laur -	6^{s}-6	
81.	Moran Tho -	12^{s}	
	Febr. 9th. 1733-4. Rx full - - -		0 - 12- 0
82	Mathews J^{n}. for Mrs Moor -	10^{s}	
	Novr. 9. 1733. Rx full - - -		0 - 10- 0

N^r.			
83.	Mathews Jo^n - Novr. 9th. 1733. Rx full - - -	2^{ll}-15^s	2 - 15- 0
84.	Moor Lewis - Rx full - - -	6^s-6^d	0 - 6 - 6
85	Masham $Rich^d$ - Novr. 9th. 1733. Rx full - - -	1^{ll}	1 - 0 - 0
86.	Murphy Jo^n - May. 3^d. 1733. Rx full - - -	5^{ll}	5 - 0 - 0
87.	Mùrphy Pat^r - Febr. 9th. 1733-4. Rx full - - -	3^{ll}	3 - 0 - 0
88.	Moor Laur - Novr. 9th. Rx full - - -	1^{ll}	1 - 0 - 0
89	$Mitch^{ll}$ Jam - Mar. 14th. 1734. Rx full - - -	1^{ll}.	1 - 0 - 0
90.	Murphy W^m - Rx full - - -	4^{ll}	4 - 0 - 0
91.	M^c an Hugh - Rx full - - -	2^{ll}-6^s	2 - 6 - 0

N^{r}.			
92	Madden Edw - Mar. 14th. 1734 Rx full - - -	2^{ll}	2 - 0 - 0
93.	McAles^{tr}. ⟨Ric^{d}⟩ for J^{n} But^{lr}. Es^{q} - Mar. 14th. 1734. Rx full - - -	1^{ll}-10^{s}	1 - 10- 0
94	M^{c}ales^{tr} Richard - Mar. 14th. 1734 Rx full - - -	0 -15^{s}	0 - 15- 0
95	Nicholson Jam - May. 3^{d}. 1733 Rx full - - -	4^{ll}-10^{s}	4 - 10- 0
96.	Newman Tho -	7^{ll}	
97	Nowland Mic. & Henly Pa^{tr} -	2^{s}	
98	Poor. Chris^{tr} - Novr. 9th. 1733. Rx full - - -	15^{s}	0 - 15- 0
99	Pearson Jo^{n} - Novr. 9th. Rx full - - -	7^{ll}	7 - 0 - 0
100	Prende^{r}grass Laur - Febr. 9th. 1733-4 Rx full - - -	2^{s}-8^{d}½	0 - 2 - 8½
101	Potter Robt - Novr. 9th. 1733. Rx full - - -	8^{ll}-10^{s}	8 - 10- 0
102.	Prat Jo^{n} Esqr - Novr. 9th. 1733. Rx full - - -	2^{ll}-5^{s}	2 - 5 - 0

N^{r}.

103 Quin Pe^{tr} - 28^{ll}-10^{s}
Dec^{b}. 20th. 1733 - Rx full - - - 28 - 10- 0

104 Quin James - 4^{ll}-15^{s}.
Mar. 14th. 1734. Rx full - - - 4 - 15- 0

105. Roan Tho^{m} for Corn^{ll} Robins - 1^{ll}-8^{s}-6
May. 19th. 1734 Rx full - - - 1 - 8 - 0

106 Rourk Edm - 2^{ll}
Novr. 9th. 1733. Rx full - - - 2 - 0 - 0

107 Reynolds Pa^{tr} - 6^{ll}-16^{s}
Mar. 14th. 1734. Rx full - - - 6 - 16- 0

108 Reynolds Jo^{n} - 10^{ll}
Febr. 9th. 1733-4. Rx full - - - 10 - 0 - 0

109. Robinson Jo^{n} - 3^{ll}
Novr. 9th. 1733. Rx full - - - 3 - 0 - 0

110. Row Hugh - 6^{ll}
Novr. 9th. 1733 Rx full - - - 6 - 0 - 0

111 Rourk Jo^{n} - 4^{s}

[11v]

N^r

112	Stubbs Robt -	5^s-5^d	
	Novr. 9th. 1733. Rx full - - -		0 - 5 - 5
113.	Sandys Pa^{tr} -	2^{ll}-6^s	
	Mar. 14th. 1734. Rx full - - -		2 - 6 - 0
114.	Sturges Cha^l - - -	4^{ll}	
	Novr. 9th. 1733. Rx full - - -		4 - 0 - 0
115	Strong $Rich^d$ -	18^s-6^d	
	Novr. 9. 1733. Rx full - - -		0 - 18- 6
116	Seaman Paul -	2^{ll}	
	Nov. 9th Rx full - - -		2 - 0 - 0
117.	Savage Thom -	12^s-6^d	
	Jun 28th 1735. $P^d$by Dr W. part 11^d onely		
118	Tool Jam -	1^{ll}-10^s	
	May. 3^d. 17ss Rx full - - -		1 - 10- 0
119	Tool. Jo^n & Frances -	9^{ll}	
	Mar. 14th. 1734. Rx on account - - -		2 - 6 - 0
120	Tint Jam. Esqr -	9^{ll}	
	May. 3^d. 1733. Rx full - - -		9 - 0 - 0
121.	Verdon Hugh & Murphy Jo^n -	1^{ll}-10^s	
	Novr. 9th. 1733. Rx full - - -		1 - 10- 0
122	Vineau for Capt Chenevix -	1^{ll}-3^s	
	Novr. 9th. 1733. Rx full - - -		1 - 3 - 0

N^r.

123 Wakely Tho. Esqr - 10^{ll}
Mar. 14th. 1734. Rx full. - - - 10 - 0 - 0

124 Wheland Cornel - 6^s

Out of the Alphabet

David Chagneau . . . . (not payd) Rx full Dec^b. 12th 5 - 0 - 0

Ld A. B. Dubl.

Tyth of 30 Acres $Wein^{tr}$ corn 5^s p^r ac. - - -	7 - 10 - 0
Spring Corn 25 Acres 3^s p^r acre - - -	3 - 15 - 0
Meadow 30 acres 2^s-6^d p^r acre - - -	3 - 15 - 0
	15 - 0 - 0
Mr Norton 13 acres Spring corn - - -	1 - 10 - 0

Tyths drawn without notice

Coleman Jo^n
Newgent Law^r
Sheridan W^m
Purcel Jo^n
Mr Talbot
Feragh Wm

W.

No^{vr}. Wor^{ll} 10^{d}. - - - 0-0-10

Dc^{b}. 24. Mrs Helsh. 6^{d}½

Febr 20 Shri^{dn} 1^{s}-1^{d}

Fe^{br}. 22 Sher^{dn} 1^{s}-1^{d}

Sherd. 1^{s}-1^{d} C. Gra^{ttn} 6^{d}½

Sheri^{d} 6^{d}½ Mar. 28 Whit 2^{d}

Ap. 2. Dr Arrogant - - - 0-1-1

May 20 Sh^{rdn}. 6^{d}½

Whitw. 2^{d} Jax^{sn} B. G. 3^{d}

Aug. 12. Whit^{w} 9^{d} ☞ -0-0-~~9~~ 10

Sep^{t}. 2. Whitew. 6^{d} Harris^{n} 4^{d} - 0-0-10

Sep^{t} 13 Whitw. 6^{d}½

Oc^{br}. 2^{d} Whitw 5^{d} --10. Har^{r} 2^{d}

Oct^{br}. 13. Whit^{w}. 5^{d}

L.

Nov. 9. Wor^{ll}. 4^{d} - - - 0-0-4

J. Gr^{tt}. 1^{s}-1^{d} - - - 0-1-1

Dc^{r}. 24. Arrogant. 1^{s}-1^{d} - - - 0-1-1

Ja^{r}. 9^{d}. Hellsh^{m} 6^{d}½ - - - 0-1-3½

p^{d} in Whitwy 1^{s}-1^{d} - - - 0-1-1

Feb. 1. Whit. 8^{d} - - - 0-0-8

She^{d}. 6^{d}½ Whitway 5^{d} - - - 0-0-11½

Whit^{w}. 2^{d} May. 9. Whit. 6^{d}½ - - - 0-0-8½

Jun. 5. Whit^{w}. 8^{d} Jun. 17. H^{ls} 6^{d}½ 0-

Whitw. 5^{d}½ Whitew. 5^{d}

Aug. 5. Dr Arrogance. us. in all 0-2-2

Aug. 24 Shed^{n} 6^{d}½ Harris^{n} 6^{d}½ 0-1-1

Whitew. 1^{d} White. 4^{d} Har^{sn} 1^{d} - - - 0-0-6

Oct^{b}. 2^{d} ⟨Whitw 5^{d}⟩ Harr^{n} 2^{d}

--10. Whit^{w}. 11^{d}. Harr^{sn} 1^{d}

Harr^{n} 3^{d}

Oct^{b}. 28. Harris^{n}. 3^{d} Whit^{w}. 5^{d}½ 0-0-8½

Account of Expences from Nov^{r}.

1st 1734 to Novr. 1st 1735

⟨16. Deadly sick at Howth⟩

Novem^{br}. Sm-- G--ts

Nov^{br}. --1734

Novr. 1. MWhit^{wy} 10^{d} --G. 2^{d} - - -	0 - 1 - 0
--2^{d}. G. 6^{d}½. 3^{d}. Church. 1^{s}-1^{d}. Wor^{ll}. 6^{d}½ ⟨Ser^{vts} 1^{s}-7^{d}½⟩- - -	0 - 2 - 4½
Ridgw. 6^{d}½ G. 1^{s}. G. 1^{s}. G. 1^{s}-7^{d}½ ⟨H. bill. 0-10^{s}-9^{d}⟩ - - -	0 - 4 - 2
⟨Whitings 7^{d}.⟩ G. 1^{s}-1^{d} G. 1^{s}. sm^{ll} 4^{d} G. 1^{s}-1^{d} G. 1^{s}-4^{d}½ - - -	0 - 5 - 0½
G 6^{d}½ G. 1^{s}-4^{d} G. 1^{s}-4^{d} Ch^{rs} &c. 3^{s}-3^{d}. G. 1^{s}-1^{d} G. 6^{d}½ - - -	0 - 8 - 1
⟨G. 5^{d}⟩	1 - 0 - 8

⟨2^{d} Week⟩

⟨Brd w. 10^{s} H. bill (allowd) 1^{s}-7^{d}½. Wash 1^{s}-1^{d}⟩

Dec^{r}. (Some part to last Month by mistake

⟨Cavoner 1^{s}-7^{d}½⟩	
--13. G. 1^{s}-10^{d}½ --15 G. 1^{s}-1^{d} G 16 at Howth 2^{s}-10^{d} --17. Han^{nl} 2^{s}-8^{d} -	0 - 8 - 6
--18 Jo. 6^{d}½. 2^{d}. G. 2^{s}-2^{d}. G. 1^{s}-1^{d} --23. Whitew. 1^{s}-7^{d}½ - - -	0 - 5 - 7
Helsh. man 2^{s}-8^{d}½ Ridg^{w}. 6^{d}½ G. 1-7^{d}½ G. 5^{d} 26. Sican 6^{d}½ - - -	0 - 5 - 9
--28. G. 11^{d} G. 9^{d}½. Por. 1^{s}-7^{d}½ G. 1^{s}-1^{d} G. 1^{s}-1^{d} G. 1^{s}-1^{d} - - -	0 - 5 - 6
	1 - 5 - 4

Jan^{ry}.

--4th G 6^{d}½ 5. G. 1^{d} Chairs. 2^{s}-2^{d} G. 2^{d} G. 1^{s}-7^{d}½ - - -	0 - 4 - 7
G. 2^{d} G. 1^{s}-7^{d}½ --G. 1^{s}-1^{d} Whit^{wy}. 1^{s}-1^{d} G. 1^{s}-1^{d} --19. Poor 1^{s}-1^{d} - -	0 - 6 - 1
G. 2^{d}. G. 1^{s}-7^{d}½ Lights 1^{s}-1^{d} G. 4^{d}. Chairs 1^{s}-7^{d}½ --G. 2^{s}-2^{d} - - -	0 - 6 -10
G. 5^{d}. G. 1^{s}-4^{d}½	

Febr

1 Whit. 7^{d}. G 6^{d}½. 2^{d} Sa^{t}. 1^{s}-1^{d} --3^{d} Jaxson 10^{d}. 4. G. 1^{s}-1^{d} - - -	0 - 4 - 4
Ridg^{w}. 6^{d}½ 5. Pig 6^{d}½ -G. 1^{s}-4^{d}½ --9. Sa^{crt}. 1^{s}-1^{d} G. 6^{d}½ - - -	0 - 4 - 1
G. 6^{d}½ G. 4^{d} G. 1^{s}-1^{d} --15 Ch^{r}. 6^{d}½ --16. G 1^{s}-1^{d} - - -	0 - 3 - 6½
17. Whit^{w}. Co^{ch}. 1^{s}-1^{d}. G. 1^{s}-1^{d} G 8^{d} G. 1^{s}-1^{d} --19. G. 6^{d}½ - - -	0 - 4 - 5½
Whitw. 6^{d}½ G. 6^{d}½ -G. 1^{s}-4^{d}½ --21. Hogs cheeks. 1^{s}-1^{d}. sm^{ll} 1^{d} - - -	0 - 3 - ½6
--22 G Land lord Cavoner. 1^{s}-1^{d} M^{c}guires man 1^{s}-1^{d} Oranges b^{il} 6^{d}½ - - -	0 - 2 - 8½
sm^{ll}. 1^{d}. Ch^{r} Sherid 1^{s} -G. 1^{s}-1^{d}. Man 1^{s} --25. Co^{ch}. Man. 1^{s}-1^{d} - - -	0 - 4 - 3
G. 4^{d} G. 1^{s}-7^{d}. Whit^{w}. 6^{d}½ --27. G. 1^{s}-7^{d}½ G. 1^{s}-4^{d}½ - - -	0 - 5 - 5½
G. Sher^{dn} 6^{d}½ ⟨Ch^{r} ⟩28 ⟨Ch^{r}. 8^{d}.⟩ G. 6^{d}½ - - -	0 - 1 - 1
	1 - 12- 1½

March.

1. G. 1^{s}-4^{d}½ 1. G. 1^{s}-1^{d}. Rid^{gw}. Din^{r} 6^{d}½ Ser^{vts} 6^{d}½ G. 3^{d} - - -	0 - 3 - 9
Co^{ch} Whit^{w}. 1^{s}-1^{d} Ridg^{y} 6^{d}½ Whit^{w}. 8^{d}½ G. 3^{d} G. 1^{s}-4^{d}½ - - -	0 - 3 -11
G. 1^{s}-4^{d}½ G. 1^{s}-1^{d}. --17. Bacon. 1^{s}-1^{d} sm^{ll} 4^{d} Ch^{r} paid 6^{d}½ - - -	0 - 4 - 5
G. 11^{d} 21. 5^{d} --22. White^{w} 8^{d} --23 G. 1^{s}-1^{d} Ser^{vts} 6^{d}½ - - -	0 - 3 - 7½
G. 1^{s}-7^{d}½ --26. G. 1^{s}-1^{d} Whitw Ch^{r}. 8^{d}½ G. 1^{s}-7^{d}½ G. 3^{d} - - -	0 - 4 - 4½
30. G. 1^{s}-1^{d} Mad^{m}. 1^{s}-1^{d} G. 9^{d}. - - -	0 - 2 -11
	1 - 3 - 0

April. Sm. G--ts

--Ridgw Din^{r} 6^{d}½ G. 1^{s}-7^{d}½ G. 4^{d} --5. Ch^{r} Whit^{w}. 6^{d}½ - - -	0 - 3 - 0½
--6. Sac^{rmt} &c 3^{s}-3^{d} Mad. 1^{s}-1^{d} G. 4^{d} --8 Watch Rub^{d}. 2^{s}-2^{d} - - -	0 - 6 -10
10 Whit^{w} Co^{ch} &c 1^{s}-8^{d} 11. Heads. G. 1^{s}-1^{d} G. 1^{s}-7^{d}½ - - -	0 - 3 - 4½
--15. G 5^{d} --16. Groom 2^{s}-8^{d} Poor 1^{s} ⟨Rid⟩ Whit^{w}. 8^{d} --18. Gard^{nr} 2^{s}8^{d}½-	0 - 7 - 5½
--20. G. 1^{s}-1^{d} Brat. 6^{d}½ --21. G. 4^{d}. G. 1^{s}-7^{d}½ --21 Whit^{w}. ch^{r} 6^{d}½ - -	0 - 3 - 7
22. Ridw -for a Play &c. 1^{s}-1^{d} --23^{d}. G. 1^{s} --24. G. 1^{s}-3^{d} - - -	0 - 3 - 4
27. Church. 1^{s}-1^{d} G. 2^{d}. --28 G. 4^{d} G. 1^{s}-7^{d}½ - - -	0 - 3 - 0½
--29 Jackson 1^{s}-1^{d}. G. 6^{d} Sm^{ll} 1^{s}. - - -	0 - 2 - 7
	1 - 13- 2½

May

--1. White^{w}. Angll. &c. 2^{s}-8^{d}½ My Bayl. 2^{s}-8^{d}½ - - -	0 - 5 - 5
1 May. dinner 6^{d} 3^{d}. G. 3^{d} --3^{d}. G. 4^{d} --4. G. 1^{s}-1^{d} - - -	0 - 2 - 2
--5 G. 1^{s}-4^{d}. 6. G. 2^{d} --7th G. 5^{d} --9. Whit^{w}. 6^{d}½ - - -	0 - 2 - 5½
--10 1^{d} 11. Sac^{rmt} &c 1^{s}-3^{d}. 12. Ridg 5^{d} 14 G. 1^{s}. - - -	0 - 2 - 7
G --- 1^{s}-7^{d}½ G -- 1^{s}-7^{d}½ G. 1^{s}-7^{d}½. Groom 6^{d}½ - - -	0 - 5 - 5
Sm^{ll} 3^{d} G. 6^{d}½ --17. G. 10^{d} Sac^{rt} 1^{s}-2^{d} --20 Whit^{w}. book 2^{s}-2^{d} - - -	0 - 4 -11½
G. 4^{d}. Whit^{w} 6^{d}½ --21. G. 1^{s}-1^{d}. G. 1^{s}-7^{d}½ --4^{d} --G. 1^{s}-1^{d} - - -	0 - 5 - 0
25. Sac^{t}. 2^{s}-8^{d} --26. Nebr 10^{d} Co^{ch} Sica^{n} White^{w} 1^{s}-1^{d} - - -	0 - 4 - 8
--28. Spargs L^{d} M^{r} 3^{d}. Whit^{w} 1^{s}-1^{d}. ha^{d} maid 6^{d}½ G 2^{d} - - -	0 - 2 - 0
Poor. 1^{s}-7^{d}½ to 31st 2^{s}-8^{d}½ - - -	1 - 14- 8½

June

1 --Sa^{ct}. 2^{s}-8^{d}½. 2. White^{w} &c 8^{d}½ G. 1^{s}-7^{d}½. G. 2^{d} - - -	0 - 5 - 1
G. 6^{d} --8. Sac^{rt}. 1^{s}-1^{d} G 1^{s}-7^{d}½ G. 4^{d}. G. 5^{d}. Sac^{rt}. 1^{s}-3^{d} - - -	0 - 4 -10½
G. 5^{d}. White &c 8^{d} G. 3^{d}. G. 1^{s}-7^{d}½ --20 G. 1^{s}-4^{d}. 23. G. 3^{s} - - -	0 - 6 - 3½
G. 1^{s}-7^{d}½ sm^{ll}. 4^{d} --28 Ven^{son}. 2^{s}-8^{d}½ G. 6^{d}½. Whit^{w}. 1^{s}-1^{d} - - -	0 - 5 - 3½
--29. Sac^{rmt} 1^{s}-1^{d} G. 1^{s}-7^{d}½ G. 3^{d}. G. 1^{s}-1^{d} - - -	0 - 3 - 9½
	1 - 5 - 4

July

--G. 6^{d}. 4th G. 1^{s}-1^{d} --Whit^{w}. 6^{d}½ --6. Sac^{t}. 1^{s}-1^{d} G. 4^{d} G. 3^{d} - - -	0 - 3 - 9½
G. 2^{d}. 8- G. 8^{d} G. 1^{s}-7^{d}½ --9. G. 1^{s}-10^{d} Harris^{n} 2^{s}-2^{d} - - -	0 - 6 - 5
G. 1^{s}-1^{d} G. 1^{s}-3^{d} G. 4^{d} --12 feu MA 1^{s}-1^{d} --13. Sac^{rt}. 1^{s}-1^{d} - - -	0 - 3 - 9
--15. G. 4^{d} G. 1^{s}-7½. G. 1^{s}. --16. G. 1^{s}-1^{d} --18. D^{r}. H. Ser^{ts} 2^{s}-2^{d} -	0 - 6 - 2½
G. 6^{d} --18. G. 1^{s}-4^{d}. Poor 1^{s}-4^{d}½ G. 3^{d} G. 4^{d} - - -	0 - 3 - 9½
Whit^{w}. &c 8^{d}. Jul. 26. Wom^{n} Venison. 1^{s}-1^{d} Din^{r} Ser^{vts} 1^{s}-1^{d} - - -	0 - 2 -10
G. 1^{s}-4^{d}½. M^{rs}. Sic^{n}. Book. 2^{s}-2^{d}. Old wom^{n} broke leg. 2^{s}-8^{d}½ Sc^{rt} 6^{d}½ -	0 - 6 - 9½
G. 2^{d} G. 5^{d} Ser^{vts} 1^{s}-1^{d} G. Ser^{t}. 1^{s}-3^{d} Poor 1^{s}-4^{d}½	

August.

White^{w} 6^{d}½ sm^{ll} 6^{d}. --2. To a poor Boy. 1^{s}-5^{d} --3^{d}. Sc^{rt} &c 1^{s}-4^{d}
G. 6^{d}. G. 1^{s}-1^{d} 6. G. 2^{s}-2^{d} G. 6^{d}½ 7. G. 1^{s} Whiteway 6^{d}½

Aug

Brought over - - -

--9. G. 9^{d} G. 1^{s}-4^{d}. ⟨11.⟩ G. 4^{d} --G. 5^{d} --18 $Whit^{w}$ & Son 1^{s}-1^{d}

G. 1^{s}-9^{d}½ G. 3^{d} $Ridg^{w}$ 6^{d}½ --20. G. 7^{d} --$Neigh^{br}$. 6^{d}½

A. Bp^{s} men 1^{s}-1^{d}

--21. G. 1^{s}-5^{d}. G. 1^{s}-9^{d} $White^{w}$. 6^{d}½. 29th. G. 1^{s}-1^{d}. G. 1^{s}-1^{d}

--30. $White^{w}$. 6^{d}½. Poor. 1^{s}-9^{d}½

Sep^{tb}.

4 G. Ser^{ts} 6^{d}½ G. 6^{d}. G. 1^{s}-9^{d} --6. G. 1^{s}-1^{d} 9 $Whit^{w}$. 7^{d} - - - 0 - 4 - 5½

G. 3^{d} --12 Dr Del. Coach. 1^{s}-1^{d} --11⟨D^{rs} D's Coachman 1^{s}-1^{d}⟩- - - 0 - 3 - 8½

Ridgw. $Halp^{n}$ 7^{d}. G. Sho^{sr} poor. 1^{s}-1^{d} --12. $Earth^{n}$ ware. 1^{s}-1^{d} - - - 0 - 1 - 4

$Whit^{w}$. boy. 1^{s}-7^{d}½. G. 4^{d}. --$Whit^{w}$ 1^{s}-1^{d}. Mol. 2^{d}½ --Church 6^{d}½ - - - 0 - 2 - 9

G. 8^{d}. --15. G. 1^{s}-9^{d}½ G. 1^{s}. $White^{w}$. 6^{d}½ --21. G. 1^{s}-1^{d} G. 1^{s}-9^{d}. - - 0 - 3 - 9½

Slmore. 6^{d}½. G. 2^{d} --G $Whit^{w}$. 6^{d}½ G. 1^{s}. G. 6^{d}½ - - - 0 - 6 - 9

--28. Sac^{rmt}. 1^{s}-1^{d} Sm^{ll} 4^{d}. M^{rs} Co^{brs} 2^{s}-8^{d}½ $Whit^{w}$. 6^{d}½ - - - 0 - 2 - 9½

Charles 2^{s}-2^{d}. 30. D. of Dorset 2^{d} G. 1^{s}-9^{d}½ - - - 0 - 4 - 7

0 - 4 - 1½

1 - 13 - 0½

Oct^{br}

--2 Whitw 6^{d}½ --G. 3^{d} Sac^{rt}. 1^{s}-1^{d}. G. 4^{d}. $Ridg^{w}$. 6^{d} - - - 0 - 2 - 8½

Whitw. 6^{d}½ G. 6^{d}½. $Whit^{w}$. 6^{d}½. G. 3^{d} $Whitew^{w}$. 6^{d}½ G. 1^{s}-9^{d}½

--17. Whitw. 1^{s}-1^{d}

--20. G. at $Webb^{rs}$. 1^{s}-7^{d}½. Whitw. 6^{d}½ Sac^{rt} 1^{s}-1^{d}. G. 4^{d} G. 1^{s}-9^{d}½

--23. $White^{w}$. 1^{s}-1^{d}. G. 1^{s}-7^{d}½ Neal 1^{s}-1^{d} Whitw. 1^{s}-1^{d} $Sriv^{l}$. 1^{s}-2^{d}

G. 1^{s}-1^{d}. G. 8^{d}. G. 1^{s}-1^{d}. Whitw 6^{d}½ Whitw. 6^{d}½ 31. G. 2^{d}

Octr. 11: den: otè

Account

Of Expences from Nov^{br}. 1st. 1734 to Nov^{br}. 1st. 1735

First Quar^{tr}

From Novr. 1st. 1734 To Feb^{r}. 1st 1734-5

Cloaths

Mend Shirts -8^{d} p^{r} shoes & Slipp^{rs} 15^{s} crv. 1^{s}-2^{d} - - - 0 - 15- 3
Decr. 8. Riding Cassock. Prenoll. 17^{s}-6 Velvet 4^{s}-7^{d} 1 - 2 - 1
Making, mending & Cheating 14^{s} --2^{d}. Wig box. 9^{d} Col^{r}. 2^{d} 0 - 15- 1
Mend wig. 3^{s}-3^{d} Tayl^{r} 14^{s} Camb^{r}. &c. 1^{s}-8^{d}

Serv^{ts} Cloaths.

Dec^{br}. 1. Boots. 12^{s}

Extr^{dys}.

Dog. 6^{d} Dogs 6^{d} Dogs 9. 6^{d} -D^{r} & Shd. 1^{s}-7^{d} - - - 0 - 3 - 1
Sm^{ll}. 3^{d} Tobac. 1^{s} Dogs 6^{d} Dog 6^{d} Raz^{r} case 4^{d} - - - 0 - 2 - 7
Dog. 6^{d} Birth Sc^{t} 1^{s}-1^{d} Gingr br. 2^{s}-2^{d} Sand 1^{s} - - - 0 - 4 - 7
Chairs. &c. 2^{s}-2^{d} Dc^{br}. 6th. Ging^{r}. 2^{s}-2^{d}. Tobac, 1^{s} Liqrice 8^{d} - - - 0 - 6 - 6
Dog. 6^{d} Decr. 15. Usque 5^{s}-2^{d}. Dec^{br}. 14 Chips. 6^{d}½ M^{l} Wat^{r} 6^{d}
Dog. 6^{d} Grocer. 12^{s}-4^{d} Milk w^{tr}. 6^{d} Dog 6^{d} D^{r}. 31. Sug^{r}. 5^{s}-10^{d}
Dogs 6^{d}. Jan^{r}. 16th. Snuff. 1^{s} Fe^{r}. 14th. gilt Pap^{r}. 1^{s}. Fe^{br}. 11. Chips. 6^{d}½

Horses.

2^{d} Smith 2^{d}-1^{d} Straw 7^{d} Smith &c 8^{d} Pillion &c 2^{s}-4^{d} - - - 0 - 5 - 8
Sm^{ll} 2^{d}. De^{cr}. 9. Oats 1s-1^{d}. Mend 9^{d} Smith 2^{s} Strap. 4^{d} - - - 0 - 4 - 4
Decr. 18th. Oats 2^{s} Girth 2^{d} Dc^{r}. 24. Straw 3^{s}-6^{d}
Smith 2^{s}

--25
Novbr. Τεβυναι

Expences

From Novr. 20 to Decbr. 4th. at Grange.

1st Month

1st Week

1st to 9.

Brd w. 12s. Wor11. 1s-1d 8th 6d½ Wor11. 6d½ - - - 0 - 14- 2

H. Bill. ⟨10s-9d⟩ 9s-8d Wash. 1s-1d Lettr. 6d Stw 1s - - - 0 - 12- 3

2d Week

9 to 16 Belcamp from 11 to 16th

Brd w 10s. Meat at Grattans. at Jacksons. 1s-7d½

H. bill. 4d 1½ H bill 2s-6d. Watr. 6d Wash 1s

3d Week

16 to 23d

Brd w. 10s H bill 5s-3d½ Wash 1s-1d

4th Week.

23d -to 30th

Brd w. 10s. H. bill. (at Grange) 1s-7d½ Wash 1s-1d

16. Deadly
Sick at Howth.

Expences to Dublin the 4th

Dece^{br} 20. 2 giddy fits in 3 minutes Took a Vomit.

1st Week

2^{d} Month

Dec^{b}. 18th. Enfin resblee pour le feu Vague

1 to 7

Brd w. 10^{s} H. 2^{s}-4^{d}½ Wash at Grange 4^{d} Wash 1^{s}-1^{d} - - - 0 - 13- 5½
Meat 1^{s}-8^{d} Sm^{ll}. 7^{d} - - - 0 - 2 - 3

2^{d} Week.

7 to 14

Brd w. 12^{s} ⟨9. 9⟩ Ch^{r} & Co^{ch} 1^{s}-7^{d}½ H. bill 5^{s}-4^{d} - - - 1 - 18-11½
--⟨11⟩12 Chair 8^{d} Mutton 9^{d} sm^{ll} 1^{d} --13. Coach. 1^{s}-1^{d} Wash 1^{s}-1^{d} - -0 - 3 - 8

3^{d} Week.

14 to 21.

--Brd w. 12^{s}. --16. Co^{ch}. 6^{d}½ --17. Co^{ch}. 1^{s}-1^{d} a fowl 1^{s}-3^{d} - - - 0 - 14-10½
--17. Co^{ch}. 1^{s}-1^{d} Sm^{ll} 2^{d}½ sm^{ll} 4^{d}½. Blue. 1^{s}-1^{d} -1^{d} - - - 0 - 2 -10
--18. Ch^{r}. 6^{d}½ Ferry 2^{d} sm^{ll} 1^{d} H. bill 6^{s}-2^{d} Co^{ch}. 6^{d}½ 0 - 7 - 6
Chair 9^{d} 0 - 0 - 9
1 - 5 -11½

4th Week

21 to 28

Brd w. H bill Ridg^{w} 7^{s}-8^{d}½ 14. Ch^{r}. 9^{d} Lett^{r}. 2^{d}
Wash. 1^{s}-1^{d}. --26 Ch^{r}. 1^{s}-3^{d} H bill 7^{s}-7^{d}½ Lett^{rs} 1^{s}-10^{d}
--1. Co^{ch}. 3^{s}-3^{d} Chi^{r} 8^{d}½

Remd^{r}.

28 to Jan^{r}. 1.

Brd w. . . Ch^{r}. 8^{d}½ Meat, Raisins. 1^{s}-6^{d}

Expences

Jan^{r} --20. Lett^{r} from Sh-- about Bs knife. 3^{d} Month

First Week

1 to 4
Brd w 5^{s}-6^{d} --3^{d} Lett^{r}. 9^{d} Ch^{r} 6^{d}½
H bill 2^{s}-11^{d} mutt^{n} 7^{d} Chick^{n} 6^{d}½

2^{d} Week

4th to 11
Brd w 5^{s}-6^{d} 9. Ch^{r} 9^{d}½ 1 Pullet 1^{s}-4^{d} Mutt^{n}. &c. 1^{s}-1^{d}
Lett^{r} 8^{d} Scotch Wash. 1^{s}-1^{d}. H. Bill 3^{s}-7^{d}. --14 Ch^{r} 9^{d}

3^{d} Week

11 to 18
Brd w 12^{s}. 17. Din^{r} Sher^{d}. 1^{s}-1^{d} --17. Ch^{r}. 9^{d} --17 Co^{ch} 9^{d}
Meat 4^{s}-1^{d}½ H bill 4^{s}-4^{d} Lett^{r}. 6^{d} Cha^{r}. 1^{s}-1^{d}

4th Week

18 to 25.
Brd W 12^{s} Ch^{r}. 8^{d} --21 Ch^{r}. 1^{s}-1^{d}
--24 Din^{r} Lightburn 1^{s}-10^{d}

Remd^{r}.

25 to Feb. 1. . . 27 Din^{r} <5^{s}-10^{d}>
Brd w. . . Chair 8^{d} 27. Ch^{r}. 8^{d}. Din^{r}. D^{r} Sh^{d}. 1^{s}-1^{d}
31. Chair 8^{d}½ 25 Meat 2^{s}-7^{d}. Meat 4^{s}-7^{d} --Chair 8^{d}½
Ch^{r} 8^{d}½ H. bill 5^{s}-6^{d} Wash 1^{s}-1^{d} <H bill>

Totals

[5]

<Account of>/Second Quart^{r}

<Expences>/from Febr. 1. 1734 to May. 1. 1735

Cloaths

Mend Gown 1^{s}-1^{d} Cap lind. 6^{d}. July 9. Hanker^{cf} lost 3^{s}-6^{d}

Serv^{ts} Cloaths

Extr^{dys}

Dogs. 6^{d} Febr. 5 Snuff. 1^{s} --Ging^{rb} 2^{s}-2^{d}

Feb. 14 Mrs Mcguire for Oranges 1^{ll}-14-6^{d} --Chips -8^{d}

Dogs. 6^{d} A Message 10^{d} Dog 6^{d} Dog 6^{d} Mar. 7 Tobac 1^{s}

Mar 8 Starch. 1^{s}-1^{d}. Ging^{r} br^{d}. 4^{s}-4^{d} Mar. 13. Sug^{r}. 6^{s}-11^{d} Dog. 6^{d}

Oranges 1^{ll}-8^{s}-6^{d} Dog. 6^{d} Port^{r} 6^{d} Mar. 24 Snuff 1^{s} Dogs 6^{d}

Mar. 26. W. Balls 10^{d} Cards. 6^{d}½ Dog. 6^{d} Apr. 9. Tobac. 1^{s}

Apr. 12 ☞ Mend repeat^{g} Watch. Dog. 6^{d}. Apr. 11. Chips 6^{d}½

--19. Ging^{r} br^{d} 2^{s}-2^{d} Dog. 6^{d} Dog 6^{d} Dog 6^{d} Watch mend. 1^{ll}-3^{s}

<Sican 7^{s}-9^{d}> Sican. 7^{s}-9^{d} Jun. 27th. Usqub 5^{s}-5

Horses.

Sm^{ll}. 3^{d}. Turnp. 3^{d} Febr. 12. Smith. 2^{s}. Mar. 5. Oats 7^{s}-7^{d}

Mar. 8. Scissors. 1^{s}-6^{d} Turnp 3^{d} Mar. 15. Straw. 3^{s}-9^{d} Turn^{p}. 2^{d} --1^{d}

--24. Smith 6^{s} sm^{ll} 2^{d}. Turnp. 3^{d} Mar. 20. Saddle 1^{ll}-10^{s}. Sad^{lr}. 4^{s}

[5v]

Febr. 1st Month

First Week

1 to 8.

B^{rd} w 12^{s}. . . Ho Bill 7^{s}-1^{d} Chair 1^{s}-6^{d} - - - 1 - 0 - 7
Wash. 1^{s}-1^{d} Meat 1^{s}-$1^{d}\frac{1}{2}$ Mutton 10^{d}

2^{d} Week.

8. to 15.

B^{rd} w 12^{s}. Ch^{r}. 8^{d}. Din^{r}. $Whit^{w}$. 2^{s}-2^{d}.
10. Chair $8^{d}\frac{1}{2}$ --13. Ch^{r}. $8^{d}\frac{1}{2}$ Meat 1^{s}-6^{d}
Mutton. 9^{d} 14. Ch^{r}. $8^{d}\frac{1}{2}$ --15. Ch^{r}. $6^{d}\frac{1}{2}$.

3^{d} Week

15 to 22

B^{rd} w. 12^{s}. 16. Din^{r} $Whit^{w}$ 1^{s}-1^{d} --18. Din Mar. 1^{s}-1^{d}
Ch^{r}. 8^{d}. H. bill 4^{s}-2^{d} Wash. 1^{s}-1^{d} --20. Din^{r} $Shrd^{n}$. 1^{s}-1^{d}
--Ch^{r}. $Sherd^{n}$. $6^{d}\frac{1}{2}$ --$Ridg^{ws}$ bill meat. 11^{s}-1^{d}

4th Week R^{ding}

22 to Mar. 1.

B^{rd}

B^{rd} w. 12^{s}. Ch^{r}. $8^{d}\frac{1}{2}$ 24 Ch^{r}. $8^{d}\frac{1}{2}$
Meat 2^{s}-$8^{d}\frac{1}{2}$ $Lett^{r}$. 6^{d}. 27. Di^{r} $Shrd^{n}$. 1^{s}-1^{d}
Meat 3^{s}-$3^{d}\frac{1}{2}$ Meat 2^{s}-$8^{d}\frac{1}{2}$ H. bill. 5^{s}-$6^{d}\frac{1}{2}$
$Lett^{rs}$ 1^{s}-2^{d} Wash. 1^{s}-1^{d} Ch^{r}. 8^{d}. H. bill -- 0 - 4^{s} - 5
$Lett^{r}$. 6^{d}

Expences.

March 2^{d} Month

First Week

1 to 8^{d}

Brd w. 12^{s}. --Co^{ch}. 1^{s}-4^{d} --5. Din^{r} Sican 1^{s}-1^{d}.	0 - 14- 5
¬-Nutmegs. 8^{d}. 7. Ch^{r}. 1^{s}-1^{d} --H. bill. 4^{s}-3^{d} Lett^{rs} 2^{s}-4	0 - 8 - 4
Wash. 1^{s}-1^{d} Co^{ch} 6^{d}½ Tobac. 1^{s} - - -	0 - 2 - 7½
	1 - 4 - 4½

2^{d} Week

8 to 15.

Brd w 12^{s} Ridg^{w} H bill. 9^{s}-½^{d} H. bill. 4^{s}-9^{d} - - -	1 - 5 - 9½
Wash. 1^{s}-1^{d} Chair 8^{d}½ --19. Din^{r} Shrd^{n}. 1^{s}-8^{d} - - -	0 - 3 - 5½
Din^{r}. Mar^{l}. 2^{s}-2^{d} - - -	

3^{d} Week

15 to 22^{d}

Brd w. 12^{s} Charw. 1^{s}-1^{d} H. bill 3^{s} - - -	0 - 16- 1
Chair &c 1^{s} --27. Ch^{r}. 6^{d}½ - - -	0 - 1 - 6½

4th Week

22 to 29.

Brd w 12^{s}. Meat 6^{s}-1^{d} Meat. 2^{s}-10^{d} - - -	1 - 0 -11
Wash. 1^{s}-1^{d} Char. 1^{s}-1^{d} Por^{tr}. 2^{d} H. bill. 6^{s}-5^{d}½ - - -	0 - 8 - 9
Arrear to Sican. 1^{s}-2^{d} --31. Din^{r} Ma^{r} 2^{s}-2^{d} Ch^{r}. 8^{d} - - -	0 - 3 -11

[6v]

Expences

April

3^{d} Month

1st Week

1 to ⟨to⟩ 5th

Brd w. 12^{s}. Ch^{r}. 6^{d}½ ⟨ ⟩ Lett^{r}. 4^{d} - - - 0 - 12-10½
--3. Din^{r} Ma^{r} &c 14^{s}-4^{d} more 3^{s}-9^{d}½ in all - - - 0 - 18- 1½
Wash. 1^{s}-1^{d} Meat 1^{s}-7^{d}½

2^{d} Week.

5 to 12.

Brd w. 12^{s}. 7--Ch^{r}. 10^{d} meat. 3^{s}-6^{d} H. bill 7^{s}-2^{d}½ - - - 1 - 3 - 6½
Lett^{rs} 1^{s}-4^{d} Wash. 1^{s}-1^{d}

3^{d} Week

12 to 19

Brd w. 12^{s} ^meat ---4^{s} ½ sm^{ll}. 1^{d}½ H. bill 5^{s}½^{d}
Wash. 1^{s}-1^{d}. Record^{r}. 3^{s}-8

4th Week

19 to 26.

Brd w. ^12^{s} ⟨1st⟩ H. bill. 1^{s}-6 Lett^{r} 4^{d} Wash. 1^{s}-1^{d}

Remd^{r}

Brd w 5^{s}. Meat 3^{s}-7^{d}½ Wash. 6^{d}
Forgot. 1^{s}

Totalls

Third Quarter

From May. 1st. 1735 to Aug. 1st 1735

Cloaths

May. 17. 4 Hankrchfs. 10^{s}. May. Make. 11 Hanch^{r}. 2^{s}. - - - 0 - 12- 0
Hanch^{fs} bought. May. wrisb Shirt 3^{d} --1^{d}½. Cloth. 3^{s}-4^{d}. - - - 0 - 3 - 8½
Jul. 17. Breches 2 pair Cloth. 1^{ll}-6-4 mak.

Servants Cloaths

May. 1. Cloath &c. 8^{ll}-9^{d}

Extr^{dys}

Dogs. 6^{d} Cob^{lr}. 6^{d} Dogs 6^{d} May. 20. Chips 6^{d} Dogs 6^{d}
May 23^{d} Tobac. 1^{s} Dog. 6^{d} May. Ging^{r} br^{d} 2^{s}-2^{d}. Sug^{r}. 6^{s}-11^{d}
May. 4 Oyl. 1^{s}-6^{d} Ink 6^{d} Dog. 6^{d} Jun. 15. Watch clean^{d} 2^{s}-2^{d}
Liquerice 6^{d} Dogs 6^{d} Jun 27. Carrw^{ys}. 5^{d}½ Dog 6^{d} :1^{s}
Tobac 1^{s} Dogs 6^{d} Dog. Doc^{tr}. 6^{d}½ Dog. 6^{d} Cards. 1^{s}-1^{d}. Dog 6^{d}
Dog sick 8^{d} --Jul. 24. Brandy 2^{s}-2^{d} --Brandy for Cherrys &c. &c. - - - 1 - 5 - 4
Brandy Rasbrys &c

Horses.

May. 2^{d}. Turn^{p}. 6^{d}. Boy 5^{d} Stable. 8^{d} Stabling. &c 1^{s}
May. 16. Smith 6^{s} --Turnp. 6^{d}. Stabl^{ig} 9^{d} Boy 3^{d}
Jul. 12th. Smith 6^{s} Sm^{ll} 2^{d}. Turnp. 3^{d}

⟨May.⟩ Expences. 3. R.

May. 7 R. 12 miles 1st Month

First Week

1 to 10

B^{rd} w. ⟨12^{s}⟩ ^ ⟨1^{11}-4^{s}-0⟩ 19^{s} 1. Meat 5^{s}-10^{d}½ Meat &c 4^{s} Wash. 7^{d}
H. Bill 6^{s}-6^{d} Wash. 1^{s}-1^{d}

2^{d} Week.

10 to 17

B^{rd} w 12^{s} 12 Sican din^{r}. 2^{s}-2^{d} Din^{r} $Whit^{w}$. 2^{s}-2^{d}
$Lett^{r}$. 4^{d} Wash. 1^{s}-1^{d}. H. bill. 3^{s}-7^{d}

3^{d} Week

B^{rd} 17 to 24

B^{rd} w. . . . 2 din^{rs}. 14^{s}-10^{d} H. bill. 9^{s}-1^{d}
Latt. 4^{d} Wash. 1^{s}-1^{d} ⟨Wash. 1^{s}-1^{d}⟩

4th Week 27th. a Vomit. 28. 30. 31 rode

24 to 31st

B^{rd} w. 12^{s}. Meat &c -3^{s}-10^{d} H. Bill 13^{s}-6^{d}
$Lett^{r}$ 1^{s}. Wash 1^{s}-1^{d} Blue &c. 1^{s}-1^{d}.

June.

2^{d} Month

First week.

May. 31. to June 8

Brd w

--2 Lett^{r}. 6^{d} --5. Chair 10^{d} --4 Ld Ham^{lt} din^{r} 15^{s}-8^{d}
H. bill 12^{s}-1^{d} Wash 1^{s}-1^{d}. H. bil 4^{s}-10^{d}

2^{d} Week

8 to 15

Brd w 12^{s} --11 Ch^{r}. 6^{d}½ H. bill 7^{s}-1^{d}½ Lett^{r}. 4^{d}
Wash. 1^{s}-1^{d}

3^{d} Week

15 to 21.

Brd w 12^{s}. 19th. Whit^{w} din^{r}. 2^{s}-2^{d} H. bill 8^{s}. Lett^{rs}. 10^{d}
wash. 1^{s}-1^{d} Mrs Sican 4^{s}-7^{d} more 10^{s}-3^{d}

4th Week

21 to 28

Brd w. 12^{s} H. Bill ⟨13^{s} 14^{s}.⟩ Wash. 1^{s}-1^{d} Mrs Sican 3^{s}-½

Remd^{r}

28 to Jul. 1. Mrs Sican 11^{s}-2^{d}. More 8^{s}-4^{d} Chick^{n}. 6^{d}
Brd w . . . .

July. 3^{d} Month

1st Week

1 to ⟨6^{d}⟩ 5

Brd w. 12^{s}. --Chair 1^{s}-1^{d} H. bill. 6^{s}-5^{d} 6^{s}-5
--2. Chickens 1^{s}

2^{d} Week

⟨6 to 13.⟩ 5 to 12
rogue
Brd w. 10^{s}-6 Stopt ⟨H. Bill⟩ --7^{d} Co^{ch} 6^{d}½
White^{w}. Din^{r}. 2^{s}-2^{d} --12. Chair 8^{d}½ --5. Chickens. 1^{s}. 9. Mutton. 8^{d}
Meat. 2^{s}-8^{d} Lett^{r}. 6^{d} Wash. 1^{s}-1^{d} H bill. 5^{s}-10^{d}

3^{d} Week

12 to 19

Brd w 12^{s} --13. Meat 3^{s}-4^{d}. H. bill 7^{s}-8^{d} Cha^{r}. 1^{s}-1^{d}

3^{d} Week --22^{d} Rode.

19 to 26

Brd w. 12^{s} --23 Sand 1^{s}. House bill. 4^{s}-2^{d} Sm^{ll}. 1^{d}
--30. Chair rain. 1^{s}-1^{d} ⟨H. bill 6^{s}-4^{d}⟩ H. bill. to Aug 2^{d} 6^{s}-4^{d}
Chair 1^{s}-1^{d} lett^{r}. 4^{d} Lett^{r}. 4^{d}

Totals

Of a Quarter from May. 1. 1735 to August 1. 1735

Fourth Quarter

From Aug. 1. 1735 to Novr. 1. 1735 ~

Cloaths

Aug. 1. Shoes. 11^{s}-6^{d} Aug 4 line whole wast coats 2^{s} Aug. Breeches
mend Boots 2^{d} Aug. 21. Night-gown Stuft &c. 1^{ll}-3^{s}-10
making Night-gown. making. 2^{s}-6 Sep^{t}. 9. Gloves 5^{s}-5^{d}
Sep^{tr}. Stockins 1^{ll}-8^{s}. run Stockins 9^{d} Girdle 2^{s}-2^{d} flannel. 6^{d}

Serv^{ts} Cloths

Aug. 26. Servant shoes & Stockins 7^{s}-6^{d} mend. Britchs 1^{s}-1^{d}
stockins 3^{s}-3^{d} Oc^{tb}. 31. great Coats Cloth 2^{ll}-1-1

Extra^{rdys}

Aug. 6. Tobac. 1^{s}. Dog. 6 Dog. 6^{d}. Poud^{r} & shot 6^{d}½ Dog 6^{d}
Dog 6^{d} Card. 4^{d} Dog. 6^{d} Dogs 6^{d} Dog. 6^{d}. Chips 6^{d} Dogs 6^{d}
Sep^{t}. 20. Ging^{r} br^{d} 2^{s}-2^{d}. Oc^{tb}. 7. Snuff 2^{s} Dog. 6^{d}. Oc^{tr}. 14. Blew. 1^{s}
Carr^{ws}. 7^{d} Dog. 6^{d}. Oc^{tr}. 17. Chips 6^{d} Dog. 6^{d} Dirt 1^{s}-1
Oc^{tb}. 28 Seal wax. 1^{s}-3^{d}. Pags 8^{d}½

Horses.

Tav^{rn} &c 4^{d} - - - 0 - 0 - 4
Aug. 1st for 20 load of Hay - - - 4 - 10- 0
--Bringing in Hay &c 6^{s}-1^{d} to Charles. Stabl^{ig}. 6^{d}
<Dogs 6^{d}> Oyl 9^{d} Smith 6^{s} Sep^{t}. 10th mend whip 6^{d}½
Oc^{tr} 25. Smith 6^{s}.

Expences.

August. 8. R. 19. R. 11. R. 1st Month

1 to 9. Brd w. 12^{s} --2. Ch^{r}. 6^{d}½ Meat 7^{s} - - - 0 - 19- 6½
Bill. 7^{s}-11^{d}½ Cha^{r}. 1^{s}-1^{d} - - -

2^{d}. Week.

9 to 16

B^{r} w. 12^{s} Lett 4^{d} Cha^{r}. 1^{s}-1^{d} H. bill 3^{s}-6^{d} - - - 0 - 16-11
Meat. 11^{d}

3^{d} Week.

16 to 23.

Brd w. 12^{s}. Brd w 12 H. bill 7^{s}

4th Week. R. 25: 29th.

23 to 30th

Brd w. 12^{s} H. Bill. 7^{s}-8^{d}½. Cha^{r}. 1^{s}-1^{d}

Expences.

Septemb^{r}. 2^{d} Month

1st Week.

1 to 6

Brd w. 12^{s} 4. Chair 8^{d}½. H. bill 4^{s}-3^{d}½
Char. 1^{s}-1^{d} Meat. 1^{s}-9^{d}½

2^{d} Week.

6 to 13.

Brd w. 12^{s} --12. Co^{ch} 8^{d}. H. bill 5^{s}-7^{d}½
Lett^{r}. 1^{s} Char. 1^{s}-1^{d}

3^{d} Week

13 to 20

Brd w. 12^{s}. H. bill -6^{s}-6^{d}½ Char. 1^{s}-1^{d}

4 Week

20 to 27th

Brd w. 12^{s} Ch^{r}. 10^{d} H bill. 5^{s}-4^{d}½ Lett^{rs} 10^{d} Char. 1^{s}-1^{d}
Bief 2^{s} Meat 4^{s}-3^{d} 3^{d}

Rem^{dr}

27 to Oc^{tb}. 1.

Brd w. . . . meat 5^{s}-1^{d} Ridg. din^{r} 6^{d}½

October | Expences | 3^d Month

1st. Week

1 to 4 Meat 3^s-3^d½ 3. Ch^r. 8^d - - - 0 - 3 -11½
B^{rd} w 12^s

2^d Week

<Oc^{tb}>4 to 11.
B^{rd} w. 12^s. Meat. 1^s-7 --7. Chair. 1^s-1^d - - - 0 - 14- 8
Chair 6^d½ $Lett^{rs}$ 1^s-4^d <H. bill. 6^s-4^d½. $Lett^{rs}$. 1^s-4> 0 - 1 -10½
H. bill 7^s-01½ Char. 1^s-1^d

3^d Week

11 to 18 Rice 3^d½ Meat 3^s-½ House bill 6^s-3^d
B^{rd} w. 12^s. $Lett^r$ 4^d. Wash. 1^s-1^d Chair. 6^d½

4th Week.

18 to 25.
B^{rd} w. 12^s Meat 3^s-2^d. H. bill 3^s-7 Char. 1^s-1^d
< >

25. to Novr. 1. $Remd^r$.
B^{rd} w. . . .
29. Chair. 8^d. Meat. 4^s-8^d.

Jul. 17th. 1735

Pd to Mr Morgan officer of the Commons for warning a Committe about Setling the piece of ground in Oxmantown Green for my Hospital to be built on - - - 0 - 6 - 8

July 17. 1735 Eatan the Glaziers Receit - - - 1 - 14- 6

Aug. 1st Keating, House Paintr &c - - - 8 - 0 - 0

--11 Laughlin's Receit Windows - - - 0 - 3 - 3

Carpenter for Step-ladder - - - 0 - 19- 3

Articles

Of Annuityes and other larger gifts from

Novr. 1st 1734 to Nov^{r}, 1st 1735 ———

M F

DD.

P^{d} at 4 times - - - 52 - 0 - 0

Christmas.

Whiteway. 1^{ll}. Ridgw. 5^{s}-5^{d} Ser^{vts} din^{r} 2^{s}-8^{d}½ DD 11^{s}-6^{d} - - - 1 - 19- 7½

⟨Wom^{n}⟩ Ser^{ts} 6^{s}-8^{d} Wom^{ns} Livery 14^{s} Half week 2^{s}-8^{d}½ 1 - 2 - 8½

⟍and & wife 16^{s}-3^{d}. Kenrick 10^{s}-10^{d} Apple wom^{n}. 1^{s}-1^{d} 1 - 8 - 2

Taylor. 1^{s}-1^{d} Smith. 2^{s}-2^{d} frgt. 2^{s}-2^{d} Mar^{s} men 1^{s}-1^{d} --2^{s}-2^{d} 0 - 8 - 8

Miss Harrison 15^{s} Miss Surstrn Cogue 2^{s}-6^{d} Mrs Ham^{l} 5^{s}-5^{d} 1 - 2 -11

Malheureuse. 11^{s}-6^{d} Turnpike. 2^{s}-2^{d}. begg^{r}. 6^{d}½ - - - 0 - 14- 2½

6 - 16- 3½

Great G--ts

At Grattans. No^{r}. 16 6^{s}-6^{d} Ser^{vnts} ^&c 5^{s}-6^{d} - - - 0 - 12- 0

De^{b}. 4th Grange 2-12^{s}-6^{d} Ach. 1^{s}-1^{d} --19. Mr Hamil^{n} Venson 5^{s}-5^{d} - - - 2 - 19- 0

Dec^{b}. Nurse D^{r} 5^{s}-5^{d} ⟨ ⟩Ja^{nr}. 17. O Bryan 5 Pris^{rs} 5^{s}-5 - - - 0 - 10-10

Feb. 6th. Mrs Whit^{w}. 1^{ll}-10^{s}-6^{d}½ Miss G. Parke G. 12^{s}-10^{d} - - - 2 - 13- 4

Mar. 18th - Nurs. daugh^{r}. 5^{s}-5^{d} Apr. 1. Yong Fitz H^{r}. 11^{s}-6^{d} - - - 0 - 16-11

May. 14 Malheureuse 10^{s}-10. ⟨ ⟩Jun. 20 Mrs Blackall 5^{s}-5 - - - 0 - 16- 3

Jun. 18th. Nurse d^{r}. 5^{s}-5^{d}. Jun. 30th. Dr Steevens. 15^{s}.

Jul. 16. Malheureuse. 1^{ll}-3^{s}. Aug. 22^{d} Miss Molly books. 8^{s} 1 - 11- 0

Aug. 29. Whit^{w}'s boy 1^{ll}-3^{s}. Oct^{b}. 2^{d} Whit^{w} Lett^{r}. Vicars fee 10^{s}-10 1 - 13-10

Oct^{b}. 17. Mr Throp 5^{ll}-15^{s}. Oct^{br}. 19 M^{r}.Ledwidge 1^{ll}-4^{s} - - - 6 - 19- 0

Oc^{tb}. 29th. Malheureuse. 1^{ll}-3^{s} - - - 1 - 3 - 0

M^{rs}. W$^{tway's}$ boy.

For Jun. 1. 1^{ll}-3^{s}

Wine

Sm^{ll} 6^{d}½
Dec^{b}. Chassalic Wine. 4^{ll}-5^{s}-8^{d}
W. 2 Hogsh^{ds} from D^{r}. H--
Ja^{r}. 31. p^{d} Dr Hel^{sh} Part of 34^{ll}. 17^{ll}. p^{d}p^{d} more 17^{ll}. - - - 34 - 0 - 0
M^{r}. Hall - 10^{ll}-1^{s} Feb. 18. Shiel 14^{ll} p^{d} p^{d} more 24 - 0 - 0
⟨Feb^{r}. 26 M. Wine 3 doz. pints⟩
Mar. 15. 1734. Shilis Bill for Wine & Mountain &c - - - 3 - 3 - 0
⟨Mr Parry⟩ Shiel Oc^{tb}. 27^{ll}-16^{s}-7^{d} - - - 27 - 16 - 7

Corks. Bottles. Porters &c

Sm^{ll} 6^{d}½
De^{cb}. 18. Bottles. 1^{ll}-3^{s} Por^{tr}. 1^{s} Corks 2^{s}. Sawdust. 10^{d} - - - 1 - 6 - 10
Febr. 18 Por^{tr}. 10^{d} Saw-dust 10^{d} Por^{tr}. 6^{d}
Febr. 26. Por^{tr} 6^{d} ‸May --23 & 26th Corks. 13^{s}-6^{d}
May 23 & 26. Mr Parrys 2 Hogsh^{ds} bottle^{d} 10^{s}-10^{d}
Coopers man 1^{s}-1^{d}. May 21. Corks. 1^{s}-3^{d} Corks 2^{s} Corks 14^{s}
Corks 1^{s} Porters 1^{s}-8^{d}. Corks 1^{s}-3^{d} Coop^{r} ale 4^{d}½ Corks. 1^{s}-3^{d}
Jun. 14 1736 p^{d} in Arrear for Bottles to Mrs Acheson on accont - - - 1 - 10 - 0

Dean^{ry} Charges and Repairs

Wnds. ⟨10^{s}⟩ 28 Sash Windows repair^{d} 4^{s}-5^{d}½ - - - 0 - 4 - 5½
Dc^{br}. 14. Chimny 10^{d} Mend locks. 1^{s}-6^{d} Febr. 25. dirt man 1^{s} - - - 0 - 3 - 4
Mar. 3. Sweep Chim. 6^{d}½ Mar 13. Kitch^{n} Chimy 10^{d} Mar. 10th Brooms 1^{s}-1^{d} 0 - 2 - 8½
Sm^{ll}. 6^{d}½ Bell-Spring 6^{d} 11^{d} Nails 3^{d} Jun. 17th Pump. 1^{ll}-14^{s}-2^{d} more 3^{s}-4^{d} - - - 1 - 19 - 0
Key 6^{d} Jul. 14. Lamp money. 11^{s}-^{d}. Sep^{t}. 1st paver 16^{s}-7^{d}½ - - - 0 - 18 - 2
Mend Grates 2^{s}-8^{d}½ Matts 1^{s}-2^{d} lock mend 4^{d} Puding bag. 5^{d}
Barl. 2^{d}

Houshold good

Houshold goods

Apr. 6. Brush^{s} 8^{d} Apr 14. Napkins & making 11^{s}-11^{d} A crock. 1^{s}-2^{d} - - 0 - 13 - 9
Jun. 9. China 6^{s} --Tin pot 10^{d} Jun 9th China tea &c. 6^{s}-11^{d} China 6^{s}-11^{d} - - - 0 - 19 - 8
Jun. Jul. 12. Plates 2^{s}-4^{d} --12 Mops. 2^{s}-8^{d}

Houshold goods ⟨Garden & Vineyard⟩

Tub men^{d} 4^{d} Hamp^{r} 3^{d}. Brooms 5^{d} Jan^{r}. 11. Ladle drug box &c 11^{d} - - 0 - 1 - 11
Jan^{r}. 16. 12 Wa^{r} glasses and dishes 8^{s}. Mnd Jack. 4^{s}-6^{d} --17 Ch. p^{ts} 1^{s}-6^{d} - - - 0 - 14 - 0
Ja^{nr}. 28. Mop. 1^{s}-1^{d} Locks &c 2^{s}-4^{d} key &c. 10^{d}. Turn Sheets 10^{d} - - 0 - 5 - 3
Oc^{tb}. 20. Glasses 2 doz. 15^{s}-3^{d}

Visitation Dinn^{r} - - - Ja^{nr}. 13th 1734-5 - - - 7 - 0 - 8

H. Goods added

Jul. 23^{d} Sweeping Brush 2^{s}-4^{d}⟨ ⟩Scouring Brush 1^{s}-6^{d}

[14v]

Defalcations from Deanry

Tallow Chancl repd annually - - - 0 - 10- 0

Defalcations from Laracor &c.

Mr Lightburn
School-mas^{tr} of Trim - - - 0 - 10- 2

Defalcations from Rath-beggan

Mr Jourdan for May. 1. 1734. - - - 8 - 0 - 0

La Chicane.

Feb. 5. Attorny. 3^{ll}-9^{s}

Fee Record^{r} Mar. 16 Mr Hale. 11^{s}-6^{d} ⟨ ⟩ Sklt^{on} 1-3^{s}

Mar. 24. to Kenrick for drawing lease to Dr Wilson - - - 0 - 11- 6

Jul. 8th. ⟨Jul. 8th⟩ 1735 P^{d} Mr Hale for entring ⟨Dr Sheri^{d}⟩ the
Judgmt on Sr W. Fowns Bond on Apr. 2^{d}. 1735 in Exchek^{r} 1^{ll}-14-2^{d}
and G ⟨to⟩ as gratis 5^{s}-10^{d} - - in all - - - 2 - 0 - 0

More Wine. 1735

May. 24. to Shiell 1^{ll}-7^{s}-3^{d}

Physick

For my self and Servants

To Mr Staunt^{n} in all 13^{s}-6^{d}½ Fe^{br}. 8. Surge^{n} 11^{s}-6^{d}

Brewing

Brew. Feb. 12th Hops &c. 2^{s}-2^{d} Mar. 29th. mend Vessel 2^{s}

Mar. 27. Hops. 2^{s}. Yest. 2^{d}. Woman 1^{s}-1^{d}. Rp^{d} mault Arrear 1^{ll}-4-9 1 - 8 - 0

Garden & Vineyard

Mar. 8. Nails 1^{s}-10^{d} Prun^{ig} &c 10^{s} ⟨Gard^{nr}⟩ Labo^{r} 10^{d}

Apr. 8. Hows 1^{s}-8^{d} Weed. 1^{s}-1^{d} sm^{ll} 2^{d} Nails 1^{s}-9^{d}

Prune knife 1^{s}-1^{d} Stone 3^{d} Aug. 20 Landry Arrear. 2^{s}-6^{d}

ground near Vineyard wall

May. 24th. P^{d} on account 10^{s}-10^{d} Jul. weed 10^{d} Nails 4^{d}

Sep^{t}. 3^{d} (A Cheat) Nayles 15^{s}-7^{d} Summ^{r} pruing &c

Sep^{t}. Scyth. 2^{s}-8^{d}

Interest for Wages.

Febr. 27th p^{d} the Woman 7^{s}-6^{d}

Memd Moves

Co^{ch}. &c 4^{s}-4^{d}

Taxes and Cesses

Jan^{r}. Kilmain^{m}. 11^{d} --Naboth. 5^{d}

May. 30. Scaveng^{r} 5. Orphans 8^{s}-5½

Jul. 10. Kilmain^{m} Cess. 2^{s}-11^{d} July. 18th. Kil^{m}. 3^{d}

Sep^{tb}. 2^{d} P^{d} for that dog Swan Chimny 4^{s} --Lights. 3^{s}

Oc^{tb}. 7. Kilmain. 1^{s}-1^{d}

Soap and Candles

Aug. 12 Soap and blue. 3^{s}-10^{d} --20 Candles 3^{s}

Oct^{b}. 11th. Soap 1^{ll}-14-2

Deanry set for 1734

N^{r}. 1. Andrews Jo^{n} - - -	4^{ll}	X
2 Ascune Jo^{n} - - -	11^{ll}	X
3 ⟨arr⟩ Barret Mic^{hl} - - -	14^{s}	
4. Barret Mic^{l} - - -	1^{ll}	
5 Bellew James - - -	6^{s}	
6 Bellew Chris^{t} - - -	3^{ll}	
7 Berming^{m} Math - - -	2^{ll}	
8. Berming^{m}. Will - - -	5^{s}	
9 Bottom Tho - - -	4^{ll}	
10. Bottom Jo^{n} - - -	4^{ll}	

Deanry. - 1734

N^{r}. 11th	Brangan Law^{r}.- - -	4^{s}-6^{d}	
12.	Brown Henr - - -	1^{11}	
13.	Brown Oliv^{r} - - -	2^{s}-2^{d}	
14	Byrn Ed^{m} - - -	2^{s}-8^{d}½	
15	Byrn Garr^{t} - - - Feb. 24. 1734. Rx full - - -	6^{11}	6 - 0 - 0
16.	Byrn Edm. - - -	2^{s}-8^{d}½	
17.	Byrn Tedy, & Jam. Eager	18^{s}-6^{d}	
18.	Byrn Pat^{r}. - - -	8^{s}-6^{d}	
19	Carol. Ter - - -	8^{s}-1½	
20	Cavan Jo^{n} - - -	1^{11}-10^{s}	
21	Colcot Sam - - -	9^{11} X	

Deanry for 1734.

N^r. 22.	Coleman. Jo^n - - -	10^s	
23	Corbill. Chri^r for Mr Reddy - - -	13^{ll}-15^s	
24.	Cougland Edw. & Chester. Jo^n - - -	4^s-4^d	
25	Chagneau Esqr - - -	6^{ll}	
26	Costello Darby - - -	8^s-1½	
27	Coughlin Edw - - -	5^s	
28	Conolly Rich - - -	10^s-6^d	
29	Cullen Jo^n - - -	9^s-3^d	
30	Curry Hew. for W. Curry - - - Febr. 25th 1734. Rx full - - -	1^{ll}-15^s	1 - 15- 0
31	Coyl Pat^r - - -	12^s	
32	Dillon Jo^n - - -	13^s	

Deanry 1734.

N^{r}. 33. Dillon Cath. - - - 12^{11}

34. Dod. W^{m} & Pat^{r} - - - 3^{11}

~~34~~ 35⟩ Dogherty. Bryan & Hogan - - - 3^{11}-2^{s}

~~35~~ 36⟩ Doyl. Alice - - - 10^{s}

~~36~~ 37⟩ Doyl Jo^{n} - - - 3^{11}

38 Eager Jam - - - 2^{s}-8^{d}½

39 Ellis Pat^{r} - - - 4^{s}-6^{d}

40 Emmerson Jo^{n} - - - 3^{11}-5^{s}

41. Emmerson Jo^{n} - - - 1^{11}-10^{s}

42 Eustace Chrs^{t}. & T Divine - - - 11^{s}

⟨X Eleaz^{r}. - - - 8^{11}⟩ Rath^{b}
Mar. 14th 1734 Rx full - - -

8 - 0 - 0

[18v]

Deanry. 1734

N^{r}. 43. Farrell Sim - - - 18^{s}

44 Faulkn^{r} Jo^{n}. Esqr - - - 1^{ll}-17^{s}
Mar. 14th. 1734. Rx full - - - 1 - 17- 0

45 Fitzsimons Ch. - - - 5^{s}-5^{d}

46 Fulham - - - 16^{s}

47. Font Tho - - - 8^{s}

48 Gibton Mich - - - 3^{ll}

49 Gibton Will - - - 8^{ll}

50. Grumly Pat^{r} - - - 3^{s}

51. Harny Hugh - - - 1^{ll}-

52. Hart And - - - 4^{ll}

Deanry. 1734

N^{r}. 53.	Hedan Jo^{n}. & Reyly - - -	6^{s}	
54.	Hewson W^{m} - - -	6^{ll}-15^{s}	
55.	Hilliard W^{m} - - -	1^{ll}-3^{s}	
56	Hill Tho. - - -	10^{s}	
57	Hilland Luke - - -	6^{s} X	
58	Hilliard Pet^{r} - - -	1^{ll}-10^{s}	
59	Hoey Tho. - - -	3-10^{s}	
60	Hoey Nich - - -	1^{ll}-	
61.	Hoyl Bart^{h} - - -	10^{s}	
62.	Hudson Ed^{m} - - -	3^{ll}-5^{s}	
	Febr. 25th. 1734. Rx full - - -		3 - 5 - 0
63	Hughs Jo^{n} - - -	1^{ll}	
	Febr. 25th. 1734 Rx full - - -		1 - 0 - 0

Deanery. 1734

N^r. 64.	Jackson Ch. - - -	16^s-3^d
65	Jordan Tho - - -	2^s-8^{d}½
66	Karny W^m - - -	8^s-6^d
67	Kering Morgan - - -	2^{ll}-5^s
68	Kegan Marg^t - - -	11^s
69	Kernan Jo^n - - -	5^s-5^d
70	Kelly Jo^n - - -	18^s
71.	Kenedy Jo^n - - -	2^{ll}-10^s
72.	Kensellah Jo^n - - -	8^s-1½ X
73	King Pat^r - - -	2^s-8^{d}½

Deanry. 1734

N^r. 74	Lawler Dan - - -	2^s-8^d½	
75	Lawler Math - - -	1^{ll}-15^s	
76	Lenan J^n. Tool Nich - - -	11^s-6^d	
77.	Lenan Ter - - -	13^s	
78	Lewis $Chris^r$ - - -	5^s-5^d	
79	Lyons Jer^m - - -	3^{ll}	
80	Lyons Jo^n - - -	7^s	
81.	Madden Edm - - -	2^{ll}	
	Mar. 14th. 1734. Rx full - - -		2 - 0 - 0
82	Madden Jo^n - - -	6^s	
83	$Mcalest^r$ & Stones - - -	1^{ll}-10^s X	

Deanry 1734

N^r. 84.	Martin Pat^r - - -	6^{ll}
85	Martin Pat^r - - -	3^s
86	Mathews Jo^n - - -	3^{ll}
87	Mathews Jo^n. R. Moor - - -	8^s
88.	Mathews Jam - - -	5^s-5^d
89	Mitchell Jo^n - - -	16^s-3^d
90.	Moony Owen - - -	2^s
91.	M^ccan Hugh - - -	1^{ll}-10^s
92	Moor Laur - - -	2^{ll}-15^s

Deanry 1734

N^r. 93. Moran Edm - - -	8^s
94. Moran Tho. - - -	2^s-8^d½
95 Moor Lewis - - -	1^{ll}-
96. Moorhouse Robt - - -	1^{ll}-10^s
97 Mullaly Pat^r - - -	7^s
98 Mullaly Ed^m & Conner - - -	8^s-1½
99 Murphy Jo^n - - -	1^{ll}-12^s
100 Murphy Jo^n - - -	5^{ll}-10^s
101. Murphy Pat^r - - -	2^{ll}-12^s-6^d X
102 Murphy David - - -	9^s

Deanry. 1734

N^{r}. 103 Murphy W^{m} - - - 3^{ll}-15^{s}

104 Murry Jam. - - - 5^{s}

105. Nugent Laur - - - 2^{ll}-10^{s}

106 Newman Tho. & J. Bottom 8^{ll}-10^{s}

107. Nowland Pat^{r} - - - 8^{ll}-0

108 Potter Robt - - - 11^{ll}

109 Power $Chris^{t}$. - - - 2^{ll}-6^{s}

110 Pearson Jo^{n} - - - 8^{ll}

111 Prat Jo^{n} Esqr - - - 2^{ll}-5^{s}
Mar. 14th. 1734. Rx full - - - 2 - 5 - 0

112. Purcel Mich - - - 2^{s}-$8^{d}\frac{1}{2}$

Deanry 1734

N^{r}. 113.	Quin Pat^{r} - - -	13^{11}	
114	Quin Pet^{r} - - -	18^{11}	
	Mar. 14th. 1734. Rx on account - - -		12 - 0 - 0
115	Quin Jam. - - -	5^{11}	
116.	Reddy Geo For D. Reddy - - -	5^{11}	
117	Reynolds Pat^{r} - - -	9^{11}	
118	Reynolds Jon - - -	11^{11}	
119	Roan Tho - - -	1^{11}-15^{s}	
120	Robinson Jo^{n} - - -	2 -10^{s}	
121	Row Hugh - - -	6^{11}-10^{s}	

Deanry 1734

N^r 122 - Sands Pat^r - - - 3^{ll}-9^s

123. Savage Tho - - - 12^s-6^d

124. Seaman Paul. and Brooks 2^{ll}-10^s

125 $Sheph^d$ W^m. Esqr - - - 26^{ll}--

126 Slattry Law & Cullen - - - 11^s-6^d

127 Strong Ric^d - - - 9^s--

128- Stubbs Robt. - - - 2^s-$8^d\frac{1}{2}$

129 Sturges Cha^l - - - 6^{ll}-10^s

130 Ternon Pat^r - - - 5^s

131. Ternon Pat^r - - - 2^s-$8^d\frac{1}{2}$

Deanry 1734

N^{r}. 132.	Tool James - - -	1^{ll}-3^{s}	
133.	Tool Jo^{n} & Francis - - -	7^{ll}--	
134	Tint James Esqr - - -	10^{ll}	
	Febr. 25th 1734 - - -		10 - 0 - 0
135	Vigneau for Capt Chenevix - - -	1^{ll}-3^{s}	
136	Wak^{e}ley Tho Esqr - - -	6^{ll}	
137	Ward Jam - - -	5^{s}-5^{d}	
138	Williams Tho - - -	13^{s}	

Disputed

Arch Bishops Tyths valued - - -	9 - 0 - 0
Shaw Ed^{m}. Claym^{d} by Mr Kane - - -	1 - 10- 0
Wilson Jos - says not in my Parish - - -	0 - 15- 0
	11 - 5 - 0

Names that gave no Bonds. 1734 Payd

Dry W^{m} - - -	p^{d} - - -	1 - 8 - 6
Masham Ric^{d}. - - -		1 - 5 - 0
⟨Moor⟩ Rourke Edm^{d} - - -		1 - 10- 0
Savage James - - -		0 - 11- 6
Coleman Jo^{n} - - -		1 - 3 - 0
Heffernon - - -		0 - 15- 0
Mr Bodkin - - -		0 - 8 - 1½
Nicholson Jam - - -		0 - 3 - 3
Purcell W^{m} - - -		0 - 2 - 8½
Clinton Alex^{dr} - - -		0 - 2 - 2
Murphy Pat^{r} - - -		0 - 4 - 4
Dempsy Robt - - -		0 - 4 - 4
		7 - 17-11

Rathbeggan. the like. 1734

Coll^{ns} Kerr - - -	0 - 16- 3
Corbelly Elias - - -	0 - 4 - 4
Wilson James - - -	0 - 4 - 4

These ⟨two⟩ above Paym^{ts} are part of a long Bill of money received by me which came to in all to - - - 161 - 14- 0

All which I have entred in my severall Books as received.

Febr. 7th. 1734-5. J: S.
I gave my Receit for 61 - 12 - 4 as receivd the same day, and likewise entred the Names. J. S

Rathbeggan. 1734

N^{r}			
1.	Brewer Rich^{d} - - -	1^{ll}-10^{s}	
2	Cardiff Tho - - -	13^{s}-6^{d}	
3	Cook. Jo^{n}. and Tho^{m} - - -	3 -5^{s}	
4	Pearson. Eleaz^{r}. - - -	8^{ll}--	
	March. 14th. 1734. Rx full - - -		8 - 0 - 0
5	Fleming Martin - - -	1^{ll}-18^{s}	
6	Lacy Pierce - - -	12^{s}	
7	Martin Jo^{n} - - -	8^{ll}--	
8.	Royne Chris^{tr} - - -	3^{ll}	
9.	Stanly Mar^{tn} - - -	4^{s}-4^{d}	
10	White Nich - - -	7^{ll}-10^{s}	

[24v]

1735 23[11]
June 17th ^ Rx from Mr R. Grattan as Proctor - - - 2 - -

Payments of Arrears

upon Account. From Dr Wilson

A. D. 1735

My 1 By Mr Farrell.	
June ⟨ ⟩17th. 1735 More by Kenrick - - -	27 - 0 - 0
Dc^{br}. 19th. 1735. Mr Clynch - - -	40 - 0 - 0

Deanry Land-rent for 1734

Fe^{br}. 3^{d}. 1735-6 Receiv^{d} from Mr Stopford by M^{r}
to make up
Dan Brown. a years rent for Michlmas 1735 - - - 170 - 0 - 0
<Febr 24th 1735 Rc^{d} from Mr Al^{dr} Pearson ½ year
for Michls 1735 - - - 40 - 0 - 0>
Febr. 24 1736 Rx from Mr Pearson for Michlm^{s} 1735 40 - 0 - 0

Deanry Groundrents

Apr. 1st. Rc^{d} from ^Morgan <Morg> 2 y^{r} Rent due L^{dy} Day 1724 - - - 5 - 0 - 0
Aug. 25 1735 Rx ½ years rent for Goodmans - - - 5 - 0 - 0
holding, due last Mi^{chlms}1734 - -
Jan^{r}. 12. Connly a year due Michl^{ms} last 1735 - - - 9 - 0 - 0
<Jan^{r}. 12 Trim Mr Cope due Octbr 5th 1735 1 year and half - - - 36 - 0 - 0>

Perquisits

Apr. 6^{d}. Lease. 11^{s}-8^{d} --Lease ½ fees. 5^{s}-10^{d} - - - 0 - 17- 6
Oct^{br}. 1. A Vicar 10^{s}-10^{d}

Interest

Mar. 8th From Mr Nugent ½ a years interest
due July 11th, 1734 - - - 60 - 0 - 0
Apr. 17th 1735. From Mrs Throp ½ a years interest
due Febr. 3^{d} last (abating 1^{ll}-5^{s}) - - - 13 - 15- 0
May. 24th. 1735 (Date of Henry's bill.) from Mr Lynch
on Account Rx - - - 100 - 0 - 0
Jan^{r}. 1735-6 Payd me 1 year and half Interest to
Oc^{tb}. 5th 1735. by Mr Cope. Executor to Sr Wm Fowns - - - 36 - 0 - 0

Money payd out

of the Weekly Collections

of the Cathedrall of

St Patrick's

From Febry. 11th to 18

1738---9.

Poor Mony to other Persons beside y^e List

1-1
3-3

Money p^{d} out of the Collections
in the Cathedrall of St Patrick's
Begun March 25 1739. to be
payd weekly⟨out⟩ or occasionaly to
those of my own Liberty.

To Mr Lyon, for a weeks Sick Poor - - -	0 - 5 - 5
To Ditto from. March 25th to April 7th to 10 ⟨People⟩ Poor People at 3$^{d}\frac{1}{4}$ and for a fortnight to each. - 6½ - - -	0 - 5 - 5.
Apr. 25 to Ditto for Ditto - - -	0 - 5 - 5
May. 3^{d} Increas^{d} to Mr Lyon by the pernicious vice and Advice Of my daily Spunge and Inmate Will's Son to 12 Scoundrels } at 6^{d}½ p^{r} week fortnight - - -	0 - 6 - 6
--19 to 12 poor per ditto - - -	0 - 6 - 6
--Ex^{trd} to a Wom^{n}. broke her arm	0 - 1 - 1
--29. To 12 poor ditto - - -	0 - 6 - 6
June 16. to 12 poor ditto - - -	0 - 6 - 6
--30 --for a fortnight.	0 - 6 - 6
July. 14. for a fortnight - - -	0 - 6 - 6

1739

Brought over.	
July. 28 to the 12 Poor - - -	0 - 6 - 6
August 11. to Ditto - - -	0 - 6 - 6
-- 25 to Ditto - - -	0 - 6 - 6
Sep^{tbr}. 8-- to Ditto - - -	0 - 6 - 6
Increase the same day - - -	0 - 3 - 6
	0 - 10 - 0
From this Date the Number of the Poor <will be> in encreased from twelve to twenty at 10 Shilling per Fortnight. Sep^{tbr}. <20> 22^{d} - - -	0 - 10 - 0
Sep^{tbr}. 29 a fortnight	
For <Oct^{br}. 5> ^ Ditto to Ditto ^ - - -	0 - 10 - 0
<Oct^{br} -7 - - -	0 - 9 - 3½>
Oct^{br}. 20th - - -	0 - 10 - 0
<28	0 - 7 - 0>
Nov^{br}. 3 - - -	0 - 10 - 0
--17. To Ditto for Ditto - - -	0 - 10 - 0
To the two Widows in Alms-House	<0 ->
for two Weeks. when Church shut - - -	0 - 4 - 4
<Dec^{br}>	
Nov^{b} 25th to Ditto by Ditto a Fortn^{t}	0 - 10 - 0
<Dec^{br}. 2. - - -	0 - 6 - 0>
a fortnight	
Dec^{br}. 15-- Ditto for Ditto	0 - 10 - 0
--26 to John Dalto - Shoemak^{r}	0 - 4 - 4
--29 To Mr Lyon for a Fortnight - - -	0 - 10 - 0
Jan^{r}. 5 to a por man - Ridg^{w}	0 - 0 - 3

1739-40

Brought over

Jan^{r}. 12. A long extra^{dry} Cold Season, and
I was Worryed by Mr Lyon to give more
than the Fund can well support. < >
However I give 20 Shillings.
a fortnight

Jan^{r}. 12 To Mr Lyon - - -	1 - 0 - 0
Jan^{r}. 9 to Flora Sanders[1] - - -	0 - 2 - 8½
March. 11. to a Blind Parson, & wife - - -	0 - 2 - 8½
To Mr Lyon for a fortnight ending Ap^{r}. 12	0 - 10- 0
To Ditto for a Fortnight end^{g} Apr. 26 - - -	0 - 10- 0
--Overplush to Flora, and a poor Man - - -	0 - 2 - 2
To Ditto for Ditto for a Fortnight May 10	0 - 10- 2
May 24 to Ditto for a fortnight - - -	0 - 10- 0
<Jun 1 Trinity Sunday very little - - -	0 - 5 - 1½ >
A Mistake of mine J: S.	
To Mr Lyon for a Fortnight to be due on Saturday next. Jun 7th. p^{d} - - -	0 - 10- 0
--Jun. 21 - - -	0 - 10- 0
July. 6th - 1740 to ditto a fortnight	0 - 10- 0
<--13. 1740. Miserable doings - - -	0 - 4 - 4 >
--19 to Ditto a fortnight - - -	0 - 10- 0
August 1. Ditto a Fortnight - - -	0 - 10- 0
Sep^{tbr}. 27. to 4 Paymts ditto - - -	2 - 0 - 0
To Oc^{tbr}. 12th to Ditto, a Fortnight	0 - 10- 0
Nov^{br}. 22^{d} to Ditto 3 Paymts - - -	1 - 10- 0
Dec^{br}. 6. To Ditto a fortnight - - -	0 - 10- 0

January. 3. to two Payments to Ditto - - -	1 - 0 - 0
--17 to one Payment - - -	0 - 10- 0
--31 to Ditto a fortnight - - -	0 - 10- 0
<Feb^{ry} 8 Ditto - - -	9 - 9>
Hanq Alba via for Blundring.	
Febr^{y}. 28 to Ditto 2 Payments - - -	1 - 0 - 0
March. 14 to Ditto a fortnight - - -	0 - 10- 0
--1741. </to Ditto>	
--28 to Ditto a fortnight - - -	0 - 10- 0
April. 25 to ditto a Month - - -	1 - 0 - 0
May. 22 1741 to Ditto a Month. - - -	1 - 0 - 0
June. 20 1741 To Ditto 4 weeks - - -	1 - 0 - 0
July 18 1741 To Ditto 4 Weeks	1 - 0 - 0
Augus 16 To Ditto - - 4 Weeks	
September. 8. 1741. to Ditto - - -	1 - 0 - 0
October 4 to Ditto - - -	1 - 0 - 0
December. 20 To Ditto - - -	1 - 0 - 7

Charity - Money

Received out <of> of

the Cathedrall of

St Patrick's

Beginning

Entered by the Dean

Poor money

Febr[y]. 11 to -18 1738-9	0 - 5 - 5
--25. 1738-9 - - -	0 - 5 - 0
Mar. 4th. - - -	0 - 13- 0
--7. Ash wednesday - - -	0 - 15- 7
--12 - - -	0 - 8 - 9
--18 - - -	0 - 8 - 2½
--25 - - -	0 - 6 - 3
Apr. 1 - - -	0 - 7 - 〈 〉
--8 - - -	0 - 11- 4
--15 - - -	0 - 6 - 0½
--19 Wednsday - - -	0 - 3 - 4½
-- Some mistake	
Apr. 29th Sunday - - -	0 - 4 - 0½
--May. 2[d] A: B[ps] Visitation	1 - 10- 3½
--6 - - -	0 - 6 - 0
--13 - - -	0 - 7 - 7
--20 - - -	0 - 7 - 7
27 - - -	0 - 8 - 9
Jun. 3[d] - - -	0 - 5 - 6
--10. Whit Sun[d] - - -	1 - 5 - 9
--17. Trinity Sunday - - onely - - -	0 - 8 - 5½
--24 - - -	0 - 6 - 6
--July. 1. - - -	0 - 6 - 6
--8 - - -	0 - 8 - 0
--15 - - -	0 - 7 - 9
--22 - - -	0 - 7 - 1½. 4.
--29 - - -	0 - 12- 1½
	12 - 2 - 4

Church money for Poor. 1739.

Brought over - - -	⟨7 - 1 - 4⟩
August 7 - - -	0 - 8 - 1
--12 - - -	0 - 19- 7
--19 - - -	0 - 5 - 4½
--26 - - -	1 - 11- 9
Sep^{tbr} 2^{d} - - -	0 - 11- 9½ $\frac{3}{4}$
--9 - - -	0 - 6 - 0
Some mistake	
--Sept 23^{d} - - -	0 - 7 - 1½
--30 - - -	0 - 5 - 4
Oct^{br}. 7 - - -	0 - 9 - 3
--14 - - -	0 - 9 - 2½
--21 - - -	0 - 7 - 4
--28 - - -	0 - 17- 6½
-- No Church - till	
Nov^{br}. 18. - - -	0 - 5 - 1½
--25 - - -	0 - 10- 8
Dec^{br}. 2. - - -	0 - 6 - 2
--9 - - -	0 - 6 - 2
--16 - - -	0 - 6 - 2
--23. before X^{mas}. Ordination	1 - 9 - 3
--25 Christmas day - - -	2 - 8 - 8
--30 - - -	0 - 8 - 4½
Jan^{r}. 7. A cruel Frost of twelve days, and still going. The Collections this day were but 2^{s}-1^{d}, but I added my usuall Shilling on comino Sunday	0 - 3 - 2
	11 - 14- 1½

Poor Money. 1739-40

Brought over - - -	
Jan^{r}. 13. - - -	0 - 5 - 2
--20 - - -	0 - 3 - 3
--27. - - 3^{s} - 9 - - -	0 - 3 - 9
Febr 3 ⟨2⟩ - - -	0 - 1 - 8½
--10 - - -	0 - 5 - 0
--24 - - -	0 - 4 -10
March. 2 - - -	0 - 7 - 0
--9 - - -	0 - 7 -10
--16 - - -	0 - 14- 7
--23 - - -	0 - 11- 4
--29 - - -	0 - 3 - 3
Apr. 6 Easter day - - -	3 - 14- 7½
--13 - - -	0 - 7 - 3
--20 - - -	0 - 5 - 3
--27 - - -	0 - 7 - 1
May. 4 - - -	0 - 9 - 0½
--11 - - -	0 - 8 - 0½
--14 - - - A. B^{ps} Visitation - - -	1 - 4 - 5½
--18 - - -	0 - 15- 2
June 1. - - - poor doings - - -	0 - 5 - 1½
--8 - - -	0 - 6 - 2
--15 - - -	0 - 9 - 3½
--22 - - -	0 - 8 - 9
--29 - - -	0 - 13- 6
--July 6. - - -	0 - 8 - 4½
--13 - - -	0 - 4 - 4
--20 - - -	0 - 6 - 6½
	14 - 1 - 6½

From July. <1740> 20th 1740
There was no Cathedrall Service
to Sunday Aug. 31

Then collected - - -	0 - 3 - 8½	
September. 7 collect^{d} - - -	0 - 4 - 1	
--14 (I guess - - -	0 - 4 - 0	
Sep^{tbr}. 21 Collected - - - 6^{s} - 4 - - -	0 - 6 - 4	
<Sep^{tbr}. 21> Sep^{tb}. 28 Collected - - -	0 - 6 - 6	
Octo Collected - - -	0 - 5 - 7½	
Oct^{br}. 12 - - -	0 - 3 - 3½	
Oct^{br} 19 - - - Collection	0 - 3 -10	
Oct^{br} 26 - - -	0 - 4 - 4	
Novembr. 2 - - -	0 - 5 -10½	
--9 Collected - - -	0 - 8 - 2	34
--16 Collected - - -	0 - 8 - 4	
--23 Collected - - -	0 - 5 - 7½	
--30 Collected - - -	0 - 4 - 0	
Dec^{br}. 7 Collected about - - -	0 - 3 - 4	
--14. No Service. Church over flown	Nothing	
--21 An Ordination then Collected - - -	1 - 4 - 4½	
--25 Christmas day. a poor Collection - -	1 - 5 - 0	
28. Sunday - - -	0 - 8 - 4½	
Jan^{ry}. 4: - - -	0 - 10- 7½	

1741. Old Stile - - -

Memorand: that Jan^{r}. 1. is
meant to the old Style, for 1741.

Sunday Jan[r]: 18 1740-1 Collect[d] 0 - 2 - 4½

6 - 5 - 7	7 - 7 - 8
5 - 19-11	14 - 1 - 6½
6 - 7 - 8½	11 - 14- 1½
18 - 13- 2½	12 - 2 - 4½
	45 - 5 - 8½
	18 - 13- 2½
	63 - 18-11

Charity received in this ~
long dismall Frost.

From the Chap^{tr}. by Mr King - - -	5 - 0 - 0

July. 23. 1741

Given at the Request of Mrs Ridgeway to a poor Family in my Liberty	0 - 3 - 3

Mony paid by ye Dean, but

not entered in his own Acc^{ts}

See ye Vouchers

		£ s d
1729	Xtmass Cloathing - - -	11 - 5 - 5
1730	Do - - -	11 - 17- 9
1732	Do - - -	11 - 10- 3
1733	Do omitted part - - -	- - 10- -
1735	Do - - -	11 - 14- -
1737	Do - - -	11 - 5 - 1
1739	Do - - -	10 - 11-11

1740-1

Account of Collections. It is in the old Style. which is January the first for 1741.

Jan[ry]. 11. Collected - - -	0 - 9 - 9
--18 Poor Collection a Trifle - - -	0 - 2 - 8½
--25. A noble Collection - - -	0 - 2 -11½
--Febr. 1 - - - 0 - 0 - 0-	0 - 7 - 8½
--8 - - -	0 - 9 - 9
Febry. 15 - - -	0 - 6 - 2½
--22 - - -	0 - 8 - 1
--28 - - -	0 - 2 - 8
March 8 Collected - - -	0 - 5 - 9½
--15. Collected - - -	0 - 4 - 5
--22 Collected - - -	0 - 3 - 3
Ester day Collected - - -	1 - 16- 0
Collected - - -	0 - 4 -10
Collected - - -	0 - 5 - 4½
...... Collected - - -	0 - 5 - 4½
April 26 - 1741. Collected but - - -	0 - 2 - 8½
May 1741 Collected about - - -	0 - 8 -
	6 - 5 - 7

Given to an honest Man one Luke. 10 Shillings: of Collections and and 10 Shillings more of my own in all - - - 1 - 0 - 0

Collections in my Cathedrall. May. the
1741 then Collected - - - - 0 - 5 - 4

May. 17. Whit Sunday Collected - - -	0 - 4 - 7½
Besides one Guinea value in	
Change. in all - - -	1 - 2 - 0
May 24. Collected - - -	0 - 4 - ½
--31 Collected - - -	0 - 3 - 0
Jun. Collected - - -	0 - 5 - 8
June Collected - - -	0 - 4 - 7
--21. Collected - - -	0 - 2 - 4
--28. Collected - - -	0 - 3 - 6
July. 5 - Collected - - -	0 - 10-10
--12 Collected - - -	0 - 4 - 4
--19 Collected - - -	0 - 8 - 1
--26 Collected - - -	0 - 3 - 7
Aug. -2^d Collected - - -	0 - 3 - 9
Aug. -- Collected - - -	0 - 3 - 3
Aug. -- Collected - - -	0 - 2 - 9
August Collected - - -	0 - 4 -10½
Aug. to Sep^t. 6 Collected - - -	0 - 4 - 4
Sep^tbr 13. Collected - - -	0 - 3 - 3
Sep^tbr -20. 41. Collected - - -	0 - 3 - 9
Sep^t - 27. -41 -No Collection in the Church, ^but I gave - - -	0 - 2 - 8½
October 4. 41.	
--Collected - - -	0 - 5 - 0
Oct^b. 11 - - -	0 - 6 - 6
	5 - 19-11

Collected in my Cathedral

October 18th. 1741: - - -	0 - 5 - 5
Oct^{br}. 25 1741 - - -	0 - 3 - 5½
Nov^{br}. 1st 1741 - - -	0 - 4 - 0½
--8 1741 - - -	0 - 6 - 6
--15	
--22	
Nov^{br} -29 - - -	0 - 5 - 4½
Decemb^{r} 6 - - -	0 - 4 - 4
--Dec^{br}. 13 - - -	0 - 5 - 3½
20 - - -	0 - 6 - 2½
Chrismass day Collected - - -	1 - 17- 0
January 17 Collected - - -	0 - 7 - 7.
February 7 - Collected - - -	0 - 4 - 7-
February 14 - Collected - - -	0 - 4 -10
February 28 Collected - - -	0 - 2 - 4½
March - 07 Collected - - -	0 - 5 - 5-o
March. - 14 - Collected - - -	0 - 4 - 4
March - 21 Collected - - -	0 - 4 - 4
March. - 28 Collected - - -	0 - 3 - 9½
April - 4 04. Collected - - -	0 - 3 - 3
April ⟨18⟩ 18 - Collected - - -	0 - 10- 3
	6 - 7 - 8½

The State of the Weekly Collections
of St Patrick's Church Rec^d by ye Dean
from 1730 to April 1742

	£ s d
By the Collections from 1730 to 11th Feb: 1738 - - -	195 -11 - 9½
By D^o from Feb: 1738 to April 1742 - - -	63 -18 -11
	259 -10 - 8½
	246 - 8 - 9
Octob^r 1742 Balance due to ye Poor	13 - 1 -11½

by Mony Disbursed

on Cloathing ten poor Boys

& by allowance p^r Month to poor People

	£ s d
From 1730 to 7th Jan: 1738 - - -	108 - 15 - 8
The same continued; with some Bills for ye poor Boys cloathing y^t had been not entered by Mistake - to Octr 1742 - - -	127 - 5 - 7
	236 - 1 - 3
By Mony given to Mr Kendrick to distribute among ye poor of ye Liberty on 24. Jan: 1739	10 - 7 - 6
	246 - 8 - 9
July 19: 1735 To Mr Worrall for ye Monthly Poor; charged in no former Ballance	7 - - 10
Augt 30: 1736 to D^o for D^o not charged before - - -	7 - - 10
July 19: 1733 A Fee with Benj: Coffee one of ye poor Boys to a Shoemaker - - -	2 - - -
	262 - 9 - 5
	259 - 10 - 8½
The Dean Cred^r to ye Poor - - -	2 - 19 - 8½

Entered as due to y[e] poor which

£13 - 1 - 11½

A Mistake - The

Vouchers being found since

to y[e] Contrary --------

The Poor D[r] to y[e] Dean

£2 - 19 - 8½

Debts and Mortgages due to me

Munday ⟨Jul. 1.⟩ Apr. 11. 1736
Alex^{dr} Lynch Mortgage to me for 2000
at 5^{ll} p^{r} cent July. 9th. 1732. p^{r} an. 100^{ll}
Dec^{br}. 11th 1733 Dean Swift Esq^{rs} Mortgage to
me for 2000^{ll} 6 p^{r} cent. p^{d} by G. Nugent who has a
lease of lives renewable on Castle-Ricard. 120^{ll}
Memd^{m} Mr Nugent did not enter till May after
so half a year more is owing to me by Mr Swift.
Dean Swift likewise owes me besides which with the
last article makes up near 1000^{ll} more. or 3000^{ll}.
Aug. 13th 1735 John Putland Esq^{rs} mortage
for the Interest 80^{ll} Debt 1500^{ll} ----- ⟨1580^{ll}⟩ -
Mrs Throps Mortgage June 16. 1725
for 500^{ll} at 5 p^{r} cent p^{r} ann -25^{ll}
Sr Wm Fowns bond and Warrant 6 p^{r} cent
is 400^{ll} ⟨at owes me⟩ Int^{ret} - - - 24^{ll}
Mr Cashor of Trim owes me many years
at 6 p^{r} cent 100^{ll} and long Arrears ----

Mr Lynch	2000^{ll}
Mr Swift	2000
Ditto near	1000
Mr Putland	1500
Mr Throp	0500
S Wm Fowns	0400
Mr Cashor	0100
	7500

Swift and Nugent's Dec^{b}. 11 1733 - 2000^{ll}. 6 p^{r} cent

Mr Nugent owes me Lady day last

Alex^{d} Lynch's Mortgage to me. July 9th

1732. for 2000^{ll} - at 5 p^{r} cent.

Dec^{br}. 11th. 1733. Dean Swift Esq^{rs} mortage

to me for 2000^{ll}. ⟨in⟩ 6 p^{r} cent Int^{rst} to be p^{d}

me by George Nugent Esqr of Castle Ricard.

Mortgage from Mr Put^{ld} for 1500^{ll} at

80^{ll} p^{r} ann Interst. Aug. 13th - 1735

Mem^{dm} Mrs Bensons lease has seven years just

expired Mar 25. 1737.

Mr Reading assign^{mt} of Throps mortage to

me for 500^{ll} June 16. 1725

Sr Wm Fowns Bond and warr^{t} for 400^{ll}

Mr Lynch's debt Commence ⟨Ma⟩ July. 9th 1732 2000^{ll}

at 5 p^{r} cent on July 29th 1737 there will be 5 -

years, which amount to 500^{ll} of which he payd me

Novr 19th	1733	-	100
June....	1734	-	50
May. 24	1735	-	100
Sep^{tb} 20		-	080
			330

So Mr Lynch is in arrear one Year and 3 quarters

⟨on the⟩ on the 9th of this instant Apr. 1737. that is 175^{ll}.

Mr Nugents and Swifts Mortgage

From De^{cb}. 11 1733 to Apr 11 1737 are 3 years 4 Month

Three years are 360^{ll}

call 4 months 1 Quar^{tr} 030

Totall 390

Then on the 11 Instant April ⟨he⟩ 1737 he owes 390^{ll}

Mr Nugent payd me on Mar. the 8 1734-5

Mar. 8 ⟨175-⟩ 1734-5	60
$_{\wedge}$1735-6 - - -	60
Nov^{r}. ⟨25⟩ 17. 1736	60
	180

So Mr Nugent owes me. on Apr. 11th instant 1737 one Year and halfs rent wch is as above 180^{ll}.

Mr Putlands mort^{ge} Aug. 13th. 1735 - 1500^{ll} at 80^{ll} p^{r} ann. Apr. 13 ins^{t}. 1737 he will ow me a year and 8 Months. 160^{ll}

Mr Putland payd me Aug.$^{9}_{\wedge}$1736 - 40^{ll}

So Mr Putland owes me 120^{ll}

Mr Lynch on Apr 9th owes me - - -	170 - 0 - 0
Mr Nugent owes me Apr. 11. 1737 above - - -	180 - 0 - 0
Mr Putland Apr. 13th 1737 will ow me - - -	160 - 0 - 0
Apr. 11. 1737 - - -	510 - 0 - 0

To George Nugent Esqr. at Castle Ricard
near Clenard Bridge -

APPENDIX I

(From Scott, I, 61n)

Account of expences from Nov. 1, 1700 to Nov. 1, 1701.

Articles per Account,	£	s.	d.
Shoes and books, - - -	3	0	0
A Servant's wages, &c. - - -	7	0	0
Washing, &c. - - - -	4	0	0
Linen, - - - -	5	0	0
Clothes, - - - -	13	0	0
Journeys, - - - -	10	0	0
J. B. - - - -	5	0	0
Accidents, - - - -	5	0	0
Horse, - - - -	12	0	0
Letters, - - - -	1	10	0
Play, - - - -	5	0	0
Gifts and charity extraordinary, - -	10	0	0
Charity common, - - -	2	10	0
Expences common, - - -	17	0	0
	L. 100	0	0

APPENDIX II

(From Mason, p. 416, note 1)

A State of my affairs, Sept^ber 8th 1718.

	£.	s.	d.
Bonds and securities in the hands of Mr. Tho. Staunton for 1000l. of which belongs to me	500	0	0
Due to me from Mrs. Benson by Mich^mas next	315	0	0
Due to me by bond from Ld. Bp. of Down	150	0	0
Due to me by John Beaumont, for which I have a mortgage of his house in Trim .	100	0	0
Due to me from Dr. Raymond 150l. on Effernock, whereof belongs to me only . .	50	0	0
Three houses in Trim, which cost me . .	205	0	0
Due to me from .... 50l. Engl. . .	54	0	0
Due to me from Jo. Beaumont, for which I have securities with the Ld. Bp. of Clogher	60	0	0
Lent in Trim to several persons for encouragement of industry, about . . .	80	0	0
	1514	0	0
From whence deduct to be laid out for building at Neilstown	200	0	0
All other debts I hope to pay out of my accruing rents.			
By a bond from Mr. Proudfoot . .	15	0	0

APPENDIX III

(From Forster 530)

p. 172 To Conolly —— Bill —— 19 - 8 - 0
More in Charity 1 -10 - 0
20 -18 - 0

---

p. 180
1 - 8 -11
1 - 9 - 1
2 -18 - 0
2 -14 - 2

---

p. 188 (Three lines drawn through entire page)

May. 19. 1736. R by —— for 1735 Kenrick from Dr Wilson ——	114 -10 - 0
May. 19. 1736 R. by Ditto	30 -12 - 0
Jul. 9th 1736 Rx by me for 1735 —— —— ——	50 - 0 - 0
Aug. 31. ^{1736} for 1735 R ——	30 - 0 - 0
Sep^{tb}. 14.th 1736 R by me for ⟨ ⟩1735 ——	40 - 0 - 0
Oc^{tb}. 27 1736 Rx by me for 1735 —— ——	50 - 0 - 0
Repair of Tallow Church ——	0 -10 - 0
	315 -12 - 0
Jan^{ry}. 22^{d} 1736 —— Rx more at the Deanry. for 1735 —5 —— ——	27 -14 - 5
	343 - 6 - 5

Jan^r. 22^d. 1736

p. 198

<Scotch	——	——	——	2 -14 - 2
				0 - 3 - 4>
Scotch	——	——	——	0 - 4 - 4
				2 -18 - 6
Scotch	——	——	——	0 - 1 - 8
				3 - 0 - 2
Taken out more		——		1 - 3 - 0
				4 - 3 - 2
Put in				4 - 0 - 0

2 - 3 - 4	2 - 3 - 4
0 - 1 - 4½	1 - 3 - 0
1 - 3 - 0	0 -11 - 6
0 -11 - 6	0 - 1 - 5½
3 -19 - 2½	3 -19 - 3½

---

p. 199

	2 - 3 - 4
	0 - 5 - 5
	0 - 6 - 8
	0 - 0 - 5½
Cess ——	0 - 2 - 3½
	2 -18 - 2

---

p. 222

1 - 9 -10
1 - 1 - 8
0 -13 - 0
0 -10 - 0
3 -14 - 6
0 - 5 - 5
3 -19 -11

(From Huntington Library MS 14338)

Horse - - -	0 - 0 - 2
Corks - - -	0 - 0 - 4
Walls - - -	0 - 0 - 8
G - - -	0 - 1 - 3½
Bell mend	0 - 1 - 1
Dogs - - -	0 - 0 - 6
	0 - 4 - 0½
	0 - 8 - 4½
	0 - 4 - 0½
	0 - 4 - 4

APPENDIX IV

From Nichols Supplement, I, xxv,
Lyon MS note, f. 9

Mem. On Wednesday between 7 & 8 at Evening May 10th 1710 I received a Letter in my Chamber at Laracor (Mr Percival & Jo: Beaumont being by) from Mrs F dated May 9th: with one inclosed, sent from Mrs Worrall at Leicester to Mrs F: giving an Account, that my dear Mother Mrs Abigail Swift dyed that morning Monday April 24th 1710, about ten o'Clock, after a long sickness, being ill all winter and lame, and extremely ill a month or six weeks before her Death. I have now lost my Barrier between me & Death; God grant I may live to be as well prepared for it, as I confidently believe her to have been. If the way to Heaven be through Piety, Truth, Justice and Charity she is there.

J: S.

REFERENCES

Ball	The Correspondence of Jonathan Swift, D.D., ed. by F. Elrington Ball, London, 1910-1914. 6 vols.
Ball, History	Francis Elrington Ball, A History of the County of Dublin, Dublin, 1902-1917. 5 vols.
BL	British Library
Blundell	Blundell's Diary and Letter Book, 1702-1728, ed. by Margaret Blundell, Liverpool, 1952
Civil Survey	The Civil Survey A.D. 1654-1656. County of Meath Vol. V. With returns of tithes for the Meath Baronies. Prepared for Publication with Introductory Notes and Appendices by Robert C. Simington, Dublin, 1940
Corres.	The Correspondence of Jonathan Swift, Oxford, 1963-[1965]-1972, ed. Harold Williams. 5 vols. Vols. IV and V were reprinted with corrections by David Woolley in 1972 and have been used in this edition.
Craik	Henry Craik, The Life of Jonathan Swift, London, 1882
CUL	Cambridge University Library, Williams Collection
Deane Swift	Deane Swift, An Essay upon the Life, Writings, and Character of Dr. Jonathan Swift, London, 1755
Delany	[Patrick Delany], Observations upon Lord Orrery's Remarks, London, 1754
Mrs. Delany	Autobiography and Correspondence of Mary Granville Delany, ed. Lady Llanover, London, 1861-2. 6 vols.
Down Survey	Down Survey Barony Maps, published at the Ordinance Survey Office, Southampton, 1908. (From Sir William Petty's original maps now in the Bibliothèque Nationale, Paris.) Also a volume of contemporary copies, Down Survey Maps of County Meath in NLI, Dublin, which includes maps and terriers of Moyfenrath and Ratoath Baronies and Laracor and Rathbeggan Parishes but not Deece Barony or Agher Parish. The Down Survey maps "were drawn by parishes, some at about three, some at about six inches to one mile, with index maps on a smaller scale for each barony and a verbal description or terrier of the forfeited land in every parish . . . as cultivable, bog, mountain or wood" (John Andrew, Ireland in Maps, Dublin, 1961, p. 10).
Ehrenpreis	Irvin Ehrenpreis, Swift, The Man, His Works, and the Age, Cambridge, Massachusetts, 1962-1967. 2vols.
Faulkner	George Faulkner, "Some Further Account of Doctor Swift in a Letter to the Earl of Chesterfield," in The Works of the Reverend Dr. J. Swift, Vol. XI, Dublin, 1762
Forster, Life	John Forster, The Life of Jonathan Swift, Vol. I, 1667-1711, London, 1875

Grierson	*Letters of Sir Walter Scott*, ed. H. J. C. Grierson, London, 1932. 12 vols.
Halliwell	James Orchard Halliwell, *Some Account of a Collection of Several Thousand Bills, Accounts, and Inventories. Illustrating the History of Prices between the Years 1650 and 1750*, Brixton Hill, 1852
Hawkesworth	John Hawkesworth, *The Life of the Revd. Jonathan Swift, D. D.*, London and Dublin, 1755
Healy	John Healy, *History of the Diocese of Meath*, Dublin, 1908. 2 vols.
HL	Houghton Library, Harvard University
Illustrations	John Nichols, *Illustrations of the Literary History of the Eighteenth Century*, London, 1817-35. 6 vols.
JS	Jonathan Swift, *Journal to Stella*, ed. by Harold Williams, Oxford, 1948. 2 vols.
Landa	Louis A. Landa, *Swift and the Church of Ireland*, Oxford, 1954
Landa, "Deanery"	Louis A. Landa, "Swift's Deanery Income," in *Pope and His Contemporaries*, Essays presented to George Sherburn, ed. by James L. Clifford and Louis A. Landa, Oxford, 1949, pp. 159-170
Lawlor	Hugh Jackson Lawlor, *The Fasti of St. Patrick's, Dublin*, Dundalk, 1930
Lyon	John Lyon, manuscript notes in a volume now in the Forster Collection (#579). The volume includes Hawkesworth's *Life of Swift*, 1755; "Some Further Account of Doctor Swift," Faulkner's appendix to his edition of Swift's *Works*, 1762; and sheets of paper of varying sizes. All were bound together after Lyon's notations were made, probably in the early 19th century. Lyon's notes can be dated by his reference to the annuity Swift provided for Mrs. Ridgeway 'which she still enjoys (1765)." With the exception of the notes on the sheets of paper, the Lyon-Hawkesworth-Faulkner volumes are referred to as *Lyon*. Lyon's notes on the loose sheets bound in to the Lyon-Hawkesworth-Faulkner volume are referred to as *Prelims*, for "preliminary material."
Mason	William Monck Mason, *The History and Antiquities of the Collegiate and Cathedral Church of St. Patrick*, Dublin, 1820
Mayhew	George P. Mayhew, *Rage or Raillery*, San Marino, California, 1967
Mayhew, "Two Entries"	George P. Mayhew, "Two Entries of 1702-3 for Swift's *Polite Conversation*, 1738," *Notes and Queries*, 206 (1961), 49-50.
ML	Marsh's Library, MS. Z.1.2.3. (1), 1693, (5), 1697. *The State of the Diocese of Meath* as delivered to the Lords Justices by Anthony, Lord Bishop of Meath, 1693, transcribed by John Stearne in 1697

NLI	National Library of Ireland, Dublin
NLS	National Library of Scotland, Edinburgh
NYPL	New York Public Library, The Henry W. and Albert A Berg Collection; Astor Lenox Tilden Foundation
Nichols	The Works of the Rev. Jonathan Swift, D.D., ed . by John Nichols, London, 1801, 1803, 1808. 19 vols.
Nichols, Supplement	A Supplement to Dr. Swift's Works, ed. by John Nichols, London, 1779. 3 vols.
Orrery	John Earl of Orrery, Remarks on the Life and Writings of Dr. Jonathan Swift, Dublin, 1752
Pilkington	Memoirs of Mrs. Letitia Pilkington, 1712-1750, London, 1928
Poems	The Poems of Jonathan Swift, ed. by Harold Williams, Second Edition, Oxford, 1958. 3 vols.
Pope	The Correspondence of Alexander Pope, ed. by George Sherburn, Oxford, 1956. 5 vols.
Prelims	Preliminary materials, loose sheets bound in to the Lyon-Hawkesworth-Faulkner volume in the Forster Collection. Cf. Lyon
PW	The Prose Works of Jonathan Swift, ed. by Herbert Davis, Oxford, 1939-63. 14 vols.
RCBL	Representative Church Body Library, Dublin
Rothschild	Rothschild Collection, Trinity College Library, Cambridge
RIA	Royal Irish Academy, Dublin
SPH	St. Patrick's Hospital, Dublin
Stevenson	John Stevenson, Two Centuries of Life in Down, 1600-1800, Belfast, 1920
Synge	Edward Synge, A Brief Account of the laws now in force in the Kingdom of Ireland for Encouraging the Residence of the Parochial Clergy . . . Together with an Appendix shewing how the Fund of First-Fruits . . . has hitherto been managed and applyed to the use for which it was given, Dublin, 1723
Tyldesley	The Tyldesley Diary. Personal Records of Thomas Tyldesley, ed. by Joseph Billow and Anthony Hamilton, Preston, 1873
Visitation	Visitation of Meath about 1733. Typescript in RCBL. The date, previously cited as 1723, has recently been corrected by the Library, following Healy, who quotes a note written on the original MS of the Visitation report by an official of the Record Office, determining the date from internal evidence. The original MS, seen by Healy in 1908, was then at the Record Office but was later destroyed.
Williams	Harold Williams, Dean Swift's Library, Cambridge, 1935

ABBREVIATIONS

The following list includes only those abbreviations which may not be immediately clear. Raised letters have not been used, as Swift's practice is variable.

A B D: Archbishop of Dublin
A Bp: Archbishop
abt: about
acct: account
Ach: Acheson
AD: Archbishop of Dublin?
Ad: Addison
agn: again
Aldr: Alderman
alld: allowed
allod: allowed
almds: almonds
ambr: amber
an: annum

B: Barber, Beaumont, Berkeley, Betty, bill, Bishop, box
B.,J.: Jo Beaumont
B---n: Barton?
B, Mrs.: Mrs. Brent
bar: barrel
bd: board
bdw: board wages
betr: better
bil: bill
blew: blue
bll: bill
Bol: Bolingbroke
Br: Brent
brchs: breeches
brd: board, bread
brdy: brandy
brechs: breeches
bred: bread
Brt: Brent
Bty: Betty
burll: burial
by: boy

C: Charles, Colonel
cadl: candle
camb: cambric
cambt: camlet
cans: canister
car: carriage
carg: carriage
carptr: carpenter
carrws: carroways
cass: cassock
cch: coach
ch: chair, chamber, charities, coach?
chand: chandler
Chapld: Chapelizod
char: chair, charwoman
chim: chimney
chiny: chimney
chir: chair
chocl: chocolate
chr: chair
Cl: Clarges, Clogher, Colonel?
cld: cleared
clk: clerk
clrd: cleared
coblr: cobbler
cochn: coachman
coh: coach
Coll: Colonel
colr: collar
colrd: colored
cols: coals
comino: communion
comn: coachman
consd: consideration
copr: cooper
cr: chair
cra: cravat
credr: creditor
crm: cream
crv: cravat
Cue: Kew
Cunyhm: Cunningham

D: Dartmouth, Davis, Dean, Delany, Dillon, Dolben, Duke
D---s: Davis
dbt: debt
Del: Delany
dgs: dogs
din: dinner
dir: dinner
Donibk: Donnybrook
Dr: daughter, debtor, December, doctor
drbs: drabs
Ds: Duchess
dtr: daughter

E: Earl
elctn: election
Esay: Isaiah
exp: expenses

F., A.: Sir Andrew Fountaine
F., M.: Mrs. Fenton
Fn: Fountaine
fortnt: fortnight
fr: for, from
frgt: forgot
Frnd: Freing
fro: from
funrll: funeral
fust: fustian

G: George, Giffard?, gifts, Gilbert, given
g---ts: gifts
gard: guard
gl: gloves
glvs: gloves
gr: great
Grat: Grattans
grm: groom
grt: great
Grtt: Grattans
gwn: gown

H: Helsham, house, Hugh
hank: handkerchiefs
hankfs: handkerchiefs
Harr: Harrison
Harrn: Harrison
hazd: hazard
Hess: Hester Vanhomrigh
Hls: Helsham
Hold: Holland

I: Isaiah
Iah: Isaiah
id: idem
imper: imperial
incl: including
Ind: India

intret: interest
intrst: interest
Is: Isaiah
Isay: Isaiah
Ital: Italian

Jaxons: Jacksons
Jn: John
joury: journey

Kilm: Kilmainham

L: Lewis, lost
lanthn: lantern
Larar: Laracor
ldys: ladies
leqrice: licorice
lett: letter
lin: linen
linn: linen
liqrce: licorice
liqris: licorice
Lnd: London
Lod: London
ltt: letter

M: mountain, Mrs.
M---y: Manley
mak::make
Manl: Manley
Mar: March, Martha, Mary
Margt: Margaret
md: maid
mdm: madam, memorandum
med: mend
memd: memorandum
mend: memorandum
mid: maid
Missess: Hester Vanhomrigh
ml: milk
mn: man
mnd: mend
mny: money
Mol: Molly Harrison
Moth: Mother
Mrgt: Margaret
Mry: Mary
mymrs: mummers

N: number
nebr: neighbor

omb: ombre
Ormd: Ormond
Ornd: Ormond
oth: other

P: paid, per
Par: Parvisol
paratr: apparitor
Parl: Parvisol
pd: paid
pecing: piecing
perwg: periwig
Petr: Peterborough
pickt: piquet
pist: pistole
pistoll: pistole
plov: plover
podr: powder
por: poor
potcary: apothecary
pothy: apothecary
poudr: powder
pr: pair, per
Prcvl: Percival
prisrs: prisoners
Prodfut: Proudfoot
prt: part, Pratt
pruing: pruning
pts: pots
pullt: pullet
Pvll: Parvisol
py: pie

R: Raymond, Robert, rode, Rolt
Radr: Radnor
Raimd: Raymond
Ranel: Ranelagh
rasbry: raspberry
Rayd: Raymond
rd: received, riding
Rding: Reeding
rdr: remainder
redr: Reader, remainder
regsr: registrar
rendr: remainder
repd: repaid, repaired
Rid: Ridgeway
ridg: Ridgeway, riding
Ridw: Ridgeway
risb: wristband
Rivs: Rivers
rostr: roaster
rt: rent
Rx: received

S: Samuel?
Sachvll: Sacheverell
sacmt: sacrament
sact: sacrament
sadl: saddle

sart: sacrament
sat: sacrament
scrt: sacrament
scrty: secretary
scty: secretary
serns: sermons
sert: servant
sevll: several
Sh: Sheridan
Shd: Sheridan
Shed: Sheridan
Shedn: Sheridan
Shilis: Shiells
shill: shillings
shoing: shoeing
shos: shoes
Shrs: Shrewsbury
sizrs: scissors
sm: small, Smith
smll: small
sp: spent
spt: spent
St. J.; St. John
Stn: Stearne
stock: stockings
Strn: Stearne
Stwd: Steward
Sumr town: Somerstown
sup: supposed
supr: supper
survry: surveyor
svll: several

T: Thomas
tabac: tobacco
tavn: tavern
tayl: tailor
thrd: thread
thy: they
tindr b: tinder box
tob: tobacco
Tr: Treasurer
Trsr: Treasurer
turn: turnpike
turnp: turnpike

usq: usquebaugh
usqb: usquebaugh

V: Vanhomrigh
Van: Vanhomrigh
Vanhom: Vanhomrigh
Van Homr: Vanhomrigh
vittls: victuals

W: wages, Wesley, Will,

Wilson, wine, won
w. ball: washball
Wabr: Warburton
war: water?
Warbr: Warburton
warrt: warrant
washb: washball
wastct: waistcoat
wch: which
Wes: Wesley
Westnr: Westminster
wg: wages
Whit: Whiteway
White: Whiteway
win: wine
Widr: Windsor
wn: wine, woman
Wr: Worrall
wrisb: wristband
wth: with
wtr: water

X church: Christ Church
Xing: christening

y: you
Yng: Young

CONCORDANCE

INDEX OF PROPER NAMES

Identification is supplied only when it is not to be found in the introduction or text or in readily available reference works. A query following the name indicates a doubtful reading. Modern spellings have been used wherever possible.